NO PLEASURE CRUISE

The Story of the Royal Australian Navy

An artists's impression of the visit of the Royal Navy's 'Flying Squadron' as part of a Naval Review held in Port Phillip Bay in 1881. (London Illustrated News)

NO PLEASURE CRUISE

The Story of the Royal Australian Navy

Tom Frame

ALLEN&UNWIN

Dedicated to
my dear friend and esteemed colleague
Mr Robert Hyslop ISO,
who served in the
Department of the Navy
1936–1970

First published in 2004

Allen & Unwin
83 Alexander Street
Crows Nest NSW 2065
Australia
Phone: (61 2) 8425 0100
Fax: (61 2) 9906 2218
Email: info@allenandunwin.com
Web: www.allenandunwin.com

National Library of Australia
Cataloguing-in-Publication entry:

Frame, T.R. (Thomas R.) 1962.
No pleasure cruise: the story of the Royal Australian Navy.

Bibliography.
Includes index.
ISBN 1 74114 233 4.

1. Australia. Royal Australian Navy—History.
2. Australia—History, Naval. I. Title.

359.00994

Index compiled by Helen Frame.
Set in 10.5 on 13pt Centennial Light by Midland Typesetters, Maryborough
Printed by BPA Print Group, Burwood, Vic

10 9 8 7 6 5 4 3 2 1

CONTENTS

PREFACE

When I joined the Royal Australian Navy (RAN) in January 1979 as a very nervous sixteen-year-old cadet-midshipman, I knew practically nothing about naval history. In fact, I had never been on board an Australian warship, or even ventured in a small boat beyond the sight of land despite being raised in the New South Wales coastal city of Wollongong. The only naval ship I had ever set foot in was USS *Monticello*, a 1950s vintage American *Thomaston* Class amphibious warfare vessel, which was opened for public inspection at nearby Port Kembla on a Saturday afternoon in October 1978. And yet, as an adolescent, I desperately wanted to join the navy and go to sea in a destroyer. Shortly after putting on my new uniform at the Naval College, my classmates and I were given varied opportunities during breaks in our academic work to spend short periods in seagoing vessels operating in and out of Jervis Bay. During our initial year, I was fortunate enough to spend some time at sea in the patrol boat HMAS *Attack*, the fleet tender HMAS *Stalwart*, the aircraft carrier and RAN flagship HMAS *Melbourne*, and the destroyer escort HMAS *Derwent*. It was in *Derwent*, despite a brief bout of seasickness, that I gained my helmsman's certificate and manoeuvred a warship for the first time. It was an exhilarating and unforgettable experience. Having decided to pursue a career in submarines, later thwarted by the onset of asthma, I spent two weeks during mid-1980 in HMA Submarines *Oxley* and *Otama* operating off the New South Wales south coast. It was in this period that *Oxley* fired the first Mark 48 torpedo and I was given a chance to participate in a dummy attack on a passing merchant ship. These were all great experiences for a young man who had by now embraced the navy in mind, body and soul.

In the years that followed, it was difficult not to be drawn also towards Australian naval history. As our college instructors were not besotted by Lord Nelson's three great victories nor preoccupied with Britain's naval administration (although they had good reason to be so), we were able to learn something of Australia's success in developing a navy of its own and the achievements of earlier classes of

Australian cadet-midshipmen. It eventually became apparent, at least to me, that the RAN was every bit as effective and efficient as the Royal Navy (RN) or the United States Navy (USN).

It was also apparent that Australian naval history was just as colourful and as controversial as the chronicles of the much older navies. There were wonderful triumphs and dismal failures; incredible feats of expert seamanship and fatal instances of poor judgement; scenes of bravery and heroism and times of uncertainty and fear; bureaucratic in-fighting and political intrigues; moments of popular adulation and years of public suspicion; and a succession of great fighting leaders who had risen above the merely competent. And yet, the written record of the RAN in the early 1980s was very thin. There were a few standard texts, such as the official histories of the two world wars, but not many works that sought to describe long-term trends or continuing themes. Not much had been published on the navy's people, its shore establishments, the many smaller ships that had supported large fleet actions, or the peculiarities of Australian naval administration. In all of this there seemed an opportunity to make some contribution to what I knew, and what others might know, about the navy that I had joined and now loved.

When I was awarded the Australian War Memorial's inaugural summer vacation scholarship in January 1985, I was able to assist the memorial's staff in preparing a large body of records relating to the Royal Australian Naval Bridging Train for public access. The 'Train' was a light naval engineering and construction unit deployed to Suvla Bay during the latter part of the Gallipoli campaign. It later served in Palestine and suffered a mutiny. Here were episodes in Australian naval history of which I was completely ignorant. This provided me with the impetus to start researching and writing naval history in the hope that someone might eventually want to publish my work. I began with short articles that examined the training regime at the RAN College during the First World War, and the conduct of public religious worship in ships and at shore establishments. I was genuinely surprised to receive a hostile letter from a service chaplain who felt my commentary on worship was advocating a hybrid form of 'naval religion'. I could not see how he or anyone else could have taken that view although it was widely known that I belonged to a denomination that elsewhere exerted the privileges of being the 'Established Church'. I was left in no doubt that Australian naval history contained much contested ground.

Since then, I have examined a number of particular events and a range of specific issues in Australian naval history. Naval battles and combat tactics have been of less interest to me than the relationship between the RAN, the Federal Parliament and the Australian people. This is why I decided to focus on the 1964 collision of the aircraft carrier HMAS *Melbourne* and the destroyer HMAS *Voyager* as the subject of my doctoral dissertation in 1989. Giving an explanation for the collision was a challenge but it was not the most important part of the thesis. Something needed to be said about why the loss of *Voyager* led to two drama-filled royal commissions, how the Australian Parliament and people felt about their navy, and what the navy learned from this terrible tragedy. To my mind, these were more significant matters. This assessment was reflected in the structure and content of the finished work. My doctoral dissertation was substantially rewritten and published by Hodder & Stoughton with the title *Where Fate Calls: The HMAS* Voyager *Tragedy*. Its release on 10 February 1992, 28 years to the day after the collision, coincided with an ABC television *Four Corners* documentary entitled 'The Cruel Legacy' and a major feature in the *Sydney Morning Herald*'s 'Good Weekend' magazine. On legal advice, 27 passages in the book were either omitted or altered to reduce the risk of legal action for defamation. I hope to be able to publish parts of the original manuscript within the next few years although the deleted sections did not affect the book's main conclusions. The *Voyager* controversy was most recently (September 2003) re-examined in David Salter's critically acclaimed television documentary *Unfit to Command*. My only regret in participating in the production of this film was that *Where Fate Calls* was no longer in print!

The only sustained examination of a naval action that I have undertaken was in regard to the genuinely mysterious and unnecessarily controversial loss of the light cruiser HMAS *Sydney* off the coast of Western Australia in November 1941. *HMAS* Sydney*: Loss and Controversy* was written at the invitation of my then publisher, Bert Hingley, at Hodder & Stoughton. He was adamant that the Australian public was still engrossed in the loss of *Sydney*. I was only mildly interested in the subject but accepted the commission because it offered an opportunity to participate in a continuing debate about respecting the limits of historical evidence and resisting the appeal of speculation. To my surprise the book sold more copies than any other naval history I have published. But there was an unexpected personal cost.

It was disconcerting to receive so much ill-informed and spiteful correspondence from unknown people that included questions about my motives in writing the book. These were magnified at the public hearings of a joint parliamentary committee into the loss of HMAS *Sydney* held during 1998. Individuals whom I had never met told the parliamentarians that I had written about *Sydney* in a manner that showed the Naval Board in a very positive light in order to rehabilitate myself within the navy after official disappointment with *Where Fate Calls* and annoyance at my public response to Captain John Philip Stevenson's unreasonable and partisan attack on my handling of *Melbourne*'s second collision with USS *Frank E. Evans* in 1969. The accusations made during the inquiry were recorded in the official transcripts although they were completely without foundation. Having decided that I would not make any submission to the committee because my book contained all I wanted to say about *Sydney*, these were insults I was prepared to bear. It remains my view that far too much effort and energy has been devoted to the loss of HMAS *Sydney* with minimal prospect of anything new or potentially conclusive being found. It is now the responsibility of naval historians to persuade the public to move on to more potentially productive inquiries.

By way of example, much more attention needs to be directed towards Australia's continuing need for partnerships and cooperative arrangements in the provision of maritime defence. It is beyond the financial and manpower resources of the parliament and people of this country to protect adequately all of our national offshore assets and principal maritime interests. The mismatch of need and provision has been of particular interest to me. Written to mark the fiftieth anniversary of the Battle of the Coral Sea, which was fought by a combined Allied force against the Japanese in 1942, *Pacific Partners: A History of Australian–American Naval Relations* was my attempt to account for and defend this country's evolving and still very healthy relationship with the United States Navy. It was a deliberately polemical work designed to promote the navy's cause. It was based on my belief that at certain points in Australian history the navy, and only the navy, was able to promote the nation's best interests while giving Australia a flexible and subtle capability to influence events far beyond its shores. It was also possible to make this point in relation to operations in Turkey during 1915.

In *The Shores of Gallipoli: Naval Aspects of the Anzac Campaign*, I wanted to highlight the flexibility of naval hardware and the ingenuity of trained personnel while contending that the Gallipoli legend had a navy-blue dimension that was not obliterated by khaki. This theme appears in a number of my books because I have always been uncomfortable with the overly expansive claims made for the Anzac spirit and its alleged enduring influence on the Australian character. In the Chief of Navy's *Strategic Intent* document produced in April 2002, Vice-Admiral David Shackleton remarked: 'Little known is that members of the RAN were first in, and last out at Gallipoli, where the Anzac legend was born.' *First in, Last Out!* was the title of my co-authored book with Greg Swinden on the role of the submarine *AE 2* and the RAN Bridging Train in the Dardanelles campaign. It was gratifying to know the book's title had become a catchphrase in the navy and that others shared my concern about the navy's service 'being somewhat understated', as Admiral Shackleton rightly had concluded.

In nearly twenty years, I have written about many aspects of Australian naval history. This book is an attempt to bring these disparate writings together in the context of five broad objectives. The *first* is to outline the threats, both real and imagined, to the Australian people and their property posed by people with ships and nations with navies. The *second* is to describe the measures taken to provide for the maritime defence of the continent and to protect seaborne cargoes travelling to and from Australia. The *third* is to identify the themes evident in planning for naval defence and the patterns apparent in its provision. The *fourth* is to argue that Australians have not fully appreciated the possibilities and potentialities of the surrounding seas in relation to both individual prosperity and collective security. And *fifth* and finally, I want to demonstrate that Australia has indeed produced officers and sailors every bit the equal of those lauded in the naval histories of Britain and America.

I also want to deal with and discount many of the misconceptions and misunderstandings associated with naval service. There is a popular perception that the navy is all about gleaming white uniforms and immaculate grey ships. That life at sea is about enjoying the bright sunshine and fresh air, and visiting interesting and exotic places where a warm welcome is assured. As the South Australian gunboat HMCS *Protector* sailed for China in 1900, tasked with suppressing the murderous Boxer Rebellion, Gunner William Blake felt the need to record in his journal that the passage to China was 'no pleasure cruise'. The conditions on board *Protector* were cramped and uncomfortable. Men lived on top of each other in hot and stifling conditions within a ship ill-suited for a long ocean voyage and the armed conflict into which they had all been drawn. The food was generally poor and sleeping difficult on the overcrowded messdecks. Seasickness and ill-health were common as the mostly young sailors prepared to engage a foe with whom they had no personal quarrel. Some were afraid of suffering and death in a dark and evil place; others wondered about their families and who would care for them should they not return; nonetheless they were keen, well-trained and ready to do their duty.

Naval personnel now serve in considerably improved conditions. Ships are better designed and air-conditioned; meals are creatively presented and nutritionally sound; many excellent facilities exist for recreation; first-rate medical care is near at hand; and communication with loved ones can be readily arranged. But officers and sailors still live in confined quarters with restricted personal space. They spend long periods away from families and friends engaged in arduous duties in places they would not care to visit were they given a choice. And the ships in which they sail are frequently the subject of hostile intent. Their home is also a weapon of war. These remain the realities of naval service. An overseas deployment is still 'no pleasure cruise'.

Much of the material in this book is not new although the content has been selected and arranged to make certain important points. Naturally, the constraints of space mean there are some omissions and gaps in the narrative. Some places and people have not been included. It could not have been otherwise. Like most general works, the book draws together and builds on the work of a substantial community of talented scholars, including a growing number of serving and ex-serving naval officers led by Dr David Stevens (presently the RAN's Director of Naval History), who have produced a steady stream of first-rate histories on Australia's naval defence over the last decade. Their work has covered naval operations, strategy and administration during war and in peacetime. With generous encouragement from the navy at an official level, they have shown the RAN to be a highly complex organism that deserves careful and consistent study. The future of Australian naval history is in very capable hands. Although this volume is intended for a general audience, I hope it will arouse the reader's interest in the more specialised works that have appeared over the last decade. They have been identified and categorised in the bibliography.

In closing, I want to thank Ian Bowring of Allen & Unwin for giving me the opportunity to write this book and for his goodwill and encouragement. Professor John Seymour very kindly provided a great deal of useful material on press discussion of naval affairs in the period 1900–10. Commander Graham Wright, Commodores James Goldrick and Jack McCaffrey, Vice-Admiral Russ Shalders and Admiral Chris Barrie read parts of the manuscript and made some helpful comments. I am especially grateful to my dear friend Robert Hyslop ISO for his continuing assistance and wise counsel. Robert served for more than thirty years as a civil servant in the Department of the Navy rising to the senior position of Assistant Secretary. Since meeting in 1988, we have maintained a very fruitful dialogue on naval policy and public administration, and have been sympathetic critics of each other's work. It is fitting, therefore, that this book be dedicated to Robert Hyslop in appreciation of his personal kindness and to honour his distinguished contribution to the Royal Australian Navy and to the study of its history. His achievements are a reminder that it is not only officers and sailors that make a navy great.

INTRODUCTION

Australia is an island. It is the most obvious feature of its geography. This has also been the most significant and lasting element in its national life although it took some time for this fact to be established. Lieutenant James Cook made the first survey of Australia's east coast in 1770 while commanding *Endeavour*. When the First Fleet under Captain Arthur Phillip arrived in 1788, it was not known whether a land bridge to South-East Asia existed. Before Commander Matthew Flinders sailed from Sydney in *Investigator* (the former 334-ton sloop *Xenophon*) in 1802, he had been instructed by Governor Philip Gidley King to ascertain whether Australia was indeed an island continent. As the Governor wrote to Sir Joseph Banks, there is a need to 'solve the doubt whether the mountains are separated from other parts of New Holland by a sea or a strait running from the Gulf of Carpentaria into the Southern Ocean which is a very favourite idea in this country'. Flinders understood the political, diplomatic and strategic significance of his journey: 'It is necessary, however, for geographical precision, that so soon as New Holland and New South Wales were known to be one land, there should be a general name applicable to the whole'. He then went on to say: 'Had I permitted myself any innovation on the original term, it would be to convert it into Australia; as being more agreeable to the ear, and as an assimilation to the names of the other great portions of the earth'.

Having determined that Australia was an island, Britain was able to claim the continental landmass without needing to negotiate and settle a common land border with any other European power. Britain also recognised that, as an island continent, a vast body of water protected Australia from potential European invaders. The British knew first hand the advantages of defending an island. An invading force had not successfully crossed the English Channel since 1066. The Preamble to the *Articles of War* proclaimed: 'It is upon the Navy, under the providence of God that the safety, honour and welfare of this realm do chiefly depend'. Just after Flinders had proved Australia was indeed an island, the Earl of St Vincent, Admiral Sir John

Jervis, said of France's threatening forces in a speech in the House of Lords: 'I do not say they cannot come. I only say they cannot come by sea'.

Australia's geography was and would remain its principal defence and strategic asset. The nation's first prime minister, Sir Edmund Barton, was quoted in the Melbourne *Argus'* editorial on 1 January 1901: 'there is a nation for a continent and a continent for a nation'. Not surprisingly, this sentiment was reflected in a song that later became the national anthem. The only hint of defence in 'Advance Australia Fair' is the reference to Australia being an island: 'our home is girt by sea'. Although this short phrase might seem obscure or even unintelligible to many, it highlights what has been perhaps the single most critical factor in this country's development. Australia's national prosperity and much of its recreation is linked to the seas. Ninety-five per cent of all Australians live within 150 kilometres of a coastline. Those living inland go for holidays to the coast. The beach has made its impact on the Australian psyche and identity while Australians have demonstrated their natural aptitudes as surfers, swimmers, fishers and sailors. And to leave the country invariably means 'going overseas'.

The vastness of the continent causes many to forget that Australia is an island. The mainland has an area of 7 682 300 square kilometres. Although the smallest continent, it is the largest island on Earth. Australia is the only nation that occupies a continent. It stretches some 3700 kilometres from its most northern to its most southern point, and about 4000 kilometres from east to west. In area, Australia is the world's sixth largest nation after Russia, Canada, China, the United States of America and Brazil. The coastline is more than 17 000 kilometres in length.

Beyond the continental landmass, Australia claims possession of 8222 offshore islands. Western Australia has 3747 islands, Queensland 1955, Tasmania 1000, Northern Territory 887, South Australia 346, Victoria 184 and New South Wales 102. The largest is Melville Island off the Northern Territory which has an area of 5786 square kilometres. It is followed by Kangaroo Island off South Australia, which is 4416 square kilometres. Macquarie Island is one of Australia's most distant possessions. Located in the Southern Ocean at a latitude of 54°30' South, longitude 158°57' East, Macquarie Island is 200 kilometres closer to the Antarctic continent than its parent state of Tasmania, which lies 1500 kilometres north-west. Measuring an area of 128 square kilometres, Macquarie Island is 34 kilometres long by just five kilometres at its widest point. It is the only place on earth where rocks from the Earth's mantle (six kilometres below the ocean floor) are being actively exposed above sea level. For over 50 years, Australia has operated an Antarctic research support station at the northern end of the island. The station (built in 1948) is home to over 40 people in the summer and around twenty through winter. Australia also boasts the largest sand island in the world. Fraser Island in Queensland is 1653 square kilometres and Australia's fifth largest island.

In addition to the continental landmass and the offshore islands, Australia also exerts territorial rights to the marine resources 200 nautical miles* from its coastline. This Exclusive Economic Zone, claimed on 1 August 1994 and recognised internationally by the Law of the Sea Convention, covers an area of 11.1 million square kilometres. The area encompassed by the continental shelf is 14.8 million square kilometres. It is about two hundred metres deep and ranges from about fifteen to 500 kilometres from the coastline. Australia lays claim to control of more water that is not ice than any other nation on the planet. Consequently, given the size of this enormous maritime zone, Australia boasts the third-largest fishing zone in the world. Commercial fishing is Australia's fifth-largest primary industry, with an annual catch averaging a quarter of a million tonnes of fish worth around $A2 billion. More than 80 per cent of the catch is exported, mainly to Asian markets. Offshore oil and gas is also a major industry in value and significance to Australia's own needs and international trade performance. Even though Australia has fewer than 0.3 per cent of the world's population and roughly 1.5 per cent of its gross national product, it is also one of the largest generators of global sea transport demand.

Until 1830 the value of imports to Australia exceeded its exports. But gradually the Australian wool industry increased its yield in volume and value and there was a trade surplus for the colony. Ships engaged in trade from Britain to Australia needed protection from the Empire's enemies. There was also a need to protect local vessels. By 1806 a fleet of coastal vessels existed of which about twenty were engaged in the Bass Strait sealing industry. The larger vessels were restricted to colonial waters but as these included the South Pacific, a lucrative trade began to flourish. From 1822 to 1840 New South Wales built

* *A nautical mile is 2035 yards and a land mile is 1760 yards.*

139 vessels totalling 6447 tons. By 1841 there were sixteen steamships running along the coast, mainly engaged in the trade between Sydney and the Hunter River region. By the end of the nineteenth century, there were three Australian shipping companies involved in overseas trade; and seven interstate shipping companies were operating before 1914. The Commonwealth Government Line of steamers was created in 1916 but sold off in 1928. Another fleet of government-operated ships was commissioned during the Second World War and survived hostilities to be known as the Australian National Line (ANL).

Australia's trade-based economy as a leading world exporter of iron ore, coal, nickel, zinc, alumina, lead, wool, meat, sugar, salt and wheat depends upon the seas and the free passage of seaborne cargoes. In terms of the number of tonnes carried and the number of kilometres travelled, Australian cargoes make up more than 10 per cent of world trade. More than 70 per cent by value and 95 per cent by volume of international cargoes are carried to and from Australia by sea, a trade that Australia relies on for its economic performance overseas and at home. Any disruption to Australian sea trade would be felt immediately and by most of the population.

The surrounding seas also create international responsibilities for Australia. As 70 per cent of the Earth's surface is covered in water, marine pollution (ship-generated and land-based waste dumping) and fishing are shared problems. There is also a need for effective management of international maritime trade, equitable resolution of disputes over maritime sovereignty and boundaries, and the need to provide all nations with access to sea lane focal points and the high seas. Then there is the need to combat piracy on the high seas, provide maritime search and rescue services, and prevent maritime accidents. The International Maritime Bureau reported in 2001 that there were 238 pirate attacks on merchant ships with a further 97 unsuccessful attacks. Sixteen of these attacks involved hijacks with 210 people taken hostage. In these incidents 21 seafarers were killed. Piracy continues to be a serious problem.

In the nineteenth century, shipwrecks were nearly as common as motor vehicle fatalities are in the twenty-first century. In the period 1875–79, there were 72 shipwrecks; that is, almost one every three weeks. The report of a ship colliding, foundering or grounding frequently ended with 'All hands lost'. Indeed, many ships sailed from Australian ports and were never seen again. Divers continue to find previously unknown wrecked ships. Ships are still lost around the Australian coast or in Australian contiguous waters.

Together with its offshore islands, territories and maritime resources, Australia has an area of immediate national interest covering 10 per cent of the Earth's surface. This means that Australians must look beyond the coastline to exploit the full extent of their national wealth and to ensure national security. The Indian, Pacific and Southern Oceans define Australia's geography and shape its security. In addition to the many defence and security tasks confronting a nation such as Australia, a range of purely domestic responsibilities demand some response: the challenge of preventing illicit drugs and other contraband from entering the country; the regulation of the immigration zone to prevent the unauthorised entry of illegal immigrants; securing our fisheries grounds; and protecting our native maritime flora and fauna. The physical security of Australia's offshore assets, such as oil rigs and navigational aids, creates another national burden.

The task of defending all of Australia's national assets and interests is immense. In fact, it is beyond the capability of Australia's small population to provide adequately for every security need. The magnitude of the task might account, in part, for the blasé manner in which many Australians regard national defence. The remoteness of the continent might be another reason. That Australians have not experienced conflict over a shared international land border demarcating people of different racial or ethnic identities could be yet another. This suggests that Australians do indeed rely upon the enveloping seas for their safety and security. They know that Australia has been able to control the extent to which it is influenced by the wider world because of the surrounding oceans. Geoffrey Blainey's phrase 'the tyranny of distance' is understood imperfectly. Blainey claimed that distance 'has worked for and against the Australian people and their interests'. In my view, it has had an overwhelmingly positive social, economic, political and strategic effect. It is the principal source of the peace and prosperity that Australians continue to enjoy.

The reason that Australians have taken the positive effects of the seas for granted is the confidence they have always had in the RAN and the Royal Navy before it. It is the mainstay of Australia's maritime defence. Responsibility for preventing any adversary from landing on Australia's shores rests primarily with the navy together with the job of ensuring the security of Australia's maritime zones. RAN ships patrol Australia's national waters, assist customs and immigration officials, and rescue seafarers from peril. The RAN also provides the national hydrographic service and plays a leading role in support of oceanography and other scientific research. For such a small population, the ability of the nation to produce so many fine naval officers and sailors for service in war and in peacetime has been a stunning achievement. For the strategic advantage of bigger ships and stronger armaments to be exploited tactically, well-trained officers and motivated sailors are needed to operate and maintain the equipment.

Since its foundation, the RAN has never failed to produce gifted personnel able to prove they were every bit as competent in all facets of naval activity as those serving in navies that have existed for centuries. Australia's naval power originates as much from the aptitudes and abilities of its people as it does from the ships, submarines and aircraft making up its order of battle. Those who have served in the navy are acutely aware of the importance of the seas to Australia's national life and are among its principal proponents. As the RAN's founding father, William Rooke Creswell, remarked in 1902: 'For a maritime state furnished without a navy, the sea, so far from being a safe frontier is rather a highway for her enemies; but with a navy, it surpasses all other frontiers in strength'. This theme was reiterated in the Chief of Navy's *Strategic Intent* document published a century later: 'Australia is the world's largest island continent, and its borders include the biggest oceans of the planet as well as one of the most complex archipelagos to be found . . . the success of the Navy depends critically on the Australian people taking ownership of "their Navy"'.

The RAN is one of Australia's oldest continuously existing national institutions and integral to its continuing survival as a sovereign nation in a violent and disordered world. As this work reveals, the strongest argument for the Australian Navy is its own history.

1

Strategic sea base? 1770–85

Most general histories of Australia begin with the establishment of the British penal colony in New South Wales. But few ask the question: why did the British Government in London ever express an interest in Botany Bay? There were, of course, a number of alternative sites more readily accessible and easier to colonise. In overlooking the matter of why the British opted for Botany Bay, historians could be missing something significant about the character of the continent that later became known as Australia. We might begin to see our national history without the alleged 'convict stain' if it were shown that Europeans settled and developed this country for more complex reasons than those usually acknowledged.

The British Government's need for a new penal colony to cope with an expanding number of convicts is the conventional view of why Australia was settled. This is usually expounded as a matter of fact rather than a product of interpretation. Sir Keith Hancock's pioneering study *Australia*, published in 1930, stated the matter simply: 'The Government of Pitt chose New South Wales as a prison, commodious, conveniently distant, and, it was hoped, cheap'. Several decades later, Russell Ward confirmed the conventional view: 'In 1788 the Australian nation was founded by and for Great Britain's surplus of convicted criminals'. Manning Clark wrote that the British Government was 'looking for a place to send convicts sentenced to transportation . . . and Botany Bay was to be that place'. At first glance, this seems a valid explanation. After the loss of the American colonies in the War of Independence (1775–83), Britain needed a new place to dump its convicts and to rid itself generally of the products of the severe social conditions that led to an explosion in criminal activity and increasingly harsh sentences. The gaols and the prison hulks had become terribly overcrowded and there was a public scandal in the making. By the mid-1780s the problem was reaching a crisis point and the Government of William Pitt (the younger) needed to do something. After a fair amount of procrastination and the surveying of several possible sites, it settled on Botany Bay as a suitable site for a penal settlement. It combined the possibility of a limitless capacity to take more convicts with the likelihood that many of them would never return to England's 'green and pleasant land'. But was there more to the choice? Did the British Government have other agendas in mind? A little known Tasmanian researcher thought so.

In an address delivered in 1952, Ken Dallas, an economics lecturer at the University of Tasmania, developed what has become known as the 'strategic sea base' theory. His interpretation did not attract much attention until 1966 when it was refined by Professor Geoffrey Blainey and incorporated into his best-selling account of the impact of distance in Australian history: *The Tyranny of Distance*. Blainey attacked the penal settlement interpretation by arguing that it was highly improbable that Australia should be colonised merely as a British gaol. It was simply too far from Britain. In 1784, the First Lord of the Admiralty, Richard Howe, had disparaged the idea as being too dangerous, too expensive and too slow a solution to an urgent problem. In July 1785, Das Voltas Bay on the West African coast was considered as a possible place of exile for criminals, but only if the commercial and political benefits justified the inevitable expense. When the site was found to be unsuitable, Botany Bay was suddenly more desirable. Why? British trade and security would be enhanced by a new settlement in such a location.

Britain needed a new sea base and refitting port to strengthen its position in the East. Botany Bay was well placed to service important British trade areas and commercial activities: the China tea trade, the Pacific coast of North America, whaling activities, and smuggling and privateering in the rich Spanish trade. As both the British and French were jockeying for position in the Indian Ocean, Botany Bay could not be allowed to become a French possession. In 1786, the French had based some of their forces in Mauritius and there were fears they might try to take India from Britain. It was also believed that Botany Bay would serve as a cheap source of high quality flax for sailmaking and timber for ships' masts and spars. This was an obvious attraction. Blainey argued:

> *In letters in which British politicians explained their reasons for selecting Botany Bay they did not have to emphasise that flax and timber were vital to their country, it was too obvious to be spelled out. The men to whom they addressed their letters knew the importance of a secure supply of naval stores and the dangers facing Britain's sources of naval stores.*

The earliest proposal to use Botany Bay as a penal settlement originated with James Mario Matra. But he also had an eye for trade opportunities and naval requirements. He put his suggestion to Evan Nepean, then Under Secretary for the Home Department, in August 1783. Matra argued that the

> *proposed colony of New South Wales might in time atone for the loss of the American colonies . . . and would improve the trade with China, and open up commercial intercourse with Japan, Korea, and the Moluccas. The timber and flax of New Zealand might become articles of commerce of great importance to the naval interests of England.*

He went on to suggest that 'the geographical position of New South Wales might give it a very commanding influence in the policy of Europe'. In the event of war with Holland or Spain, it would furnish England with 'a naval station of the greatest value'.

Sir George Young, a distinguished former naval officer with a private commercial interest in British overseas settlements, saw the advantages of the proposal.

> *The geographical position of the country placed it within easy communication with the Spanish settlements in South America on the one hand, and with China, the Spice Islands, and the Cape of Good Hope on the other. The facilities for extensive trade thus disclosed were not all; for should war break out between England and Spain, English ships would then have the tremendous advantage of a great naval station in the South Sea.*

The convicts, Young considered, could be sent to the colony to assist in its construction. They could be conveyed in 'the China ships of the

East India Company, which, by altering their route after leaving the Cape of Good Hope, might land the felons on the coast of New South Wales, and then proceed to their destination'. The proposal met with a favourable response from Lord Sydney, Attorney-General Pepper Arden and Sir Joseph Banks, who offered a first-hand recommendation. In 1784, the Admiralty was consulted. But the First Lord, Admiral Richard Howe, rejected the idea.

A number of other sites for a settlement were proposed around the same time. They were led by Das Voltas Bay (at the mouth of the Orange River on the south-west coast of Africa), Gromarivire Bay (on the Caffre Coast east of Cape Town), Tristan da Cunha (in the South Atlantic), and Madagascar. These four were located within a circle of radius of 1000 nautical miles. Botany Bay, on the other hand, was 7000 miles further to the east. Yet, it was the site ultimately chosen. There would appear to be only two grounds on which the British Government would have selected Botany Bay given its distance from London. First, it offered significantly greater potential for settlement to compensate for its distance from Britain. Second, it must have offered some special advantage not offered by the others. The attitude of the Admiralty in all of this was pivotal. For its part, the Royal Navy showed no initial resistance to the plan or any hesitation either in accepting command of the First Fleet or later in nominating naval officers as the first four governors. In those years the Admiralty had enormous power and influence. It literally did only what it wanted to do. Although Cabinet decided plans for overseas expeditions, the First Lord, who was invariably a Cabinet minister and the only person publicly accountable for the administration of the navy, ensured that Cabinet's decisions reflected his personal view. As British historian Nicholas Rodger has pointed out, 'although Cabinet orders began with the phrase: "Your Lordship will require and direct", most often the First Lord had himself decided the tenor of the orders he was to receive'. This did not mean, however, that the Admiralty always managed to secure the funds it needed to protect Britain or its interests at sea. In the 1770s and 1780s, the Admiralty believed it was desperately short of funds and reminded the Government that Britain was an island nation that needed to be a sea power and its people seafarers if it was to survive and flourish. A revitalisation of the navy and greater attention to maritime security abroad coincided with renewed interest in Botany Bay. It was also prompted by a series of naval and military disasters between 1776 and 1782.

The American war was a severe blow to Britain. France joined in the war with Britain in 1778, to be followed by Spain in 1779 and the Dutch in 1780. Revenge was the motive and Britain was thrown back on home defence for its survival. At the same time its solid grip on the Mediterranean had begun to falter. Britain lost Minorca for the second time; and as its forces were engaged in relieving the blockade of Gibraltar, a French squadron was able to leave Brest for the Indian Ocean. On the way it defeated a British expedition sent to capture the Cape of Good Hope, then in Dutch hands. The French Admiral, Pierre André de Suffren, captured Trincomalee in Ceylon and Britain came very close to losing its precious colony of India. If the French were to secure South Africa, India would be virtually lost as France would gain complete control of the sea route to India and, effectively, those waters would be closed to the British. Trade would cease. The French had also won at Ushant and gained the strategically vital island of Grenada in the Caribbean.

By 1782 Britain had experienced one of the blackest periods in its history. It had been almost evicted from North America and the Mediterranean. The navy had clearly been neglected and the funds destined for maintenance and expansion had been embezzled. Sir Geoffrey Callender, in describing the state of the navy from the mid-1760s, argued that:

> *Not even in early Stuart times was speculation so rampant and embezzlement so rife. The First Lord [of the Admiralty] divided his time between the gaming table and the political arena. Funds voted for the Fleet were deflected by [the First Lord] to party needs or private purposes, and his subordinates at the Navy Office and elsewhere trafficked and bartered with the maritime stores committed to their keeping.*

There was another disastrous consequence of the long period of decline after the Seven Years' War. The lack of interest in the navy had led to an absence of planning and foresight when it came to ships' timbers. The principal source of oak for British ships had been the forests of England. But these had been consumed to provide for past fleets and, despite a vigorous planting program instituted in the reign of King Charles II, the new trees were not sufficiently developed. Europe had become the navy's chief source of trees, despite its timbers being inferior to Britain's. The chief fear was that Britain might be excluded from Europe by a protracted war and so denied access to the vital forests with which to build and repair its warships.

The successive defeats starting with the American war had such an impact on Britain that things had to change and from the top. The dockyards and victualling yards were overhauled and administrative practices reviewed. Trustworthy men guarded the storehouses and stocktaking became more regular. In a logistic sense, the navy began to prosper as it had not done since the time of Oliver Cromwell's Commonwealth, over a century earlier. In 1778 when the French declared war on Britain, naval expenditure was £875 000; just five years later it had risen to approximately £2 000 000, which was actually spent on the purposes for which it was intended. By 1783 Britain was on the verge of a new era in its naval power and was ready to regain what it had lost over the previous decade.

The peace achieved by the signing of the Treaty of Versailles in September 1783 marked the start of a new phase in Britain's naval development and the creative use of sea power. The overall British strategy was straightforward. By restricting or hindering the use of the seas by the other European powers, Britain would curtail their economic progress and arrest their national development. By guaranteeing the secure use of the seas for its own purposes, Britain could find new markets to exploit and consistently enlarge its economic and trading base. This would enhance its ability to maintain a navy and further establish a global empire. Thankfully, the Royal Navy had survived the traumas of the previous decade, if only because its enemies were in a state of disarray. It was an opportunity for it to lick its wounds and rebuild without the enormous and complicating pressure of war. Barely three months later the administration of William Pitt (the younger) took office. Pitt was the prime minister the navy needed if it was to recover its ascendancy. He knew well that it was the condition and efficiency of the navy that had enabled his father to achieve such striking success in the Seven Years' War. Putting aside Britain's poor financial position in the early 1780s, he was determined to build a strong navy. His administration conducted some sweeping reviews of the dockyards and allocated funds for the building of 24 new ships of the line. To man this enhanced fleet, the navy grew from 15 000 to 18 000 men.

Pitt was also aware that Britain's position on the European continent would always be tenuous at best and that Europe could not be considered a reliable supply of materials, particularly for shipbuilding. In the event of a sustained war with European powers it would be Britain's colonies, along with the massive expansion of the internal economy under the Industrial Revolution, which would sustain the

Empire. The crucial link between the colonies and Britain was its merchant fleet, which would carry the cargoes, and the navy, which would protect the sources of supply and the transportation of commodities while searching for new markets and new areas to exploit. Owing to the location of its colonies, Britain needed to exert control of the seas. This involved guaranteeing the safe passage of its own trade and denying the seas to its enemies. All of this was reflected in the navy's strategic outlook at that time.

The Royal Navy had a 'trinitarian' understanding of its functions as military, diplomatic and policing. The *military* function consisted of engaging the enemy and principally destroying his fleet. The *diplomatic* dimension consisted of using naval force in every situation short of war to highlight national interests and demonstrate national resolve. *Policing* took the form of protecting and safeguarding national interests, particularly the seaborne trade plying the world's oceans.

The old Admiralty maxim was 'The seas are the world's highway'. Britain needed to ensure its trade could enjoy the freedom of the seas in the absence of interference. It was also evident that a country with a navy is potentially an ally or an enemy to all countries with a coast. Britain needed the seas to sell the commodities it produced and could hope to expand that trade with seaborne access to nearly every region on the globe. The possession of a large navy was also the source of immeasurable national prestige. This was not just a matter of appearance but a concrete advantage. It won Britain respect, authority and deference in the international arena. The power of the Royal Navy was one of Britain's chief propaganda weapons and gave it diplomatic strength that outweighed its actual potential. Oliver Cromwell, a man with a grasp of naval strategy that has been largely ignored, used the navy to great effect in the days of the English Commonwealth and remarked that a warship is 'a country's best ambassador'.

The protection of trade was Britain's foremost objective in the East and was particularly important with respect to France, which was steadily expanding its trade in the region. Heightening British concerns, there were rumours that the French were considering amalgamating their East India Company, which had been provided with ships of the line mounting 64 guns made redundant by the peace of 1783, with that of the Dutch. For their part, the Dutch controlled the Cape of Good Hope and although they were not at war with Britain, the British needed a safe harbour in the region to afford some protection for its India trade. The best Britain could do was to occupy the Andaman Islands in the Bay of Bengal. However, the Andamans had proved a disastrous place for European settlement. Attempts by French Jesuits in 1711, the Danes in 1756 and the Austrians in 1778 had all ended in failure. An alternative was needed and was sought. Given its size and location astride three great ocean basins—the Indian, Pacific and Southern—Australia was too large a landmass to ignore and would inevitably become of some strategic value. As a storehouse for the Royal Navy, Botany Bay was remote from the major trading routes and therefore from potential areas of conflict, and was ideally protected by distance. It was considered to be possibly the best site for the purpose for which it was intended. It would need wharfage and some refit facilities, in addition to stores and accommodation, before it would be of any use. But that was not a great problem. Its enormous strategic potential would surpass the cost of building local facilities and infrastructure.

In his groundbreaking study published in 1981, *Convicts and Empire*, Alan Frost argues that Botany Bay was primarily to serve as a base for naval operations against the Spanish in South America and as a means of excluding, or at least counterbalancing, the French presence in the East. Britain's trade with India was so crucial that the sub-continent could no longer go unprotected and New South Wales would serve as a strategic outlier to the Indian trade routes. Frost also attacked the trade and commerce theories by showing that Governor Phillip was given the most explicit instructions not to permit any kind of private trade between New South Wales and the European centres in Asia. There was also the closely guarded monopoly on trade held by the British East India Company. According to Frost, the need for a new penal settlement played only a minor part in the British Government's thinking in regard to the establishment of a settlement at Botany Bay.

The best known response to the strategic sea base interpretation championed by Blainey and developed by Frost is Robert Hughes' account of the convict element in Australia's history: *The Fatal Shore*. As the book argues that the convict experience is integral to the evolution of Australian nationhood and the creation of an Australian identity, Hughes has little choice but to enter the debate with a commitment to discarding the strategic and commercial theories and their claims. His ten pages of refutation are persuasive and perhaps conclusive to those unfamiliar with the debate. On closer inspection they are highly questionable and cannot be left unchallenged.

Hughes opens his criticism of the strategic sea base theory by denigrating the author of the first proposal to use Botany Bay as a commercial and maritime base, James Mario Matra, whom he derides as an opportunist and a man bent on personal gain. He then suggests that the failure of Lord Frederick North, Secretary of State for the Colonies, to reply to the proposal is evidence that the suggestion was 'ignored' because of its silliness. But Hughes neglects to point out that North's character would have prevented him from being interested in Matra's proposal. He was, according to one biographer, a 'man of peace; cultured, charming, adept at political manoeuvre and incapable of leadership'. He was dominated in all discussion of naval matters by the First Lord of the Admiralty, Lord Sandwich. In fact, North had told the First Lord in September 1772: 'I do not recollect to have seen a more peaceful appearance of affairs as there is at the moment'. It is highly unlikely that he would have acted on Matra's proposal, let alone given it support when he held those sentiments. It would have seemed irrelevant.

Hughes also fails to mention Lord Sydney's response to Matra's suggestion. He uses the 'argument of silence', for which he is critical of Blainey, to say that William Pitt was not impressed by the strategic idea based on the attractive supply of flax. He does not say why the views of Alexander Dalrymple, the East India Company's hydrographer, should have had the most weight in official circles. One would have thought his opinions would have been heavily biased given that he was, as Hughes admits, in the employ of a company whose monopolistic charter would have been violated by the supply of flax. There is no reason why Dalrymple's opinion should have been judged more expert when it came to the assessments of the quality of flax or its growth anywhere else in the region.

That Hughes is determined to give no credence to the strategic sea base theory is obvious by his use of invective when it comes to describing the manner in which the strategic proposals were handled. Lord Howe 'curtly' rejected them while their illogicality was 'sharply' pointed out by Dalrymple, who saw them as 'ridiculous'. On the matter of their rejection by Lord Howe, Hughes forgets that Howe was not the principal adviser on naval affairs to the young Pitt. The scheming Comptroller of the Navy, Sir Charles Middleton, had Pitt's ear. Yet Hughes implies the navy was against the idea because the First Lord was unconvinced. Of those whom Hughes names as having anything to do with the proposal, five are either advocates or supporters: Matra, Banks, Sir George Young, Colonel John Call (formerly of the East India Company) and Pepper Arden (Pitt's Attorney-General). Three—Pitt, North and Sydney—have no definite view ascribed to them. Only Dalrymple and Lord Howe were opposed, although Hughes fails to say why Howe rejected Matra's early proposal. In sum, his critique is far too narrow and fails to give enough weight to Britain's external concerns, particularly the protection of merchant shipping and its limited presence in the Indian Ocean.

It is hard to deny that the state of British prisons by the mid-1780s was little short of critical and that something had to be done. Hughes is right to point out the urgency of the problem and the role Botany Bay could have in alleviating such a situation. This is reinforced by the British Government's subsequent actions. If anything was in abundance in New South Wales it was convicts. The supply of convicts was constant and seems to have borne little relationship to the colony's ability to sustain them. The penal settlement interpretation is still, however, inadequate in accounting for the selection of Botany Bay. The settlement of New South Wales was fundamentally a complicated maritime question with a number of dimensions. Would a new settlement on the coast charted by James Cook in 1770 serve Britain's maritime interests and national security? The answer must be considered in context.

Europe showed little interest in the island continent during the seven decades following William Dampier's voyage to the South Seas in *Roebuck* and his landing on the west coast of Australia in 1699. In 1769, Lieutenant James Cook was given command of *Endeavour* and placed in charge of a scientific expedition in the South Pacific to observe the transit of the planet Venus. Although exploration was a secondary objective, Cook rounded the south-east coast of Australia and followed the coast as far as Cape York Peninsula. He was impressed with what he found. Cook told the Admiralty that a place he had named Botany Bay was most suitable as the site for a new settlement, although he did not comment in detail on its purpose. In the years that followed, however, there was much to distract Britain's attention from establishing a new settlement so far from its shores. The American colonies had declared their independence and were unavailable for the transportation of British convicts after the last shipment arrived on board the *Jenny* at Virginia in April 1776. In 1779 the House of Commons ordered a commission to inquire into the problem of transportation, and if possible to develop a plan to relieve the congested state of the prisons and hulks. Transportation to Africa was abandoned in 1785 owing to the high rate of mortality from the harsh climate. There was a successful attempt to smuggle a shipload of convicts to America in 1783–84 but the number was very small. In any event, it did little to relieve the overcrowded gaols in Britain. But the problems associated with a growing convict population were not deemed to be as compelling nor as immediate as the fears that Britain's enemies, especially the Spanish, were rapidly improving their position in the New World.

Alan Frost and Robert King have argued that it was not a fear of the French or the Dutch that had the central role in the selection of Botany Bay. They point to the Spanish and their growing colonial interests. Both historians provide a wealth of evidence to show that Britain was frustrated by its inability to attack the Spaniards in the Pacific, particularly their settlements on the western coast of America. There had also been two failed attempts to capture the Falkland Islands from the Spanish. The first was in 1749 while the second, between 1764 and 1770, nearly led to war. By the mid-1780s, British resentment of Spanish action in claiming a right of exclusive navigation in the Pacific and the exclusive possession of the western coast of America had reached crisis level. For Britain to establish the empire it desired there was no alternative but to challenge the Spanish, primarily over their domination of the entire eastern Pacific Ocean littoral.

A British base at Botany Bay would give the navy its best chance to mount an attack on the Spanish possessions with fresh ships and at a time that suited the Royal Navy. This was precisely what Sir George Young told Captain Arthur Phillip on his departure from England in command of the First Fleet. The purpose of Botany Bay was not to directly attack the Spanish settlements but to establish 'ports of shelter, and refreshment for our ships should it be necessary to send any into the South Seas' in a war with Spain. Britain would strive for the demise of Spain in the Pacific in carving out for itself an empire in the East. The existence of an imperial inclination is, however, disputed vigorously by historians holding the penal settlement interpretation. David Mackay argues:

> *those who put the foundation of the . . . [Botany Bay] . . . settlement in the context of a 'swing to the east', and those who see its establishment as part of some great commercial endeavour, greatly overestimate the policy-forming resources and enterprise of the metropolitan government. They assume a capacity for long-term planning which did not exist. They assume the existence of*

> *a philosophy of empire without specifying exactly where such a philosophy might reside or how it might be expressed. In this way the New South Wales example poses the question of how well adapted the government was at this time to view any imperial question in a wider context of direction or purpose.*

In response to Mackay, it can be said that the place for such a philosophy was within the Royal Navy and its expression was the determination by Britain to achieve 'command of the seas'.

By the mid-1780s Britain needed an imperial strategy to extend and enhance its economic and trading position that in turn gave rise to the need for Britain to have command of the seas and this, completing the circle, required an imperial outlook. The basis for and the validity of such a strategy already existed in Britain's recent history. Britain's maritime power was virtually interchangeable with its economic power. When it suffered naval defeats, as it had done since the mid-1750s, the entire nation suffered a setback. Control of the seas was vital to ensuring that Britain prospered and its enemies did not. The British naval strategist and historian, Sir Julian Corbett, argued that the high seas had important positive value as a means of communication and that this was at the heart of Britain's interest in controlling them:

> *For the active life of a nation such means may stand for much or it may stand for little, but to every maritime state it has some value. Consequently by denying an enemy this means of passage we check the movement of his national life at sea . . . It is obvious that if the object and end of naval warfare is the control of communications it must carry with it the right to forbid, if we can, the passage of both public and private property upon the seas.*

By denying other powers the use of the seas, Britain would curtail their economic progress and arrest their national development. By guaranteeing the secure use of the seas for its own purposes, Britain could find new markets to exploit and consistently enlarge its economic and trading base. This would enhance its ability to build and maintain a navy and detract from the ability of others to do the same. By the mid-1780s, the East held the greatest prospect for the expansion of trade. Trade with Atlantic countries accounted for £3 000 000 in exports and £4 000 000 in imports, while that with the East was less than £1 000 000 in exports and £2 000 000 in imports.

There was little doubt that trade with the East would expand and that 'the flag', carried by the ships of the Royal Navy, would need to follow.

It is very hard to believe that in the entire administration and the totality of the machinery of government there was no thought devoted to the future and no attention given to planning. This was patently not true of the Admiralty. It was constantly concerned with the future as a product of the long-term character of building and maintaining naval power. The Admiralty, which had historically stressed the oneness of the seas and the importance of Britain being guaranteed secure use of trade routes, favoured Britain developing an imperial outlook to assist it in achieving command of the seas. This accounts for the enthusiasm of the navy to assist with undertakings throughout this period such as the Botany Bay settlement. It was to be expected then that men like Sir Charles Middleton of the Navy Board, Phillip Stephens at the Admiralty and Lord Mulgrave played such a significant role in formulating a coherent imperial policy and strategy for Britain from the beginning of the Pitt administration.

The ships of the Royal Navy would build for Britain the empire it needed to sustain its economic growth while undergirding its security in Europe. But for warships to perform the myriad tasks that were expected of them, they had to be served and supported by a network of bases. At these naval bases, ships would be refitted and reprovisioned with ammunition and supplies, the ships' companies would rest and replacements would be provided for those who had either died or were too ill to continue at sea. Without these bases the fleet could neither go to sea nor stay afloat in a distant colonial station. The availability of nearby bases also offered a vital tactical advantage. Most naval actions did not proceed to the entire destruction of an enemy fleet. Rather the fight was broken off when smashed spars, torn sails and a lack of cordage left the ships unable to fight but capable of returning to a friendly port. The nation that was able to repair its fleet first gained an enormous tactical advantage. It could either defeat a depleted enemy or blockade its harbours.

Botany Bay was meant to add to Britain's already considerable tactical advantage in the Pacific with a ready supply of flax, hemp and ships' timbers. However, the supply of these items for the repair and maintenance of warships was principally for the dockyards in India, which had already gained a reputation for efficient refitting and shipbuilding. However, there are some grounds for being sceptical of the extent to which the British Government was led to make a decision in favour of Botany Bay on the basis of flax and Norfolk pine. In the first instance, there was little evidence that the flax was of superior quality or the timbers were as good as reputed. There was the word of Sir Joseph Banks, although his survey had been conducted well over a decade before and had been queried by others besides Alexander Dalrymple. At best, the possibility of obtaining those commodities was the subject of speculation and the measures taken for the manufacture of sailcloth from flax grown in the East were very rudimentary. Had Pitt placed great importance on a new supply of the materials coming from Australia more effort would have been expended and the British Government's interest in the early results would have been much greater. But if New South Wales was 'too far' and 'too expensive' for the dispatch of convicts, then should not the same be said about flax? Alan Frost points out that the flax was initially meant for India rather than for British manufacturers, thereby diminishing the significance of distance.

It was for these reasons that the selection of the site for a naval base was so important. Naval men nurtured their bases with care, constantly sought their improvement and development, and defined their requirements expansively. There were never enough bases and naval officers never tired of telling this to anyone who would listen. Such was the enthusiasm of naval officers for bases and support facilities that Lord Salisbury complained that 'if they were allowed full scope they would insist on the importance of the moon to protect us from Mars'. In spite of the natural reluctance to admit all of the navy's demands, the advantage of bases and facilities for a maritime force operating at considerable distance from home was self-evident. In sustaining a naval presence wherever its interests were located, the Royal Navy would shorten the time necessary for intervention in local conflicts, increase the length of deployments, enhance the refreshment of ships' companies and expedite replenishment. A string of bases also allowed local repairs and maintenance and avoided the risk of losing ships returning to England. Naval bases also served a diplomatic function. Their existence was a symbol of Britain and a sentinel of its naval power. Well-supplied and fortified bases and tactically deployed ships meant that Britain's political and economic hegemony would not be challenged without good intelligence and superior firepower. And the particular appeal of New South Wales was its location on a distant island beyond the usual commercial routes. There would be no immediate need of an army to protect the new settlement from a land attack or to prevent its occupation by another power. Britain would claim the island and there would be no serious threat from France, Spain, Portugal or Holland.

For its part, the Royal Navy was not in the least bit interested in the Government's convict problem. It saw in the New South Wales expedition a wonderful chance to extend British naval supremacy. The expansion of British naval power and the extension of its reach were national preoccupations by the mid-1780s. They were manifestly the strength of Britain. After 1783, the revitalised navy maintained by Pitt was looking to spread its influence and to engage in some diplomacy of its own. Sparing a few minor ships and some available officers for such a task was just the thing the navy was looking for. As much of the work would be performed by convicts and at no expense to the Admiralty, the navy would have been foolish not to make the most of this wonderful opportunity. Botany Bay was to be a low-cost experiment that met a number of needs while offering some general, attractive prospects for the future. For the navy it would be one of those 'come in handy' bases bound to meet a need in the future. Given its location, there was no chance of the Australian continent not taking on some strategic significance. Although Botany Bay was not the best site in relation to the established trade routes, it appeared that a settlement there would stand a great chance of survival and offer prospects of imperial expansion into the South Pacific.

At each point of the formal preparations for the fleet's voyage after 1786, some provision was made for the settlers to meet every need and every hope embodied in the decision to establish the colony. There was just enough equipment to allow some refit work to be conducted; just enough equipment to allow the local flax to be tested for its potential as sailcloth; and just enough stores and equipment for the whole colony to survive. It was the navy's timeless custom to give no more than the bare minimum it thought was required for the execution of the task. Some commentators point to the paucity of naval resources as a weakness in the strategic sea base interpretation. Mollie Gillen argues:

> *They . . . [the British Government] . . . sent 700-odd convicts to this marvellous source of naval supplies to struggle for more than two years without support before a single ship was sent to follow up—not with artisans, shipwrights, naval and military advisers to build a strong presence, but with a thousand more convicts, half of them sick and feeble . . . The flax was not exploited, the naval experts were not sent, the convicts did not build dockyards.*

Gillen quite rightly points out that, had the British been serious about establishing a strategic base, they would have done in New South

Wales what they did in Halifax 40 years earlier. There they sent a series of transports not with convicts but

> *with carpenters, shipwrights, smiths, masons, joiners, bricklayers and all other artificers necessary in building or husbandry, a hospital ship, military and naval advisers, surveyor, engineer, military stores. Even then there were difficulties, but the town was built, fortified, and became in truth a strategic base, with money voted to maintain it.*

Even Frost is forced to concede that 'one cannot say that the New South Wales colony's playing of its strategic part in the years between 1793 and 1802 was more than tentative'.

This aspect of the debate has not been the subject of adequate attention. An historian could reasonably expect the attitude of the British Government to the colony before 1788 to have been reflected in its actions over the first five years of settlement. And given that communication with the colony was extremely limited and the picture they were able to gain of it was at best very rough, the emphasis on transporting convicts to New South Wales strongly suggests at least part of their motive in establishing the colony. The counter-argument would be to say that the convicts were the vital source of labour necessary to create the strategic outlier that the colony was meant to be, but this fails to account for the absence of the other requirements for a naval base. It was not until 1795 that a navy yard was established and even then its capacity to serve as a place of refreshment and repair for ships other than the two formally attached to the colony was virtually non-existent. The only purely naval purpose the colony was able to perform by 1800 was to be a guaranteed friendly place for ships to anchor. In other words, it was known not to be hostile. Except for the valuable survey work that was carried out continuously from the earliest day of the settlement and which had great naval value, along with the availability of convicts to serve as seamen in ships plying the waters of the East, little else was achieved. In fact, it would not be until the mid-1850s that New South Wales effectively had any naval value to Britain of consequence, and it was then more the product of local efforts than of the result of imperial policy.

The decision to settle Botany Bay should be seen as being influenced by a combination of factors, but we are still unable to reliably determine the essential significance of those various elements in the formulation of British policy. Much that was critical in the decision-making process was never written down. We can speculate and offer interpretations based on the best evidence and greatest plausibility, but those interpretations should not be treated as fact to the exclusion of other theories that undeniably have some merit. Botany Bay was arguably the 'best fit' for the British Government in 1786. It offered the most attractive option based on the best information of the time. The combined force of the commercial, strategic and social imperatives, and a measure of speculation led to New South Wales being chosen. This should not surprise anyone who is familiar with bureaucratic decision-making. As Paul Appleby remarked: 'in the executive branch as elsewhere . . . must be weighed sympathy, compassion, magnanimity, beauty, welfare and human unfolding along with order, defence, self-interest, bread, brick and machines'. Thus, Robert King properly concludes: 'Two of Pitt's most pressing concerns in 1786 were convicts and preparations for expeditions against Spanish America—in a single measure, one could serve the end of the other'. Convicts were the means, attacks on the Spaniards the end.

By 1786 the British Government had observed two things about Botany Bay. First, the continent is situated astride the two great ocean basins of the southern hemisphere. Its strategically significant location could not be overlooked. For the British in the 1780s, its initial occupation and subsequent development by an adversary would have threatened directly its possessions in Central and East Asia. Second, as an island it afforded certain unique advantages to the occupying state. Mindful of the difficulties faced by a succession of aggressors in attempting to cross the English Channel after 1066, the Royal Navy recognised that occupation of the entire continent could be achieved with a minimum of fuss and a minimal demand for continuing protection. Once the Royal Navy had achieved command of the seas, the British Government could develop Botany Bay at its leisure and without substantial expense on naval defence.

These two factors—the continent's location and its island geography—have been of enduring significance and the principal reasons for this land being largely spared the ravages of war. The following narrative assesses the extent to which these entirely natural advantages were either exploited or forgotten by both civil governments and naval administrations.

2

Pax Britannica 1786–1855

The selection of Botany Bay as the site for a new British colony was finally announced in July 1786. His Majesty's Transport Office was given the task of finding a fleet of ships for this special mission into distant and unfrequented waters. Having gained recent valuable experience in chartering vessels to carry troops and convicts to the American colonies and elsewhere around the globe, a small fleet was hastily assembled. It consisted of two naval escorts: the frigate HMS *Sirius* and the brig HMS *Supply*; three store ships, *Golden Grove*, *Fishbourne* and *Borrowdale*; and six transports, *Alexander*, *Charlotte*, the brig *Friendship*, *Lady Penrhyn*, *Scarborough* and *Prince of Wales*. They were the eleven ships of the First Fleet. The merchantmen were comparatively new vessels, *Lady Penrhyn* and *Prince of Wales* having been completed in the year they were chartered. Three of them met the rigorous standards set by the East India Company and would continue their voyage from Botany Bay to China where they would take on cargoes of tea. The others would be ballasted and return to England.

The fleet's flagship boasted a varied career. Referred to at the time as a sixth-rate frigate of 540 tons with an armament of twenty guns, *Sirius* was originally an old East India Company ship named *Berwick*. Under that name she had been burnt out to the waterline during loading some years before and had been left untouched for some time in Deptford Yard. Lieutenant Philip Gidley King, who sailed with the ship to Botany Bay, recorded in his journal that: 'She had been purchased on the stocks by Government in 1781, and was sent once to

America as a store-ship during ye war, and once after ye peace to ye West Indies'. Apparently the Admiralty purchased what remained of the burnt-out hull and rebuilt it for war service, retaining the name *Berwick*. When the requirement for First Fleet ships needed to be met, *Berwick* was taken up and her name changed to *Sirius*, the bright star in the southern constellation. Her complement was 160 men and boys, while the ship's original armament of six carronades and four six-pounders was supplemented with ten additional six-pounders and their carriages, which were not mounted. Captain Phillip's intention was to use any of the guns not required on board to form fortifications at the new colony. The other warship, the armed tender *Supply*, was a much smaller ship of 170 tons, armed with eight guns and sailed by a ship's company of just 50 men. *Supply* had been a navy transport and was really too small a ship for so long a voyage. Although considered a ship with very poor sea-keeping and 'very improper for this service', she was in use continuously until returned to England as unfit for further service.

The appointment of an officer to command the fleet and serve as the founding governor was the most crucial decision to be made. The officer would need to be discreet and capable with some experience of war in case the fleet or the settlement should come under attack. It appears that Sir George Rose, Treasurer of the Navy, chose his neighbour at Lyndhurst to command the expedition. Captain Arthur Phillip was then on forced retirement at half pay, farming at Lyndhurst. Phillip's last appointment had been to the ship of the line HMS *Europe* of 68 guns. An active and zealous man, Phillip was known as a capable officer, prudent, and possessed of sound judgement when it came to assessing character and human nature. But not everyone agreed he was the right choice for the task. Viscount Richard Howe, First Lord of the Admiralty, on hearing of the appointment wrote to Lord Sydney (Thomas Townshend), Secretary of State for the Home Department: 'I cannot say that the little knowledge that I have of Captain Phillips [*sic*] would have led me to select him for a service of this complicated nature'. Perhaps Lord Howe's failure to pen the captain's name correctly was evidence enough of how little he did in fact know of the officer and his many attributes.

The fleet sailed from Motherbank on 13 May 1787 with Captain John Hunter in *Sirius* and Lieutenant Henry Ball in *Supply*. HMS *Hyaena* would escort the fleet 200 miles to the west of the Scilly Isles where they would be beyond the dangerous French and Spanish coastlines and largely safe from mid-ocean attack. On board were

568 male and 191 female convicts; the guard consisting of one major-commandant and three marine captains, twelve subalterns, 24 non-commissioned officers and 186 private marines. Their departure met with little interest in England. Two other matters had grabbed public attention: the rumoured marriage of the Prince of Wales (later King George IV) and Mrs Fitzherbert which occasioned the payment of his considerable accumulated debts; and the impeachment and trial of Warren Hastings, the first Governor-General of India, for oppression and cruelty towards the local population.

The fleet called at Tenerife, Rio de Janeiro and the Cape of Good Hope for supplies, livestock and seeds en route to Australia. The voyage took over eight months to complete. When they arrived at Botany Bay in mid-January 1788 they found it hardly resembled the place Cook had visited in April 1770. There was very little arable land and the bay was too open to afford a comfortable anchorage. Phillip's instructions from Lord Sydney included the direction not to 'delay the disembarkation of the establishment upon the pretence of seeking a more eligible place than Botany Bay'. With this in mind he gave orders to have ground cleared for landing and tents erected. But Phillip was not happy to remain at Botany Bay without surveying the possible alternatives along that immediate area of coastline. One thing was sure, Botany Bay offered few natural features that would serve either a strategic sea base or a convict settlement.

Phillip decided to locate the colony in the next major inlet nine miles to the north of Botany Bay. Cook had named the feature Port Jackson after Sir George Jackson of the Admiralty. Phillip recorded his actions in a letter to Lord Sydney: 'I went round with three boats, taking with me Captain Hunter and several officers, that by examining different parts of the port at once less time might be lost'. Captain Hunter recorded that Phillip actually set out to examine Broken Bay not Port Jackson, but decided to have a look anyway. 'We got into Port Jackson early in the afternoon [the 20th], and had the satisfaction of finding the finest harbour in the world in which a thousand sail of the line may ride in perfect security.' They sailed around the harbour for two days. Hunter later wrote: 'examining every cove or other place which we found capable of receiving ships; the country was also particularly noticed, and found greatly superior in every respect to that round Botany Bay. The Governor, being satisfied with the eligibility of this situation, determined to fix his residence there, and returned immediately to the ships'. There is no doubt he also sighted the islands in the harbour as he sailed into Port Jackson. He went on to say:

> *The different coves were examined with all possible expedition. I fixed on the one that had the best spring of water, and in which the ships can anchor so close to the shore that, at a very small expense quays may be made at which the largest may unload. This cove, which I honoured with the name of Sydney, is about a quarter of a mile across at the entrance, and half a mile in length.*

On 23 January, Phillip returned to Botany Bay and found that the ground being cleared was of poor quality. Seven days after he had arrived in Botany Bay in *Supply*, Phillip sailed for Port Jackson, leaving Captain Hunter to follow with the transports.

Just before the fleet moved from Botany Bay, an ominous sight appeared on the horizon. It aroused the worst fears of the naval men and no doubt reinforced the reason for their enterprise. Two ships drew near and they were observed to be flying French colours. They were *La Boussole* and *L'Astrolabe* commanded by Comte de La Pérouse. On 24 January, they anchored on the northern side of the bay. Captain Watkin Tench of the Marines noted:

> *I flew upon the deck, on which I had barely set foot, when the cry of 'another sail' struck my astonished ear. Confounded by a thousand ideas which arise in my mind in an instant, I sprang up the barricado, and plainly descried two ships of considerable size standing in for the mouth of the bay. By this time the alarm had become general.*

They were not expected but the import of their presence was clear. The French had designs on the continent and perhaps even the infant settlement. Their timing could not have been better to achieve a maximum impact; forts and harbour defences would need to be established in Port Jackson immediately and the colonists would need to remain vigilant in watching for the untrustworthy French. The French sailed on 15 March and were lost on a reef at Vanikolo in the Santa Cruz Islands. There were no survivors and, accordingly, the French Government remained ignorant of the existence of the British settlement.

At ten o'clock on 26 January 1788 the fleet weighed anchor and in the evening reached Port Jackson. The majesty and strategic potential of the harbour met with universal acclaim. Daniel Southwell wrote: 'As a place for shipping it is perfectly landlocked, and has several capital arms furnished with many inlets, caves, and bays, where whole fleets might lay in safety, with good water under them and fine holding ground at the bottom'. The fleet surgeon, Dr John White, remarked: 'Port Jackson, I believe to be, without exception, the finest and most extensive harbour in the universe, and at the same time the most secure'. The Governor's commission was publicly read as were the letters patent for establishing the civil and criminal courts, the Union Jack was hoisted and the health of His Majesty King George III was toasted. The colony of New South Wales had been founded although the formal proclamation did not take place until 7 February. It was then that Phillip addressed the convicts:

> *we are here to take possession of this fifth division of the globe on behalf of the British people and to found a state which, we hope, will not only occupy and rule this great country, but will also be the beneficent patroness of the entire southern hemisphere. How grand is the project which lies before the youthful nation.*

Captain Phillip was faced with a tremendous task. He had to found a penal settlement and the beginnings of a strategic sea base with the most unpromising material and even that was in short supply. But his selection for such an undertaking had not been made with haste. He had the right background. Indeed, Lord Palmerston had proclaimed: 'Whenever I want a thing done well in a distant part of the world; when I want a man with a good head, a good heart, lots of pluck and plenty of common sense, I always send for a Captain of the Navy'. He had also earned the hardest praise of all, that of contemporaries. Captain J.F. Fortesque, on hearing of Phillip's appointment wrote in a letter to the Reverend W. Butler: 'I do think God Almighty made Phillip on purpose for the place, for never did man know better what to do, or with more determination to see it done; and yet, if they'll let him, he will make them all very happy'.

It was not long after the First Fleet entered Port Jackson that Captain Phillip ordered a full survey of the harbour. During the morning of 28 January, Captain Hunter with Lieutenant William Bradley commenced a series of day surveys.

After the construction of the basic settlement Phillip began to think about maritime facilities around Sydney Cove. Phillip knew from experience that once land was portioned out it would remain in the long-term possession of the owners. If the navy got certain parts of the harbour they could retain them for as long as they wanted, or so Phillip probably thought. He had to plan for both the short-term and the long-term defence of the colony. If Sydney were to serve in any capacity as a strategic sea base, it needed to have the facilities available to support naval ships, especially after La Pérouse had pointed to what the future might hold. On the western side of Sydney Cove a primitive wharf was built and named the Hospital Wharf, and later the King's Wharf. On the southern side of the cove, a small wharf was erected for the use of the Governor. These were short and of little use in ferrying cargoes from ships at anchor. Any repair and maintenance work was carried out adjacent to the King's Wharf, although the obvious preference was to sail the ships back to England for any major work. Although Garden Island—so named because it was given to the ship's company of *Sirius* to grow vegetables—had a beach ideal for careening ships it seems its isolation as an island negated any immediate naval advantage it may have offered. Phillip also attempted to give the settlement as much naval protection as he could, deploying the additional guns from *Sirius* to best effect. He gave the task of building forts to an officer of the Marine detachment, Second Lieutenant William Dawes. He first built a simple earthen redoubt on the eastern side of Sydney Cove, that closest to any would-be aggressor, on the site of what is now Bennelong Point. There he installed two six-pounders. He then turned his attention to the western side of the cove, where he mounted a battery of eight six-pounders. The site was named Maskelyne after the Astronomer-Royal of the day, the Reverend Nevil Maskelyne. The battery on Bennelong Point very soon fell into disuse whereas the battery on the western side was developed into a major defensive position. A third battery was to be built on Garden Island but at some later time.

Phillip left the colony on 10 December 1792. He had established a new colony, laid the foundations for naval defence and given the Royal Navy a leading role in civil affairs. His immediate successors, Acting Governor Grose and Captain Paterson, were military men who did not share Phillip's enthusiasm for establishing essential naval infrastructure. It was not until 7 September 1795 that Captain John Hunter arrived as governor and immediately took up where Phillip had left off.

To assist in ship repair, Hunter established His Majesty's Dockyard on the western shore of Sydney Cove and appointed Thomas Moore as master boatbuilder on 13 September 1795. Hunter later added a 'commodious stone house near the naval yard for the Master boatbuilder. Paled in a naval yard on the western side of the cove, and erected a joiner's and blacksmith's shops; sheds for repairing vessels, and for the workmen'. But it was never more than a very modest facility. Captain James Colnett of HMS *Glatton* described it as 'confined—badly situated—not capable of improvement; I have seen a dog-kennel larger'. This was a rather scathing and uncomplimentary assessment. However, the depot continued to fill an important role in the life of the colony. One of the first vessels to be constructed at the yard was *Cumberland*, a small schooner of 29 tons, which was launched in 1801 and placed at the disposal of Matthew Flinders in 1803 after *Porpoise* was wrecked 740 miles north-east of Sydney. While Hunter had enlarged the colony's ability to support naval operations and maritime trade, a crisis had developed in his dealings with the military establishment.

In the three years between Phillip's departure and Hunter's arrival, the New South Wales Corps, formed to provide a garrison in the new colony, had managed to gain economic and political ascendancy. Indeed, such was the extent of the corps' sway that it could directly challenge Hunter's decision to end its monopoly on the trade of rum. Although the exercise of arbitrary authority was needed, Hunter tried a personal approach, believing he was dealing with fellow officers who could be trusted to act honourably. He was wrong. He was subjected to unscrupulous denigration by the corps, and critical letters were sent back to England which further tarnished his professional reputation. His recall came as no surprise, not even to Hunter himself. The standing of a gentle, humane and charitable man was destroyed by a group of men lacking respect for either Hunter or his office. As governor, he should have acted decisively to enforce his authority while steadfastly refusing to admit any challenge to his near-absolute power to regulate the affairs of the colony, especially its defensive preparedness. This was an instance in which a naval officer did not utilise the full extent of his prerogatives of command to fulfil the instructions given to him by government. The legacy of Hunter's administration was a mutinous military that resented authority, especially when it resided in a naval officer.

When the newly promoted Captain Philip Gidley King arrived at Sydney in the transport HMS *Speedy* in April 1800 to replace Hunter, the navy's position needed bolstering. King acted as *locum tenens* until a formal appointment was made. By letters patent dated 20 February 1802, Hunter's commission was revoked and King was appointed Captain-General and Governor-in-Chief. Following Hunter's initiative, King appointed himself to the command of *Porpoise* on its arrival in the colony. King had actually been appointed to *Reliance*, although that ship had returned to England in 1799. King did not, however, propose to lose his status as senior officer as this would allow him to supervise naval activity in the region. He wrote to Lord Nepean on 30 November 1800:

> *I have to acquaint you that His Majesty's armed vessel* Porpoise *arrived here the 6th November, and I have taken it upon me to appoint Mr William Scott, master in the navy (and who brought the* Porpoise *out under the Naval Board direction, and no other naval officers being here), to act as Lieutenant and Commander of that Vessel in my absence, but without any additional pay or wish on his part to be confirmed as a Lieutenant.*

The Duke of Portland replied on 19 June 1801: 'In consequence of the representations which I have made to the Lords Commissioners of the Admiralty, their Lordships will order the *Buffalo* to return to New South Wales as soon as she can be got ready, and they will send out by her the necessary commission'.

Nepean also wrote to King on 2 December 1801 advising him that the Admiralty had put him in command of *Buffalo* with Lieutenant Kent second commander. However, concerning his self-appointment to the command of *Porpoise*, Nepean wrote on 5 May 1802: 'The Lords Commissioners of the Admiralty acquaint you that under the circumstances you have stated, they will not disapprove of what you have done although the proceeding has been irregular'. But the situation was still somewhat unsatisfactory from King's point of view. In a dispatch to the Secretary of State for the Colonies, Lord Hobart, dated 9 May 1803, King again inquired about his naval status and his ability to direct all naval activity around the continent. The matter prompting this correspondence was the arrival in Port Jackson of HMS *Glatton*. In command was Captain James Colnett, who was actually senior to King by date of promotion. He wrote: 'I have requested Captain Colnett, who is my superior naval officer, to order a survey of the *Supply* hulk'.

King had reason to be concerned about the sufficiency of the colony's maritime defences. The moorings and anchorages used by warships in the early days were all in Sydney Cove with ship's boats conducting their business from King's Wharf. The first moorings sent to the colony appear to have been sent in 1796 or 1797. With the difficulty of building wharves and jetties, Governor King sought some additional equipment in a letter to Under Secretary John Sullivan written on 7 August 1803.

> *Three sets of mooring chains were received in this colony one of which was laid down for the* Supply*—another set has just been laid down for the* Investigator *hulk to which has been attached small chains for the use of smaller vessels and as a third remains to be laid, that beneficial object is to be retarded for the want of a swivel and three Jew Harps, which cannot be found from which I conclude they were omitted to be sent.*

King asked Hunter to look into the matter and to arrange for the delivery of a further two smaller swivels and bridle chains to accommodate the increased amount of shipping that was using the harbour. But they would probably take years to arrive. This made the people acutely conscious of how far they were from Britain and the protection afforded by the Royal Navy. As replies to communications with London could take as long as one year to be received, the settlement could be destroyed before the Admiralty was even aware that it was under threat of attack. Captain Watkin Tench of the Marine detachment remarked as the ships of the First Fleet departed Port Jackson in July 1788:

> *it was impossible to behold without emotion the departure of the ships. On their speedy arrival in England perhaps hinged our fate . . . The Dread of want in a country destitute of natural resources is ever peculiarly terrible, we had long turned our eyes with impatience towards the sea.*

The presence of the French had caused alarm when the First Fleet arrived in 1788. This was the first of many worrying incidents over the next fifty years. David Collins commented with some suspicion on the visit of the Spanish corvettes *Descuvierta* and *Atrevida* in 1793. There was also the visit of the American brig *Philadelphia* in December 1792. The arrival of the French ships *Le Géographe* and *Le Naturaliste* under the command of Captain Nicolas Baudin in June 1802 prompted concerns about French interest in the west coast of the Australian continent and the South Pacific. Although the British and the French had signed the Treaty of Amiens, two members of Baudin's party, Francois-Auguste Péron and Lieutenant Louis-Claude de Freycinet, were engaged in spying on defences around the continent. Although the French were treated politely, new settlements were promptly ordered on the Derwent and in Port Phillip. Later Péron reported to General Decaen, the French Governor of Mauritius, on the best strategy for attacking the British settlement at Port Jackson. Although the attacks never came, the first three governors understandably felt themselves to be in a relatively vulnerable position. For the first fifteen years of settlement, the presence of warships was irregular and progress on naval infrastructure was slow. In effect, the security of New South Wales had been effectively guaranteed by events elsewhere.

The Battle of Trafalgar on 21 October 1805 was Britain's finest hour at sea. After more than two years of hostilities, a much smaller force commanded by Admiral Horatio Nelson had destroyed a combined French and Spanish fleet. Although retaining control over a massive area of continental Europe, the French forces commanded by Napoleon Bonaparte could no longer take the war to the British on the seas. The Royal Navy now sailed the world without fear, confident in the awesome and unrivalled power that it alone possessed. There was little Napoleon could do outside of Europe. He had neither the ships nor the bases to support a distant campaign against a British outstation. Most of the brighter French naval officers had been butchered during the Revolution as enemies of France. Yet Napoleon still tried to exert some naval strength. In 1810 he instructed the French Governor of Mauritius to seize Port Jackson. The British blockaded Mauritius and sent a ship of the line to Sydney. Such was Britain's capacity for the exercise of sea power anywhere in the world, the French Governor did not even attempt to carry out his desperate Emperor's direction.

Indeed, Britain's entire position in the East had significantly improved since the establishment of the settlement in 1788. In 1793–94, Britain captured French bases and islands in Canada and the West Indies, and Pondicherry in India. By the end of 1794, they had captured the Cape of Good Hope, Trincomalee and Malacca. In 1796, the Royal Navy had seized Colombo, Amboina in the Moluccas and the Banda Islands. Britain countered French victories on the continent by the deprivation of colonies and the destruction of shipping. In 1810–11, the British Government led by Spencer Perceval authorised a series of operations against French and Dutch possessions in the Indian Ocean and Far East. The British captured Mauritius, Bourbon, Madagascar, the Seychelles and Java. Just as New South Wales had the capacity to contribute to the strategic equation in the Indian and Pacific Ocean basins, the need diminished dramatically. Even the Admiralty thought New South Wales was secure because no fleet powerful enough existed anywhere in the world to mount an attack across the seas. After Trafalgar, their Lordships reduced the naval presence in Sydney to ships of less than twenty guns and then withdrew warships altogether for the foreseeable future. The southern continent would remain safely in British hands without the protection of naval power.

The Royal Navy had nonetheless enjoyed relative freedom of action in the colony for more than twenty years and had not ignored naval requirements. But none of the first four governors managed to achieve satisfactory relationships with the military units deployed to New South Wales. King was unable to control the New South Wales Corps and spent much of his time and energy in conflict with its officers. Captain William Bligh, a veteran of two naval mutinies in 1789 (HMS *Bounty*) and 1797 (HMS *Duncan*), was unable to bring the more rebellious elements of the corps to heel and found himself the victim of a third mutiny. The Royal Navy's ascendancy in New South Wales came to an abrupt end with the appointment in 1809 of Lieutenant Colonel Lachlan Macquarie as governor to replace the deposed and imprisoned Bligh. When Macquarie arrived in Sydney on board the 50-gun frigate *Hindostan* (accompanied by the 20-gun store ship *Dromedary*) he made a prompt tour of the more immediate parts of the colony.

As the years passed he made further tours to the more distant parts of the settlement. While concentrating on development of the hinterland and exploitation of its potential, Macquarie seems to have shown little enthusiasm for the navy's activities. As a soldier with only passing acquaintance with naval operations and the exercise of sea power, Macquarie seemed to believe that the defeat of the French and Spanish fleets at Trafalgar in October 1805 had removed any continuing threat to Britain or its expanding empire. He overestimated the extent to which the Royal Navy was able to act independently and the scope of its self-containment. In spite of victory over Napoleon and the rise of the Royal Navy as the premier naval force in the world, Britain's colonial possessions around the world remained modest. They consisted of Newfoundland, Canada (east of the Great Lakes), the Cape Peninsula, certain parts of India, a string of islands and the eastern seaboard of New South Wales. It was not until after the Battle of Waterloo in 1815, which saw Napoleon finally defeated, that Britain used its naval and military power almost solely for the purposes of trade protection and extension, and territorial expansion. Although Britain claimed to 'possess' Australia, it would have been of little use in any sea fight in this quarter of the globe other than being able to provide a friendly port in which British ships could take refuge. Consistent with the strategic outlook, Port Jackson still had very limited capacity for ship repair and maintenance. Macquarie's faith in the Royal Navy and confidence of the benign state of this corner of the world may have contributed to his undertaking an enormous expansion of the interior without the fear of external aggression. He also failed to see that Britain still needed a string of bases and support facilities around the world if it were to maintain its naval dominance and be prepared for any aggression against its national interests. The nearest port which could sustain a warship was Singapore (seized by the British in 1819)—much too far from Australia should Britain's interests be challenged. Macquarie may also have felt that there were imbalances to correct.

With the rapid growth of trade to and from Australia, the need for a naval presence increased rather than diminished despite the Royal Navy's pre-eminence. The fear of privateers remained well into the nineteenth century while shifting alliances in Europe had the ability to turn friends rapidly into foes. Consequently, the navy would be needed to protect convoys of British traders fearful that Bass Strait, discovered in 1797, would become a haven for raiders. Thinking that the French would most likely establish a base in the south-east corner of Tasmania, a settlement was established on both sides of the strait, at King Island and at Port Phillip Bay.

Australia was a place whose value was based on the fact that it lay on the route to somewhere. Britain prized the harbours more than it valued the land. But from 1820 and with the continuing growth of a lucrative local industry in wool and whale oil, Australia became 'a terminus instead of a wayside station'. The Australian continent now needed protection in its own right and the Admiralty needed to rethink its provision. So with Australian trade increasing rapidly in value, the Admiralty established the Australia Station in 1821 as a division under the East Indies command with ships from the East Indies Squadron occasionally detached for service in Australian waters. Over that twenty-year period HM Ships (sixth-rate) *Alligator*, *Caroline*, *Conway*, *Imogene* and *Rattlesnake*, and the sloops *Hyacinth*, *Pelorus* and *Zebra* were all based for a time in Port Jackson. Their presence tended to balance the number of foreign vessels sailing into and through Australian waters.

French ships were frequent visitors during the 1820s. Their official purpose was 'discovery' but the British feared a more sinister intent. *La Coquille* visited in 1824, *La Thetis* and *Esperance* in 1825 and *L'Astrolabe*, commanded by Dumont D'Urville, in 1826. D'Urville had been ordered to explore islands off the west coast of Australia in preparation for the possible establishment of a French penal colony near the Swan River. After Major Edmund Lockyer was sent on an expedition to the west in December 1826, Captain James Fremantle in HMS *Challenger* took possession in May 1829 of that part of the continent not included in the declaration of New South Wales.

But this was not to suggest that Sydney itself was secure. William Charles Wentworth's *Australian* newspaper was the first to express concerns about the poor state of naval defences. Should nations like Russia ever declare war on Britain, 'that gingerbread work, Macquarie Fort, and all the pop guns at Dawes Battery, could not for one hour oppose an armed force of any power, Russian or American . . . what defence a hindrance against blowing the town about our ears, but a levy of a good sound contribution by way of ransom'. While a squadron might be detached from India, the *Australian* asked what would be left 'after the mischief were done?' There was a wave of general anti-Russian sentiment prompted by the devastating Russian suppression of a Polish uprising in 1830–31. Russian warships had been visiting since the *Neva* sailed into the harbour during Bligh's governorship. The Russians were subsequently given permission by Macquarie to establish an observatory and ship repair facility. Ten Russian ships visited Sydney between 1820 and the Polish suppression. After Russia formed an alliance with Turkey in 1835, the local press remarked with some relief: 'HMS *Rattlesnake*, 28 guns, under the orders of Captain [William] Hobson RN we are gratified to learn, is to remain on this station until relieved by another ship from the East Indies Squadron. A permanent man-of-war of respectable force has long been a desideratum'. The colonists remained suspicious of the Russians until the Crimean War of 1854–56 when there was a transition to open and unrestrained hostility. The Russians had replaced the French as the principal threat in colonial minds.

In addition to the Russian Navy, the colonists were wary of the Americans after 1835 when the US Navy created its own East Indian Squadron. Part of its purpose was protecting and extending American interests in an enormous area bounded by Africa to the west, the Bering Sea to the north, Hawaii in the east and Australia to the south. This was the most remote of the American distant stations established in this period. The first visit of American warships to Australia was on 30 November 1839 when two ships, *Vincennes* and *Peacock*, of an

American naval exploring expedition under Commander Charles Wilkes USN, sailed into Sydney Harbour unannounced. Seeking to give his ships' companies some rest and recreation after fifteen months at sea, Wilkes arrived off Port Jackson in darkness and brought his ships through the heads to anchor in Neutral Bay without being challenged by the port signal station on South Head. An editorial in the *Herald* spoke for many when it remarked:

> *The Governor some time ago remarked, we believe, that with a few guns, in a few hours, he could sink anything that attempted to come into the harbour. This speech excited a smile from the thinking portion of the people. The circumstance was recalled forcibly to our minds when we observed on Sunday morning an American squadron anchored off the town, which had come in during the night, without pilot, or any knowledge on the part of the authorities. It is a lucky thing that we are at present at peace with [the United States] or we should have been mauled 'pretty considerably I guess' in spite of the Governor's great guns. We trust the Government will see the propriety of immediately erecting batteries for our defence.*

Wilkes himself later commented: 'Had war existed we might, after firing the shipping and reducing the great part of the town to ashes, have affected [*sic*] a retreat before daybreak in perfect safety'. After the initial embarrassment of seeing the inadequacy of colonial defence plainly demonstrated, the people of Sydney extended a warm welcome to Wilkes and his men. As a final farewell gesture, Wilkes and his officers organised a gala ball held at Fort Macquarie with more than a thousand guests. The visit was an enormous success and created a most favourable impression of the US Navy among the colonists. When the ships departed on the next leg of their expedition to Antarctica, forty American sailors had deserted.

The unexpected and undetected arrival of Wilkes' ships added to residual concerns for self-defence among the people of Sydney. The comparative strengths of the British and American navies contributed to continuing caution as well. With European interest in the South and South-West Pacific increasingly rapidly from the early 1840s, the relative standing of the Royal Navy and its ability to protect British interests in the region had begun to decline. By 1846 the combined fleets of America and France in the Pacific outnumbered the Royal Navy, 27 ships to fifteen, and in firepower, 682 guns to 392. In that year alone, the United States had deployed to the

Pacific one 100-gun ship, two 50-gun ships, three carrying 24 guns and one of 24 guns. By comparison, the British had stationed a number of capable ships in the Pacific. They included *Collingwood* (80 guns), *America* (50 guns), *Grampus* (50 guns), *Fisgaard* (42 guns), *Modeste* (28 guns), *Juno* (26 guns), *Carysfort* (26 guns) and *Frolic* (16 guns). When tension developed over the role each nation would play in Pacific affairs, Britain realised it could not take on the Americans without drawing in the French as well. Although another naval war with America was unlikely, the British feared the development of a Franco-American alliance directed against the British. There was no doubt the Americans were seeking to play a larger role in Asia and the western Pacific.

By the 1840s American domestic demand for trade with Asia gave the US Navy a vital role in national economic growth. Navy Secretary William Preston wrote in his first annual report of 1849 that: 'The trade of the Pacific is now the great commercial prize for which the world is contending . . . Activity and energy will make it what it ought to be—an American commerce and an American trade'. This led Preston to ask Congress to increase the number of naval steamers it had authorised. Consequently, the US Navy was able to press an 'Open Door' trade policy on Japan. Not without reason, the authorities in New South Wales were alarmed. The commander of the imperial troops in Sydney, Sir Maurice O'Connell, had earlier on 15 February 1842 informed the Commander-in-Chief of the Horse Guards: 'There is moreover no naval force on this station, and, as there is both an American and a French squadron in the South Seas, we might in case of war with either of those powers anticipate an attempt on their part to levy contribution in New South Wales'. Britain's disputes with America over borders in Canada were also contributing to continuing diplomatic ill-will.

In his study of war scares in Australia in the nineteenth century, Robert Hyslop lists nearly two hundred separate incidents in which the colony's recognised enemies included France, Germany, Russia and America, and less often China, Holland, Japan and Spain.

France figures consistently throughout the period as a potential enemy. Russia appears in the first 30 years because of visits from Russian naval ships; then from the 1850s through to the end of the century. The United States features as the opponent of England in the war of 1812 but thereafter as sometimes a potential enemy mostly in respect of American activities in the Pacific and because of visits by American ships of war.

What are we to make of these sentiments? Were they justified? Quite apart from understandable concerns generated by the colony being so far from the sources of naval and military assistance, the defence of seaborne trade and the security of the principal harbours was clearly inadequate. Substantial investment was required as a matter of priority. In addition to Fort Macquarie on Bennelong Point in Port Jackson, the earliest attempts to give some protection to the trade route north of Australia were the establishment of Fort Dundas (on Melville Island) in 1824 and Fort Wellington (on Raffles Bay at the east end of the Cobourg Peninsula) in 1827. Other smaller fortifications were established in the decade that followed. But after the embarrassment of Wilkes' arrival, the imperial military commanders in New South Wales had moved to strengthen the harbour from attack by sea with the construction of Fort Denison on Rock Island in the middle of Port Jackson after 1841.

> *It now appears that the principal works consist of two batteries which the late Commanding Royal Engineer had constructed for the defence of the harbour and town of Sydney at a time when the public mind was ill at ease in consequence of an apprehension of hostilities between this Country and America.*

But the work suffered from parsimony. Although a small installation, work on Fort Denison was halted by a lack of funds from Britain a year after construction began. It was not until 1855 that work was resumed. British attention was also turned more towards India, which had plainly become too precious to leave as unprotected as it had been, and China, a rapidly growing destination for opium grown in India and a source of china, tea and other highly desirable commodities. Britain seized Singapore, the gateway to East Asia in 1819, and Aden, the postern between India and the British Isles in 1839. The only threats to existing British interests had been rumours of a French settlement in New Zealand in 1832 and the departure of a large French squadron in 1841 bound for the Pacific. The French established colonies in Eastern Polynesia and seemed, for the moment, to be content with that. Emperor Napoleon III of France apparently considered privately the possibility of seizing the Australian colonies in 1853. The colonists do not seem to have been aware of this although they still feared the French. The Russians, however, presented a different proposition.

In the early 1850s, deteriorating relations between Great Britain and Russia alarmed the colonists in view of the concentration of

Russian naval power in the North Pacific. There were also reports in Australia that a Russian warship was cruising off Cape Horn; four others were said to be in transit for Valparaiso, and fourteen others were at Vladivostok. At the time there were only six small ships of the Royal Navy in Australian waters. They were *Calliope*, a sailing frigate of 26 guns; *Herald*, a brig with eight guns; *Electra*, a sloop armed with fourteen guns; *Fantome*, a sloop of twelve guns; and the two small paddle-wheeled steamers, *Acheron* with five guns and *Torch* with nine guns. This was a totally inadequate force to cope with the firepower at the Russians' disposal. In March 1854, war broke out on the Crimean Peninsula and the subsequent departure of four Russian warships southward from Manila was interpreted as a definite threat to Australia. There was also a strong feeling that Australia was now worth defending in its own right; that it was no longer just a matter of denying its possession to the enemy. Australia was an important source of many commodities, particularly wool. By the 1850s, rich deposits of gold were being discovered. As a people, Australians were already developing pride in their colony and looking forward to the prospect of nationhood. Clearly, the Australian people and their property needed to be defended from the threatening Russians. To this end, HM Colonial Ketch *Spitfire* was launched at Sydney in 1855. This was the first warship built locally for an Australian colony's defence. It was a demonstration of commitment and resolve. The colonists also wanted the prestige of having warships in their ports: ships of their own but more importantly at the time, ships of the Royal Navy. But the Governor of New South Wales during the crucial period of the 1850s, Major General Sir William Denison of the Royal Engineers, saw Australia's defence needs from the perspective of a soldier, and an engineer at that.

Denison took a narrow view of local requirements. He proposed making fortresses out of the harbour entrances. Given that Australia's greatest interest at that time was the safe passage of cargoes around the coast and abroad, the strategy outlined by Denison and the other soldier-governors was parochial and largely futile. Denison wrote to his friend Sir Roderick Murchison on 21 May 1855, explaining his view of Sydney's security problems.

> *You laugh, and with reason, at the panic which led people in these Colonies to insist upon fortifying themselves against the Russians. I never partook of this panic, but I have gone into the question of the defence of Sydney for the purpose of keeping off much more*

unpleasant neighbours than the Russians, namely our friends the French and our relations the Americans. The access to this harbour is so easy that unless we have some batteries ready to open upon vessels lying off the town, a few frigates might run in under cover of the night, and the first notice I should have of their arrival would be a 32lb shot crashing through the walls of my house. Of Russia I have no fear.

That this was a most unlikely scenario explains why it never happened and why the coastal defences were of little real value. There was no need for any enemy ship to venture near Port Jackson and to make itself a target for the short-range shore batteries. They could have remained on the horizon off Sydney and inflicted great damage on the colony by capturing inbound and outbound shipping. This would have effectively closed the port. It was arguable whether the erection of gun batteries on the headlands or in the harbour itself would have prevented the surreptitious arrival of enemy ships in any event. There was an alternative: a mobile squadron of frigates. Warships were better suited to protecting the ships and the harbours. But the problem of repairing and maintaining any ship deployed to the large and far-flung Australia Station remained a challenge to the Governor in Sydney and the Admiralty in London.

The Government Dockyard was closed in 1833 with, it appears, little disruption to naval activities. In the period that followed, Royal Navy ships anchored or moored usually in Farm Cove with stores issued from a number of store ships under the direction of a small naval administration section located at Fort Macquarie. The smaller ships visiting the port, and in this period most were minor vessels, could practically complete their refit with their own labour and expertise. To encourage this would have suited the local authorities as it avoided any expenditure or administrative action on their part. Private firms enjoying a monopoly provided naval stores. As there was little chance of the monopoly being broken, the Sydney merchants could be left to make good profits while the local economy would remain relatively buoyant. The only time some attention was given to the requirement for naval stores in Australia was when five vessels visited Port Jackson during a four-month period in 1827. The Navy Board was directed to consider establishing a dedicated naval store as the colony was unable to meet the ships' demands. However, the matter came to nothing and the demands of 1827 did not re-occur. The stores themselves were procured from local sources through the army commissariat officer. This proved to be a satisfactory arrangement until 1870 when imperial troops were finally withdrawn and the navy was forced to seek alternative arrangements.

The absence of adequate naval facilities drew comment from the Admiralty in 1846. Their Lordships noted:

> *there is no arsenal or port in the Pacific in which any material assistance can be provided in effecting repairs to Her Majesty's ships, nor is there any place between the north west coast of America and New Zealand where the damaged spars of even large frigates can be replaced.*

Only two options were available to ships requiring hull repairs (usually leaks). Ships could either attempt to work on the hull timbers from the bilges or the ship could be careened. This entailed grounding and beaching the vessel at high tide with the ship supported and made fast in low tide to permit access to the hull. But this became increasingly unsatisfactory. A busy port could not operate without a dock, and a number of options were raised.

When the colony was in a position to build its own graving dock, the site selected was Cockatoo Island. It was the largest island in Port Jackson with an area nearly twice that of Garden Island. Cockatoo Island was first used before 1800 as a gaol for hardened convicts awaiting transportation to Norfolk Island or Van Diemen's Land. It was proclaimed a general gaol for convicts in June 1841. Stone from Cockatoo Island was found to be ideally suited for building and convicts were employed in cutting the stone used for the wharf at Circular Quay, the island's own wharf and a wheat storage. In 1851 work commenced on excavating the 150-yard long Fitzroy Dock on the eastern side of the island, four years after the newly established New South Wales Legislative Council gave its approval. Work was completed in 1857 and HMS *Herald* was the first ship to be docked. Prior to that time the navy had been forced to use Morts Dock, a commercial facility, which had opened two years earlier. The prison on Cockatoo Island, a useful source of labour, continued to operate until 1871.

There were several good reasons for the Admiralty deciding against funding the construction of a purpose-built naval dockyard in New South Wales. In the first instance, the dockyards had been an administrative nightmare in Britain. They had been the scene of enormous corruption and mismanagement for well over a century even after several attempts by the Admiralty to curb the many excesses. The idea of setting up a dockyard in Australia, although it was administratively a clean slate, was not very attractive. The navy was also extremely pressed for finance. Those who might have been aware that such a need existed had not argued in the right places or with adequate conviction the need for such a facility. Ship maintenance and repair facilities since the colony had been established had shown no great need for a permanent, purpose-built dockyard in Australia. But this in itself was a misleading argument. In New South Wales, the ships visiting Port Jackson were clearly not worthy of repair or were in such good condition that repair was not required. Neither option would cost the Admiralty vast sums nor require a decision on whether to repair a ship or build a new one. There was not a great deal the Admiralty had to decide about naval affairs in Australia. It is apparent that the Admiralty was not well acquainted with the challenges facing New South Wales nor did their Lordships appear to trouble themselves greatly over such a far-flung and minor naval station. It was, after all, still only an offshoot of the East Indies Station. There remained, however, a strong feeling against using merchant or commercial facilities for naval work. This largely accounts for the navy yard remaining for as long as it did within the confines of Sydney Cove. As late as 1848, the principal ship surveyor of Lloyd's Register expressed the view that warships ought to be built in the naval dockyards because only there were the workers accustomed to the necessary standards of construction, which required a combination of the best possible skill and materials.

Although it was universally recognised that any threat to Australia had to come by sea, the facilities required for sustaining warships remained woefully inadequate. The navy's base was effectively an area around Fort Macquarie made available by the Commanding Royal Engineer for minor ship refitting and repair. When all forts and barracks were handed over to the local colonial government in 1849, the navy requested the use of Fort Macquarie as the basis for a future depot. The request was granted in 1851 only to have control of the fort return to the British Army when belated news arrived of the outbreak of war in the Crimea. The navy's presence in Sydney was, at best, of a temporary character and little was permanent. The development of steam plants for ships was to be one of the most important factors leading to the development of naval shore infrastructure. Whereas smaller ships like *Beagle* could be virtually refitted without shore support, new ironclads like the revolutionary HMS *Warrior*, which was fitted with a steam engine, required the use of engineering machinery and technical equipment to keep them running. It was time for the colonies to contribute to the naval defence of the continent and the protection of the merchant ships that were the cause and effect of its prosperity.

3

Colonial navies

1856–1900

After the scare prompted by fears of the Russian Navy during the Crimean War and growing public recognition of how vulnerable British and colonial shipping was to attack and seizure, it was by now plain that the Australian colonies urgently needed naval ships and adequate infrastructure. In 1858, the Governor of Tasmania, Sir Henry Young, wrote to the Colonial Secretary urging 'the necessity of making the Australian colonies an Admiral's station and for maintaining in Australian seas a Naval Squadron equal at least to that maintained therein by any other power'. Although there was no shortage of goodwill towards the Royal Navy in New South Wales there was, according to local politicians, insufficient public money available to fund naval development. As the colonists were increasingly afraid of pirates and commerce-raiding vessels, they appealed to London for help. But there was little the Admiralty could do in the short term. The neglect of the Royal Navy in the fifty years after Trafalgar by a succession of complacent British governments was an enormous blot on the Victorian era; and rather unexpected given the rate at which the Empire was expanding. There was a swift and devastating reduction in the size of the King's Fleet with the defeat of the French and Spanish at Trafalgar in 1805. In 1812 there had been 543 ships in commission with 130 000 officers and men in the navy. Five years later, only 20 000 of them were still serving. Of the 98 sail of the line, a mere thirteen remained in commission. The fighting navy had been gutted and a mere shell remained. In both absolute terms and in comparison with the leading foreign powers, the Royal Navy was the smallest it had been at any time since the reign of King James I in the early part of the seventeenth century.

Ashore, the problems and upheavals were just as great. The Admiralty was weakened and marginalised. It now made very few of the decisions relating to the deployment of Britain's naval power. Cabinet determined the size and composition of the naval forces to be maintained in the various stations. This was acknowledged with some bitterness by the First Lord of the Admiralty, the Earl of Haddington (Thomas Hamilton), when writing to the Prime Minister, Sir Robert Peel, in 1844 concerning the naval defence of New South Wales: 'I have no right on my own to add a ship to the number on any station fixed by the Cabinet. I must therefore trouble you so far about the *Daphne* as to say that I will be obliged to you to let me know whether I may retain her on the Pacific station or not'.

Cost-cutting measures were the feature of the period as the navy estimates were successively trimmed with or without claims that efficiencies had been achieved by any standard or rule. Nicholas Rodger has argued that the 'Royal Navy had gained an Empire but lost a role'.

The colonial ministers from around Australia came together in late 1858. Defence was high on the agenda for discussion. The colonies of Victoria and Tasmania felt most vulnerable to attack and least able to respond. By this time there were only two ships of the Imperial Squadron on the station and they were rarely seen in Victorian or Tasmanian waters. In March 1859 the Admiralty considered Sir Henry Young's earlier pleadings together with a separate dispatch from the Executive Council of New South Wales. In reply, the Secretary of the Admiralty stated:

> *As regards the question of local defence and the amount of naval force required to be stationed for the general protection of the trade of the Australian Colonies and of Tasmania and New Zealand, my Lords deem it probable that the amount of force hitherto maintained in the seas adjacent to those colonies will in future require to be larger than at former periods, and two additional ships have recently been ordered to proceed from China to join the Senior Officer at present commanding the ships stationed for that service.*
>
> *My Lords also have under consideration the expediency of a complete separation of the Squadron in the Australian seas from that under the command of the Flag Officer on the East Indies*

Station, but they are of the opinion that an officer with the rank of Commodore will be sufficient for all general purposes at present.

Several days later on 26 March 1859, Captain William Loring was ordered to hoist a blue pennant in HMS *Iris*. He was appointed the first Commodore-in-Command of a separate and independent Australia Station. His promotion to Commodore Second Class brought him an additional £1 per day. He was an officer with a record of gallant service in China, and later achieved high naval rank. It was a thankless and inglorious appointment although Loring was content with his duties. Many of his men were not so happy. The number of floggings on the Australia Station during 1862 was three times higher than the average for the whole Royal Navy, while desertion was always a critical issue. There was no shortage of places visited by warships around the continent or in the islands where men could make a fresh start in life and perhaps achieve great wealth. Many left their ships and never returned despite perennial threats of punishment.

The new Australia Station was bounded to the north by the Torres Strait, to the east by Samoa, to the west by St Paul and to the south by the Antarctic Circle. It covered about one-sixth of the Earth's surface. The ships at Loring's disposal in exercising his command were the frigate *Iris*, the corvette *Pelorus* and three sloops *Niger*, *Elk* and *Cordelia*. This was an important advance for the Australian colonies. By agreeing to augment British naval forces in Australian waters and establishing a separate station, the Admiralty recognised its increasing responsibility towards the Pacific colonies as well. But their Lordships also felt the colonists should themselves accept a greater share of the defence burden. A departmental committee of the British Government consisting of representatives of the Treasury and the Colonial and War Offices (known as the Mills Committee after the chairman, Liberal parliamentarian Arthur Mills) met in 1859 to consider the matter of colonial military expenditure. After taking evidence from a vast number of witnesses, the committee presented its report to the House of Commons on 11 July 1861. Arguing against the contention that some colonies were simply indefensible, the Chancellor of the Exchequer, William Gladstone, perhaps the most eminent witness to appear before the committee, was adamant that the time for action had come.

The whole question is one of the supremacy at sea. That is absolutely vital to our existence. England will no longer be England the moment she has lost it. So long as she has supremacy

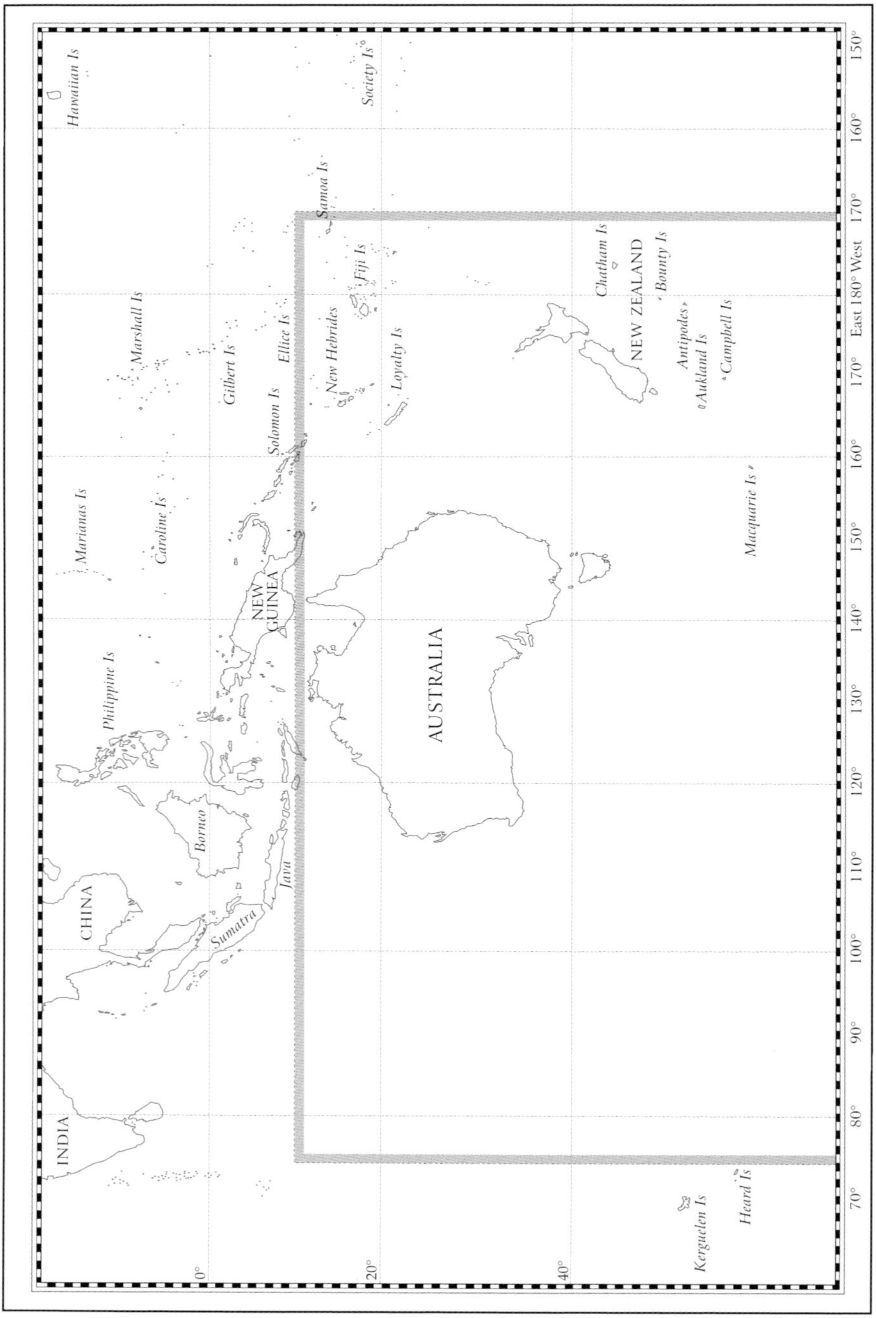

The area confined by the original Australia Station, 1859.

> *at sea her Colonial Empire is virtually safe, and many of our present garrisons are little, if at all, required.*

The report to the British Government stressed that the colonies should indeed accept some responsibility for the defence of their trade and the security of their infrastructure. The report did not prompt much of a response in New South Wales or at the Admiralty. This was largely because the committee was satisfied with the adequacy of the squadron then attached to the Australia Station and because it avoided encouraging the development of local navies or coastal defences. But the Admiralty did accept the need for enhanced refit facilities at its modest base on Garden Island. These were deemed vital to keeping the squadron at sea where any aggressor would be met. As these were shore facilities, the Admiralty contended that their development and maintenance were the responsibility of the local legislature. The New South Wales Government felt, however, that maritime defence was an imperial matter and the responsibility of the Admiralty. Politicians in Sydney believed that keeping Britain's fighting ships at sea was London's responsibility although the local population was, of course, the principal beneficiary of imperial expenditure. Commodore Loring tried unsuccessfully to encourage the colonists to take a more active and a rather more generous view of their own defence requirements. He was assisted when the principle of 'self-help' in colonial defence matters was endorsed by a unanimous resolution of the House of Commons on 4 March 1862:

> *This House (while fully recognising the claims of all portions of the British Empire to Imperial aid in their protection against perils arising from the consequences of Imperial policy) is of the opinion that colonies exercising the right of self-government ought to undertake responsibility of providing for their own internal order and security and ought to assist in their own external defence.*

While there was debate about who should bear the cost of naval defence in New South Wales—the colonial legislature or the Admiralty—the mindset in Victoria was markedly different. After being declared a separate colony in August 1850 by the *Imperial Act*, Captain Sir Charles Hotham RN was appointed Governor of Victoria. He quickly developed an appreciation of the colony's particular maritime defence needs. A select committee of the Victorian Legislative Council was appointed to inquire into ways of strengthening

Victoria's maritime defences. As Royal Navy ships were rarely seen in Victorian waters, the first move was to acquire the armed vessel *Victoria* (of which more will be said later) and establish the repair facilities needed to keep the ship at sea. In 1856, work commenced on a government patent slipway at Williamstown at the head of Port Phillip Bay. Two years later the slipway was completed and immediately put to good use. A report by William Fairfax published in the *Argus* the following year explained the great service the slipway would perform for the colony.

> *Until very lately all vessels over 600 tons when damaged below the water line either had to resort to heaving down first on one side and then the other or proceed to Sydney or India for repairs. This state of things, however, is now altered, as the Government patent slip is completed at an expense of £75 000 and is able to haul up all descriptions of vessels that frequent this port, except, perhaps the very largest, and for these the Government contemplates constructing a large graving dock.*

In October 1858, the Victorian Government had decided to build a graving dock adjacent to the slipway. Another slipway was also planned to accommodate ships up to 1000 tons although this was to be privately funded and constructed. By 1860, a floating dock capable of taking ships up to 700 tons was added to Port Phillip's ship repair facilities. After plans were drawn up, the first contracts for the graving dock were let in 1863. Work proceeded slowly. Prince Alfred, the Duke of Edinburgh, set a memorial stone on 4 January 1868. The dock was officially named the Alfred Dock in his honour. A cofferdam was completed in July of the following year to allow the dock walls and floor to be started. Pumping out the water commenced in August. The only major stoppage during construction was in March 1872 when part of the cofferdam collapsed during a heavy storm. The dock was completed in September 1873 with caisson work completed in February of the following year. The official opening was on 2 March 1874 with the docking of the former battleship HMVS *Nelson*. The dock was 476 feet long, 80 feet wide at the entrance with a water capacity of 6 million gallons at sea level. From 1874 to 1918 the Alfred Graving Dock was operated by the Victorian Government and met all the ship repair demands placed upon it.

By the early 1860s, both the Admiralty and the colonial governments were starting to invest heavily in naval infrastructure development. It was now possible for British ships to remain in Australian waters for considerable periods. Enhanced shore facilities allowed the Admiralty to schedule longer deployments to the South Pacific where Britain was looking to expand its empire further. In an effort to bolster their own security and to assert something of their growing prosperity, status and importance, the governments of Victoria and New South Wales expressed an interest in creating navies of their own. The ketch *Spitfire* had been a modest start in New South Wales and an indication of the colony's intent. As independence brought with it the burden of defence, the colonists recognised they had to consider the prospect of providing for their own security whenever they united as a sovereign nation. Although there was no suggestion that the task would not be shared by the Royal Navy for the time being, the moment for progress had come.

When the House of Commons passed the crucial *Colonial Naval Defence Act* in 1865, it was a turning point for the Australian colonies. The Act's full title disclosed something of its purpose: 'An Act to make better provision for the naval defence of the colonies'. For the first time there was legislation on the statute books providing for a definite colonial naval defence policy. It also granted to the colonies the right to form their own navies—a prerogative they had previously been denied. The legislation's most important aspects were the right of colonies to provide, maintain and use their own vessels of war when required for self-defence. They could also offer them for such purposes 'as Her Majesty-in-Council from time to time approves, and to place those vessels at Her Majesty's disposal when any such vessel would become to all intents a vessel of Her Majesty's regular navy'. The Act also allowed the colonies to 'raise and maintain seamen to serve in such vessels', together with volunteers and emergency volunteers 'so raised to form part of the Royal Naval Reserve'.

The Act was overdue. The colony of Victoria had already played a part in the long-running Maori wars in New Zealand. In 1840, the Maori chiefs signed the Treaty of Waitangi in which they acknowledged Queen Victoria as their sovereign in return for a commitment that they would be treated as British subjects whose rights and property would be respected. New Zealand formally became a British colony the following year. Although the British Government hoped to establish a system of land titles that would prevent the Maori from being deprived of their land, there were two challenges to the plan. Those who signed the treaty did not represent every Maori tribe, while the New Zealand Company felt its commercial operations

Colonial sailors engaged in cutlass drill.

would be impeded by the document. There was no surprise when Maori resentment caused alarm among white settlers at Wellington in 1842. HMS *North Star* landed 50 men of the British 80th Regiment based in New South Wales during August 1843 and tried to demonstrate British resolve by 'showing the flag' at Port Nicholson and Wellington. This strategy worked for a while. The first Maori War began in 1845 when a group of Maori from the top of the North Island led by Hone Heke Pokai sought to resist British colonial expansion and to assert their independence from Britain. A naval squadron of five ships mounting 117 guns led by *North Star* and *Hazard* was deployed to New Zealand waters to assert British sovereignty. This was not work greatly appreciated by the Royal Navy generally or by the officers and men sent to New Zealand. Sailors were not soldiers and resented shore service of this kind, despite its frequency. It did not accord with their temperament nor make use of their specialist skills. Many naval personnel also felt that the colonists had unnecessarily provoked Maori passions. Officers and sailors from the two ships were formed into naval brigades while the guns were landed and used as heavy artillery. The combined British naval–military force defeated the Maori but indigenous hostility remained.

In 1860, 350 British troops were massacred in the Taranaki Province and the 40th Imperial Regiment was sent from Sydney to restore order. Commodore Loring embarked in *Iris* and sailed for New Zealand leaving orders for *Pelorus* and *Cordelia* to follow. *Niger* had already been sent to New Zealand and was retained after her replacement, HMS *Fawn*, arrived at the colony. The ships' companies were reduced to a minimum as officers and men were sent ashore to fight land battles. The Maori proved to be a formidable enemy and fiercely resisted the combined naval–military force brought against them. The campaign took seven months and there were 238 British casualties before a temporary truce was made in April 1861. By this time, an acrimonious debate had developed between the Governor of New Zealand, Sir George Grey, and the Royal Navy. Grey wanted more ships deployed to New Zealand than the Commodore was prepared to commit. He also preferred to deal personally with the senior naval officer present in New Zealand rather than relaying his requests for assistance to Sydney. The Admiralty resisted a scheme to make New Zealand a separate naval station and became annoyed with Grey's incessant demands. It did agree, however, to the newly arrived Commodore, William Wiseman, temporarily establishing his headquarters in New Zealand.

Open warfare was resumed in July 1863 when the Governor refused to accept the demands of the Waikato-based Maori King Movement. More than 2500 men in Australia volunteered to join the New Zealand colonial forces with eleven chartered vessels transporting them to New Zealand for service in the four locally raised Waikato regiments. As imperial troops under Leiutenant General Duncan Cameron invaded the Waikato, the colonists organised a small fleet of protected vessels for operations along the Waikato River. They were manned partially by officers and sailors from *Curacoa*, *Harrier* and *Eclipse* in late September. A total of 365 naval officers and men were landed for river or shore operations. Fighting continued until April 1864 with the loss of Captain Hamilton and three men from *Esk*, Commander Hay and three men from *Harrier*; a lieutenant and a sailor from *Curacoa*, and a lieutenant and eight men from *Miranda* during a hostile encounter near the port of Tauranga on the east coast. By this time the Maori cause was lost. Commodore Wiseman sailed for Sydney in June 1864. Although sporadic hostilities would continue until 1870, and the navy's headquarters remained in New Zealand until 1866, the navy's effective involvement in the campaign ended in 1864. Thereafter, Wiseman was instructed by the Admiralty not to detach naval personnel for military operations. The navy's role was to provide maritime communications, transportation of personnel and stores, and the landing and working of heavy guns. The army would fight whatever land battles were required.

The Maori wars were significant for the colonies in several respects. This was the first occasion on which Australians had participated in a foreign campaign. It also highlighted the need for sea transport and naval logistic support for land operations. In 1860, the colony of Victoria made its only warship, the graceful steam sloop *Victoria* (armed with eight 32-pounders), available to transport 120 troops of the 90th Regiment to New Zealand and to fight the Maori if needed. *Victoria* had been acquired by the Victorian Government to provide local defence, conduct surveys, recover passengers and crew from stricken vessels, collect mail and serve as a lighthouse tender. Prior to her departure for New Zealand, the Victorian Parliament passed the *Armed Vessels Regulation Act* to give legal status to the ship and her complement. Believing that this effectively created an independent Victorian Navy, the Act was struck down by the British Government. *Victoria* sailed to Hobart on 19 April 1860 and embarked 134 troops from the 40th Regiment. On arrival in New Zealand, the ship was used for shore bombardment, coastal patrol and logistic resupply between Auckland and New Plymouth. In July, *Victoria* sailed for Sydney, returning the following month with Major General Thomas Pratt and the regimental headquarters staff. When the Maori attacked the New Plymouth fortifications, *Victoria* evacuated women and children to Nelson. After a refit at Wellington during October, the sloop was on hand to deploy fresh reinforcements from Britain. By this time, the Victorian Government asked for the ship to be returned for some urgent survey work. *Victoria* returned to Melbourne in March.

But *Victoria*'s involvement in the Maori wars created something of a legal quandary that required close and immediate attention. Was a colonial ship operating in international or foreign waters, such as in New Zealand, a British man-of-war or a privateer? The best legal minds in England gave their opinion on 21 December 1860: 'We think that all vessels of war in the Colonies intended to navigate beyond these territorial limits should be commanded by officers holding commissions from the Crown, and be essentially part of the Royal Navy of England'. This meant that any ship owned and maintained by the various Australian colonies had to be specially commissioned as one of Her Majesty's ships with its commanding officer given a temporary commission in the Royal Navy. This position was maintained over the next four decades.

This did not deter the Victorians, who continued to fund naval activity. An armoured monitor, later named HMVS *Cerberus*, would be built for the colony in England. The cost was shared unequally. The British Government agreed to pay £100 000; the Victorian Government's contribution was £25 000. *Cerberus* was ready to sail in October 1870, not long after the similarly designed HMS *Captain* capsized killing almost the entire ship's company. There were real fears that this new class of ship, with its big guns, was inherently unstable and actually quite dangerous in heavy weather. Despite encountering gales and high seas en route to Australia, *Cerberus* arrived safely in Melbourne during April 1871. Eighty permanent personnel manned the ship with the complement raised in wartime to 155; the additional men to be drawn from the Naval Reserve. A training ship, the elderly and obsolete wooden ship *Nelson*, would also be made available on permanent loan from Britain. The ship was re-commissioned, refurbished and deployed to Victoria in July 1867. Although beyond involvement in naval combat, the ship's 74 guns provided local defence for Melbourne and offered a suitable platform for seamanship training. Despite Victoria's enthusiasm for naval defence, the Admiralty was nonetheless wary of colonial involvement and its lack of control over colonial naval affairs. The colonists had little expertise in naval defence and often embarked on infrastructure works without seeking the Admiralty's technical advice.

Undeterred by any anxiety in London, the New South Wales Government dedicated Garden Island in Port Jackson 'as a depot for the use of Her Majesty's ships'. But when it came to acquiring funds for its development, the Comptroller of the Navy indicated that he 'considered with great apprehension the commencement of a new naval establishment in the Antipodes. These establishments are already too numerous and the expenditure upon them is in no way under the control of the Home authorities'. No additional imperial money was made available. The only buildings on the island were a small residence, a boatshed and a blacksmith's shop, hardly sufficient to keep a fighting squadron at sea. The Australian Squadron was plainly not well supported ashore. Nor had New South Wales made much progress on local provision for imperial needs. The Government considered acquiring the more modern battleship HMS *Brunswick*, but could not afford the £150 000 required to convert the wooden ship into an ironclad.

After reviewing the colonies' naval defence requirements in 1869, the Admiralty concluded that it was not in favour of expanding the colonial navies. Instead, it preferred a subsidy scheme, under which a permanent Australian naval force would be established with the colonies to pay half the cost of operating and maintaining the squadron. Ships sent to Australia would be fitted out in Britain before departure and would return home when in need of major repair. This would reduce the requirement for maintenance and repair on the station and provide work for the dockyards in Britain for which Australia would pay. Protracted discussions followed, but no agreement was reached and the scheme lapsed. But by this time, the maintenance and logistic needs of the Australian Squadron were acute and the Royal Navy decided to build a dedicated naval storehouse on Garden Island. The colonial architect was asked to produce some plans even as the Commander of the Station, Commodore James Goodenough, considered alternative sites for the depot, including Fort Macquarie. After months of waiting and little activity, Goodenough ran out of patience. He revealed his frustration in a personal letter to the Admiralty Director of Works, Colonel Pasely, while embarked in HMS *Pearl* off Fiji on 20 June 1875.

> *Dealing with these Colonial Governments is precisely like dealing with a foreign Government. They are all suspicion and alarm. Of course I keep in view the possibility of our preferring Auckland to Sydney as a Headquarter. Its disadvantages would be that every ton of coal will cost 27/- or 30/- instead of 15/- or 16/- but for Island purposes one saves in consumption to and from of what is equal to that difference. There is however no dock at Auckland and this is of course a drawback. In point of climate they are much alike. Possibly Sydney is more relaxing of the two.*

It was a remarkable letter for what it revealed about the attitude of one senior naval officer towards the New South Wales Government and the contempt in which some naval officers held it. Goodenough's thinking was obviously dominated by the matter of finding a suitable site for the navy's stores. He conceded that Garden Island had merit as a navy yard but that seems not to have been foremost in his mind. This was partly a product of his ambition to see the Australian Squadron as a highly mobile naval force, able to sustain operations around the continent and in New Zealand, with minimal dependence on shore facilities which nonetheless remained very basic. Goodenough mentioned Auckland in such a way as to suggest that it was, or at least had been, seriously considered as an alternative to Sydney.

A showdown was building. The New South Wales Government claimed that the provision of Garden Island was based on the understanding that Port Jackson would be the Royal Navy's headquarters in the Pacific. If the squadron headquarters moved, Garden Island would be resumed.

Goodenough drafted a letter to the Admiralty setting out his thoughts and his plans for Sydney. It was never sent. On 20 August 1875 the Commodore died from the effects of arrow wounds he had sustained at Santa Cruz in the Solomon Islands. He had sailed there as part of his effort to suppress the activities of the blackbirders (recruiters of indentured labour) in the islands. Although Goodenough attempted to befriend the people of the islands, they were bent on revenge for those taken by the blackbirders and attacked Goodenough's party when it landed on Carlisle Bay. Two sailors were also killed. They were buried with their commodore in the graveyard at St Thomas' Anglican Church in North Sydney.

Despite his predecessor's views, Commodore Anthony Hoskins recommended Sydney as the most convenient port for the Royal Navy's headquarters in Australian waters. In his view, Sydney's considerable strengths were its ideal location in the Pacific; the appealing climate and availability of water and supplies; the dock accommodation and the capacity of private industries to meet the navy's needs; a cheap and abundant coal supply; and the perfectly formed harbour. The only rivals to Sydney in Hoskins' estimation were Auckland and Hobart, but neither of these was fortified and both were unsuited for land defence. The Royal Navy's headquarters would remain in Australia and in Sydney.

The following year, the British Government again broached the question of Australian colonial defence, this time adopting a new approach by detailing two representatives, Major General Sir William Jervois and Lieutenant Colonel (later General Sir) Peter Scratchley, to report on the means required to put colonial naval and military defences in order. They spent ten months visiting each of the Australian colonies. The Jervois–Scratchley naval proposals were based on a policy of leaving offensive action entirely to the Royal Navy; but it was recommended that the colonies should provide ironclad gunboats to protect trade and a few torpedo boats for harbour defence. It was further recommended that Australian crews should man all local vessels, and that all floating defences should be under the sole control of the officer commanding the Australian Squadron. Victoria had already anticipated many of these recommendations but in New South Wales and South Australia, for a variety of reasons, the scheme failed to go much beyond the planning stage.

The colonies were nonetheless determined to reach a common position on naval and military defences. The Premier of South Australia revived the Admiralty's subsidy proposals of 1869, but they were rejected by the larger eastern states on the grounds that as large British interests were involved, the maintenance of naval defences at sea was entirely the responsibility of the British Government. For its part, it felt that the Australian colonies could and should contribute to their naval defence. A Royal Commission under the presidency of the Secretary for the Colonies, Lord Carnarvon (Henry Herbert), was appointed in September 1879 to inquire into the defence of British colonial possessions and commerce abroad. The Royal Commissioners' report was tabled on 23 March 1882. They concluded:

> *the time, in our opinion, has arrived when the Colonies may reasonably be expected to take upon themselves some share of that defence—a burden hitherto exclusively borne by the Mother Country. Looking at the fact that only one Colony has availed itself of the powers vested by the* Naval Defence Act *(1865), and that the vessel acquired by Victoria as a sea-going ship (HMVS* Cerberus*) has practically been converted into a vessel for harbour defence, we do not suggest that these Colonies should maintain sea-going ships for action beyond their territorial waters. But we see no reason why the Australian Colonies should not make a contribution in money towards the cost of that squadron which is maintained by the Mother Country for the protection of interests common to the Colony and Herself.*

The commission said the British Government could reasonably be 'called upon to contribute in some measure to the expense of defending a harbour, if it should be thought desirable that one should be specially selected for coaling, repairing and refitting your Majesty's ships'. Although coastal defences were the responsibility of the colonies, the committee conceded there were facilities warranting an imperial contribution. Sydney was one such place. But the question of where the navy would be based in Sydney was still the subject of almost constant debate despite the Admiralty's continuing possession of Garden Island. Hoskins' successor, Commodore John Wilson, was instructed to consider either Fort Macquarie (the location of the present Opera House) or Dawes Point (on which now stands the southern pylon of the Sydney Harbour Bridge) as alternatives to Garden Island. By this time, the New South Wales Government decided that it desperately wanted the return of Garden Island while hinting at its reluctance to spend money on a naval depot. For the colonial politicians, it was all a matter of competing priorities.

Successive New South Wales governments exhibited a characteristic of most governments during peacetime: a reluctance to spend adequate sums of money on defence and security. This is not to suggest that colonial governments were characteristically parsimonious. After the colony of New South Wales achieved 'responsible government' in 1856 the pressures on public revenues for infrastructure development were enormous. There were the competing priorities of building bridges, roads, telegraphs and railways as a means of dealing with the huge distances that were the cause of so much commercial expense throughout the colony. For example, the first railway line from Sydney was commenced in 1850 and completed in 1855 at a cost of £70 000—six times the projected cost. In 1860 there were only 70 miles of rail open for traffic; by 1872, 400 miles had been completed with expenditure on railways in that year alone being estimated at £183 000. In the same year £50 000 was spent on all public works in the colony; the figure ten years later was £4 100 000. The next few years witnessed a slightly depressed economy with £38 000 spent on relief works from total outlays of £2 10 000. To pay for railways, bridges and roads, the colony needed an extensive loans policy. But such a policy was not always able to secure sufficient funds. In this context, a naval depot was but one of a number of competing demands and, as it appeared to be unproductive in terms of output, it was likely to receive a low priority. In addition, there remained the stalemate over where the navy's principal base ought to be.

Its patience exhausted, the Admiralty issued an ultimatum to the New South Wales Government. If agreement on a suitable site was not forthcoming, the navy's ships would be based elsewhere, possibly even in New Zealand. This was a return to the desperation of a decade before. The Colonial Secretary, Alexander Stuart, prepared a long minute, approved by Cabinet on 19 March 1883. He stated:

> *I wish at once to place on record my conviction of the desirableness of making this Port the Headquarters of the British Navy in these seas [and that] no mere consideration of economy should be permitted to interfere with the attainment of so desirable an object.*

The New South Wales Government also offered £50 000 for naval construction on Garden Island with the possibility of additional funds being made available. The Admiralty decided to accept the offer of Garden Island, which it would develop simultaneously with Spectacle Island, located in the western reaches of Port Jackson. Encouragement was provided by the visit to Australia in 1881 of the Royal Navy's Detached or 'Flying Squadron' led by the frigate *Inconstant* and consisting of the corvettes *Cleopatra*, *Carysfort*, *Bacchante* and *Tourmaline*. The *Bacchante* attracted the most interest as her complement included Queen Victoria's grandsons, Prince Albert Victor and Prince George. The squadron visited Brisbane, Sydney and Melbourne. The delights of colonial Australia again proved too appealing to many British sailors with a large group deserting from each of the ships: about 15 per cent of sailors did not return to service. As press-ganging had been abolished more than sixty years before, finding trained sailors in Australia was no easy task. To sail without an adequate ship's company was something every captain dreaded, especially when there was a fear of hostilities. Some of these fears were justified; others were less so. The visit of a Russian naval squadron consisting of the corvettes *Afrika* and *Platon* and the sloop *Vestnik* to Sydney, Hobart, Melbourne and Adelaide in 1882 prompted virtual hysteria in the minds of more paranoid colonists, especially those in the press. The Russians were accused (probably rightly) of covertly surveying coastal naval defences and secretly lying in wait to attack the four main colonial cities. Although the stories were subsequently discredited, politicians were nonetheless alarmed by the inadequacy of colonial defences.

This increased awareness coincided with continuing efforts to establish local naval forces in line with the Jervois–Scratchley proposals. New South Wales acquired the old HMS *Wolverine* (a 2431-ton screw corvette carrying seventeen guns) as a training ship for the local naval brigade and two second-class torpedo boats, *Avernus* and *Acheron*; Victoria had *Nelson* and *Cerberus*, the first-class torpedo boat *Childers*, and two gunboats sentimentally named *Victoria* (530 tons armed with one 10-inch gun, two 13-pounders and two 3-pounders) and *Albert* (370 tons armed with one 8-inch gun and one 6-inch gun); Queensland maintained two gunboats based on *Albert*'s design, *Gayundah* and *Paluma*; and South Australia had its own small navy based on the cruiser *Protector*. More of a very heavily armed gunboat than a cruiser, *Protector* was lightly armour-plated. She displaced 960 tons and carried one 8-inch gun, five 6-inch guns, four 3-pounders and five machine-guns. *Protector* was, in fact, quite

Garden Island viewed from 'Mrs Macquarie's Point' in 1888. The Rigging Shed and Sail Loft are visible at the southern end of the island.

a formidable ship. After a formal inspection, the Commander of the Australia Station remarked that the cruiser 'was not only better kept than any ship on the Station, but was so much better kept that there was no ground for comparison'. But none of this particularly impressed the Admiralty in distant London. Their Lordships considered the duplication of naval forces and defence administrations across Australia to be wasteful. It wanted the colonies to contribute to the superior defence that the Royal Navy provided at sea, as distinct from what it believed were essentially ineffective harbour and coastal defences.

The appointment of Rear Admiral George Tryon in January 1885 raised the Australia Station to flag rank status and signified its growing importance in the naval scheme of things. Tryon had earlier established an Admiralty intelligence department, was considered the ablest tactician in the fleet and, before arriving in Australia, held the very influential position of Secretary to the Admiralty. It is likely that he was personally responsible for the Australia Station command being upgraded to flag rank. The station's increased prestige demanded local recognition. But the Admiralty did not insist on the New South Wales Government providing an official residence because it realised this could, and probably would, be an avenue for the colonists to exert improper personal influence on the Commander-in-Chief. A residence was nevertheless purchased by the New South Wales Government at Kirribilli and named Admiralty House. A parcel of land over three acres came with the building, with the New South Wales Government attempting to resume a strip of ground on the west side of the property owned by the Pastoral Finance Association 'in order to render the Admiral's residence more private'. When the association strongly objected, a deal was struck and the association agreed not to build within three feet of the western boundary. Tryon's biographer, Rear Admiral Penrose Fitzgerald, notes that

> *Admiral Tryon was not accompanied to Australia by his wife. During the early part of his command threatening war clouds were in the air; and besides this there was no house ready for him to occupy . . . the rent of a house for the Commodore in the Town of Sydney, had recently given a house in a beautiful site on the north shore of the harbour, opposite to the town, and overlooking the man-of-war anchorage, which is almost at the foot of the garden, but the house required alterations, and it was some months before it was ready for occupation. But as soon as Tryon did get into it, he entertained Sydney society with a hospitality which was remembered for many years after.*

One suspects that the New South Wales Government was almost enthusiastic about the provision of a suitable house. Colonial politicians realised they would be the prime recipients of the Admiral's hospitality and showed none of the hesitance that had marked discussions over the site of a navy depot. Admiralty House quickly became the 'best night out in Sydney'. It was said that

> *To the young Society Miss an invitation to a man-o-war was bliss, no matter how small or how grubby the little ship might be. To the Society Matron an invitation to Admiralty House was a command, the hallmark of high social standing treasured even beyond an invitation to Government House. Admiralty House was a force in the land, a social force of considerable national value and influence.*

Despite fears in London, Tryon was more influential than influenced. He was keen to reshape the colonists' ideas on naval defence. But they were still not convinced that the defence of Australia based on British naval power was assured and there was always the concern that some of the squadron's ships could be deployed elsewhere in the region in response to emergencies. This would effectively leave Australian cities vulnerable to seaborne attack.

To counter these fears, the Admiralty directed Tryon to negotiate with the colonial governments for the formulation of an 'acceptable' naval defence scheme. An Imperial Conference was held in 1887 to consider an agreement between the colonies and the British Government for the provision of an Australasian Auxiliary Squadron. Subject to parliamentary ratification the agreement reached at the 1887 conference would see the Admiralty build and equip five cruisers of 2575 tons displacement and two torpedo gunboats of 759 tons displacement. Of these vessels, three cruisers and one gunboat were to be kept continually in commission, the remainder held in reserve. The *Australasian Naval Defence Act* (1887) stipulated that the colonies

> *should pay five per cent annually on the prime cost of the Squadron, such payment not to exceed £35 000 per annum and provide maintenance costs, including retired pay to officers and pensions to ratings provided that the annual charge under this heading did not exceed £91 000 [including New Zealand's contribution].*

The colonies agreed that the squadron would be under the sole control of the Commander-in-Chief of the Australia Station, but would be deployed within the limits of the station and only otherwise employed with the consent of the colonial governments. The agreement, which would be in force for ten years, was duly ratified before coming into operation in 1891. But before the squadron arrived, a great deal of preparation was needed in Sydney where the Government, despite promising to establish a naval depot to the navy's 'entire satisfaction', was resisting direct requests from the Admiralty for assistance.

In 1889, the New South Wales Government finally made good its word. Garden Island was beginning to function as the Admiralty intended although it was rapidly becoming a more substantial facility, requiring a more sizeable staff than the Admiralty had reckoned for a 'small Dockyard Reserve dealing with minor defects'. It had grown so large that it depended upon local private firms for heavy engineering support. By this time there was a number of other dockyards that the navy could use throughout this part of the world although distance remained a factor in relation to damaged vessels. Alternatives included the docks at Bombay, Singapore, Whampoa and Shanghai. There was also the Calliope Dock in Auckland and the Alfred Dock in Melbourne. As all of the facilities in Australia and New Zealand belonged to the government or harbour trusts, they were available at no charge to the navy. The Admiralty did not want to go overboard with Garden Island but recognised the growing importance of the station.

The Captain-in-Charge of the Naval Establishment, Captain W. St Clair, was appointed in June 1890 and immediately pressed the Admiralty for additional staff. By this time the facilities in Sydney were nearly equal to those in Hong Kong and Bermuda. This made sound economic sense. Ever since Commodore Goodenough's time, the navy had complained about the quality of shore labour hired to effect ship repairs. Goodenough preferred to use his own men for the most demanding tasks and even asked the Admiralty if they could be paid a special allowance to undertake the tasks normally carried out by shore tradesmen. The extra staff sought by St Clair was approved. The naval depot on Garden Island was finally completed in 1891 and handed over to Rear Admiral Sir Cyprian Bridge, the Commander-in-Chief, on behalf of the Admiralty.

The Australasian Auxiliary Squadron had arrived in Sydney during 1891. It consisted, as promised, of five third-class protected cruisers of 2575 tons originally laid down for the Royal Navy—*Katoomba*, *Mildura*, *Ringarooma*, *Tauranga* and *Wallaroo*—and two torpedo-gunboats—*Boomerang* and *Karrakatta*. The name of each vessel represented the six Australian colonies and New Zealand with each paying a share of their construction and maintenance. The ships' companies received a hearty welcome from the local population. The Australia Station was accordingly elevated to a Vice-Admiral's command. On 2 September 1896, Sir Cyprian conducted his first inspection of the naval establishments and reserve ships. He was pleased with progress on the naval depot. The Commander-in-Chief was not so pleased with the reserve ships. *Boomerang* and *Tauranga* were below the standard 'which is maintained in the home ports'. This was unacceptable. There would be no reduction in professional naval standards in the colonies. He directed that they receive special attention. But some of the colonists were still critical of the ships comprising the new squadron. They argued that third-class cruisers were unsuitable for service on a station characterised by vast expanses of open sea and heavy weather. This proved not to be the case although their operational capabilities and sustainability would never be seriously tested. From the late 1890s to the first decade of the twentieth century, the number of ships on the station was steadily expanding and Britain's colonial possessions in the Pacific increasing.

The final four years of the nineteenth century were ones in which the navy was able to make substantial progress in enhancing its position in Sydney, free from the administrative wrangles and the uncertainty that had been a feature of most of its dealings with the colony of New South Wales for over one hundred years. The local press supported the expanding naval activity, especially when the Boxers rebelled against European colonial rule in northern China in early

New South Wales Naval Brigade completing minelaying drill.

1900 after months of unrest. By July 1900, Garden Island was the scene of busy preparations for the first Australian military operation in Asia. After receiving a request from the British Government, HMS *Wallaroo* of the Auxiliary Squadron and *Mohawk* and *Lizard* of the Imperial Squadron were released for service in China. With the bulk of Australia's military forces deployed in the Transvaal and the Orange Free State in a drawn-out war against the Boers, it was left to the colonial navies and the men of the naval brigades, also known as 'bluejackets', to rescue the foreign legations in Peking from the anti-Western and virulently anti-Christian Boxer rebels. This was usually soldiers' work, but there were simply none available. More than 450 000 men, including in excess of 16 000 Australians, had been committed to the war in South Africa. And there was the political question of whether Australians ought to be engaged in a war with questionable moral or strategic justification. In the Victorian Legislative Assembly, Henry Bournes Higgins remarked: 'The people will be wanting to know whether we in these colonies are to be expected to volunteer each time to contribute valuable lives and money in aid of wars which may not interest us directly'. Apparently they were.

While the Australians in South Africa tried to conclude what had become an increasingly unpopular campaign, a contingent consisting of 500 men from the New South Wales and Victorian naval brigades sailed to China in SS *Salamis* (requisitioned by the Admiralty and renamed HMT *105*). They were to join an international force under the Commander-in-Chief of the China Station, Admiral Sir Edward Seymour, with the objective of restoring civil order and Western supremacy in China. Also bound for China was the South Australian gunboat HMCS *Protector* and her complement of 100 men commanded by Captain William Creswell. The imperial authorities declined Queensland's offer of its two gunboats, *Paluma* and *Gayundah*. They were considered to be 'too old and too slow'.

SS Salamis *being prepared for service in China.*

HMT *105* had sailed from Sydney bound for China on 8 August 1900. She proceeded independently and made no contact with the South Australian gunboat. Following her arrival in Sydney on 10 August, *Protector* lay off Garden Island to take on coal and essential stores. After taking on board all the requisites for the mission including several stands of Lee-Enfield rifles from the Royal Navy's storehouses, *Protector* sailed for Brisbane on Sunday, 12 August. Gunner Blake joined the ship in Townsville on 18 August and was impressed by the cruiser's state of readiness and the smartness of the ship's company.

> *My first glance at the ship's company convinced me that they were a hardy lot of men, fit to go anywhere. Events proved I was*

> *right. I could see it was no pleasure cruise for these men. From the day I set foot on board until we returned, both officers and men were kept incessantly at drill, either at the guns, small arms, general quarters, man and arm boats, collision and fire drill. Going to quarters was no make believe, as every time we went to quarters, the ship was prepared for battle, and all the top hamper taken down. Everything in the ship that could give any protection to the quick-firing gun's crews, such as awnings, sails and hammocks, was used.*

Protector skirted a typhoon, but reached Hong Kong without any machinery or equipment defects. The only problem seemed to be the limited space available for stores and water. In a development prompted by *Victoria*'s service in the Maori wars, *Protector* was commissioned into the Royal Navy while alongside. The South Australian colonial flag was exchanged for the naval white ensign.

When HMT *105* arrived in Hong Kong on 26 August, the naval brigades learned that the Boxers, aided by elements of the Chinese Army, had forced back Admiral Seymour's force at Tientsin and inflicted heavy casualties. Seymour called for reinforcements. An international force of approximately 20 000 men relieved the foreign legations on 14 August. On arriving in the Yangtse River, the Australians learned they would be sent to north China to garrison the forts at Taku. The Australians were put ashore on 15 September, deeply disappointed they had apparently missed most of the action. After several changes of plan, on 10 October the New South Wales contingent was ordered to march a hundred miles from Taku to Peking. They were expected to cover ten miles each day before reaching the British Legation compound in Peking where they would be accommodated and commence garrison duty. The first bit of excitement came when they apprehended a notorious Boxer who was attempting to set fire to a house situated between the contingent's headquarters and a store of silk they had been ordered to guard. The man was later executed by a five-man firing squad drawn from the New South Wales bluejacket contingent. He was the first of many. The number of condemned men was so great that firing squads were limited to three men, supplemented by the use of a bayonet or a revolver bullet when necessary to complete the task. The bluejackets acknowledged they were 'growing callous' by the extent of death and destruction around them.

By this time *Protector* had arrived off Taku. In preparation for an attack on the Chinese fort at Ching-huang-tao, a shore party was landed and combined with a naval detachment from HMS *Dido*. Before they could advance on the fort, it became apparent that the Russians had got there first. The remainder of *Protector*'s time in Chinese waters was spent on minor logistic support tasks. There being no continuing use for the ship, *Protector* sailed from north China on 7 November and reached Sydney six weeks later.

This was not the first time that the distance between Australia and the rest of the world had caused Australian forces to arrive too late to see action. In 1885, the colonial gunboats *Victoria* and *Albert* together with the torpedo boat *Childers* were alongside in Malta en route to Victoria when they were offered to the British Government for service in the Sudan to avenge the death at Khartoum of General Charles Gordon, the famous British military officer. The offer was accepted and they were ordered to Suakin on the Red Sea for service under Admiral Sir William Hewitt. On 3 March 1885, the people of Sydney watched 522 colonial troops and a battery of six guns embark in *Iberia* and a further 212 men and 200 horses board *Australasian* bound for the Sudan. As the conflict was brief and fighting quickly moved inland, the three colonial ships were not required for naval operations and continued their passage to Australia. Being an island at the bottom of the world had its advantages.

As the men from New South Wales trekked towards Peking, the Victorian bluejackets were ordered a hundred miles inland to Paoting fu, the capital of Chihli province, while their stores and equipment were transported by junk. This expeditionary force also included a substantial colonial contingent from India. Their task was to restore civil order, free any besieged Westerners and guard condemned prisoners found guilty of killing European missionaries and traders. The Victorians were particularly surprised by the bloodthirstiness of the German troops and their willingness to loot and sack every town they entered, ostensibly to avenge the death of Baron Von Kettler, the German minister killed by the Boxers. After 25 days in the field, the Victorians had not encountered a single Boxer. It seemed to have been a largely pointless operation and most were relieved when ordered back to Tientsin where they undertook policing and municipal duties until the entire Australian naval contingent was withdrawn at the end of March 1901. The bluejackets embarked in SS *Chingtu* and arrived in Sydney on 25 April. Seven men had died as a result of various sicknesses or other non-combat related causes during the campaign. By the time they returned, Australia had become a sovereign nation and the naval brigades would be remembered as the first naval personnel to serve abroad as Australians and not as representatives of a colonial government. The British commander in China, Lieutenant General Sir Alfred Gaselee, told Prime Minister Edmund Barton: 'It only remains for me to say how excellent an effect has been produced by the appearance in so remote a stage as North China by these fine contingents from the Australian Commonwealth'.

Able Seaman William Bertotto, a member of the Victorian Brigade, concluded his diary with a poetic lament: 'Nobody knows what happened to us, nobody knows or cares, only those who fought old Kruger, are allowed to put on airs'. The reference to Kruger—President Paul Kruger of the Transvaal—revealed the extent to which the bluejackets felt marginalised by the much larger military force raised for the South African campaign. But the wider significance of the deployment to China was not lost on the local press. The 11 August 1900 edition of the *Adelaide Observer* remarked:

> *For the first time in the history of British colonisation a self-governing province was sending 'to the front' a fully equipped ship of war to take its place in the fighting line with vessels of the Royal Navy. The contrast—of soldiers returning from South Africa and sailors departing for China—is suggestive of the stirring times in which we live, the demands of Empire, and the cheerful response of loyalty and the enthusiastic colonists to show practical sympathy with the mother country.*

As a sovereign state, Australia had to accept greater responsibility for its own defence. The 26 May 1900 edition of the *Spectator* pronounced:

> *To hold intercourse with mankind, to share in their fortunes, to enrich themselves by commerce, above all to be great in the world's affairs, the Australians must take to the sea. By the sea they will sell everything, through the sea they will buy everything; and that fact, which they cannot alter, will in the end—which may not be as far distant as we now imagine—force upon them ships, fleets to protect the ships, and, if we may look yet a few decades further ahead, political ambitions. A great commerce implies fleets to protect it, fleets require maritime stations, and both commerce and ambition point out to the Australians the same path.*

An entirely new fleet was needed. The old monitor *Cerberus* was virtually useless and would much later be stripped and used as a breakwater in Port Phillip Bay. *Victoria* and *Albert* would soon be sold for civilian use as towing vessels. *Paluma* and *Gayundah* would be retained for training Naval Reserve personnel in local waters (until 1916 and 1922, respectively). Some of the smaller vessels were still suitable for harbour patrol and defence work. Not surprisingly, the well-maintained cruiser *Protector* was the only ship really suitable for twentieth-century naval operations. She would serve until 1924.

The ships of the colonial navies had provided Australians with an opportunity for training in the basics of seagoing and the rudiments of naval warfare. Other than the steam sloop *Victoria* and the cruiser *Protector*, none of the colonial warships was capable of being deployed to foreign waters. They were, at best, gestures at local maritime defence and, it must be said, they did serve as a deterrent to any would-be naval raiding party with hostile intent. While the Australian colonies were more active in providing for their naval defence than any other in the British Empire, a whole new vision was now required as the colonies moved towards forming a Federal Commonwealth and becoming a sovereign country. Naval officers, such as Captain Robert Muirhead Collins of Victoria, could see the critical relationship between the new nation and the naval defence provided by a responsible government: 'It is important for Australia, from her geographical position and her manifest maritime future, to develop her own resources. This cannot be done if her naval defence is restricted to the payment of subsidies'. The Australian people would soon demand their own navy.

4

National navy 1901–13

After a decade of consultation, negotiation, compromise and determination, the six Australian colonies formed a Federal Commonwealth on 1 January 1901. Australia had become a sovereign nation. The Royal Navy had looked forward to this development for some time. The Admiralty hoped that administrative arrangements for its operations around and beyond the continent would be streamlined in dealing with one rather than six governments. But the progression to independent nationhood inevitably produced criticism of continuing imperial control of Australian naval defence.

The return of the naval brigades from China became the subject of political debate in Australia, and objections were voiced over the actual and proposed future British use of Australian ships and men for causes that did not directly concern Australia. On the other hand, the Admiralty expressed its concern with the limitations already placed on the control of the Auxiliary Squadron and began to propound the creed that naval defence should no longer be a matter of local interest. A single undivided navy—the Royal Navy—was imperative to Australia's security at sea and the wellbeing of the Empire. This would be the Admiralty's line of argument for the next few years. Both perspectives—imperial and local—sounded the death knell for the 1887 agreement. When the *Australasian Naval Defence Act* (1887) expired in 1901, neither party was interested in its renewal. The way was now open for a new agreement. But opinion in Australia was sharply divided between two schools of thought:

those advocating a separate Australian navy; and those supporting the creed of one empire, one navy.

The foremost proponent of an Australian navy was William Rooke Creswell, a former Royal Navy officer who had settled in Australia in 1878, after his father's death. In turning to farming, he hoped to make a new life for himself. He had no private income and could not survive on the half pay he received from the Admiralty for a disability he had sustained during active service. By 1885, however, the lure of the sea had proved too strong and Creswell was appointed first lieutenant of HMCS *Protector*. By the time of Federation, Creswell had been involved in Australia's naval defence for two decades and had a clear vision for a local navy which he was to pursue to realisation. Creswell believed the proclamation of Federation made Australia an independent nation. As the first responsibility of any national government was to guarantee the safety and protection of its citizens, Creswell argued that Australia should have its own navy. But there was more to his argument than a desire to promote expensive statecraft. Creswell positively believed that Australia needed naval defence to secure its territorial integrity and to protect its overseas interests. As an island nation keenly sensing its remoteness from friends and allies, an adequate navy was paramount to national survival. In 1902 he wrote: 'For a maritime state furnished without a navy, the sea, so far from being a safe frontier is rather a highway for her enemies; but with a navy, it surpasses all other frontiers in strength'.

Following service with the South Australian colonial navy, Creswell became the Naval Commandant of Queensland on 1 May 1900. Shortly afterwards on 28 September 1901, he produced a report on 'the best method of employing Australian seamen in the defence of commerce and ports'. Creswell attacked the extant naval agreement as irrelevant and inadequate. He advocated construction of four 3000-ton cruisers for training local personnel; the acquisition of a training ship for boys; the creation of an Australian naval reserve; and the establishment of specialist naval training schools. The four cruisers would be minimum-manned in peacetime and raised to a full fighting complement in wartime for deployment as a reserve flotilla in the Imperial Squadron. Creswell claimed that his proposals would not exceed current expenditure on naval defence with the four cruisers to be delivered over a four-year period.

The nation's leading press appeared to support the development of an Australian navy that was owned, operated and maintained by

Australians. In response to Creswell's report, the 20 December 1901 edition of the *Age* praised his strategic outlook.

> *The Australian Navy is not mere sentiment. It is a policy, and wise policy too. Captain Creswell has rendered a service in trying to bring it out of the clouds and place it on the basis of a practical scheme . . . Clear thinkers have long since been practically unanimous that the sea must always be not alone Australia's first line of defence but her chief line. An invader can reach us only in ships. He can come in sufficient force only if convoyed by strength enough to land forces without danger of serious molestation. No foreign power would be mad enough to transport a large aggressive force over the sea to attack Australia unless it first made provision against serious intervention on the sea . . . Moreover, we have to remember the vast risks of landing anything short of a large army in Australia.*

The *Age* had already expressed a firm commitment to the development of Australian maritime power.

> *Australia cannot avoid her destiny as a sea power, and it is equally clear she must be dominant in this part of the world. In the fulfilling of this end she must have a navy. The beginning of the Federation era is the suitable time for the beginning of this navy. The one is the adjunct of the other. The laying of the foundations of a nation like ours must commence on a scheme of national defence for the wealth we are accumulating.*

The *Age* also accepted Creswell's assessment that an adequate local navy would cost as much as the present subsidy scheme while giving Australia an asset to show for its expenditure. In any event, the *Age* noted, Australia already had the genesis of a navy.

> *There are some 1800 men in the naval forces of the various States. The lack of training facilities has told against their efficiency in some States. Under Federal organisation and with proper training afloat in the Federal ship of war, they could be made an effective body of men for sea service. Seeing, therefore, that in any provision for the future we must spend some £300 000 a year out of the Federal Treasury for the maintenance of naval defence, the question very opportunely comes up again whether we cannot spend this money much more advantageously for ourselves than by handing it over to the British Admiralty.*

In adding its support to Creswell's scheme for Australian naval defence, the *Sydney Morning Herald* remarked on 20 December 1901:

> *There is an element of incongruity in the spectacle of some five million Anglo-Australians with an army splendidly equipped but unable to prevent the burning of a cargo ship in sight of Sydney heads. Of course there is a pardonable touch of rhetoric about this because we have the protection of His Majesty's ships and the auxiliary squadron as a first line of defence. We contribute largely to the maintenance of this squadron mainly because we recognise the necessity for some such provision and our moral obligation to bear a share in its cost. But Captain Creswell's contention is that we can arrive at the same result in another way, which, while probably less burdensome on the mother country, would ensure to us a permanent result.*

The *Sydney Morning Herald* stressed the need for self-help and self-reliance but felt the lack of Australian ships made it impossible for the new nation to train its own naval personnel.

> *Clearly, then, the first requirement of any scheme for federal naval defence is the provision of the necessary ship or ships to form the nucleus of a squadron. Since we in this State lost the* Wolverine, *we have had no means of giving our men training afloat, yet the services of our Naval Brigade in China showed that we are as capable of taking part in the Empire's wars with this arm of the service as with the Bushmen and Mounted Infantry who served in South Africa. What is wanted is the opportunity for training afloat. Once that is forthcoming we shall be better able to judge the amount of effective material that can be drawn from the available total of nearly 30 000 men engaged in the sea and river and fisheries services of the Commonwealth.*

Anticipating fears in London that Australia would abandon its links to the Empire, the 21 December 1901 edition of the *Brisbane Courier* explained that:

> *The creation of an Australian navy would in no sense mean the separation of Imperial from Australian defence, but rather the co-operation for a certain definite purpose. It may easily happen*

> *that the whole strength of the Imperial navy would be engaged in another part of the world in opposing the ships of other countries, or in protecting British commerce and at such a time it would be of extreme importance to have the Australian coastal trade protected by our own fleet from raiding cruisers.*

It was obvious that the assumption of independence and sovereignty by the Australian colonies would not be an empty achievement. Within the first months after Federation, Australians were expressing a sincere commitment to accepting all of the responsibilities of nationhood, including naval defence. But the Colonial Conference held the following year at which the extant naval agreement was to be renegotiated overshadowed Creswell's creative plan. The First Lord of the Admiralty, Lord Selbourne (William Palmer), had made the imperial position very clear.

> *It is desirable that the populations of the Dominions should become convinced of the truth of the proposition that there is no possibility of the localisation of naval forces, and that the problem of the British Empire is in no sense one of local defence. The sea is all one, and the British Navy, therefore, must be all one; and its solitary task in war must be to seek out the ships of the enemy wherever they are to be found, and destroy them.*

The Australian Prime Minister, Edmund Barton, and his ministry generally subscribed to this view, but there were many who voiced their disapproval. The member for Bendigo, Sir John Quick, pointed out that more than a decade earlier Admiral Tryon had favoured some form of local naval control, arguing that: 'It is blood rather than gold that is the basis of every true force; and to awaken the proper spirit, the Government of each Colony, the people of each Colony, should manage as far as possible, their local naval forces during times of peace'. Billy Hughes noted that the Government's attitude was 'the death blow to the budding aspirations for an Australian Navy'.

In spite of all the opposition, a new naval agreement was signed in 1903 which provided for the stationing in Australian waters of one armoured first-class cruiser (HMS *Euryalus*), two second-class cruisers (*Challenger* and *Cambrian*) and five third-class cruisers (*Psyche*, *Pyramus*, *Pioneer*, *Pegasus* and *Prometheus*) and four sloops. Article IV of the agreement stated:

Of the ships referred to in Article I, one shall be kept in reserve and three shall only be partly manned and shall be used as Drill Ships for training the Royal Naval Reserve, the remainder shall be kept in commission fully manned.

In explaining the government's decision and in seeking approval for payment of the subsidy, Barton told Federal Parliament:

I wish to say at the outset that I do not decry, but on the other hand, fully appreciate, the spirit of local patriotism which animates those who hold that our seagoing defence should be provided for wholly by means of an Australian navy. There are two reasons in the main why the Government cannot adopt that proposal for the purposes for which this agreement has been entered into. The first of these is the principle of the unity of control in naval defence, and the second the cost of any minimum adequate defence provided for in that way.

Australia agreed to pay a subsidy of five-twelfths of the annual cost of maintaining the squadron to a maximum of £200 000. Barton compared this amount with the £500 000 he claimed it would cost to maintain an Australian squadron of comparable capability. A former commander-in-chief of the Australia Station, Admiral Sir Cyprian Bridge, was critical of the British Government for proposing a subsidy policy. He expressed the view that

badgering our fellow subjects beyond the seas for money payments towards the cost of the Navy is undignified and impolitic. The greatest sum asked for by the most exacting postulant would not equal a twentieth part of the Imperial naval expenditure, and would not save the taxpayer of the Mother Country a farthing in the pound of his income.

It was a pity he had not made the point so strongly during his service in Australia.

The Australian press reflected popular disappointment with the Government's policy. The *Adelaide Register* made no secret of its opposition: '[For] the Commonwealth to request an outside body to perform any act of defence, which the people are able to do for themselves, is to enfeeble the national character and lower Australian prestige'. The English *Spectator* was afraid that the Commonwealth's decision would have regrettable broader consequences: 'Canada, Australia and New Zealand will never attain to that Naval spirit which is the life breath of maritime empire if they hire their naval protection in Britain or merely pay in money'. But the *Sydney Morning Herald*, previously reticent about Australia's capability to provide for its own needs, supported Barton's position by arguing that those proposing an Australian navy overstated the size and capability of the squadron Australia could purchase for the proposed outlay. The newspaper claimed on 12 November 1902:

> *There is, of course, something flattering to the new Federation about the idea of its possessing and directing a fleet of its own; but the very circumstances that make it so would reduce this miniature navy for all practical purposes to a nullity . . . Sir Edmund Barton condemned the theory that the fleet could be kept selfishly at home as hopelessly wrong, insisting that to be of any real service it would have to be part of the general defence scheme of the Empire, and liable to work with ships of His Majesty's navy under common direction. This view of the case has been so often urged that it only needs to be mentioned here to ensure due weight being given it in debate.*

However, the *Sydney Morning Herald* was attacking 'straw men' when it accused the 'Creswell' group of advocating an independent navy.

> *The Admiralty must have single and undivided control of the national sea power if it is to be effectively used for purposes of Imperial defence. A number of isolated fleets under independent direction would be a source of weakness rather than of strength to the nation, and a standing invitation to the enemy in critical times. Our security lies in cooperating with the British Navy as to make such ships as we have on the Australia Station an integral part of it. This is a portion of our heritage of Empire, and we must not forget nor depart from it.*

The strongly nationalistic *Bulletin* was the most strident opponent of naval subsidies. After claiming that Australia received 'nothing that is of any value' in return for the subsidy, the 4 October 1902 edition of the *Bulletin* railed against the terms of the new agreement which it thought gave the Commonwealth Government

> *some sort of shadowy control over the fleet in its waters by a clause providing that the ships are not to leave 'the Australia Station' (which embraces nearly all the South Pacific)—without permission. But it was never pretended that this limitation would be respected in a time of crisis. If Britain called, the ships of the Australia Station would go to the Mediterranean, to China, or to the English Channel. The proposed new agreement dispenses with the hypocrisy of the control condition, and frankly allows that the subsidy is to Britain's defence not Australia's. This continent can have the benefit of the warships' presence in peacetime; when war breaks out they may continue in her waters or they may not, just as it suits Britain. Obviously, this is a bad bargain for Australia.*

The *Bulletin* further argued that Australia did need 'a few swift cruisers to protect her coastal commerce in wartime against a sudden swoop from a privateer or a vagrant warship' but that these could and should be built by Australia in due course. Consistent with its aggressive nationalism, the *Bulletin* told the Parliament that 'doubling the subsidy . . . will in no way assist Australian defence, will in no way help to dispense with an Australian fleet, and is purely and simply an addition to the charity grant now paid to a rich uncle'. The *Bulletin* stepped up its criticism of Barton's administration a week later on 8 October.

> *Unofficially, yet very openly and significantly, [Barton is of the view] that any idea of Australia creating a fleet of its own must be severely discouraged. This is a broad and conspicuous hint that Australia can't be trusted or that the marine glory of the empire, with the pomp, dignity, salary, and brass buttons attached thereto, are not for common people like Australians, but for the superior Briton only; and that Australia must be compelled to rely on Britain for defence—and be reminded unpleasantly at intervals that it doesn't defend itself but hides behind the skirts of its venerable parent. The theory that the empire's great weapon of offence must be wholly in the hands of that small fragment of the empire called Britain, embodies the idea of subjection and inferiority on the part of the rest of the empire.*

The debate continued into the new year. It was universally recognised to be a matter of national importance. The *Age* featured a long article entitled 'An Australian Navy: Policy of Self-Reliance' by 'A naval officer' in its edition of 7 April 1903.

> *It is not singular that the proposal to increase the naval subsidy to Great Britain, and simultaneously abandon all voice in the disposition of our coastwise defence, should be received with distrust and dislike, even by those who can claim no special knowledge of matters naval. But while the man in the street resents the course to which Sir Edmund Barton, when amid the seductive surroundings of the conference in London agreed to commit Australia, the man who has devoted his whole life to naval questions is able to show incontrovertibly that on the broadest basis of imperial policy the establishment of a locally owned, officered and manned fleet would make immeasurably more for the safety of the Empire and the weal both of England and Australia than any naval subsidy.*

The writer—probably Creswell—was keen to deny the assertion that an independent navy was being proposed and posed the question: 'why should the idea that a portion of the Empire's sea forces could be raised and operate from Australia be interpreted as a desire for separation and as the most wicked naval blasphemy and infidelity?' The writings of the great American naval strategist Captain (later Rear Admiral) Alfred Mahan were cited as an authority for the wisdom of 'the defence of the commerce of the great self-governing dependencies by the dependencies themselves, by their own ships and men'. 'What Australia needs,' Mahan wrote in 1902, 'is not a petty fraction of the Imperial Navy, a squadron assigned to her in perpetual presence. A continent in itself with a thriving population and willing apparently to contribute to the general naval welfare, let Australia frame its schemes and base its estimates on sound lines . . . recognising that local safety is . . . best found in local precaution.' But against the might and persuasive power and prestige of the Admiralty, could local precaution prevail? Australia's maritime geography was depicted as a strength to be exploited rather than a difficulty to be overcome.

> *The length of the coastline is not a weakness but an element of solid strategical advantage to Australia's defence. It multiplies the ports and places at which Australian warships can coal and refresh in security denied to the enemy, and for roughly 7800 miles the coast offers nothing to attack. For all practical purposes the*

main ports are islands situated at convenient distances and constituted, from the naval point of view, coaling bases. Commerce attack, according to Captain Mahan, is the only risk Australia is open to in war. The idea that towns are to be attacked is to suppose that the enemy's cruiser commanders would be mad enough to empty their magazines with no base at which to refill them, and with the risk of meeting a foe when they are in that condition.

The *Bulletin* resumed its campaign against Barton's decision on 4 April 1903 with a sense of wounded national pride after the Commander-in-Chief of the Australia Station, Vice-Admiral Sir Arthur Fanshawe, took a swipe at Australian naval aspirations by warning against the establishment of 'little petty navies' in a speech he delivered in New Zealand. Fanshawe subsequently argued that 'Australia and New Zealand's sole defence for many years to come rests upon the capacity of the Royal Navy to maintain command of the Eastern seas'. The *Bulletin*'s editor pronounced:

Under these circumstances all true Australians naturally revert to the idea of creating and gradually strengthening and building up our own fleet, and against this view the present British government has set its face hard. Its servile subordinates naturally follow its lead. The ill-bred sneer of Admiral Fanshawe at the 'petty fleets' which would naturally represent the first beginnings of the Australian marine, reflects the latest turn of the British political kaleidoscope. Yet Fanshawe's tall, bloated scoff comes badly from the representative of a country which was glad so very lately to get the aid of Australia's petty army, and which is cadging so hard for Australia's petty cash in the shape of a naval subsidy, and which boasts so much of the petty dependencies which, added together, make up its empire. If a separate Australian marine force is a matter of such utter absurdity, then a separate Australian land force is equally ridiculous, likewise a separate Australian subsidy.

The *Bulletin* also pointed out that the Admiralty seemed to have reversed its policy on local arrangements between 1887 and 1902.

[It] had been for many years agreed by practically all British authorities that Empire defence depended for one of its essentials on local defence of outlying dependencies. Australia had received

no intimation that this opinion had altered, and that these local defences were no longer regarded with a friendly eye. Then the information was sprung upon this country, after dinner, that local defences are no longer looked upon with a friendly eye; that they are rather regarded as wicked and almost insurrectionary.

The *Bulletin* also criticised the Australian Labor Party in its edition of 6 June 1903 for failing to assert its ideals in relation to naval defence.

The party professes to be White Australian and democratic in its ideals, and should have fought from the first, with tooth and nail, a scheme which, in the case of war, might leave Australia at the mercy of the fleet of Britain's ally—Japan.

A week later on 20 June, the *Bulletin*'s editor was attacking the Governor of Victoria, Sir George Clarke, and other former British service officers holding vice-regal appointments for supporting the naval subsidy proposal. Its form of attack was to lampoon those it felt were improperly interfering in what was a purely political matter.

The fact that a man has walked fiercely up and down the quarterdeck of a British ship for many years with a brass telescope under his arm, isn't evidence that he knows anything at all about the political aspects of the case. It doesn't go to show either that he knows anything about naval administration; that he knows anything about the necessities of Australian defence; it doesn't even show that he knows much about war. It only shows that he is an interested party with a telescope under his arm. That applies to the Naval governor who interferes with Australian naval questions; but if a purely military governor like Clarke attempts, however covertly, to advocate the naval subsidy folly, then he doesn't even rank as the most obscure kind of expert. It is difficult to say what he ranks as unless it be some kind of horse-marine.

Political opposition to Barton's decision continued.

During parliamentary debate on the Naval Subsidy Bill in August 1903, Senator Alex Matheson criticised the 'pauper dependency' of the Defence Minister, Sir John Forrest, who was firmly opposed to an Australian navy. It was also noted that Britain spent £1/5/0 per head of population on the Royal Navy where Australia was spending fractionally more than one shilling. Matheson pointed out that if Australians contributed at the same rate as the British there would be £5 000 000—more than the sum required for Australia to provide for itself. But the Commonwealth was, of course, caught by the 'Braddon clause' requiring three-quarters of all revenue from customs and excise collected by the Commonwealth in the first decade after Federation to be returned to the states. For politicians like Billy Hughes, the provision of a navy was fundamentally about accepting the responsibilities of nationhood.

> *[It] is calmly proposed by this agreement to remove the local Imperial fleet now stationed here and—though not in so many words—to give the death blow to the budding aspirations for an Australian navy . . . no matter what it costs, we must have it if it be necessary.*

There was fierce debate but the Bill was passed and the agreement was finally ratified. Although Alfred Deakin voted in favour of the agreement, he later contended that it was 'incompatible with the status and dignity to which the new Commonwealth should aspire'.

With the Naval Agreement ratified and public funds made available for the subsidy, Federal Parliament was in a position to consider draft legislation for the internal regulation of Australia's naval and military affairs. The ships and personnel of the former colonial navies were transferred to the Commonwealth Government on 1 March 1901 under Section 51 of the Australian Constitution, although they continued to be administered under State Acts and Regulations until the proclamation of the *Defence Act* on 1 March 1904. The Australian Commonwealth Naval Board (ACNB) was constituted on 12 January 1905 and headquartered in Melbourne. The Board originally consisted of the Minister for Defence, the Director of Naval Forces and a Finance Member. Captain Creswell was appointed the first Director of Naval Forces. His task was less to do with command and leadership and more to do with moulding the various propositions raised by politicians, the press and the Australian people into a policy acceptable to both the Commonwealth and the Admiralty in London. Creswell had to help the Government strike a balance between Australia's diplomatic and strategic responsibilities as a dominion of the British Empire and its operational and tactical needs as a nation at the foot of the Dutch East Indies Archipelago far removed from Europe, its maritime geography and the internal and domestic political struggles of the day.

In 1905, the indefatigable Creswell put forward a scheme for a local squadron of three 3000-ton cruisers, sixteen destroyers, five first-class and eight second-class torpedo boats. Creswell envisaged the local manufacture of munitions and an assumption of responsibility by Australia for local defence. He was very forthright in putting his case and was rarely concerned about allegations of political partisanship.

> *The pledge given, when Parliament assented to the Naval Agreement Bill, that local defences would be maintained, has not so far been observed. No ships have been obtained for more than twenty years. It is the same with personnel. Practically, there have been no officers entered on the permanent staff for the same period. There are [at] this moment [September 1905] only two Lieutenants on the active list really fit for duty and the whole Lieutenants List (Permanent) numbers only three.*

Creswell's views were, however, unpersuasive to a section of the public and many politicians despite the nationalistic mood prompted by Federation. There was reluctance to spend large sums of money on a navy given the alleged absence of an adversary. The strategic situation in the Pacific and Indian Ocean basins was apparently benign and an Australian navy would be of limited practical value. The 1907 edition of *Brassey's Naval Annual* commented that the retention of a Commonwealth naval force was the product of the enthusiasm of a few 'naval commandants'. It concluded that Creswell's idea for a flotilla of destroyers 'will not be of much value against any attack that is likely to be made on Australia'.

It would have been easy for Creswell to simply give up in the face of political opposition and public ridicule. But he did have some well-placed supporters who encouraged him and lobbied those to whom he addressed his proposals. The army had retained something of a stranglehold on the vice-regal office in New South Wales after the arrival of Lachlan Macquarie in 1810, but in 1902 Admiral Sir Harry Rawson became the first former naval officer to be Governor of New South Wales since Captain William Bligh. Serving until 1909, Rawson was a well-known and widely respected governor and a champion of the dominion navies. The army had used the vice-regal position to great effect for nearly a century. It was now the navy's turn.

Barton's successor as prime minister, Alfred Deakin, supported the idea of an efficient local naval force and voiced his criticism of the 1903 naval agreement, suggesting that the subsidy should be applied to 'securing up-to-date ships usefully engaged in commerce during times of peace, but capable of being employed economically and at short notice in time of war'. Deakin was a staunch and most vigorous proponent of the need for an Australian navy.

> *But for the British Navy there would be no Australia. That does not mean that Australia should sit under the shelter of the British Navy. We can add to the Squadron in these seas from our own blood and intelligence, something that will launch us on the beginning of a naval career and may in time create a force which will rank among the defences of the Empire.*

The Admiralty turned a deaf ear to these suggestions except to agree that the Imperial Defence Committee should frame a scheme of defence for Australia. In May 1906, the committee issued its report confirming that the naval agreement was adequate. The Australians were not going to be put off that easily. Efforts to reach some sort of acceptable agreement continued with Deakin suggesting in 1907 that Australia should provide 1000 sailors for the Royal Navy at Commonwealth expense with the cost estimated at £100 000 per annum, 'the remainder of the present subsidy' to be applied to a local defence force. The Admiralty refused to accept this scheme as the basis for a new agreement.

At the Imperial Conference held in London in 1907, Alfred Deakin and Sir William Lyne, the Minister for Trade and Customs, put the case for an Australian navy. Deakin took a great personal interest in the navy. His contemporaries described him as the last of the patriot statesmen and the 'greatest imperialist of them all'. The Admiralty proposal was for Australia to have a naval force consisting of small coastal destroyers and a small submarine flotilla. Lord Tweedmouth (Edward Majoribanks), the first Lord of the Admiralty, speaking on 23 April 1907 in response to the Australian proposals, stated that Australia would need to build locally 'the smaller craft which are necessarily incident to the work of the great fleet of modern battleships'. His reason for saying this was straightforward: 'You cannot take the smaller craft such as torpedo boats and submarines across the ocean'. He suggested very strongly to the Australians that they should have submarines.

The 1907 Imperial Conference. Prime Minister Alfred Deakin is seated in the front row (third from right). A young Winston Churchill is standing in the second row (extreme left). (RAN official)

> *above all things in this work, the submarine is probably the most important and most effective weapon . . . That is the view that is very strongly taken by some of the leading men in the French Navy, who think the submarine is really the weapon of the future.*

This view no doubt reflected that of the First Sea Lord, Admiral Sir John Fisher, who favoured submarines and had his own ideas on how Australia should support the Royal Navy. He did not support the establishment of a dominion navy that did not also meet pressing imperial needs. Tweedmouth also asserted that such an acquisition would be useful to Britain as well, 'supposing as it were, as I hope it may not be, drawn into a war abroad'. The conference closed with the decision that the Admiralty would wait for formal submissions from the colonial governments as to the form of assistance with naval defence that was desired.

As Deakin's delegation returned home, the Commonwealth Government learned that a large American fleet would be undertaking a worldwide tour starting in 1908. Deakin wanted the ships to visit

Australia. In his invitation to President Theodore Roosevelt, Deakin remarked:

> *No other Federation in the world possesses so many features [in common with] the United States as does the Commonwealth of Australia . . . and I doubt whether any two peoples could be found who are likely to benefit more by any thing that tends to knit their relations more closely . . . Australian ports and portals would be wide open to your ships and men.*

In conveying the invitation to President Roosevelt, Secretary of State Elihu Root remarked: 'The time will surely come, although probably after our day, when it will be important for the United States to have all ports friendly and causes of sympathy alive in the Pacific'. Roosevelt readily perceived the long-term value of accepting the Australian invitation. 'Some day the question of the Pacific will be a dominant one and it will be necessary to know the sentiment of Australia and New Zealand.' Roosevelt then decided to make public Deakin's invitation. This produced a cool reaction at the Admiralty because the Royal Navy could not mount a comparable show of naval strength in the region at that time.

Deakin was not embarrassed when the details were made public and widely reported. He was delighted when the Americans accepted and told Federal Parliament: 'The least we can do is give three cheers for the United States . . . I venture to say that a welcome such as no fleet has ever seen outside its own country will be given in Australia to the American Fleet'. Shortly afterwards a rumour began circulating in Australia that President Roosevelt was planning a visit to coincide with the arrival of the American Fleet. When American expatriate Labor politician King O'Malley asked Deakin in Parliament whether Roosevelt was coming to Australia, such a visit being the first by an American president to Australia, Deakin replied that he was not. [Lyndon B. Johnson would be the first US President to visit Australia when he toured the eastern states in October 1966]. Apparently, said Deakin, the President was planning a big-game hunting trip to Africa and another to New Zealand to study that country's 'modern industrial economic methods'. One suspects that Roosevelt's real interest in New Zealand was probably trout fishing. Whatever the reason, Australians were naturally disappointed as the visits of national dignitaries were always met with great public enthusiasm. Roosevelt explained in a private letter to King Edward VII, however, that he was closely watching international reactions to visits by the fleet and hoped the King would share his opposition to spreading Asian influence in the Pacific region.

> *I am much interested in the trip of our Fleet to the Pacific; the ships have just come out of the Straits. I feel very strongly that the real interests of the English-speaking peoples are one, alike in the Atlantic and Pacific; and that, while scrupulously careful neither to insult nor to injure others we should yet make it evident that we are ready and able to hold our own.*

There was no doubt that Japan was the unnamed pariah. After the victory of the Japanese over the Russian fleet at Tsushima Strait on 27 May 1905, the *West Australian* claimed the Imperial Japanese Navy was a threat to White Australia: 'After Tsushima, the British withdrew their battleships from the East and Australians were, to put it in Billy Hughes' words, worried "that we should now rely on the Japanese for the maintenance of British naval supremacy in Eastern seas"'. Japan was now seen as a credible threat to Australia. This made the American fleet visit crucial. The *Age* took the lead in suggesting the messages that would be conveyed and lessons that should be learned.

> *It is no less our proper business, while the Fleet is here, to use the object lesson of patriotic effort and achievement it will furnish us to steel our resolution to obtain as soon as possible a navy that will not disgrace us in comparison. Australia is an island continent. Our destiny lies on the sea. No friend or enemy can reach us save by the sea. A friend is coming to us soon along the ocean highways; but who shall dare to say that almost as powerful an enemy may not one day steam into our waters in ironclad might to fight us for our heritage? Nothing is plainer than that we must have a navy. We must arm, and inasmuch as the sea while we possess no warships puts us at the mercy of any hostile Power possessing ships, it is our first duty to arm navily. That is the lesson of the forthcoming visit—that and the fact that without a navy we should be useless to the Motherland or to a friendly Power like America as an ally.*

The sixteen white-painted American warships, dubbed the 'Great White Fleet', departed from Hampton Roads in Virginia in December 1907 for a fourteen-month cruise including 29 international ports of call. It attracted enormous attention during its visits to Sydney and Melbourne, which each hosted the fleet for one week. (After departing the eastern seaboard, the fleet also spent one week in Albany—with a population of 4000—while it took on fuel.) The Australian response to the visit was overwhelming. Public holidays were declared and funerals were delayed as a carnival spirit enveloped the host cities with balls, parades, receptions, concerts and parties for the 14 000 American sailors.

The visit of the American 'Great White Fleet' to Sydney in 1908. (RAN official)

The visit of the Great White Fleet was a clear indication that Britain was not the only nation possessing naval might and not the only nation which shared a 'natural' bond with Australia and its people. This notion of a 'natural' bond was central. As Rear Admiral Charles Sperry USN, the commander of the American fleet, told a crowd in Melbourne, the visit of his ships and men 'bring on both nations a realisation of their close relationship and common interests, and foster sympathy and mutual understanding more binding than treaties'. The sentimental component of the relationship, an important motivator for building and sustaining the trans-Pacific friendship, was reflected in Deakin's proposal of 1909 that the Monroe Doctrine be extended to all countries around the Pacific Ocean, supported by guarantees from Britain, Holland, France, China and the United States. Perhaps caught up in the euphoric aftermath of the Great White Fleet's visit, the *Age* stated that people in Australia were 'always cheered to know America is watching their efforts with more than a friendly interest and ready at a pinch to show that blood is thicker than water'.

The visit of the Great White Fleet could not have been better timed to assist the Australian navalists in their campaign to create an Australian navy. There was a growing fear of both Japanese expansionism and German imperial aspirations in the Pacific. After the Colonial Conference, Deakin proposed a variation of the increasingly unpopular naval agreement. The Commonwealth offered to substitute the subsidy with the provision of 1000 Australian sailors for service on the Australia Station with the remainder of the subsidy to be applied to local naval construction. It was proposed that 400 sailors would man two P Class destroyers retained in Australia, notwithstanding prevailing strategic conditions elsewhere, while another two cruisers would be lent for training purposes at a cost of £60 000 per annum to the Commonwealth. On 20 August 1908, the Admiralty said that it 'had difficulty in fully comprehending the extent of the scheme' outlined by Deakin and pointed out that the cost of the Australian naval proposal consisting of six destroyers, nine submarines and two depot ships was £1 277 500. Their Lordships believed that this was beyond Australia's means. Having given careful consideration to Deakin's scheme, the Admiralty 'could not see their way to accept the proposals as a basis for a new agreement'. The Admiralty waited for the Australians to respond.

Deakin's party lost office at the polls in November 1908 and was replaced by the Labor Government led by Andrew Fisher. The new administration promised immediate action on naval defence and the cost and the conditions for sharing the overall responsibility for Australian naval defence became the subject of great debate over the next twelve months. Deakin's proposals had not met with much domestic support and the only action taken had been to earmark £500 000 of surplus revenue for naval defence. The new Defence Minister, Senator George Pearce, asked Creswell to produce some plans for a destroyer program. The Government announced that two destroyers would be built in England with a third to be fabricated in England for subsequent transport and construction in Australia. In clear defiance of Admiralty advice, the design selected was an oil-burning, turbine driven torpedo-boat destroyer of 600 tons. This destroyer was twice the size suggested by the Admiralty and featured a high forecastle to permit sustained speeds in heavy seas. Australia's isolation, according to Creswell, was the principal reason for their acquisition.

> *We are at the end of the world. We are nearly at the exact point of the antipodes to the heart of the Empire. Asia, with its illimitable*

> *and perhaps threatening possibilities, is to the north of us. Foreign bases are being established in the Pacific around us. Political changes in Europe, not regarded as improbable, may later determine the ownership of the immense archipelago stretching from east to west to the north of us.*

According to Creswell, defence of coastal and international trade was the first consideration followed by the threat of continental invasion. Because aggressors would come by sea, Creswell argued that Australia needed a navy on which it could rely. Creswell's views had gradually gained currency within the community. In its editorial on March 1909, the *Age* complained that

> *Germany has stolen a march on Britain, and Britain's naval supremacy is threatened. A war may occur in a few years when one Dreadnought might turn the scale. The crisis is without parallel since the time of the Armada. The question arises therefore, is Australia rich and loyal enough to give Britain the wherewithal to build a Dreadnought? The people of the Commonwealth will be eager to make the gift, and being a gift, it will not interfere with the issue of the naval subsidy which Britain realises is doomed.*

This sparked a spirited public reaction which the Government could not ignore. But there was another view. The *Bulletin* thought the Australian people were responding with 'mental drunkenness' and asserted that the gift might result in an 'embarrassing ironclad'. While two state governments pledged assistance, the Commonwealth Government took a broader view. Prime Minister Andrew Fisher contended that Australia needed its own navy quite apart from British needs in relation to Germany. Creswell pointed out that Australian seaborne trade in 1909 was worth £170 million and that at least 1 per cent of its value ought to be invested in its protection. At that time, he stressed that Australia's expenditure including the subsidy was merely a tenth of 1 per cent.

But much of the debate was overtaken by the 'Imperial Conference on the Naval and Military Defence of the Empire' that began in London on 9 July 1909. In calling this conference, the British Government admitted that it had to reconsider the propositions of the dominions again in a broader context and recommended that the whole system of Pacific defence should be recast. The conference concentrated on finding the best means for dominion governments to participate in the burden of imperial defence. The conference adopted a general proposition that: 'Each part of the Empire is willing to make its preparations on such lines as will enable it, should it so desire, to take its share in the general defence of the Empire'. It was decided to form a Pacific fleet of three units, one on the Australia Station, one in the East Indies and one on the China Station. Each unit would consist of a battle cruiser, three light cruisers, six destroyers and three submarines with the necessary depot and store ships. It was agreed that the East Indies and China units should remain under Admiralty control whereas the Australian unit would be funded, controlled and ultimately manned by Australians. New Zealand agreed to contribute towards the cost of the unit based in China. The Admiralty claimed that: 'Such a fleet unit would be capable of action not only in defence of coasts, but also of the trade routes, and would be sufficiently powerful to deal with small hostile squadrons should such ever attempt to act in its waters'.

A meeting was then convened between the representatives of the Admiralty and of the Australian Government. They met on 19 August 1909 with the Australians provisionally adopting the Admiralty's suggestion of a fleet unit. The total initial cost of such a unit was £3 695 000. The Commonwealth Government would also pay Britain approximately £750 000 for maintenance, pay and allowances for loan personnel, training and other associated costs. The Minister for Defence, Joseph Cook, put the scheme for an Australian 'Fleet Unit' to Federal Parliament on 29 November 1909. Speaking in support of the proposal he said:

> *We must remember, first of all, that Australia is part of the Empire, and that within our means we must recognise both our Imperial and local responsibilities. The Empire floats upon its fleet. A strong fleet means a strong Empire, and therefore it is our duty to add to the fleet strength of the Empire. Our first object is the protection of our floating trade and the defence of our shores from invasion or hostile attack . . . Should the motion be carried, we shall turn over a new leaf in the book of our evolution. Our tutelary stages are past, our time of maturity is here.*

The motion was accepted and a *Naval Loan Act* was passed shortly afterwards to provide funds for the construction of the Australian Fleet Unit.

On 9 December 1909 the Governor-General, Lord Dudley, dispatched a cable to the Secretary of State for the Colonies at the request of Prime Minister Deakin. The Admiralty was asked 'to arrange for construction without delay' of the armoured cruiser (*Indefatigable* Class) and the three unarmoured cruisers. 'The destroyers and the submarines,' said the cable, 'would be the subject of special despatch.' But the armoured cruiser was to be superseded by a new battle cruiser: the Dreadnought. Battle cruisers were heavily armed but fast and comparatively lightly protected ships designed to support cruisers in their scouting operations, and also to destroy enemy cruisers. Their lighter armour made them unsuitable for action with battleships. Not surprisingly, the Commonwealth Government decided that its battle cruiser would be named HMAS *Australia* and that it would have the honour of serving as flagship. The light cruisers were also reasonably well protected. The Admiralty had been conducting experiments with the old ironclad HMS *Edinburgh*.

> *[These experiments] showed that ships protected only by a thick deck near the water line would be exposed to great damage from high explosive shell . . . An entirely new method of protection for light cruisers was therefore introduced into the ships of the 1910–11 programme, known as the* Chatham *Class, which were protected amidships by 3 inches of protective plating consisting of side plating 1 inch high tensile steel behind 2 inches of nickel steel.*

Australia was to gain the benefits of the latest technology in the crucial area of ship's side armour.

British shipyards would construct two of the light cruisers, to be named *Sydney* and *Melbourne*. A third, to be named *Brisbane*, would be built in Australia. When Andrew Fisher became prime minister again in April 1910 he repealed the *Naval Loan Act*. The cost of the naval unit would be paid from revenue. He also decided against accepting the British Government's offer of assistance with paying for the ships. Australia, he proudly stated, would meet the whole cost. With the decision made to establish an Australian navy, Federal Parliament debated the Naval Defence Bill. The *Argus* on 14 October 1910 wanted to enlighten its readers about the nature of naval defence and the need for Australia to cooperate with the Admiralty.

> *It is utterly inconceivable that the Imperial fleet should be working out some great plan of Imperial strategy, and that at the*

The first HMAS Sydney, *a light cruiser built in Britain for the Royal Australian Navy. (RAN official)*

> *same time the Australian unit should be obeying orders framed apart from the general scheme. Australia would sacrifice none of her dignity and ambition if the control of her ships in wartime went without question to the powers commanding the whole great Imperial fleet . . . When the need comes, the naval principle—with which is bound up the Imperial principle—will triumph irresistibly by the force of logical necessity, and with the fervently expressed approval of Australians. Our ships will form part of the Imperial fleet, since, saving in that character, they cannot operate in war, or count so much as a single gun in Imperial or Australian defence. Therefore, however much we may claim for our political individuality in naval control during peace, in time of war there will be only one course for our ships to travel, and that will be the course ordered by the Imperial plan. In that way Australian defence will be best realised for it is not upon any naval unit or upon the fleet in any one ocean that Australia depends, but upon the giant strength of the whole Imperial navy.*

This sentiment was echoed by the Commander-in-Chief of the Australia Station, Admiral Sir Richard Poore, during a speech reported in the *Argus* a month later:

> *The first and most obvious danger to Australia in any war of the high seas will be danger to her shipping . . . the immense peril to which Australian trade would be exposed travelling through the Suez Canal and its approaches. The canal itself is less than 100 miles long but on both sides of the canal there are narrow seas for 3000 miles and right along this vast stretch of water a happy hunting ground will exist for hostile commerce destroyers. Consequently, war will almost certainly drive Australian shipping around the Cape of Good Hope and he warns shipbuilders to prepare accordingly. What must be the influence of such an expectation upon naval defence in Australia? [The nation] must not rest content with coastal ships to protect us against the possibilities of invasion—possibilities which are happily distant while the Imperial navy is triumphantly strong—but [it] must possess cruisers able to patrol the ocean and guard our seaborne trade from hawks in the shape of commerce destroyers. It is quite natural to suppose that in time of war Australian cruisers would be expected to protect Australian shipping as far as the Cape. But without strength in ocean-going cruisers to shelter trade, Australian will not be providing the defence which it most obviously needs.*

To assist the Commonwealth Government in determining its naval infrastructure needs, Admiral Sir Reginald Henderson was invited to Australia in June 1910. The Government had asked the Admiralty for the services of Admiral Sir John Fisher, who had recently retired after six years as First Sea Lord. During his term of office Lord 'Jacky' Fisher had achieved a small revolution in preparing the Royal Navy for possible war. The Australian Government was informed that Lord Fisher was unavailable but that he had recommended Admiral Henderson, who was considered to be an expert on dockyards. Henderson proposed an elaborate scheme of sixteen bases and a long-term development program involving a fleet of 52 ships and 14 844 personnel. Henderson's report was much more grandiose than Australia could ever afford. Prime Minister Andrew Fisher declared that the Admiral's recommendations 'could not in any way serve as Australia's share in the defence of the Empire. Sir Reginald Henderson has only concerned himself with the local aspect of defence, and has not gone into matters affecting the Empire generally'. This was as good as saying Henderson had neglected to mention the role of the Royal Navy and Britain's share in the financial burden. In any event, other events overtook Henderson's inquiry.

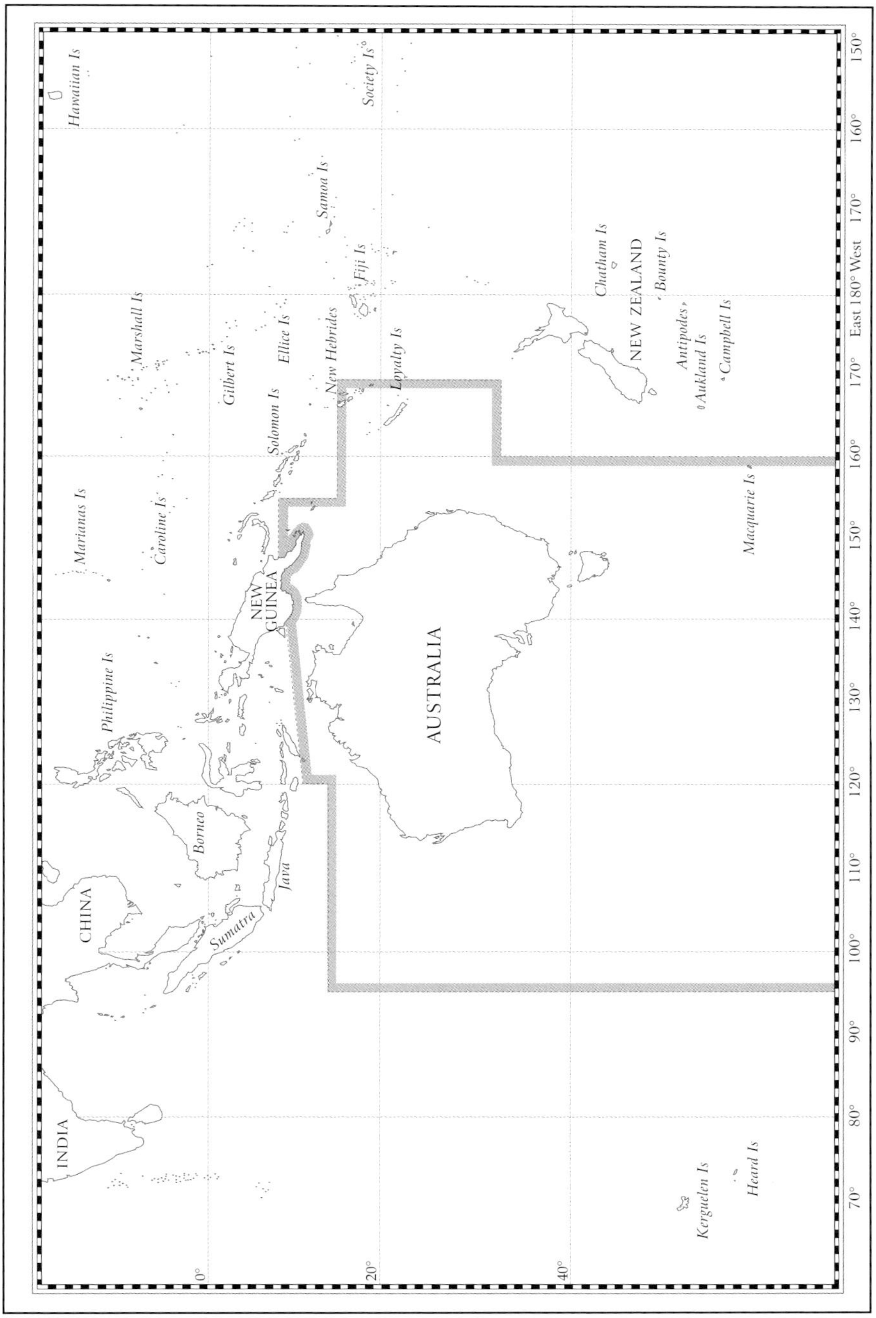

The area confined by the Australia Station at the time of the RAN's creation in 1911.

As the Australian ships were being built, the Admiralty was planning for the withdrawal of its squadron. At that time it consisted of the 14 200-ton first-class cruiser HMS *Powerful*, three second-class cruisers, five third-class cruisers and three survey vessels. With the proclamation of the *Naval Defence Act*, all was ready for the Commonwealth Government to assume responsibility for the naval defence of Australia. On 10 July 1911, King George V granted the title of 'Royal Australian Navy' to the Permanent Naval Forces of the Commonwealth and the title 'Royal Australian Naval Reserve' to the Citizen Naval Forces. The acronyms 'RAN' and 'HMAS' were also authorised. A Naval Forces Regulation stated that 'all ships and vessels of the RAN shall fly at the stern the White Ensign as a symbol of the authority of the Crown, and at the Jack Staff the distinctive flag of the Australian Commonwealth'. The administration of the Australia Station by the Royal Navy also ceased in favour of the Australian Commonwealth Naval Board (ACNB) on that date. For the next two years, the Naval Board prepared for the arrival of the Fleet Unit by recruiting officers and sailors, establishing state-based naval administrations, acquiring supports vessels and building shore facilities.

On 1 July 1913, all of the Admiralty's establishments in Australia were transferred to the Commonwealth. This marked the formal end of the Royal Navy's direct responsibility for the naval defence of Australia. It also marked the conclusion of a long and drawn-out effort to create an Australian navy that could meet the burden of responsibility which had now passed to the Commonwealth Government. The use of Garden Island and Admiralty House was transferred to the Commonwealth Government by the Admiralty, with formal possession of Admiralty House being accepted by Rear Admiral Sir George Patey, Commander-in-Chief of the Australian Fleet, as a representative of the Commonwealth Government on 'Monday, the 13th October 1913 at 9.30 a.m.', Admiral Sir George King-Hall surrendering it on behalf of the Admiralty. There were, however, certain items the Royal Navy was not prepared to give the Commonwealth Government from the naval depot at Garden Island although the arrangement was for the establishment to be passed over as a going concern. These items were HMS *Penguin* (purchased for £2000), a coal hulk, *The City of Hankow* (£1650), steamboats (£2965), lighters (£3120), an admiral's barge (£1050), pulling boats (£151) and a battle-practice target (£2000). The Commonwealth also purchased the Admiralty's coal stocks stored in Sydney and Melbourne although those held at Vila and on Thursday

Island were turned down. HMS *Encounter*, which had served on the Australia Station from 1906 to 1912, was on loan to the RAN until HMAS *Brisbane* was completed. In addition, the cruisers *Pioneer* and *Psyche*, and the sloop *Fantome* remained in Australian waters and were subsequently transferred to the RAN.

The Australian Fleet Unit ceremonially entered Sydney Harbour on the morning of 4 October 1913. The Commander-in-Chief of the Australia Station, Admiral King-Hall, struck his flag in the second-class protected cruiser HMS *Cambrian* anchored off Fort Denison with Rear Admiral Patey hoisting his flag as Commander of the Australian fleet in the largest warship in the southern hemisphere, HMAS *Australia*, which was under the command of Captain Stephen Radcliffe RN. Displacing 21 300 tons and with a complement of 820 men, *Australia* was armed with eight 12-inch guns, sixteen 4-inch guns, four 3-pounders, five machine-guns and two 18-inch torpedo tubes. The new RAN flagship was a truly impressive vessel and a decisive asset in major actions. Then followed the light cruisers *Sydney* (Captain John Glossop RN) and *Melbourne* (Captain Mortimer Silver RN), which were ideally suited for long-range patrol and escort duties. Both displaced 5400 tons with eight 6-inch guns as their main armament. Their sister ship, *Brisbane*, would be completed in October 1916. The two new Australian cruisers were followed by HMS *Encounter*. The two River Class torpedo boat destroyers, *Yarra* and *Parramatta*, were the fastest vessels in the Fleet Unit being capable of 28 knots. Their sistership, *Warrego*, had earlier been completed at Cockatoo Island Dockyard in Sydney. In addition to their three 18-inch torpedo tubes, they were armed with one 4-inch gun, three 12-pounders, one machine-gun and three Lewis guns. Three other ships of the same class were built at Cockatoo—*Swan*, *Huon* and *Torrens*—and entered service in 1916. Vickers Maxims at Chatham built the two submarines, *AE 1* and *AE 2*, which were to arrive at Sydney in late May 1914. They displaced 725 tons on the surface and were powered by two sets of 8-cylinder diesels. Their passage to Australia would be the longest submarine transit in history.

The entry of the Fleet Unit was by far the proudest moment in Australia's short national history. Enormous crowds gathered from dawn right around the harbour to gain a good vantage point. To mark the occasion, all schoolchildren in New South Wales were granted a special holiday and given a small silver medallion commemorating the event. Rudyard Kipling even wrote a short verse for the arrival:

Carry the word to my sisters,
To the Queens of the North and the South.
I have proven faith in the heritage.
By more than word of mouth.

In his address at the Sydney Town Hall that evening, Prime Minister Joseph Cook remarked:

The coming of our Australian Fleet marks a place in the naval history of the Empire. We enter upon it regretting the international necessities which make it urgent, yet feeling proud of our Australian public spirit which makes it possible. We face the future grateful for the protection of the Mother Fleet in the past, while we have acquired the ability and resource to build our own. Our resolve is greater than ever to link our destinies with those of our brethren overseas, who are, day by day, using their naval strength to guarantee the peaceful development of the Christian civilisation of the Empire and the World. A definite place has already been assigned it in the scheme of imperial defence. It is the Australian section of the Imperial Fleet.

The Defence Minister, Senator Edward Millen, shared the same sense of euphoria.

Since Captain Cook's arrival, no more memorable event has happened than the advent of the Australian Fleet. As the former marked the birth of Australia, so the latter announces its coming of age, its recognition of the growing responsibilities of nationhood, and its resolve to accept and discharge them as a duty both to itself and to the Empire. It is the expression of Australia's resolve to pursue, in freedom, its national ideals, and to hand down unimpaired and unsullied the heritage it has received, and which it holds and cherishes as an inviolable trust. It is in this spirit that Australia welcomes its Fleet, not as an instrument of war, but as a harbinger of peace.

The local press exhibited an unrestrained sense of pride. The *Daily Telegraph* declared that:

Australia's claim to nationhood finds endorsement in the arrival in Sydney of a fleet which, though but a unit of a naval fighting

> *force, is her earnest of a determination to assist in building up a buttress to Old England's naval prestige . . . It was certainly an epoch in nation building when they steamed in stately dignity into Sydney harbour on Saturday.*

In London, the *Daily Mail* reported that 'as the world views such matters, it was a small naval display. But that was hardly the point. The sight of the *Australia* and the *Sydney* . . . was an expression of an Australian patriotism . . . The spectacle was inspiring, the soul of it was patriotism'. But the *Daily Mail* pointed to a wider significance for the day's events.

> *The achievement is a feather in the Australians' cap, and the rest of the Empire will frankly envy the exploit which, with the very useful work in the Pacific already standing to their credit, overwhelmingly justifies the prescience and patriotism that led them in 1909 to start a naval unit of their own.*

Having acquired the ships and gained control of the shore establishments, the greatest challenge facing the RAN was the training of officers and sailors for service afloat and ashore. The Naval College, temporarily located on Corio Bay near Geelong, had received its first intake of cadet-midshipmen. The training ship *Tingira* (the old sailing ship *Sobraon*) was purchased in 1911 and commissioned in 1912 to prepare boys aged between fourteen and sixteen years for naval life. Civilians were recruited to provide an administrative staff to implement the Naval Board's resolutions. While the Commonwealth Government turned its attention to other aspects of national life, the newly formed RAN prepared for operations at sea under the tutelage of experienced British officers and senior sailors. As none of the other British dominions had attempted to create its own navy, the audacity of the Commonwealth Government was tempered by the realism of men like Creswell who knew the continuing importance of learning from the strongest naval power the world had ever seen: the Royal Navy. As the strategic situation in the Pacific deteriorated and the stability of Europe was subjected to a succession of disturbances, the beginning of 1914 brought a sober realisation that the RAN had not been formed a day too soon. Australia was threatened and the nation was prepared to respond.

5

First test

1914–19

The Royal Navy had enjoyed unrivalled supremacy on the seas since the Battle of Trafalgar and remained in 1914 the largest, most capable and best trained of all the major navies. On 17 March 1914, the 39-year-old First Lord of the Admiralty, Winston Churchill, intimated in the House of Commons that there would be no grand naval manoeuvres in July of that year. Instead, the reserve Third Fleet would be mobilised, manned by nucleus crews and augmented by Royal Fleet Reserve personnel who would be called up from their civil occupations for seven days' training. On 20 July the long line of warships passed before King George V, who reviewed their procession from *Victoria and Albert* near the Nab Lightship off the Isle of Wight. They disappeared into the English Channel for what most thought were ordinary exercises. They were, in fact, the preliminary moves of a war that had been coming for some time.

Germany under Kaiser Wilhelm II sought a political and imperial role consonant with its industrial strength. This meant challenging Britain's world supremacy. For its part, Austria wanted to curb an increasingly militant Serbia and the threat it posed to its own Slav lands. Russia feared Austrian and German political and economic aims in the Balkans and Turkey. This suspicion led to a naval and military arms race. By 1914 the German Army numbered more than two million men. Britain, Russia, France and Austria each had over one million enlisted men. The assassination of Archduke Franz Ferdinand of Austria in Sarajevo by a Serbian radical on 28 June 1914 was the pretext for war. The extant system of alliances meant the conflict would engulf most of Europe and be fought on land and at sea.

The mobilisation of the British Third Fleet was concluded by 24 July and the sailors and marines who had been called up were sent home. There was some measure of confidence at this stage that fall-out from the troubles in Serbia would not spread further, but four days later when the Austrians sent an ultimatum to Serbia, as a matter of caution, the First Sea Lord, Prince Louis of Battenberg, ordered the First Fleet not to disperse as had been planned. On 1 August Germany declared war on Russia, which had mobilised its army in response to the Austrian declaration of war on Serbia. Russian troops crossed the German frontier and German soldiers entered Cirey in France. By 3 August the mobilisation of the British Fleet was complete. At 11.00 a.m. on 4 August 1914, Britain declared war on Germany.

As war clouds gathered over Europe, the Australian Fleet was embarked on its annual winter cruise and was deployed off the Queensland coast. The Minister for Defence was campaigning for the next election and the First Naval Member of the ACNB and Chief of Naval Staff (a dual appointment), the now Rear Admiral William Creswell, was taking recreational leave. But his rest was shattered by the ominous news of 26 July.

> *A great crisis had developed in Europe, owing to the action of Austria in issuing an ultimatum to Serbia and demanding a reply by 6 p.m. yesterday . . . Early in the evening it was definitely announced that the ultimatum had been rejected . . . The best informed circles in Buda-Pest consider that war is inevitable . . . The Austro-Serbian differences are the first symptom of a gigantic Slav-Teutonic struggle.*

The prospect of war in both eastern and western Europe had caused enormous concerns in London. On 30 July the Admiralty sent out a warning that preparation should be made for an outbreak of war and that Australian warships should begin to move towards their war stations. By an arrangement first mooted at the 1911 London Imperial Conference and more recently confirmed, the Australian ships would be controlled by the Australian Government while in home waters but in times of war the entire fleet would be placed at the Admiralty's disposal. The leading fighting ships of the service comprised *Australia*, *Melbourne* and *Sydney*; the torpedo boat destroyers *Parramatta*, *Warrego* and *Torrens*; the cruiser *Encounter*; the small cruiser *Pioneer* (a gift from the Admiralty); and the old ships from the colonial navies, *Protector*, *Paluma* and *Gayundah*. Some 3800 men were serving in the Permanent Naval Forces in August 1914, around a fifth of whom were Royal Navy officers and sailors on loan to Australia. Command of the Fleet was vested in Rear Admiral Patey.

The political situation in Australia at the time was a curious one: as part of its strong commitment to imperial defence Australia would clearly have to enter the war. The Australian Prime Minister, Joseph Cook, had already told his countrymen: 'If there is to be a war, you and I shall be in it'. The Leader of the Opposition, Andrew Fisher, had pledged that Australia would 'stand beside the mother country to help and defend her to our last man and our last shilling'. Australia indicated its willingness to dispatch a land force of 20 000 men 'of any suggested composition to any destination desired by the Home Government'. Although the cost of deploying and supporting the Australian troops would be carried entirely by the Commonwealth Government, the force was at the complete disposal of the British Government. It had already been agreed that the RAN would be 'effectively placed' under Admiralty control in the event of hostilities. In stark contrast to its earlier concerns about the level of imperial naval strength in the Pacific and Indian Oceans, and its insistence on the need for an independent Australian naval force, the Commonwealth Government led by Joseph Cook expressed enthusiastic support for both the British Government and the Admiralty. Previous suspicion and reticence dissolved as the European diplomatic crisis worsened. Enlistment for the Australian Imperial Force (AIF) opened on 10 August 1914. Recruits could be aged between 18 and 45 years although those under 21 years were required to present a written letter of consent from their parents. Very soon, every position in the AIF's specialist categories was full. The Government was well on its way to providing a force of 20 000 men.

The navy's problem was obtaining the ships necessary to transport the soldiers to whatever theatre of operations they were assigned. A committee consisting of representatives from the navy, the army, the Commonwealth Department of Public Works and the Australasian United Steam Navigation Company was established on 4 August to take control of Australian merchant shipping. Those vessels in port and those known to be approaching the coastline were listed and assessed by the naval transport officer, Commander C.R.W. Brewis RN, for their potential to transport troops and stores at the first available opportunity. The Commonwealth naval ship constructor, Joseph Leask, inspected those considered suitable and prepared plans for their conversion into transports. The Government then formally requisitioned the ships under federal legislation. The first list of 28 requisitioned vessels included nine steamships exceeding 10 000 tons (the largest was the Aberdeen White Star ship *Euripides* displacing 15 050 tons). The smallest was the 4594-ton Bucknall liner *Saldanha*. Of those requisitioned, ten did not have provision for refrigerated cargo. Converting merchant ships into military transports was a major undertaking. In most instances, the passenger lounges, saloons and cabins were completely stripped of their fittings in order to accommodate the maximum number of troops. They were rarely comfortable. As for messing, military personnel would be fed by the ship owners from a fixed scale of rations depending upon the individual's rank. By 27 September 1914, 28 Australian transports were ready to sail.

The main naval threat to the Australian continent was from the German presence in the Pacific and East Asia. Germany's possessions spread from Kiaochow on the Chinese Shantung Peninsula to Kaiser Wilhelmsland in northern New Guinea. These territories were capable of providing fleet support facilities and communications for naval forces. While the number of German nationals spread across this 'empire' did not exceed 6500, the German East Asiatic Squadron of Vice Admiral Count Maximilian von Spee was considered a genuine threat to Australian settlements and ships. The force consisted of two 11 600-ton armoured cruisers, *Gneisenau* and *Scharnhorst*, each armed with eight 8-inch guns and six 6-inch guns, and three light cruisers, including the *Emden*. When war was declared, the last known position for *Gneisenau* was Nagasaki. Japan was still neutral but joined the British side on 23 August 1914. Nothing was known of the whereabouts of the other major naval menace, her sister ship *Scharnhorst*. Facing the Germans was the Royal Navy's China Squadron, the ships of the RAN and those of the Imperial Japanese Navy. The Allied ships were given the single task of searching out and destroying the German squadron. In a letter to his wife, von Spee remarked that HMAS *Australia* was 'in itself an adversary so much stronger than our squadron that we should be bound to avoid it'. Indeed, his strategy was to avoid any major fleet action at sea. When the war began, the German squadron was at Ponape in the Caroline Islands but there was a real possibility that von Spee might have taken refuge at or near Rabaul.

Rabaul, the main settlement on the island of New Britain, was the centre of government for Germany's Pacific colonies: the Pelews, Marianas, Carolines and Marshalls in the Central Pacific; and New Guinea, New Britain, the Bismarck Islands, Ellice Islands, Samoa and the Solomons in the South-West Pacific. The Japanese quickly captured the poorly defended Central Pacific islands and were to retain them as a colonial possession after the war. Patey's ships sailed for Rabaul. After raiding the harbour on 11 and 12 August, they found no sign of the German squadron or any evidence of a wireless telegraphy station. As there was no refuelling capacity at Rabaul, the squadron withdrew to Port Moresby. Patey suspected that the German ships had probably headed towards Nauru where the ships could be coaled before crossing the Pacific and rounding South America. There was also the possibility that they might stop at Samoa in transit. Patey's assessment was reasonably accurate. The Germans did call at Samoa en route to South America but they set out from Ponape, 1500 nautical miles to the north of the position reported by naval intelligence when the war began. After refuelling, the two cruisers in Patey's force proceeded to destroy the outlying German wireless stations. *Melbourne* arrived off Pleasant Island at Nauru on 9 September. A small shore party arrested the German Administrator before destroying the wireless station which the Germans were in the process of building.

By this time, the Australian Naval and Military Expeditionary Force (AN&MEF), a hastily gathered contingent consisting of naval reservists and recently recruited infantry, arrived in Port Moresby. On 7 September the force departed for Rabaul in the liner *Berrima* with an escort consisting of *Australia*, *Sydney*, *Encounter*, *Warrego*, *Yarra*, *AE 1* and *AE 2*. The objective was to capture two German wireless stations thought to be operating at Kabakaul and Herbertshohe. A small detachment from the Australian Naval Brigade component of the AN&MEF was landed near Rabaul and advanced towards the German headquarters. One party, commanded by Lieutenant R.G. Bowen, was landed at Kabakaul at 9.00 a.m. on 11 September. On the road to Bitapaka a scout from the brigade engaged a German soldier. The advance was halted and Bowen asked for reinforcements as the enemy had taken cover in a trench beside the road. The 'enemy' force consisted of 52 Europeans supported by 240 New Guineans commanded by nine German officers. A party of 50 from the Naval Brigade under the command of Lieutenant Commander Clive Elwell RN came forward. Elwell decided to charge the trench. He was shot through the heart and died instantly. Able Seaman John Walker was hit by a sniper's bullet and later died. But the native troops, fearing that the main body of the AN&MEF had landed, would not fight on. Three German officers then negotiated a surrender. The Naval Brigade detachment achieved its objective. The wireless station was captured and German naval communications in the Pacific were disrupted. The following day, the Naval Brigade marched to Herbertshohe and Patey demanded that the whole colony surrender. There was no point in fighting. The surrender was agreed to and German New Guinea was occupied without further loss of life on 11 September 1914. Australia had unexpectedly gained a small empire in the South-West Pacific.

HMA Submarine AE 1, *lost at sea with all hands off Cape Gazelle, 14 September 1914.*

Three days later the RAN suffered its first loss at sea. While on a patrol off New Britain, *AE 1* vanished without trace. All hands, including the commanding officer, Lieutenant Commander Tom Besant RN, were lost. The wreck of *AE 1* has never been located. It seems most likely that *AE 1* struck a submerged reef which ripped open its thin hull, sending the submarine to the bottom in waters between Cape Gazelle and the Duke of York Islands. *AE 2* was now the sole Australian submarine and to a degree ineffective on its own. By this time von Spee's force had been located. It was reported on 14 September that *Emden* had been active in the Bay of Bengal. The Governor of New Zealand, the Earl of Liverpool (Arthur Foljambe), learned two days later that *Scharnhorst* and *Gneisenau* had appeared off Samoa. *Australia* was heading south to escort the Anzac convoy when Patey was ordered back to Rabaul to protect the small Australian occupation force. *Sydney* was then sent to Augaur in the Pelew group to destroy the German wireless station. By this time, Patey had become frustrated. He wanted to engage the German squadron rather than force the surrender of small enemy outposts.

On 1 October *Australia* sailed for Suva in Fiji ahead of commencing a systematic search for von Spee's ships around the western Pacific island groups. Patey spent the next month in waters around Fiji 'like a dog tethered to his kennel'. The Admiralty was conscious of political pressure in Australia and New Zealand aimed at keeping the battle cruiser in the Pacific until the threat of German naval activity had passed. *Australia* remained von Spee's greatest threat, a fear that was justified. The German official history of the war described *Australia*'s strategic value in very clear terms:

> *The situation regarding the relative strengths on the China, Australian, and East Indies Station [at the outbreak of war] if no account is taken of the battlecruiser* Australia, *was not absolutely unfavourable for the German fighting force in East Asia. By bringing up the* Australia *the British could, it is true, at any time establish an unconditional superiority over the German naval forces.*

Unknown to Admiral Patey, whose ships were patrolling waters between Samoa and New Caledonia, the whole German squadron had already reached Easter Island in the eastern Pacific. Von Spee had enjoyed the most remarkable good fortune in avoiding detection throughout his escape across the Pacific. He believed that by making for South America he would place his squadron beyond the reach of the Japanese Navy and *Australia* and possibly breach the British naval cordon and return to Germany. On 1 November 1914 von Spee's squadron met the ships of Rear Admiral Sir Christopher Cradock, Commander-in-Chief of the North American and West Indies station, off Coronel on the Chilean coast. It was a one-sided affair. British naval historian, Sir Geoffrey Callender, described the ensuing battle in dramatic terms.

> *The German Admiral, with every advantage save one, declined action till evening threw its cloak around him, and the setting sun behind the English ships silhouetted them like targets against the western sky. Then satisfied that he could give, without receiving, punishment, he opened fire with his unanswerable weapons, and the [armoured cruisers]* Good Hope *and* Monmouth, *fighting till the waves closed over them, went down with their colours flying.*

The immensely popular Cradock perished with 1439 men.

While some at the Admiralty thought that von Spee might show a little more daring and attempt to attack the Australian and New Zealand transports bound for Europe, Patey always believed he would probably head for South America. It seems von Spee had been assisted by the dispatch boat *Komet*, which had been lying off Rabaul and sending out wireless messages about the disposition of the Australian cruisers. When the news of Coronel came through, *Australia* was sent at once to reinforce the pursuing Allied forces and, passing Fanning Island on 14 November, the RAN flagship joined several Japanese cruisers in Magdalena Bay in California. They were to prevent von Spee from sailing to Canada or attempting a passage through the Panama Canal. Together they swept down the west coast of South America where a British squadron, including two battle cruisers detached from the Grand Fleet and commanded by Vice-Admiral Sir Doveton Sturdee, was waiting. While *Australia* was searching the Galapagos Islands, Sturdee's squadron engaged von Spee's ships at the Battle of the Falkland Islands. The eight 12-inch guns of Sturdee's battle cruisers and their superior speed gave the British an enormous advantage over von Spee's 8.2-inch gun cruisers. *Dresden* escaped but only to be sunk three months later in Chilean waters off Juan Fernandez. Von Spee, two of his sons and 1800 men were killed. This German defeat on 8 December 1914 brought the war in the Pacific to a close, less than four months after hostilities began. Although *Australia*'s men felt robbed of an opportunity to engage their elusive foe, their ship's sheer firepower had contributed indirectly to the destruction of the German squadron. The naval war in the Indian Ocean was also short-lived.

By October 1914, the 20 000 troops promised by the Australian Government for service in Europe had been recruited and completed basic training. The first contingent would be ready for embarkation for the sea passage to Europe by the end of the month. The British Army Council proposed that the contingent be organised into four brigades: two infantry, one light horse and one field artillery. However, the officer commanding the first AIF contingent, Major General William Bridges, believed that Australia should provide a complete division which, at the time, numbered around 19 000 troops. The commitment to providing a large Australian unit reflected some of the lessons learned during the Boer War when small Australian units were attached to larger British forces. These units had suffered from isolation and a lack of cohesion at any higher level of command. As recruiting continued, the deployment of a complete division became possible.

The Australian division was to consist of three brigades each consisting of four battalions. Where possible, the Australian units were recruited, trained and deployed along state lines. The First Brigade originated in New South Wales; the second in Victoria; and the third from the four other states. Reinforcements were also needed. The British War Office believed that reinforcements numbering 60 per cent of the original force would be needed in the first twelve months to cover those killed or wounded in action. This task was left with the Commonwealth Government, which was also asked to agree to the training of reinforcements in Britain. 'Their presence so near the theatre of operations would ensure the speedy replacement of wastage.' In the space of seven weeks, the greatest armed force ever to leave Australian shores was preparing to embark in a hastily gathered flotilla of merchant vessels. The German Asiatic Squadron was still at large, which delayed the departure of the first AIF contingent for four weeks, but the navy would play a vital role in ensuring troops from Australia and New Zealand reached their destination. While the War Office and Admiralty were frustrated by the delay in their departure, diplomats understood that a German naval attack on dominion troops would have had far-reaching consequences on the colonies' future readiness to supply combatants for Europe. The Australian Prime Minister, Andrew Fisher, was anxious not to diminish the zeal of Australians for the war. He felt that caution was justified until intelligence reports confirmed the probability that *Gneisenau* and *Scharnhorst* were proceeding to South America.

The light cruisers *Sydney* and *Melbourne* were to escort the convoy of 38 transports from Albany, Western Australia across the Indian Ocean to the Suez Canal. The transports had come from around Australia and had already rendezvoused with the New Zealand force and its escort of four warships. On 1 November 1914, the convoy sailed into King George Sound off Albany bound for

Europe. The aggregated tonnage of the convoy was 237 885 and 21 529 men and 7882 horses were embarked. The two RAN cruisers joined the British cruiser *Minotaur* and the Japanese cruiser *Ibuki* as the escort screen.

SMS Emden *wrecked on North Keeling Island, as seen from the deck of HMAS* Sydney, *9 November 1914. (RAN official)*

Nine days out *Minotaur* received a message that the raiding cruiser SMS *Emden* was about to attack the wireless station at the Cocos-Keeling Island group, a hundred miles to the north-east. The mere mention of the name *Emden* created absolute panic among shipping companies and Allied governments in the first few months of hostilities in the Pacific and Indian Oceans. *Emden* had been launched on 26 May 1908 and was described by the Imperial German Navy as a 'small cruiser'. It was steaming through the Yellow Sea towards the Russian port of Vladivostok under the command of Captain Karl von Muller when news was received that Germany and Russia were at war. Von Muller decided immediately to raid merchant shipping in the sea lanes between Vladivostok, Nagasaki in Japan, and a number of Chinese ports. Within the first 24 hours of hostilities, von Muller had captured the Russian mail-passenger ship *Rjasan*. After rendezvousing with von Spee in the Mariana Islands on 12 August, von Muller was given permission to detach from the main

German squadron and commence operations as a lone merchant raider. In company with the supply ship *Markomannia*, von Muller called at the German colony of Angaur before heading for Koepang in Dutch Timor. By this time, Japan had entered the war on the Allied side and von Muller was denied a secure base for his operations. After a brief period in the Lombok and Sunda Straits, the first officer in *Emden*, Lieutenant Commander von Mucke, suggested that the raider hoist a fourth funnel to disguise herself as the British Town Class cruiser HMS *Yarmouth*.

On 9 September, von Muller claimed another victim: the Greek steamer *Pontoporos*. The ship with its cargo of coal was captured and became part of von Muller's supply line. For the next eight weeks, *Emden* operated in the Bay of Bengal and the Indian Ocean sinking another eighteen ships, totalling more than 74 000 tons; capturing another five; and intercepting a further four of which three were used to transport the crews of sunk or captured ships to friendly or neutral ports. *Emden* also shelled British oil installations at Madras. The fact that not one German mariner was killed throughout this period is testimony enough to von Muller's enormous skill as a raider captain. By this time, *Emden* had tied up a substantial squadron of ships. Allied warships, such as the four escorting the AIF convoy, were deployed to protect merchant shipping from the German raider; others, including the Japanese *Yahagi* and *Chikuma*, the Russian *Askold*, and the British *Hampshire*, *Yarmouth*, *Weymouth*, *Gloucester*, *Empress of Russia* and *Empress of Asia*, were ordered to find and sink *Emden*—the most hunted ship in the world.

By late October 1914, von Muller decided on a change of tactics to boost the morale of his men, who had been at sea for a long period in trying conditions without respite. With sixteen ships from five navies in pursuit, *Emden* would attempt to raid the Cocos Islands. Von Muller later wrote:

> *Apart from the material damage the enemy would have suffered by the destruction of the cable and wireless station and the temporary interruption of telegraphic communications between Australia on the one hand and England and other countries on the other, I hoped also to effect (1) a general unrest among shipping to and from Australia by creating the impression that the* Emden *would proceed to harry steamer traffic south and west of Australia, (2) a withdrawal from the Indian Ocean of at least some of the English cruisers which were taking part in the hunting down*

of the Emden. *My intention was, after carrying out the raid on the Cocos Group, to make for Socotra and cruise in the Gulf of Aden and then on the steamer route between Aden and Bombay.*

Emden took on coal from the prize ship *Exford* before dawn on 8 November, 30 miles north of North Keeling Island, but the raid was postponed until the next day after *Emden*'s wireless operators noted unusual coded radio transmissions between the Cocos Islands and ships at sea. When *Emden* signalled the collier *Buresk* on the morning of 9 November, in a code not known to the wireless operators on the Cocos Islands, the brief signal, 'Strange warship approaching' was transmitted and received at the naval signal station in Perth. *Sydney* then intercepted a second signal from *Emden.*

Melbourne proceeded to investigate, but as she was the senior ship in the absence of *Minotaur*, which had been detached from the convoy, she passed the order to *Sydney*, which detached from the convoy to intercept the 'strange warship'. Meanwhile, *Emden*'s second-in-command, von Mucke, had landed on Cocos Island with a party of 50 heavily armed men, intent on destroying the cable and wireless stations. They had not completed their task when a smoke plume was sighted from *Emden*'s bridge and von Mucke was ordered to 'speed up the work at hand'. Before the shore party could return to the ship, *Emden* weighed anchor and proceeded to sea. *Sydney* sighted the German cruiser at 9.30 a.m.

Captain John Glossop in *Sydney* believed that the maximum range of *Emden*'s 4-inch guns was 9000 yards. It was actually 13 347 yards and at more than 10 000 yards *Emden*'s third salvo struck *Sydney*'s gunnery fire control room. Another round hit the foremost rangefinder but did not explode. Four men were killed. The Australian cruiser's main armament then had to be operated in local control. At 9500 yards, Glossop opened fire with *Sydney*'s 6-inch guns and inflicted heavy damage on the German raider before closing to 5500 yards for a torpedo attack. Although the torpedo attack was unsuccessful, *Emden*'s steering gear was not functioning and von Muller had few options available. He later wrote: 'I decided to put my ship . . . on the reef in the surf of the weather side of North Keeling Island and to wreck it thoroughly in order not to sacrifice needlessly the lives of the survivors'.

With *Emden* beached, the Australian cruiser ceased fire at 11.20 a.m. and started to chase the collier *Buresk*. After the German crew scuttled the collier Glossop returned to the raider on North

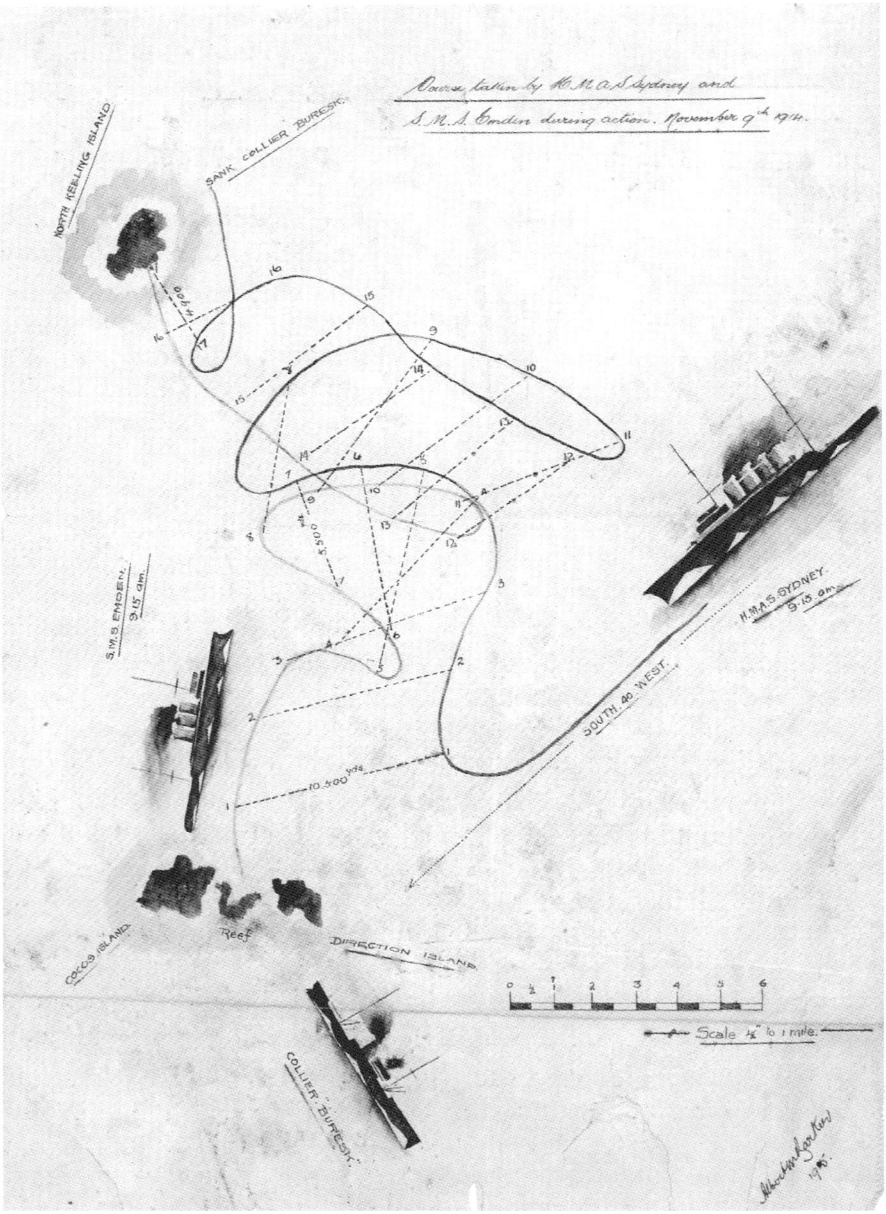

A water colour sketch of the Sydney–Emden *action on 9 November 1914.*

Keeling Island. As *Sydney* aproached *Emden* at 4.00 p.m., Glossop observed that *Emden*'s battle ensign was still flying. This signified, to Glossop at least, that Captain von Muller had not surrendered. A signal sent by light and flag-hoist from *Sydney* asked 'Do you surrender?' This was effectively a request that the German ensign be struck from its staff. Glossop was answered with 'What signal? No signal books.' The signal 'Do you surrender?' was sent to *Emden* a second time. When this was apparently ignored by the stricken raider, Glossop signalled 'Have you received my signal?' It must be asked whether Glossop was justified in thinking the battered and burning *Emden*, wrecked on a coral reef, still had the capability to fire on *Sydney*, but when there was no reply to his signals and the German ensign continued to flutter in the breeze, two salvos fired from *Sydney* crashed into the upper deck of *Emden* and twenty more men were killed. Von Muller was indignant.

> *I had not expected her to resume the attack and was very astonished when she suddenly opened up again. As I afterwards learned from the* Sydney*'s captain, they twice made the signal 'Do you surrender?' but this was not understood onboard* Emden. *As there was no reply, the* Sydney *assumed that the* Emden *wished to continue the fight, the more so as an ensign was still flying from the top-mast. In order to avoid the useless sacrifice of my men's lives, and as the* Emden *was no longer a warship but a wreck, I showed a white flag as a sign of surrender and ordered the ensign from the top mast to be taken down and burned. I am not quite certain what judgement will be passed on my decision to wreck the* Emden *and on the final surrender of the remaining crew.*

Meanwhile, von Mucke had seized the old yacht *Ayesha* from Cocos Island and sailed towards Asia. After a long and dangerous voyage, von Mucke and the *Emden* shore party reported to the German admiral at Constantinople in Turkey in June 1915. *Emden*'s brief but highly successful raiding career was over. Glossop in *Sydney* sent a signal conveying the exciting news: '*Emden* beached and done for'. In all, 134 men died in the German ship, 65 were wounded and 110 taken prisoner. The overall death toll could have been greater as only five of the fifteen shells hitting *Sydney* exploded.

Despite Glossop's questionable decision to fire on *Emden* and subsequent German complaints, the engagement brought instant

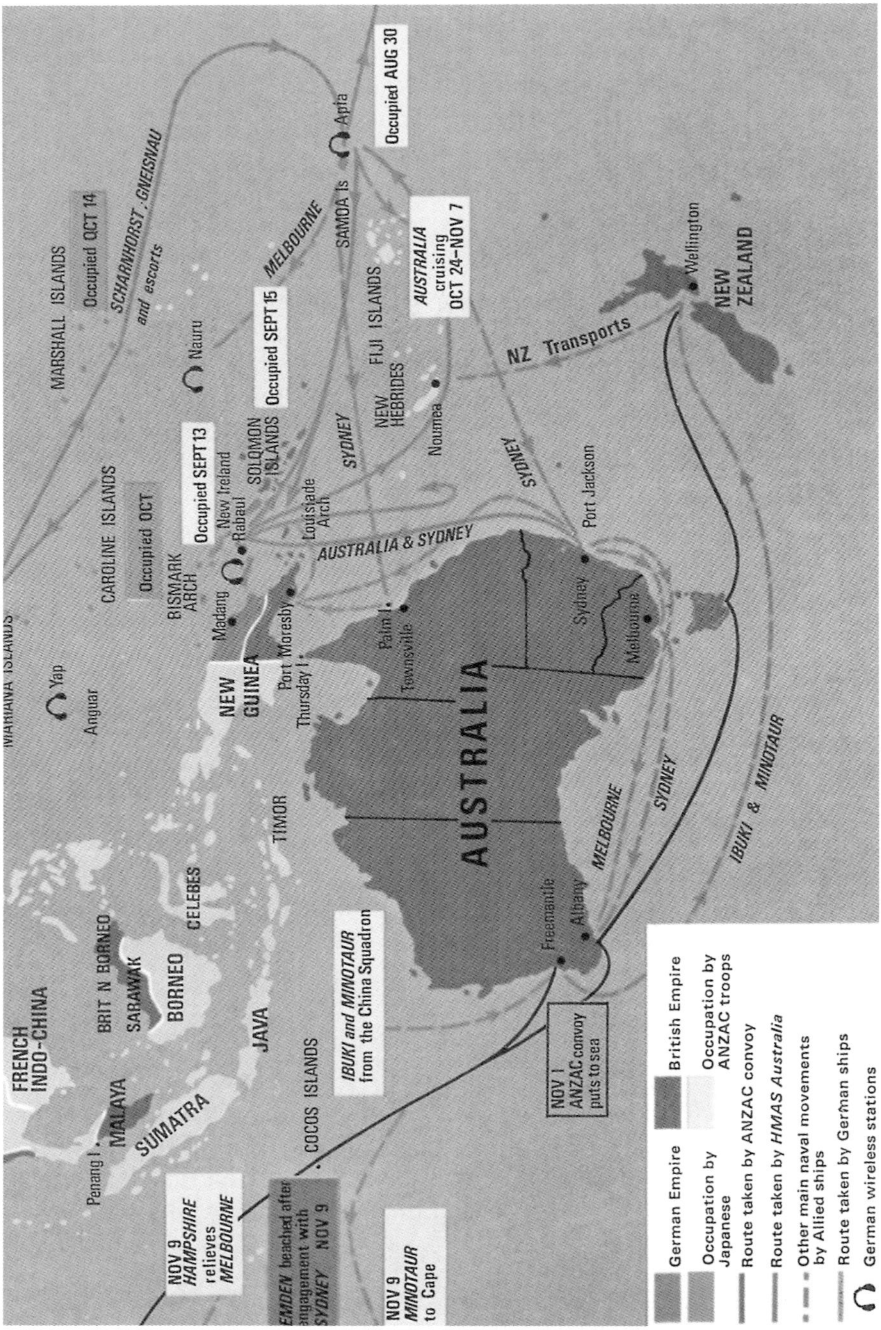

A diagram showing the disposition and movement of Australian naval forces in 1914.

international attention and fame to the fledgling dominion navy. The Australian Prime Minister, Andrew Fisher, told Parliament: 'I do not think that there is a soul in Australia that is not pleased that such an opportunity arose and such success was achieved by our own ship'. The Admiralty sent a message to Glossop. 'Warmest congratulations on the brilliant entry of the Australian navy into the war. Signal service has been rendered to the Allied cause, and peaceful commerce by the destruction of *Emden*.' '*Emden* 1914' was added to the ship's battle honours and Captain Glossop was awarded the Companion of the Order of the Bath (CB). Von Muller was awarded the Iron Cross First Class, while the Kaiser announced that 'a new and stronger *Emden* shall arise, on whose bow the Iron Cross shall be fixed'.

By this time, *AE 2* had proved to be of little use on her own and the Commonwealth Government offered her to the Admiralty for operations in European waters on 16 December 1914. The offer was accepted immediately. *AE 2* would have to repeat her record-breaking trip around the globe within eighteen months of arriving in Australia. On this occasion, she would provide some protection to the second AIF contingent bound for Europe. In December 1914 the Aberdeen liner *Themistocles* was berthed at Williamstown in Victoria, along with a number of other ships being fitted out to carry 15 000 troops and 3000 horses of the second contingent of the AIF to the Middle East. The convoy was to number sixteen ships. Among them were six enemy ships that had been seized in Australian ports at the outbreak of war. They had been taken over as 'prizes' by the Admiralty and given to the Australian Naval Board to use as they wished. The recently promoted Captain C.R. Brewis RN, the principal naval transport officer, was in charge of the convoy. He was embarked in the Blue Funnel liner *Ulysses*, which led the centre of three columns when the convoy took up its cruising disposition.

It was an enormously varied group of ships that sailed from Port Phillip Bay on 23 December 1914. With *Sydney*'s destruction of *Emden* in the preceding month, the Admiralty again felt able to move ships through the Indian Ocean without armed escorts. The only warship was *AE 2*, which was under tow by *Berrima*, on her way to the North Sea. Fortunately, neither offensive nor defensive action was required. The voyage across the Indian Ocean was uneventful for the convoy group, the troops and the horses. After a two-day delay when the wire-towing hawser tangled in the propellers of *Berrima*, the convoy finally anchored off Suez on 27 January. They arrived to the

> *smell of fuel oil drifting across the still water from the tanks ashore as we lay at anchor and the khaki hills to the south-west tinged pink to the rising sun. Here we felt we were entering the war area. The Turks, under Djemal Pasha, were staging their abortive attack on the Canal, approaching from the east across the Sinai desert, and at Suez our bridge was built up with sandbag protections. But they were not needed. We made the passage of the Canal before the Turkish columns reached the bank. The only fire we experienced was that of backchat and persiflage exchanged between our own troops and those of the defence posts on the Canal banks.*

After a day of rest, *AE 2* led the troopships through the canal, protecting herself from occasional Turkish shore and sniper fire, before receiving a hero's welcome from the men of the AIF. They, too, were now in Port Said and the reality of war surrounded them. And then fresh orders were received. *AE 2* was to sail for the eastern Mediterranean for participation in what became known as the Dardanelles campaign.

After an Allied battle fleet failed to penetrate the heavily defended Narrows at the entrance to the Sea of Marmara before a

HMA Submarine AE 2, *lost in the Sea of Mamara, 30 April 1915.*
(RAN official)

planned attack on the Turkish capital of Constantinople, the Allies decided to land on the Gallipoli Peninsula and destroy the forts along the Dardanelles in the hope of reaching the capital and knocking Turkey out of the war. On 14 April Commodore Roger Keyes, chief of staff to Vice-Admiral John de Robeck (Commander-in-Chief of the Eastern Mediterranean Fleet), summoned a group of experienced submariners to a conference on board HMS *Queen Elizabeth* in anticipation of the landings later in the month. Each was asked whether it was possible to penetrate the heavily fortified and defended Dardanelles under cover of darkness and disrupt Turkish shipping in the Sea of Marmara. It was a question every submarine captain in the Eastern Mediterranean had pondered for months.

After a routine patrol which finished on 21 April, the men of *AE 2* arrived back at their base at Mudros Island to the news that *E 15* had made an attempt on the Narrows just four days earlier but that she struck the bottom at Kephez Point and was forced to surface. This made her an easy target for the Turkish shore batteries, which forced the submarine further aground. The commanding officer and three of his ship's company were killed outright by a direct hit on the conning tower. A second shell hit the ammonia tank, with crewmen succumbing to the resulting fumes. The remainder became Turkish POWs. An embargo was then placed on further submarines attempting passage through the straits.

The enthusiasm of *AE 2*'s captain, Henry Stoker, was undaunted by *E 15*'s destruction. There was still a chance that the Australian submarine could be first to penetrate the straits. The opportunity came when Keyes gave Stoker permission to try. Within a few hours *AE 2* was ready to face the Dardanelles with de Robeck's words fresh in Stoker's mind: 'If you succeed, there is no calculating the result it will cause, and it may well be that you will have done more to finish the war than any other act accomplished'. The likelihood of failure was high and the consequences would be grave. They would either die in their submarine, be taken prisoner by the Turks, or accomplish the crucial advantage of which de Robeck had spoken.

Stoker was to attack, and sink if possible, any mine-laying ships found in the Narrows. Because the heavy fire support ships would be operating in the vicinity of the Narrows in support of the troop landings, Keyes wanted to ensure they would not be vulnerable to damage from mines floating down the Narrows with the strong current. Stoker was told then to have *AE 2* 'Generally run amok' off

Chanak as a diversion for the landings on the other side of the peninsula. He took an extra large white ensign with him to help advertise *AE 2*'s presence in the Marmara.

The submarine left Tenedos just after midnight and waited at the entrance to the Dardanelles until the moon set. At 2.30 a.m. on 25 April, *AE 2* approached the straits. *AE 2* held to the northern shore, passing a number of searchlight positions. After nearly an hour of avoiding mines, Stoker brought his submarine to periscope depth: 'Having risen twice for observation in the minefield (which I considered necessary, as *E 15* had run ashore in this vicinity), on rising the third time I found the vessel in good position, rather over to the northern side of the straits, and approaching the Narrows, some two miles distant. The time was then about 6 a.m.' The sun was rising. He was now only 300 yards from the Narrows. 'In order to take stock of the situation,' Stoker later wrote, 'I remained at 20 feet depth with periscope up.' It was immediately spotted by the forts which lined this stretch of water and fired on. The Turks now knew a submarine was roaming the Dardanelles.

Three hours before, as the moon had set and the night had become pitch black, the Anzacs had prepared to leave their transports for smaller boats and then to be towed ashore by steam pinnaces. The first wave of Australians to land on the Turkish beaches consisted of the third Brigade's 4000 men recruited from Queensland, South Australia, Western Australia and Tasmania. At 4.30 a.m. the first boats slid onto the smooth shores. The Turkish forces perched on the hills above opened fire immediately.

Meanwhile in the straits, *AE 2* went deep again with only a general sense of direction. The periscope was raised once more off the small but imposing town of Chanak. Unknown to Stoker his submarine was sighted by a Turkish battleship in the Narrows which was shelling the anchorage off the landing beaches. This had already forced the Allied transports to move to a safer position much further from the shore and disrupted support to the Anzac forces on the peninsula. The realisation that a submarine was lurking in the water had a profound psychological effect on the Turks. On sighting *AE 2*'s periscope, the battleship ceased firing and ran for safety at a time when its shelling was becoming most effective. This was not to be the only influence *AE 2* would have on the land campaign. What Stoker saw through his periscope was most inviting—an old battleship and a small cruiser. But further up the Narrows a number of destroyers and small craft were approaching at great speed with a definite purpose. He fired a torpedo successfully at the small cruiser from a range of 300 yards, then dived to avoid a destroyer which was attempting to ram *AE 2* on the port side.

For 45 minutes *AE 2* sailed up the Dardanelles at 70 feet, making good progress. Stoker thought he had eluded the enemy craft until he next raised the periscope. *AE 2* was surrounded by small craft and coming towards her were two tugs with a wire snare between them. Anti-submarine warfare was in its infancy: there were no underwater detecting devices and all surface ships could do was to fire their guns at the submarine, ram it or drag wires and chains through the water in an attempt to damage its hull. The only escape avenue for *AE 2* was to dive and turn 90 degrees to the approaching snare. The emotional and physical pressure on Stoker and his men had been enormous. They needed rest, but first they had to shake off a persistent enemy who was overdue for success. Stoker decided the risk of raising the periscope again was too great and attempted to round Nagara Point without another look. Having altered course, *AE 2* rose to twenty feet and Stoker raised the periscope again. The submarine was in the centre of the strait and heading for the Sea of Marmara. He could see some small craft chasing him, who could now see him and opened fire. Stoker took *AE 2* back to 90 feet and remained at that depth for 30 minutes. At 11.00 a.m. he thought it wise to look for another hiding place, but at midday *AE 2* was struck by a heavy object being towed along the bottom by a ship passing overhead. The impact cracked her hull and water began to collect in the motor bilges. It was impossible to pump out the water without oil also escaping and immediately giving their position away.

At 9.00 p.m. *AE 2* surfaced to charge her batteries. By this time the submarine had been shut down for sixteen hours. The air was starting to become foul and most of the oxygen had been used up. The enemy ships had given up the chase and it was time to send a signal to the fleet telling of their success. The destroyer instructed to listen for *AE 2*'s messages had been reporting 'Nothing received' for some time and Keyes and others were becoming concerned. The wireless operator in the Australian submarine did not receive an answering signal and repeated the message several times in the hope of it being received. Although purple-blue sparks from the damp aerial were the only visible result, the flagship received the signal. *AE 2*'s message came at a crucial time for the Anzacs who were engaged in a desperate struggle up the heights above Ari Burnu, having been pinned down along a mile-long front about 1000 yards inland during the first day ashore. A few minutes after midnight, *Queen Elizabeth* arrived at the anchorage with a message from the Australian commander General William Birdwood for the Allied Commander-in-Chief, General Sir Ian Hamilton. Re-embarkation of the land forces was recommended. Hamilton conferred with his staff in the admiral's dining room.

Just as Hamilton was about to write a reply, a signal arrived 'from *AE 2* for the Commander-in-Chief'. It was slightly garbled but reported that the Australian submarine had achieved its objective and inflicted damage on the enemy. Keyes added to it: 'Tell them this. It is an omen—an Australian submarine has done the finest feat in submarine history and is going to torpedo all the ships bringing re-inforcements, supplies and ammunition into Gallipoli'. It was marvellous news which Keyes later had to confess 'could not have been received at a more opportune moment' in the whole Dardanelles campaign. Hamilton then wrote his reply to Birdwood and after a few minutes read it aloud: 'Your news is indeed serious, but dig yourselves right in and stick it out. It would take at least two days to re-embark you . . . Meanwhile the Australian submarine has got up through the Narrows and torpedoed a gunboat at Chanak. Make an appeal to your men to make the supreme effort to hold their ground. P.S. You have got through the difficult business. Now you have only to dig, dig, dig until you are safe'.

The assault on the peninsula was to continue. The news of *AE 2*'s achievement was passed to the Anzac troops ashore and greatly spurred them on. Most had known *AE 2* from the convoy to Suez and had heard of her more recent operations. It was not long after Hamilton's message was sent ashore that the Anzacs became known as 'Diggers'. A tradition was born. As for *AE 2*, she would remain in the Marmara for the next four days before being sunk by a Turkish gunboat after a mechanical failure on 30 April 1915. *AE 2*'s crew were POWs for the rest of the war and four would die in captivity. Another RAN unit had made worldwide naval headlines.

As the Gallipoli campaign continued, a third convoy of Australian ships was able to transit the Indian Ocean without armed escort. Over the next two years, transports were regularly dispatched to Europe and the Middle East. Most travelled as part of the 27 convoys which sailed from Australia as requisitioned vessels. They carried a total of 253 000 troops and nearly 25 000 horses. For the most part, the convoys reached their destinations without incident although disputes over control of the Suez Canal and its inhospitable climate continued to cause problems.

The Turkish torpedo boat Sultan Hissar *that disabled* AE 2 *in the Sea of Marmara.*

One of the two 37 mm canons on board Sultan Hissar *that fired into* AE 2.

The former crew of AE 2 *as prisoners of war in Belemedik, Turkey, in 1918. (RAN official)*

With von Spee's squadron fleeing towards German home waters and the Pacific and Indian Ocean basins rid of any German presence, there was little left for the RAN to do in defence of Australian sovereign interests. Both *Sydney* and *Melbourne* were dispatched initially to Malta before being transferred to the West Indies Station where fast cruisers were needed urgently. By January 1915 *Australia* had reached the South Atlantic and caught the German Hamburg liner *Eleonore Woermann* off the Falkland Islands. After one 12-inch round was fired to stop the liner, she was scuttled. *Australia* then proceeded to British home waters, arriving in Plymouth on 28 January 1915. The following month she became the flagship of the Second Battle Cruiser Squadron commanded by Admiral Sir William Pakenham and tasked with monitoring the German High Seas Fleet.

By now the Australian Fleet Unit had been completely dispersed. *Encounter* was patrolling the Pacific from Fiji. *Pioneer* was deployed to German East Africa where she helped to destroy the *Konigsberg* in July 1915. It appeared that Australian sailors would get their first glance of the Persian Gulf in July 1915. The situation there was becoming of concern to the Allies with Germany threatening oil supplies in the region. The Admiralty responded by asking the RAN to man two ageing British cruisers, HM Ships *Psyche* and *Fantome*, which were laid up in Sydney at the time, and to sail them to the Gulf. With its customary haste, the Australian Government agreed and the ships were recommissioned with RAN personnel. However, en route to the Gulf both ships were diverted to the Bay of Bengal to contain a German-inspired uprising in Burma and India with various reports of rifle smuggling to local resistance groups. Neither ship would see the Gulf.

For the remainder of the 1914–18 war, Australian ships in the Indian Ocean went only as far as the Gulf of Oman in convoy escort work. After reasserting British authority in the more volatile larger cities of Burma and India, *Psyche* joined the China squadron based at Singapore and was ordered to patrol the Bay of Bengal. *Fantome* was based at Port Blair for patrol duties around the Andaman and the Nicobar Islands in the Bay of Bengal. *Warrego*, *Yarra* and *Parramatta* supported the occupation of the former German colonies in New Guinea before returning to Australia for maintenance and subsequent deployment to the Dutch East Indies where it was believed the Germans had a munitions base which they might attempt to relocate to Europe. When no such facility was discovered, the three small destroyers patrolled the waters between Java and Siam (Thailand), frequently boarding suspect ships. In August 1916 they were replaced in the Philippines by their three recently completed sister ships, *Huon*, *Torrens* and *Swan*. The official historian's commentary of this period sounded distinctly like a lament: 'Only three destroyers on the Queensland coast were left to remind Australians that they ever had a Navy of their own'. But the strategic situation in the region would not remain benign.

Despite the early successes in the Pacific and Indian Oceans and the Allied blockade of German ports, the war returned to Australian waters in 1917 with the arrival of the commerce raiders *Wolf* and *Seeadler*. After leaving Kiel and eluding the Royal Navy during November 1916, *Wolf* sailed for South Africa and laid mines off the principal harbours. The raider then proceeded into the Indian Ocean and began to attack merchant shipping before mining the major Indian ports. With the Allies alerted to the raider's presence, Commander Karl Nerger decided to take his ship to the south of Australia in the hope of avoiding Allied vessels while laying more mines near Gabo Island on the major coastal sea lane around south-east Australia and off New Zealand. The existence of the minefield was unknown until the British steamer *Cumberland* struck a mine and sank off Gabo Island on 6 July 1917. This led to the formation of the minesweeping section of the RAN Brigade. A number of trawlers were requisitioned for minesweeping duties and thirteen of *Wolf*'s mines were detected and destroyed. The newly commissioned HMAS *Brisbane* returned from the Mediterranean to the Indian Ocean to hunt down and sink the German raider. As *Wolf* was known to be operating aircraft, a Sopwith Baby Seaplane was transferred from the carrier HMS *Raven II*, which was deployed in waters near the Maldive Islands in the northern Indian Ocean, to *Brisbane*. The Sopwith was a useful asset for patrol duties and extended exponentially the area a ship could search. In June 1917, *Brisbane* returned to Australia as *Wolf* continued to avoid detection. The raider arrived back in Germany during February 1918 after attacking another fourteen Allied vessels. *Seeadler* was not as fortunate.

The newly commissioned light cruiser HMAS Brisbane *in Woolloomooloo Bay. She has 'dressed ship' for a special occasion.*

Disguised as a Norwegian timber vessel, *Seeadler* was a converted merchant vessel commanded by Count Felix von Luckner. After sailing from Germany in late 1916, *Seeadler* seized fifteen ships, including three large British steamers, in the North Atlantic before proceeding west into the Pacific Ocean. This proved to be a tactical error as there were few targets. When wreckage from three sailing vessels sunk by von Luckner was sighted on the main shipping route from the United States west coast to Sydney, *Seeadler*'s presence became known. With every warship in the Pacific directed to watch for the German raider, von Luckner sailed to the Society Islands to give the ship's company some respite from the rigours of war. On 2 August 1917, the raider was driven by the weather onto a reef and later destroyed by fire.

With the light cruisers *Sydney* and *Melbourne* engaged in patrols off the American coast, Admiral Patey transferred his flag to HMS *Leviathan* and took command of the North American and West Indies cruiser squadrons. His task was to counter the German U-boat threat while observing neutral American ports where a total of 91 enemy vessels had taken refuge. Although Patey was obliged to respect American neutrality, several incidents led him to doubt the sincerity of some American officials. There were 32 enemy ships in New York Harbour, many of which were capable of being converted for service as auxiliary cruisers. On 10 March 1915, the German armed merchant cruiser *Prinz Eitel Friedrich* took refuge in the American port of Newport News. International law allowed the ship to seek neutral territory for effecting necessary repairs. But as the cruiser had her hull scraped and cleaned to give her additional speed, Patey protested to the American authorities. In reply, they cited Article 17 of the 1907 Hague Convention permitting repairs to defects caused by long periods at sea. Whether a dirty hull constituted a 'defect' and a bottom scrape a 'repair' was debatable. *Melbourne* waited off Chesapeake Bay for *Prinz Eitel Friedrich* to proceed to sea beyond the three-mile limit, but the protests and the wait were in vain. On 8 April 1915, Patey was informed that the ship was to be interned for the duration of the war. Duties on this station were proving to be tedious and dull, so in June 1916, Patey proposed reassigning *Sydney* and *Melbourne* to the Grand Fleet where the ships' companies stood a chance of seeing action. The Commonwealth Government concurred and the Admiralty agreed. In September 1916, the two cruisers were attached to the Second Light Cruiser Squadron based at Scapa Flow in Scotland.

From the Western Atlantic, *Australia* proceeded to British home waters. It was only the cruel misfortune of a minor collision (ironically with HMS *New Zealand*!) on 22 April 1916 that prevented her from taking part in the Battle of Jutland during the following month. The ship sustained slight damage made worse when she was dry-docked. Other than firing at a suspected U-boat in December 1916, *Australia* was never to engage the enemy or to fire her mighty 12-inch guns in combat again. Some of *Australia*'s men did see action even though their ship did not. In April 1918, a party of volunteers from *Australia* joined men from other ships in a daring raid on the U-boat base at Zeebrugge. The attack was a success and the harbour entrance was choked when block-ships were deliberately sunk in the canal. The action was hard-fought, however, and British casualties were high. Six Victoria Crosses were awarded and a number of Australian sailors also received awards for gallantry.

Melbourne and *Sydney* saw only limited action. *Melbourne*'s first operation in the North Sea was a sweep of the waters off Norway in October 1916. Two months later, *Sydney* was also deployed into the North Sea. With the blockade of the German fleet continuing, there was no variation in operations until May 1917 when a combined force consisting of *Sydney*, HMS *Dublin* and four destroyers engaged the German zeppelin *L43*. After attempting to lure the Allied ships into submarine-infested waters, *L43* dropped bombs on both *Sydney* and *Dublin* before making good its escape. After this unconventional attack, the three Australian cruisers were fitted with a revolving aircraft launching platform. A short deck was also rigged over *Australia*'s waist turrets and a reconnaissance aircraft and a Sopwith Camel fighter added to the battle cruiser's already considerable armaments. Both *Sydney* and *Melbourne* launched their aircraft during a cruiser raid on Heligoland Bight in June 1918 but neither aircraft inflicted any damage on the enemy. The rest of the war was largely uneventful for the leading Australian ships although *Australia*, *Sydney* and *Melbourne* would be present for the surrender of the German High Seas Fleet. In fact, *Sydney*'s feat in sinking the first *Emden* was honoured when she was nominated to escort the second *Emden* on that triumphant occasion. On the way home to Australia, a landing party from *Sydney* quelled a civil disturbance at Penang in Malaya. The next day another shore party dispersed a riot in Singapore.

Absent from the surrender were the River Class destroyers. *Warrego*, *Yarra* and *Parramatta* were deployed to European waters for anti-submarine duty in May 1917 after a specific request from the Admiralty. The Commonwealth Government had no hesitation in sending the ships together with *Huon*, *Torrens* and *Swan*, all then based at Singapore. The six ships sailed to the Mediterranean and, after refitting at Malta in October 1917, were ordered to the Adriatic Sea. From their base at Brindisi in Italy, the ships maintained a routine of four days at sea followed by four days ashore. Their task was to support the 'Otranto Barrage', a line of light fishing vessels equipped with anti-submarine nets, depth charges and small calibre guns tasked with hampering U-boat operations. The Australian ships were pitted against the larger Austrian warships based at Pola at the northern end of the Adriatic. By mid-1918, the Otranto Barrage force had grown to some 36 destroyers with the six Australian ships becoming part of the Fifth British Destroyer Flotilla. *Swan* and *Warrego* escorted Allied light cruisers during a bombardment of the Albanian port of Durazzo. Following the German surrender, *Swan* was deployed with a French destroyer in the Sea of Azov as part of a British mission to support anti-Bolshevik forces. *Brisbane* had earlier transported a detachment of Royal Marines to Sevastopol to support White Russian forces resisting a Bolshevik advance.

While the RAN's ships were deployed to every major body of water, back at home Garden Island became the principal Allied naval asset for the fitting out and arming of transports and troopships in the southern hemisphere. Although most of the RAN's ships served in waters away from Australia for the greater part of the war, the island still refitted and repaired 79 vessels. The total number of ships which used Garden Island was 852, including special purpose ships such as transports, the hospital ship *Grantala* and six minesweepers. All the smaller warships were refitted at Garden Island. The torpedo boat destroyer HMAS *Parramatta* was overhauled five times; the light cruiser HMAS *Encounter*, six times. The captured German yacht *Komet* was converted into HMAS *Una* at Garden Island. Ships of the Royal Navy, the French Navy and the Japanese Navy were all supplied and repaired at Garden Island. It initially met urgent needs from its reserve stocks and a store ship, the *Aorangi*, was commissioned to give mobile support for the fleet while national naval supply arrangements were being expanded. The number of men on the island rose from around 950 when the war broke out to 1270 by 1916 and to 3000 by the end of the war. And despite the difficulty of obtaining war and technical materials, the island met every demand that was placed upon it.

The war had prompted frenetic activity across Australia. A sense of relief swept across the country when the armistice was signed. Ten million people had died in four horrific years. The human cost to the Australian nation and people was enormous. Approximately 417 000 were raised for service in the army. Of that number, 330 000 served overseas. In all, 58 132 men were killed and 156 228 were incapacitated as a result of combat. In contrast to the AIF, the peak personnel strength of the Permanent Naval Forces was 5668 men of whom 825 belonged to the Royal Navy. About 350 Australians served in the Royal Navy. The Reserve numbered 5772 personnel. The Royal Australian Naval Brigade consisted of between 1646 and 2670 men together with 3834 sea cadets. During the four years of war, the RAN lost 171 personnel comprising fifteen officers and 156 sailors of whom six officers and 57 sailors were on loan from the Royal Navy. The loss of *AE 1* was the largest single loss of life. The only other RAN ship to be lost during hostilities was *AE 2*.

Arthur Jose concludes his official history of the RAN in the Great War with a memorable tribute to those who had served.

> *So, unostentatiously as they had slipped away at the first signs of war, the Australian ships came home again. Admitted as equals into the greatest service the seas have known, their keenest effort had been to prove that honour fully deserved. They had fulfilled the purposes of their creation. They had saved Australia from raids and bombardments and the other concomitants of actual war. They had helped to protect nearly every trade route, nearly every dominion and colony and protectorate, within the bounds of the Empire. They had seen Canadian ports, and West Indian, and East African: they had safeguarded the peace of our Eastern Empire, and hunted down destroyers of Indian and Chinese and South African commerce over five of the great oceans of the world. They had shared in the defence of the Mediterranean, where through went all the succours of Britain's Eastern campaigns and no small part of the food that sustained Britain herself. They had toiled under the eyes of the Empire's best admirals in the very centre of the naval war. Primarily Australian, and persistently Australian, they had taken their full share of Imperial tasks, and everywhere had upheld the honour of the country which gave them being and owned them. Every prophecy of their detractors had been proven false, every hope of their upholders justified and exceeded . . . Our children will discover, and realize with pride, not so much what the Australian Squadron did in the Great War, as what it was . . . the symbol, alive and ubiquitous, of its country's energy and versatility, and incomparable gift of comradeship.*

In the years of peace that followed, it would be the latter quality that would be most sorely tested.

6
Trials and tribulations 1920–38

When the German fleet surrendered in November 1918, ten Australian ships were either employed or expected in European waters. Many required a refit before returning to Sydney. The last two RAN ships to depart from Portsmouth—*Australia* and *Brisbane*—were farewelled formally by the Prince of Wales and the First Sea Lord, Admiral Sir Rosslyn Wemyss, on 22 April 1919. *Australia* sailed the following day. Many of the ship's company had not seen their homes during the four years of war and were restless. Limited shore leave and arrears of pay had contributed to low morale in some quarters of the messdeck. The fixed-service enlisted men had expected to be paid a sum related to their deferred pay on the expiry of their agreed period of service, although their enlistment had continued until the end of the war. But this payment had been delayed for reasons that were not understood clearly by those affected. There was also the tedium of maintaining a strict shipboard routine when, on the cessation of hostilities, there seemed to be less need for the rigour of wartime discipline. Australian frustrations were exacerbated by perceptions that British sailors were being promoted faster and monopolising the leading positions on the lower deck of Australian ships. There were also high rates of illness: several men had died of measles and its complications during 1915. But these concerns arising from wartime service were left behind as *Australia* headed home.

When the battle cruiser arrived in Fremantle it was met with a rousing welcome and extensive hospitality. There was an open day for the local citizens and thousands of people visited the ship. However, the ship's stay was limited to three days ashore, which further increased tension among the ship's company. Representatives of the ship's company went to their commanding officer, Captain Claude Cumberlege RN, and asked if the ship could delay its departure by a day. This was their first time home after four years of war service. The captain replied that the request could not even be considered because *Australia* had to comply with a strict timetable of port visits.

Australia prepared to sail early on Sunday morning. By 10.30 a.m. the ship was ready to proceed to sea. Cumberlege was then startled to see between eighty and a hundred men emerge from the messdecks and assemble on the quarterdeck in front of 'P' gun turret where they could face and be seen from the captain's position on the bridge. The men again requested an immediate extension of their shore leave. The captain went to the quarterdeck and told those assembled that their 'request' was effectively a demand to delay the ship's sailing. As he had explained earlier, other commitments made this impossible. He allowed no further comment and ordered the men below decks. They obeyed and dispersed, but they clearly were dissatisfied. Further unexpected actions were to follow. Just as the captain gave orders to let go the aft lines, the engine room staff left the boiler rooms *en masse*. *Australia* could not maintain sufficient steam to get under way. After the quarterdeck incident, a number of sailors had apparently donned black silk handkerchiefs and gone to the boiler rooms to persuade or intimidate the on-watch stokers to leave their posts.

The situation was now becoming embarrassing as well-wishers on the wharf sensed something was wrong. The delay was obvious even if its cause was not. With the combined efforts of the petty officers and men on duty drafted from other parts of the ship, *Australia* cast off and proceeded to sea. Once at sea, the stokers returned to duty and the rest of the ship's company resumed their normal seagoing duties. The captain and his officers then held an urgent inquiry into the incident, with the result that 32 men were charged with mutiny. They were acquitted of that charge but were found guilty of refusing duty. Another five, whose ages ranged from 18 to 22 years, were accused of the more serious charge of inciting a mutiny. One of the accused, Dalmorton Rudd, had volunteered for the Zeebrugge raid and had been awarded the Distinguished Service Medal (DSM).

The five were tried when *Australia* arrived in Sydney three weeks later. The entire ship's company of the battle cruiser was sent on leave and the ship was closed to public inspection. The Naval Board stated that the influenza epidemic then present in Sydney posed a risk to any public assembly. At their trial, the accused did not deny any of the facts, the jurisdiction of the court or the validity of the indictment. They pleaded guilty and asked for leniency. It was argued in their defence that they did not understand the seriousness of the actions they contemplated nor were they aware that those actions would be considered mutiny. The sailors pleaded that they 'had no desire to be disloyal to our officers or to bring discredit on our ship'.

Two of the accused were sentenced to imprisonment for one year. A third received a gaol term of eighteen months. The other two men were dismissed from the navy and sentenced to imprisonment for two years with hard labour. The court martial was closed and the prisoners were led away to Goulburn Gaol to serve their sentences. With the trial over, differences in public and official opinion started to emerge on the outcome of the proceedings. As the RAN was still under Admiralty operational control, discipline on board *Australia* was entirely a matter for the Royal Navy. Some thought the sentences were too lenient. Others described them as 'vicious and cruel'. In the four months from July to October 1919, debate raged in the popular press and in Federal Parliament about the severity of the sentences and the necessity of the Admiralty retaining operational control of the RAN. (The RAN returned to Australian control on 1 August 1919.)

After receiving representations from the Commonwealth Government, on 10 September 1919 the Admiralty advised that the sentences would be halved. This did not satisfy the Government. On 19 September, statements were tabled in the Senate concerning the 'need of having a regard for Australian ideals and sentiment' and also 'the need for impressing upon Imperial officers that it was the Parliament of Australia, and not the imported officers, who had the last say in the administration of the affairs of the Navy'. On 6 November, the Government bypassed the Naval Board and communicated directly with the Admiralty, seeking the men's release by Christmas 1919. The Admiralty agreed. The sentences of each of the men would be reduced as an acknowledgment of the gallantry and service of the Australian forces during the war. When the men were released in December, they had served six months of their sentences.

But the Government's actions outraged the Naval Board. The Chief of Naval Staff, Rear Admiral Percy Grant, and Commodore Dumaresq, as Commodore Commanding the Squadron and president of the court martial, threatened to resign, and later did so. Only after receiving assurances from the Commonwealth Government that the Naval Board and the Fleet Commander would be consulted in all future discussions with the British Government were the resignations withdrawn. It was a very sorry affair that strained relations between the Commonwealth Government and the Royal Navy, which had supplied the bulk of the RAN's senior leadership. Although a dominion navy, the RAN would not be allowed to stray too far from British control within what was still its formative period. If anything, Australia and the RAN were tied more closely than ever to Britain and the Royal Navy as a consequence of the Great War. In 1913, Australia had acquired a fleet but not a navy. As naval historian James Goldrick has argued, problems arose not from the 'strength of British connections but from the sheer lack of Australian connections'. This is evident from a comment made by the Minister for the Navy, Sir Joseph Cook, in December 1918:

> *The war has shown us that every part of the Empire can make an effective contribution to the common cause of Empire defence. Australia counts herself fortunate that she was able to contribute in the great war by both sea and by land. The RAN has been working in and with the Royal Navy. During the war it has therefore been relatively easy to work to a single standard. It is fundamental to the idea of Empire naval defence that there should be a complete standardisation of personnel and ships and equipment and that this should be to the level of the best. Only the best is good enough for any navy in the British Empire.*

But there were real problems with the peacetime command and control of the navy. Between 1918 and 1920, there were three major inquiries into the naval defence of Australia. The first, announced in early 1918, was a Royal Commission into defence and naval administration. Soon after the outbreak of war it had become apparent that the Department of Defence could not cope with the demands being placed upon it, especially those relating to the RAN. A separate Department of the Navy was established on 12 July 1915 and Jens August Jensen was appointed Minister for the Navy to be followed in February 1917 by Sir Joseph Cook. But there remained a number of very complex questions to be faced about the allocation of administrative and command responsibilities within the Naval Board, about the limits of political involvement in operational matters and liaison with the Admiralty and about the relationship between the Defence and Navy departments.

The Royal Commission report was tabled in Federal Parliament in September 1918. It identified many problems, including excessive ministerial control, and recommended a restructuring of the Naval Board together with the promulgation of well-defined statements of responsibility and clearer lines of authority.

Soon after the Royal Commission report had been received and some reforms initiated the Prime Minister announced that Admiral of the Fleet Lord Jellicoe had been invited to advise the Commonwealth Government on postwar naval defence requirements. He arrived in Australia in May 1919 and toured the country for three months. Jellicoe's observations and recommendations were contained in his *Report on the Naval Mission to the Commonwealth* conveyed to the Australian Government in August 1919. In sum, Jellicoe stressed the continuing need for a close relationship between the RAN and the Royal Navy. After surveying the postwar strategic situation, Jellicoe proposed the creation of a large Far Eastern Imperial Fleet consisting of capital ships and aircraft carriers to be based principally at Singapore. The costs were to be borne by Britain, Australia and New Zealand in proportion to the value of their overseas trade. This translated into 75 per cent of the cost being borne by Britain, 20 per cent by Australia and 5 per cent by New Zealand.

The Australian Fleet would consist of two battle cruisers, one aircraft carrier, eight light cruisers, one flotilla leader, twelve destroyers and one depot ship, eight submarines and one parent ship, one minelayer, two sloop-minesweepers (with another two in reserve) and one fleet repair ship. The annual cost would be £4 024 600. Commonwealth revenues at that time could not sustain such a level of expenditure. Jellicoe also commented on the need for additional naval bases and improved logistic support, enhanced administration and the appointment of new specialist directors to support the naval staff with expert advice. And why maintain such a large navy and expensive shore infrastructure? The answer was straightforward. Japan was rapidly building a formidable naval force and resentment of Britain was increasing steadily among the Japanese. Jellicoe hinted that while the White Australia policy remained, Japan posed a threat to Australia because it had the means and the motive to attack both imperial and Australian interests. His summation was consistent with public recognition that the Japanese found the White Australia policy hurtful and that Japan was not happy with the distribution of League of Nations' mandates in the Pacific which had, in any event, brought Australia and Japan physically diplomatically much closer together with bordering territories. As a prudent measure, *Melbourne* embarked on a northern cruise in 1920 to reinforce the colonial administration in those former German territories that still possessed a German community. *Brisbane* conducted a similar visit the following year to encourage native acceptance of the new colonial rule. While there was always the threat of uprisings and insurrection, the Australian aim was to avoid giving any British colony or protectorate reason to welcome or prefer Japanese intervention or presence. The 20 January 1920 edition of the *Bulletin* warned that:

> *If the Japanese cherish or develop a grievance against Australia or America, or if either of the two gets hold of something which should belong to Japan in the latter's opinion, then Japan will*

SLEEPING AT HIS HOMEWORK.

The Bulletin *left its readers in no doubt that the Imperial Japanese Navy posed a serious threat to Australia. (Lionel Lindsay cartoon)*

> *select a favourable moment, and it will fight . . . If Australia happened to be the enemy selected, and if it were required to fight 'on its own', it would not have a dog's chance on the sea in the present condition of the Navy. The RAN is relatively of the same standard of effectiveness as the old subsidized or hired fleet of six years ago and earlier: 'too weak to fight and too slow to run away'.*

The *Bulletin* was adamant that Japan indeed posed a credible threat to Australia. It told its readers on 20 May 1920 that, in the absence of the British, trusting in the US Navy was national folly. The *Bulletin*'s editorial claimed that the Japanese

> *are born sailors. A glance at a map will supply the explanation. The best class of Japanese brain tends to enter the navy of the Mikado for much the same reason that the best American brains turn to business: the man who rises in the services in Japan is well paid, as Asia understands the term, and he is more esteemed than one in any other calling . . . The Yankees may be as good at sea as their politicians profess to think: it is 100 years since they had had anything like an opportunity to prove it in action. As to the quality of the Japanese there is no doubt.*

Shortly after Jellicoe's report was received and handled with masterful inactivity, another Royal Commission was convened into naval administration. On this occasion the focus was Cockatoo Island Dockyard in Sydney. The immediate impetus for the inquiry was alarm that the cost of naval work at Cockatoo Island was well in excess of budget allocations. There were reports of poor financial control and accusations of misappropriation and malpractice. The Government decided to inquire into the general operation of Cockatoo Island and, at the last minute, expanded the terms of reference to include Garden Island. This made sense. The war had revealed that the facilities at Garden Island were inadequate for the navy's expanded needs and that Cockatoo Island was required for specialist functions and to undertake work beyond the capacity of Garden Island.

A plan for the development of Garden Island was devised in 1920. It contained a proposal to spend £200 000 over the ensuing five years on alterations and additions to the facilities. It was considered that this investment would equip Garden Island to meet the navy's ship repair needs for the following ten to fifteen years. The docking of ships and the fitting out of submarines would, under this plan, be

An aerial photograph of Garden Island taken in the early 1920s.

carried out at Cockatoo Island. The plan was put to the Naval Board but rejected on the grounds of cost. In its place a series of improvements and enhancements was authorised but the approach was piecemeal. Surprisingly, the end of the war did not lead immediately to a downturn in the island's work as many of the merchant ships which had been fitted out as troopships and transports had to be reconverted for their peacetime roles. After 1920, however, men were laid off in large numbers. A general reorganisation of the dockyard was also commenced in 1920 in order to 'achieve a more efficient usage of men and repair facilities available'.

At Cockatoo Island, the collier *Biloela* was practically finished but progress on a light cruiser to be known as *Adelaide* remained slow as the men feared this ship would be their last. (The island would build only three ships over the next twenty years: the seaplane carrier HMAS *Albatross*, completed in 1928; and the two sloops, *Yarra* and *Swan*, completed in 1935 and 1936 respectively.) The Royal Commission found that there was

> *not sufficient work at present to keep both establishments fully employed, until a fixed Naval Base is established under the complete control of the Navy Department and/or until such time as the naval activities in the Pacific render it necessary for Cockatoo Island Dockyard to be transferred wholly to the Navy Department, all work in connection with the Fleet should be carried out by the Board of Control at Cockatoo Island under the direct supervision of naval officers selected by the Navy Department.*

This meant that no funds could be spent on Garden Island although it continued to be less than adequate as the main Australian naval base. The more than 3000 civilian staff employed in 1918 would be reduced to a mere 382 by 1931. Shortly after the Royal Commission's report was debated in Federal Parliament, there was further upheaval when the Navy Department was absorbed back into the Department of Defence.

As the Commonwealth Government tried to make up its mind about the shape of naval administration and arrangements for shore support, the Australian fleet became larger rather than smaller. Acknowledging the generous assistance it had received from Australia during the war, the Admiralty transferred six destroyers (*Anzac*, *Tasmania*, *Swordsman*, *Success*, *Stalwart* and *Tattoo*) and a flotilla of six J Class submarines (*J1*, *J2*, *J3*, *J4*, *J5* and *J7*) to the RAN. With the arrival of these ships, the Australian Fleet now consisted of 26 surface vessels and six submarines together with a number of different auxiliary ships with *Adelaide* and *Biloela* under construction. Despite the expense of operating and maintaining the fleet and notwithstanding the international political mood for multilateral disarmament treaties, Prime Minister Billy Hughes asked in Parliament whether Australia was 'spending too little' on national defence. But by the end of 1920, a naval reduction program was inevitable. There was simply not enough money to maintain every active fleet unit, provide sufficient fuel and stores, and pay every officer and sailor serving at sea and ashore. An economy drive initiated by the Naval Board was complemented by diplomatic pressure to reduce the size of the RAN, but none of this dampened enthusiasm for the first RAN Review during which 29 ships gathered in Port Phillip Bay to coincide with the visit of the Prince of Wales in May 1920.

Before he departed for the 1921 Imperial Conference, Prime Minister Hughes expressed his anger at Britain's announcement that it could no longer provide naval defence for the whole Empire. He stated that Australia had spent more on naval defence than all the other dominions put together and that the RAN was 'ludicrously inadequate' for the task of providing for the nation's defence. At the conference beginning in June 1921, the delegates agreed that sea power was vital to the safety and security of the Empire and that Britain and the dominions ought to have a naval force at least equal to that of any other power. As Australia would be unable to hold back a Japanese naval advance, the RAN would provide a diversion until the 'main fleet' arrived from a new strategic base to be built at Singapore. The need for close cooperation between navies was agreed upon. However, its substance was not debated as American President Warren Harding had invited the principal powers to attend a naval disarmament conference in Washington scheduled for November 1921.

The conference accepted a scheme limiting naval armaments according to an agreed formula. The three main powers—Britain, the United States and Japan—would limit their capital ship and aircraft carrier ratios to a 5:5:3 basis. The British Empire and the United States would each be limited to 135 000 tons while the Japanese would have 81 000 tons. The upper displacement for all capital ships was set at 35 000 tons while the largest armament would not exceed 18-inch guns. Aircraft carriers could not displace more than 33 000 tons or be armed with larger than 8-inch guns. The United States had wanted to limit the total tonnage of all other ships but the proposal was rejected. A British proposal, supported by Australia, to abolish submarines was not accepted. Non-capital ships, however, could not exceed 10 000 tons or have greater than 8-inch armaments. In return for Japan's pledge not to fortify the Kurile Islands or islands south of the Japanese home islands, the British Empire agreed not to establish any bases east of Singapore while the Americans undertook not to fortify any possession west of Hawaii. The treaty produced by the conference would remain in force until 31 December 1936.

As the prevailing wisdom held that war had been postponed for at least ten years, there was no surprise when the Commonwealth Government announced large reductions in the naval estimates from £3 091 138 in 1921–22 to £2 457 250 for 1922–23. To fulfil part of Britain's obligation under the treaty, HMAS *Australia* was scrapped and sunk off Sydney Heads on 12 April 1924. The submarines were paid off immediately while other ships were placed into reserve. The squadron was now reduced to three cruisers, three destroyers and one sloop, in addition to support vessels. Training depots were closed and work on a west coast naval base at Cockburn Sound was abandoned.

The battle cruiser HMAS Australia *is scuttled off Sydney Heads in 1924 in compliance with the Washington Treaty. (RAN official)*

There were further reductions and more ships were decommissioned. Jellicoe's Far Eastern Fleet never proceeded beyond paper, but the idea of a great naval base at Singapore remained an attractive prospect. At the 1923 Imperial Conference, four principles for Empire and Dominion defence were laid down. First, each part of the Empire was to have primary responsibility for its own defence. Second, the major maritime lines of communication and trade needed adequate protection. Third, naval bases to repair and fuel warships were vital to the mobility of the fleet. Fourth, there was a need to maintain at least comparable naval strength with any foreign power in accordance with the Washington Treaty. But there was considerable debate as to whether the so-called 'Singapore strategy' was sound. Would it be adequate? More importantly, could Singapore be defended?

Admiral Henderson thought in 1910 that the 'main base for a Fleet for the defence of Australia and the Pacific must be in Australia itself'. But the First Lord of the Admiralty, Leo Amery, argued that while Sydney was an ideal base for Australia's defence, it was not well placed to support any defence of the Indian Ocean shipping routes. The Singapore base would be ideal for the battle fleet with Hong Kong serving as a forward defensive position. For its part, Britain pledged to send the 'main fleet' when it was needed to defend Australia and New Zealand. The Nationalist–Australian Country

Party Coalition Government led by Stanley Bruce embraced the 'Singapore strategy' whereas the Labor Opposition advocated air defence supported by coastal vessels and submarines. To bolster Australian confidence in the mobility and power of the Royal Navy, the British Special Service Squadron, led by the battle cruisers *Hood* and *Repulse*, visited Australia between February and April 1924. The seven-ship squadron received a rapturous welcome and the visit led to a ship exchange program that saw *Adelaide* serve on the China Station until April 1925. *Brisbane* was the next ship to serve with the China Squadron, becoming the first RAN ship to visit Japan, followed by the now aged *Melbourne*.

As the security situation in China was becoming increasingly unstable, with Chiang Kai-shek's Nationalists and Mao Tse-tung's Communists engaging in disparate skirmishes across the country, Australian ships and personnel were used to exert British authority and to protect British interests although war had not been declared. Shore parties from *Brisbane* had been used during a general strike in Hong Kong to run the public transport system and provide harbour surveillance. In October 1927, *Adelaide* was deployed to Malaita in the Solomon Islands after native warriors refused to pay tax to the colonial authority and massacred the district officer and eight of his staff at the town of Sinalagu. As the white population feared (wrongly as it turned out) that this was the opening of a major campaign against them, the resident commissioner cabled the Colonial Office in London and sought the dispatch of a warship as a demonstration of colonial power and resolve. On arrival at Tulagi harbour, it was decided that *Adelaide* would provide logistic support and communications facilities while the ship's company would provide an armed shore party to assist the native police. The cruiser was withdrawn a month later when it was evident that this was an isolated incident and a general uprising was unlikely. The native police force captured the warriors responsible for the massacre and placed them on trial at Tulagi. Some were sentenced to death, others to lengthy prison sentences. On returning to Sydney, *Adelaide* was designated the training cruiser.

When Britain decided to delay construction of the Singapore naval base in 1924 (the project would be revived when Stanley Baldwin replaced Ramsey MacDonald as British Prime Minister in October 1924), the Commonwealth Government embarked on a five-year naval development plan. The new fleet would centre on two 8-inch County Class heavy cruisers, *Australia* and *Canberra*. After a controversy as to whether they ought to be built at Cockatoo Island in Sydney or Clydebank in Scotland, there were many who felt the ships were nonetheless operationally deficient. It was alleged that this class had a number of serious weaknesses, particularly the inadequacy of its armour plating which directly affected its ability to withstand damage in action. This would prove not to be the case. The plan also included two ocean-going submarines, *Otway* and *Oxley*, and the 6000-ton seaplane carrier, *Albatross*. The 'carrier', whose acquisition was a surprise to both the RAN and the Royal Australian Air Force (RAAF) did not have a flight deck. It was to be equipped with six Seagull Mark III seaplanes from RAAF Number 101 Flight. *Sydney* and *Melbourne* were both paid off in 1928. *Brisbane* was placed in reserve in 1929 with the River Class destroyers which had been laid up since 1922. When the development plan ended in 1929, the RAN was on the verge of acquiring its second generation of ships. It was also about to enter the most sudden and serious reduction in its history.

The Wall Street stock market crash in New York and the onset of the Great Depression in October 1929 were disastrous events for Australia and the RAN. As there was no imminent or obvious naval threat to Australia, expenditure on the RAN would need to be further reduced in line with an international review of the Washington Treaty at the London Naval Disarmament Conference in early 1930. In 1930–31, the Naval Board decided to reduce the seagoing squadron to the new heavy cruisers *Australia* and *Canberra*, the carrier *Albatross* and one S Class destroyer with a reduced complement. The survey vessel *Moresby* and the submarines would be placed in reserve. *Otway* and *Oxley* would later be given to the Royal Navy. The six River Class destroyers were broken up, the collier *Biloela* was sold and the sloops *Marguerita*, *Geranium* and *Mallow* were scrapped. Sixty-one officers and 639 sailors serving in the Permanent Naval Forces were no longer required, and the RAN College at Jervis Bay was closed with the staff and cadets transferred to Flinders Naval Depot (HMAS *Cerberus*) on the Mornington Peninsula in Victoria. Many of the sailors were discharged 'Services no longer required'. This meant the men forfeited their deferred pay, the contemporary equivalent of superannuation. In 1929, the basic wage of an able seaman had been reduced from 7 shillings to 5 shillings and 8 pence per day. At the same time, the Naval Board secured exemptions for officers from various cost-cutting measures, although an offset was required in the form of reduced allowances, with increased workloads demanded elsewhere. While a greater proportion of sailors than officers was retrenched during the Depression, curiously the number of flag officers increased in the same period. This prompted a parliamentarian to comment that in 1930 the navy had more admirals for four commissioned vessels than it did in 1920 when the RAN operated 30 ships. By 1932 the Permanent Naval Forces consisted of 340 officers, 25 cadets and 2776 sailors. Civil staff and dockyard workers were also retrenched. These were dark and desperate days.

While the strategic situation was still judged benign, the Commonwealth Government reduced defence expenditure to an extent that was certainly inadequate for operations at even the lowest contingency levels. In 1927–28, defence spending was 1.04 per cent of national outlays. The figure dropped to 0.6 per cent in 1932–33. Although this level of spending was higher than in the other dominions, it was less than half that of Britain expressed in terms of expenditure per head of population. The RAN needed a thoroughgoing audit of the effects of expenditure reductions on its operating capacity and the wellbeing of its personnel. This was unlikely to take place. In Britain, where naval reductions were just as acute, there was a mutiny in the Atlantic Fleet based at Invergordon. In Australia, political decisions had created a climate of dissatisfaction, but wherever it became obvious naval administrators and commanders either denied that there was a problem or censured those involved.

Throughout 1931 and 1932 there were signs of heightening messdeck unrest, including incidents of sabotage in a number of ships. The engines of the seaplane carrier HMAS *Albatross* were damaged in November 1931 and again in September 1932. Naval authorities put these problems down to the re-entry of men into the navy 'whose associations have tended to give them extreme views'. In other words, it was not the fault of the navy or its leadership, but of regrettable influences exerted by groups in the outside world such as communists. But the problem would not go away if simply ignored. In October 1932, there was a mutiny in HMAS *Penguin*, a depot ship permanently based at Sydney. There are no official reports concerning the event. The commanding officer was sympathetic to the complaints of his men and agreed to convey their grievances to the Naval Board after giving an assurance that he would not lay charges against them. He was criticised by the Naval Board for his generous attitude, the board considering that the men's grievances were 'subversive of discipline', and the matters at issue were not even considered.

Further evidence of poor morale and deep dissatisfaction is evident in welfare committee requests made to *Penguin*'s commanding officer from the early 1930s. Essentially, the sailors believed they had no proper avenue for airing their grievances. The principal complaint was that their pay and conditions had been eroded. They asserted that the Naval Board 'have shown that they are apparently unable to ensure that members of the Lower Deck shall receive humanitarian treatment'. The men had no one to speak on their behalf or to embrace their cause. Consequently, their pay had, by default, been 'reduced beyond that required for bare necessities'. It was no wonder that the welfare committee in *Penguin* complained that 'those in authority' were 'dictators' who cut the 'sustenance and living of members of the Naval Service'. It is perhaps not surprising that the Naval Board refused to consider the men's complaints and instead chose to admonish their commanding officer. The Chief of Naval Staff expressed regret that the Board could not discipline the men because the commanding officer had given his word that they would not be punished and his word had to be respected. But the Board wanted to make it very clear that the 'Government is determined to dispense with the services of any men who refuse duty'. This was an instance of poor leadership driven by political convenience.

Conditions within the navy improved after 1932 for two reasons. First, the worst of the Depression was over and the Government was in a position to increase defence spending. Second, Japan invaded Manchuria and northern China during 1931 and seemed far from satisfying its hunger for territory. RAN ship visits to the Japanese home islands were suspended. When the League of Nations proved powerless to act against Japan, and Japan withdrew its membership, it became clear that Britain, the United States and Australia would need to take their own action to prevent future Japanese aggression. Multilateralism had failed. Japan's growing belligerence was compounded by apprehension over the political situation in Germany with the Nazi consolidation of power after 1933.

An Australian defence build-up began modestly in 1932 when the RAN arranged for the loan of a flotilla of destroyers (*Stuart*, *Waterhen*, *Vampire*, *Vendetta* and *Voyager*) from the British Government. In April 1934, the Government approved a three-year development program which would include the purchase of the Modified *Leander* Class light cruiser, HMS *Phaeton*, which was still under construction at Swan, Hunter & Wigan Richardson's shipyard at Wallsend-on-Tyne. The Modified *Leander* Class cruisers were built to a basic late-1920s' design which the Admiralty constantly altered and developed as flaws and weaknesses were detected. The first five ships of the Unmodified

Class—*Leander*, *Neptune*, *Orion*, *Achilles* and *Ajax*—were launched between 1931 and 1934. The Modified Class consisted of three ships: *Amphion*, which was ordered first, *Apollo* and *Phaeton*.

The light cruiser HMAS Adelaide *took so long to be completed that she was nick-named 'HMAS Longdelayed'. (RAN official)*

The news that Australia would purchase HMS *Phaeton* caused political controversy. Although the Government announced at the same time that a second sloop (*Swan*) would be built at Cockatoo Island Dockyard, the first (*Yarra*) having been ordered in 1933, the Leader of the Federal Labor Opposition, James Scullin, argued that 'whatever is needed for the defence of Australia should not be purchased overseas if it can be made in Australia . . . with thousands of Australians unemployed and eking out a miserable existence on sustenance, the placing of a contract overseas is monstrous'. But there were some doubts about the local shipbuilding industry. HMAS *Adelaide* took seven years to build at Cockatoo Island. In 1922, the afternoon *Sun* newspaper had the banner headline 'HMAS *Longdelayed* launched at Cockatoo'. In addition to the time and cost involved, Australian naval shipbuilding lacked the experience necessary to build a vessel as complex as the latest British light cruisers. With war looming, there was not the time to let them slowly gain that experience. At any rate, construction of the ship offered by Britain was already well advanced.

HMS *Phaeton* was taken over by the RAN and launched on 22 September 1934 as the second HMAS *Sydney*. Although the old sailor's superstition promised ill-fortune for a ship whose name was changed, the ship needed to have an Australian name to highlight the dominion's active involvement in world naval affairs. One year later, the new *Sydney* completed her trials and sailed to Portsmouth under the command of Captain John Fitzgerald, an officer on loan from the Royal Navy. On 29 October 1935, *Sydney* sailed for Australia but was diverted to Gibraltar after the Italian invasion of Abyssinia (later renamed Ethiopia). The ship saw service with the British Second Cruiser Squadron, enforcing League of Nations' sanctions against Italy, and remained at Gibraltar until January 1936. On 26 February *Sydney* sailed for Malta en route to Alexandria where she would join the First Cruiser Squadron under Admiral Sir Max Horton. After exercises and an independent cruise to Cyprus designed to rid the ship of mumps which had affected the ship's company since late 1935, *Sydney* docked again at Malta before arriving at Alexandria in July. The light cruiser finally sailed for Australia on 14 July 1936 visiting Gallipoli with HMAS *Australia* en route.

After being delayed many months, the arrival of *Sydney* in her home port was a major occasion for the city and the RAN. After a short maintenance period, *Sydney* joined the normal peacetime exercise program including longer cruises, such as to New Zealand for exercises with the New Zealand Squadron, and shorter port visits. In July 1937, Fitzgerald handed over command to Captain J.W.A. Waller RN with Commander John Collins RAN being relieved as second-in-command by Commander I. Macdonald (who died on 15 December 1937). As the Australian Government and the Naval Board were pleased with *Sydney*'s performance, Prime Minister Lyons announced in March 1938 that a new three-year defence program would include the purchase of the other two Modified *Leander* Class light cruisers. The two ships, both of which were completed in 1936, had been commissioned into the Royal Navy as *Apollo* and *Amphion*. On joining the RAN they would be renamed *Hobart* and *Perth*. The seaplane carrier *Albatross* would be transferred to the Royal Navy as part-payment for the new cruiser *Hobart* in 1938. But by this time, another major European war appeared imminent.

The strategic situation had taken a turn for the worse in 1935 when Japan withdrew from the Washington Treaty before its official expiry. The following year, Germany militarised the Rhineland and started construction of two giant battleships that exceeded 40 000 tons: *Bismarck* and *Tirpitz*. While Germany rebuilt its naval forces, the Royal Navy would be preoccupied with the North Sea and few ships would be available for service in Asia or the Pacific. With the world situation deteriorating rapidly, there was little question that Australia's defence would depend upon a combined Allied naval effort. The Government concluded that:

> *The first line of security against invasion is naval defence, with the army and air force supplementing and cooperating. If the enemy attempts aggression and must be resisted, it is far preferable to fight him away from our shores than when he is seeking to land on our coasts or has actually established himself in our territory.*

An Admiralty memorandum of 1937 suggested that Australia should consider ordering a capital ship. In other words, the RAN needed a battleship. It was a matter considered by the Australian Council of Defence in December of that year. The Chief of Naval Staff, Vice Admiral Sir Ragnar Colvin, stated that while the Admiralty would welcome the presence of a battleship in Australian waters and that the presence of the ship would be an enormous asset for the Empire in the regional strategic environment, he doubted Australia's ability to afford the ship and the capability of the shore facilities to support its operations. A battleship would require a number of destroyers as escorts, in addition to docking and repair facilities. For these reasons, his preference was for cruisers to defend Australia's global seaborne trade.

By this time, the Commonwealth Government had substantially increased spending on the navy. Prime Minister Joseph Lyons was assured that with Australia's help Britain could defend the Empire's sea lines of communication. Part of that help was the need to provide docking facilities for British capital ships deployed to Australian waters. It was firmly believed that in the event of a Pacific war victory would depend on control of the vast area of ocean basin, and this would cost ships. The rate at which ships could be repaired seemed to be one of the most important factors bearing on the duration of any war. It was on these grounds that emphasis was placed in Australia on repair and maintenance of ships rather than on shipbuilding. The dockyards on the west coast of North America were, simply, too far away. Facilities located in Sydney would be vital in keeping the combined Australian, British, American, Dutch and French fleets, as well as the vast merchant fleet operating in the western Pacific, at sea and in good repair. This did not represent new thinking, but rather old thinking that had taken on an added dimension of persuasiveness by the urgency of Australia's security concerns.

A graving dock could have been built in Australia after the Great War of 1914–18 to complement the 'Singapore strategy'. But Australia was still hampered by a shortage in docking facilities for its own ships. To use the dock in Singapore, opened in 1938, would entail a round trip of 8000 miles from the east coast of Australia; and that depended on a damaged ship having the ability to steam that far. The largest graving dock in Port Jackson was located at Woolwich under the control of Morts and was 850 feet long, 83 feet wide at the entrance, and 26 feet over the sill at mean high water. There was no need to remind the Commonwealth Government that Australia was an island. Its distance from Asia and remoteness from friends and allies were all too clear.

In 1938, Cabinet approved in principle the construction of an Australian naval graving dock. The Australian Government approached the Admiralty with its assessment of the requirement and asked for its assistance. One of the first options considered was the purchase of the Southampton floating dock belonging to the Southern Railway Company. It was a tempting offer. The price for the floating dock was quoted to be £175 000; the cost of a graving dock would run to around £3 000 000. Admiral Colvin was not in favour of the floating dock. He saw it as a short-term and second-rate solution to meeting Australia's real need. It would have a limited life, be expensive to maintain and would not meet the estimated minimum ships' draft requirement, not to mention the risk involved in towing it halfway around the world to Australia. The Admiralty concurred with Colvin's assessment. The Admiralty had been considering acquiring the same dock for use in the Eastern Mediterranean, an arena they saw as a higher priority than Australia.

Accordingly, the Australian Naval Board recommended the construction of a graving dock despite the enormous cost. The Admiralty advised some changes in the proposed dock dimensions, increasing the length by 40 feet and width by ten feet. The Admiralty also suggested that Australia seek a consultant to advise on the site of the dock and specific engineering aspects. Prime Minister Robert Menzies told Parliament on 1 May 1940:

> *A dry dock of a larger size than any in Australia has been an important strategic consideration since the size of capital ships has increased so greatly. I do not need to elaborate the great value to Australia of a dock capable of accommodating not only the largest warships but also merchant ships of great tonnage. The possession of such a dock would make Australia a fit base for a powerful fleet and would, in certain contingencies, enable naval operations to be conducted in Australian waters without the necessity for ships to travel 4000 miles to Singapore for purposes of refit or repair . . . It is estimated that three years will be occupied in the construction of the dock. The estimated cost of the dock on the selected site is, in Australian currency, £2 997 000 compared with £3 039 000 for the other Sydney site [above the Harbour Bridge], and £3 839 000 for the Adelaide site. The Government has decided to accept the recommendation, and the work will be put in hand at the earliest possible moment.*

This would be the greatest engineering feat in Australia's history to that time, surpassing even the Sydney Harbour Bridge. It would involve the reclamation of 30 acres between Potts Point and Garden Island and the construction of a graving dock measuring 1139 feet 5 inches long, 147 feet 7.5 inches wide with 45 feet draught of water on sill at spring tide. This was unprecedented government investment in naval infrastructure.

Despite the debilitating effects of the Great Depression, the defence program that began in 1937 resulted in the RAN facing the outbreak of war in 1939 with a substantial but still inadequate force including two heavy cruisers (*Australia* received a substantial modernisation in 1936), three light cruisers, two sloops (with another two—*Warrego* and *Parramatta*—under construction at Cockatoo Island), six destroyers (with two new Tribal Class destroyers—*Arunta* and *Warramunga*—ordered in January 1939), a survey vessel (*Moresby*) and a number of support craft. Of the three armed services, the RAN had the largest number of permanent members with 430 officers and 5010 sailors. While there was bipartisan political recognition that the surrounding seas offered Australia the best protection against a possible Japanese invasion, a strong navy would be needed to protect its trade. The adequacy of this provision and the protection it afforded would soon be tested.

7
Global war
1939–41

On 1 September 1939, German forces invaded Poland after a series of expansionary operations that had placed Austria, the Sudetenland and then all of Czechoslovakia under German control. Meanwhile, Mussolini's Fascist Government in Italy had already disclosed a common cause with the National Socialist regime in Germany, and the militarist Government in Japan revealed its imperial ambitions by asserting that it would be 'independent' rather than neutral in the event of war. As a consequence of Germany's continued aggression and refusal to leave Poland, Britain and France declared war on Germany. Because Australia was part of the British Empire, Prime Minister Robert Menzies made a national statement at 1.15 p.m. on 3 September 1939: 'it is my melancholy duty to inform you officially that, in consequence of a persistence by Germany in her invasion of Poland, Great Britain has declared war upon her and that, as a result, Australia is also at war'.

As Prime Minister Menzies addressed the nation, *Perth* was steaming off the Venezuelan coast. A yeoman of signals serving on board recalled receiving a message from the Admiralty:

> *'Commence hostilities at once with Germany'. We immediately sped towards the islands of the Dutch West Indies where it was known that at least twelve enemy ships were lying. 'Lower deck' was cleared and the Articles of War read by the captain, who at the conclusion called for three cheers for His Majesty the King.*

> *Never in my life have I heard such a rousing response, and it came as from the bottom of the men's hearts with the will to serve. Within three hours we sighted a vessel which, on sighting us, turned away. We immediately altered course to intercept her. The vessel completely ignored our signals to stop and to reveal her nationality by hoisting her ensign. Gun crews were closed up at their stations and the order was given to train our secondary armament on the defaulting vessel. This apparently had the desired effect and the Dutch Tri-colour fluttered from her ensign staff. Ascertaining that her destination was Curacao in the Dutch West Indies, we allowed her to continue her voyage.*

Perth continued to search for German ships caught in open water or neutral ports when hostilities commenced. Other Australian ships were either at sea or hastily prepared to put to sea as the scope of the war widened.

The Union of South Africa declared war on 6 September and Canada four days later. By this time, the German Army had overrun Poland and on 17 September the Soviet Union also invaded Poland. When the last large Polish force surrendered on 5 October, the partition of the country between the two aggressors was complete. After lightning invasions of Denmark and Norway, the German Army launched a massive assault on Belgium, Holland and France on 10 May 1940. Striking through the Ardennes, German armour separated the British Expeditionary Force from the French Army. Six weeks later, France capitulated and the British Army was withdrawn from Dunkirk across the English Channel. Shortly after the German Army entered Paris on 14 June, Italy entered the war on Germany's side. Not unsurprisingly, these developments caused great concern in Australia.

Two weeks after declaring war on Germany, the Commonwealth Government had announced its intention to recruit 20 000 men for the Second Australian Imperial Force (AIF). The AIF would form a division and auxiliary units for service either in Australia or overseas. The Government also decided to call up the militia in two drafts to receive one month's intensive training. On 15 November 1939, the Government proposed that conscription be introduced for military service within Australia before announcing that the newly created Sixth Division of the Second AIF would leave for Europe on 10 January 1940, together with selected units of the Royal Australian Air Force (RAAF) and the RAN. Earlier, on 7 November 1939, the commissioned ships of the RAN were made available to the Admiralty. A week later, the Department of Defence was divided into three single service departments to cope with the expanded demands of the war effort. An Examination Service and a Naval Control Service were created to seize enemy ships, protect harbours and regulate merchant ship movements.

The Directorate of Reserves and Mobilisation was almost overwhelmed by the number of prewar Naval Reserve men who were willing to serve as gunners in defensively equipped merchant ships (DEMS). Those on the Emergency and Retired Lists returned to service. In the space of a few months, the navy almost doubled its size as men from all walks of life volunteered or were called up for service at sea and ashore. The training establishment HMAS *Cerberus* at Westernport was rapidly expanded to cope with new entry officers and sailors. Along with other shore bases around the country it provided specialist training in communications, gunnery, anti-submarine warfare, intelligence and engineering. The new recruits could elect to serve for three years or for the duration of the war. The Women's Royal Australian Naval Service (WRANS) was also formed as a separate service in 1942. It soon became apparent that the navy could not do without the WRANS. A contemporary account explained that those women trained as naval telegraphists were

> *recruited with the primary objective of releasing male ratings for service afloat, their efficiency has enabled that aim to be attained in very considerable measure. Apart from the nurses, they are the only group of women who are officially 'part and parcel of the Navy', and, before being accepted, they are required to have attained a specified, and appreciable, degree of efficiency. The majority of them staff the naval wireless station in the Federal Capital Territory. They are subject to the same discipline and conditions as men, and they do the same work.*

Those who served at sea very quickly became members of a special fraternity with peculiar customs and a language all of its own. After overcoming the trauma of seasickness and the cramped and confined conditions in which they were obliged to live and work, those who joined for wartime duty were faced with uncertainty about where they would serve and whether they would return home alive. Those posted to corvettes faced the hardships and deprivations of being in a small ship; those in cruisers endured long periods at sea in ships that were not designed for the tropics. Whether engaged in convoy escort work or as part of a major fleet action, every ship was under constant threat of submarine or air attack. When a watch-keeping officer or lookout believed he had sighted a periscope plume or when an unidentified aircraft was noticed above the horizon, the ship was brought to action stations and prepared for combat. Every man was assigned his place and given a task to perform. Those not involved in operating the ship's weapons were formed into fire-fighting, evacuation and medical parties. Many were away from their families and friends for the first time in places they had never heard of, let alone ever visited. War was a new experience for most people and little had prepared them for its horrors.

In September 1939, the Dominions Office in London had outlined its views on how Australian naval assets could be most effectively employed in Europe. Australia was asked to contribute a light cruiser and five destroyers to join HMAS *Perth*, which was already under Admiralty operational control.

> *So long as Japan remains neutral it is considered that Australian waters may be regarded as unlikely to suffer submarine attack. The most likely danger to be guarded against on [the] Australian station under present conditions is that of attack on shipping by enemy raiders. It is considered that two cruisers and HMAS* Australia *(when ready) should prove adequate for this purpose.*

As the V and W Class destroyers were technically on loan from the Royal Navy, there could be no reasonable objection to the request. But the Cabinet stipulated that the second cruiser should not proceed further west than the Suez Canal. However, after further consultation with the Chief of Naval Staff, Admiral Colvin, the Cabinet was persuaded that there was no realistic submarine threat and accepted a recommendation from the Naval Board that

> *a second 6-inch cruiser (HMAS* Hobart *or* Sydney*) should be made available forthwith for service when required. With two cruisers playing their part in the defence of sea communications to and from Australia in distant waters, and the remaining cruisers employed in Australian waters, the best distribution of our available force is achieved.*

On 6 October, the War Cabinet agreed. *Sydney*, now under the command of Captain John Collins, a member of the inaugural entry of cadet-midshipmen at the RAN College, was chosen. Before departing for the Mediterranean, *Sydney* was involved in countering the immediate naval threat posed by the two German 'pocket battleships' *Graf Spee* and *Deutschland* which were tasked with attacking British merchant shipping in the South Atlantic. The Royal Navy formed a number of naval 'hunting groups' to find and destroy the enemy ships. After the tanker *Africa Shell* was sunk by *Graf Spee* in the Indian Ocean off East Africa on 19 November, *Sydney*, in company with the Australian 8-inch heavy cruisers *Australia* and *Canberra*, patrolled the Indian Ocean shipping routes in search of the German vessel. After a fruitless four-day search commencing on 28 November, the ships returned to Fremantle. *Sydney* was relieved on station by the aged *Adelaide* on 13 December. Four days later, *Graf Spee* was driven into Montevideo after the Battle of the River Plate and scuttled outside the port by her ship's company.

Sydney rejoined the fleet in late January 1940 and formed the first Anzac convoy, US 1, with *Canberra* and HM Ships *Ramillies* and *Leander*. The light cruiser returned to Fremantle on 8 February and resumed her duties patrolling the shipping routes and escorting merchant ships off the coast of Western Australia. Collins described this period, 'which included intensive exercising, operating aircraft, high angle and surface firings and torpedo running' as the 'most valuable in the strenuous days ahead'. *Sydney* escorted convoy US 2 over April and May, and planned to escort US 3 before receiving a signal directing her to make best speed to Colombo, where she arrived on 8 May to be joined by *Hobart* for the remainder of the convoy. It was from here that *Sydney* was ordered to the Mediterranean where the Admiralty was building a fleet to counter possible Italian entry into the war. *Canberra* and *Australia* continued to escort convoy US 3, which was diverted to the Cape of Good Hope during its passage from Fremantle to Colombo on 31 May. When the convoy arrived safely the following month, *Canberra* was offered for service at the Cape and *Australia* for European waters. The Admiralty accepted the offer immediately.

When hostilities with Italy commenced after midnight on 10 June 1940, *Sydney* was in Alexandria Harbour with the ships of the Australian 'Scrap Iron Flotilla'. The ships of the Tenth Destroyer Flotilla, consisting of *Stuart*, *Vendetta*, *Vampire*, *Voyager* and *Waterhen*, were so named after the Nazi propagandist 'Lord Haw Haw' referred to the aged ships scathingly as 'another consignment of scrap iron from Australia'. The First Division of the Seventh Cruiser Squadron proceeded to sea and patrolled between Benghazi and the Ionian Islands. After refuelling in Alexandria, it proceeded to Bardia, which was bombarded on 20 June by the British cruisers *Orion* and *Neptune*, the French battleship *Lorraine* and *Sydney*. With the French surrender looming, the British Fleet returned and remained in Alexandria to prevent the French ships from falling into enemy hands. *Sydney* sailed from Alexandria again on 27 June when the Seventh Cruiser Squadron proceeded to cover the passage of a Malta-bound convoy. The following day, three Italian destroyers were spotted by an Allied flying boat and engaged at long range in the deteriorating light.

The *Espero* initially suffered minor damage and lost speed. But as the Australian cruiser approached the Italian destroyer, she returned fire and dispatched torpedoes. As Collins had prudently kept *Sydney* 'bows on' to the enemy ship to reduce the size of the target area, he was able to avoid the torpedoes before sinking *Espero*. In the darkness, Collins could hear the cries of the Italian sailors and commenced a rescue operation. The next morning *Sydney* rejoined the squadron just as Italian bombers attacked south of Crete. No damage was sustained during the attack and the ships returned to Alexandria on 1 July. By this time, five destroyers including *Voyager* had sunk two Italian submarines off Crete.

Sydney returned to sea and, as part of the Mediterranean Fleet, prepared to engage the Italian Fleet in a major action. The Allied force, led by the carrier *Eagle* and including *Sydney*, *Stuart*, *Vampire* and *Voyager*, was subjected to intense Italian air attack on 9 July. Later in the day, three enemy battleships, six cruisers and a number of destroyers were reported to be north of Benghazi. The Allied Fleet then manoeuvred to cut the route between the Italian Fleet and its base. At 3.00 p.m., *Sydney* sighted smoke and eight minutes later the enemy force was in sight. The Italians opened fire at maximum range. The 6-inch cruisers of the Seventh Cruiser Squadron did not return fire until the range had closed to 23 000 yards. The Italian Fleet made for Calabria at full speed behind a smokescreen. The only enemy ship to be sunk was the destroyer *Zeffiro*. The next day the Italians launched more unsuccessful air attacks. Between 8 and 12 July, more than 1350 bombs were directed at *Vampire* and her consorts without a direct hit, although Commissioned Gunner J.H. Endicott was fatally wounded and became the first RAN combat death at sea (although he was a member of the Royal Navy). The Allied Fleet returned to Alexandria on 13 July. By this time, *Australia* had been involved in an operation to prevent French warships at

Oran (North Africa) and Dakar (Senegal, West Africa) from entering the war on Germany's side before escorting US 3 into the Clyde and joining the First Cruiser Squadron at Scapa Flow. Nearer to home, from June 1940 three German raiders—*Orion*, *Komet* and *Pinguin*—were active in and around Australian waters, laying mines and attacking Allied shipping. These were constant reminders that the war was never far from Australian shores.

Sydney returned to sea on 18 July in support of an anti-submarine sweep north of Crete. Although *Sydney* was able to operate independently after escorting the anti-submarine destroyers through the Kaso Strait, Collins remained approximately twenty miles to the north of the destroyers rather than proceeding towards Piraeus, the port of Athens, in search of enemy shipping. The Kaso Straits are approximately fifteen to twenty miles wide and run between Crete, which was then in Greek hands, and Kaso Island to the east, which was the site of an Italian fast attack craft and air base. Shortly after dawn on 19 July, *Sydney* received an enemy sighting report from HMS *Hyperion*. The destroyers turned towards *Sydney* and were followed by the Italian cruisers *Bartolomeo Colleoni* and *Giovanni Delle Bande Nere*. Both ships displaced over 5000 tons, were armed with eight 6-inch guns and were reputed to be capable of speeds of over 40 knots. *Sydney* turned towards the destroyers at full speed but kept radio silence to avoid detection.

Collins took a risk in engaging the Italian ships as the weather conditions reduced his ability to determine fall of shot. But just as *Sydney* sighted the Italian cruisers, Collins sent an enemy report and, making best use of the available light and the prevailing misty conditions, engaged *Bande Nere* at 20 000 yards apparently undetected. In his report Collins stated: 'It was not possible to distinguish what type of cruisers they were and I was concerned in case they were heavy 8-inch cruisers. However, I decided to go for them and opened fire'. The Italians were caught completely by surprise and took some time to determine the origin of the bombardment. By this time the destroyers were in a suitable position to launch their torpedoes. In the mistaken belief that the destroyer HMS *Havoc* was a cruiser, the two Italian ships made smoke and turned away. The Allied ships chased the enemy cruisers with *Sydney* concentrating her fire from her forward gun turrets on *Colleoni*. Nearly one hour after the initial sighting, *Sydney* altered course to bring a broadside salvo to bear on the Italian cruiser. *Colleoni* lost speed. She was on fire and appeared to be down by the bows.

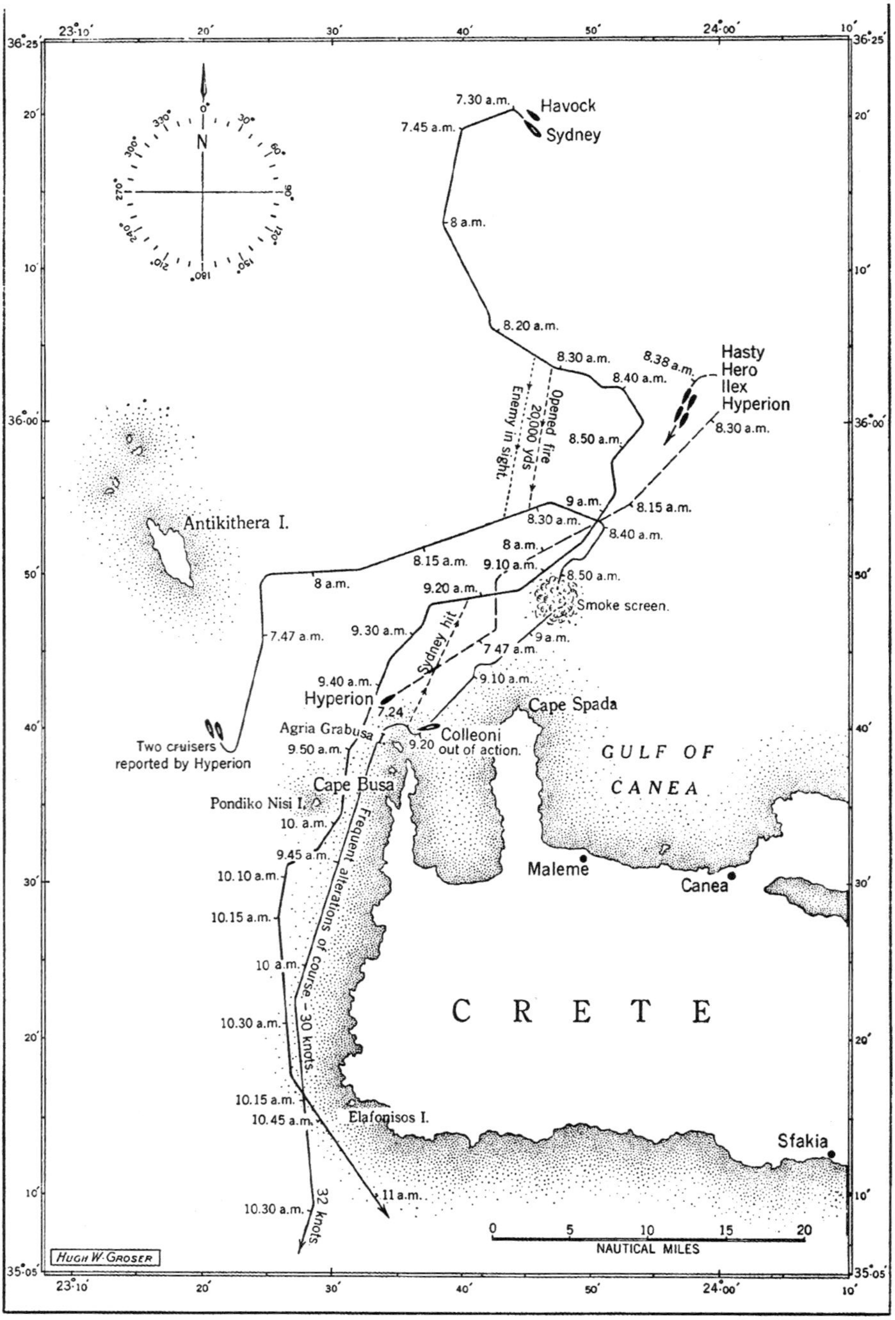

The Battle of Cape Spada, 19 July 1940.

For a moment it appeared that *Bande Nere* would remain with the stricken *Colleoni*. But after firing a salvo which struck the fore funnel of *Sydney*, she fled at full speed. While destroyers sank the *Colleoni*, *Sydney* proceeded to chase *Bande Nere*, but there was very little prospect of success. Although a shell from *Sydney* managed to hit the Italian ship, she was too fast and escaped. With *Sydney*'s supply of 6-inch ammunition practically expended, Collins had reason to be alarmed when he heard that another enemy force was expected and that *Havoc* was operating at reduced speed after a near miss disabled the boiler room. But that threat did not eventuate. *Sydney* rejoined *Havoc* and headed back towards Alexandria after rescuing some 550 Italian officers and sailors.

Sydney returned to Alexandria on 20 July after what became known as the Battle of Cape Spada. The Commander of the Mediterranean Fleet, Admiral Sir Andrew Cunningham, was overjoyed with *Sydney*'s morale-boosting success. Mussolini's son-in-law, Count Ciano, noted in his diary entry for 22 July that the Duce 'was depressed on account of the loss of the *Colleoni*, not so much because of the sinking itself as because he feels the Italians did not fight very brilliantly'. The captain of the *Colleoni*, Captain Umberto Navaro, died in an Allied hospital ship from wounds he received during the action and was buried in Alexandria on 24 July. *Sydney* had finally achieved a surface action with the Italian Fleet and demonstrated the Allied superiority in that mode of warfare. Like the first ship to bear the name, the second *Sydney* had earned a worldwide reputation.

After repairs, minor maintenance and the provision of a new Walrus aircraft, *Sydney* was refuelled, rearmed and made ready for sea on 27 July. That afternoon in another convoy escort operation, *Sydney* again came under attack from enemy bombers, but avoided being struck. The following morning in company with *Neptune*, the Australian cruiser was detached from the main force to intercept and sink the tanker *Ermoini*, thought to be in the Aegean Sea delivering fuel to the Dodecanese Islands. After repelling another unsuccessful bomber attack, *Sydney* identified the *Ermoini* at 9.30 p.m. and, after disembarking the crew, sank the tanker. *Neptune* and *Sydney* then returned to Alexandria on 30 July in time for final preparations for another patrol operation in company with *Orion*, which lasted until 2 August. *Sydney*'s ship's company was then granted a well-earned rest. Also in early August, *Hobart* was used to transport British troops from Aden to reinforce Berbera, the capital of British Somaliland, which was being attacked by Italian forces. *Hobart* patrolled along the coast and deployed her RAAF amphibian aircraft for a bombing mission at Zeila, which the Italians had occupied on 5 August. When Berbera was abandoned on 19 August, *Hobart* shelled the port to deny valuable equipment to the advancing Italians.

Sydney, impressively camouflaged for the first time, returned to sea on 12 August. Her mission was to locate enemy shipping off the North African coast and in the Aegean Sea. The operation lasted two days, but she failed to locate the enemy.

Australia returned to waters off West Africa on 23 September to support the insertion of Free French forces to subdue what remained of the Vichy French garrison in Dakar. An able seaman serving in the cruiser *Australia* described what followed when action stations was heard over the ship's main broadcast not far from the West African port.

> *To the thrill of that command every man moved swiftly to his station. Across a misty sea, big ships and little ships glided like shadows. We stared through the mist at the grim outline of those threatening cliffs. A lookout was staring through his glasses. A shaft of sunlight through the mists showed us the big guns from the fortress, trained on our movements. The suspense made our flesh creep. Something would happen soon. The ship could have been a scene in Hades. Weird figures in modern battle dress crouched like waiting demons behind the guns. In the bowels of the ship, grimy devils toiled and sweated in their anti-flash hoods, their gloves and their gas masks, and all the paraphernalia.*

In the fighting that followed, *Australia* damaged a French destroyer and fired on several cruisers inside the harbour before sustaining two shell hits and the loss of the Walrus and its crew. The operation was abandoned on 28 September and *Australia* returned to Britain.

There were problems with the Vichy elsewhere. The French Resident Commissioner in the New Hebrides (now known as Vanuatu), Henri Sautot, had declared his administration loyal to the Free French under de Gaulle while the French Governor of New Caledonia, Georges Pelicier, was similarly inclined but wavering. The arrival in Noumea of the sloop *Dumont D'Urville* commanded by Toussaint de Quievrecourt, and her captain's sympathy for the Vichy regime—which he believed was the only lawful government of France—altered the mood. When the Vichy regime replaced Pelicier with Lieutenant Colonel Maurice Denis, the local garrison commander believed that the time for some demonstrative action had come. *Adelaide*, commanded by Captain H.A. Showers RAN, was dispatched to the New Hebrides in early September to ensure the continuation of good economic relations with the French possessions and to prevent Japan from gaining any advantage in the region. This was not the first time that an Australian warship had been involved in the colonial affairs of the New Hebrides or *Adelaide*'s first visit to the colony. HMAS *Una* had been part of a punitive expedition against rebellious natives on Malekula in 1916. Two years later a shore party from *Fantome* had put down another native uprising at Malekula. When France formally acquired New Caledonia as a colony in 1921, *Melbourne* visited Noumea on a goodwill visit. Six years later *Adelaide* visited Noumea to assess its defences in the event that the port needed to be seized from France to prevent its use by enemy commerce raiders. It proved to be a wise precaution.

The plan approved by the governments of Australia and Britain was to foment a local coup, install Sautot as Governor of New Caledonia on the authority of de Gaulle and secure the colony and the *Dumont D'Urville* for the Free French while avoiding the use of force. Allied intelligence had also reported that the sloop *Amiral Charner* had sailed from Indochina with 100 troops on board bound for Noumea to preserve France's neutrality and to prevent the colony's possible annexation by Britain. In a carefully staged and conscientiously executed operation, *Adelaide* entered Noumea Harbour with Sautot embarked. After a tense exchange, Lieutenant Colonel Denis relinquished control to Sautot and de Quievrecourt was persuaded to take *Dumont D'Urville* to sea and leave the area. In contrast to the confused conflict in Dakar, *Adelaide*'s mission had been a complete success. The cruiser then sailed for Sydney on 5 October.

At the end of October 1940, *Sydney* sailed with the main battle fleet into the central Mediterranean in an effort to prevent attacks on Greece from Italy. Another short stay in Alexandria on 3–4 November preceded *Sydney*'s departure for Port Said in company with *Ajax* for the embarkation of military stores, guns and ammunition destined for Crete. After supporting the establishment of a new base at Suda Bay, *Sydney* returned to the main battlefleet, which was preparing for Malta convoy MB 8 and the Fleet Air Arm attack on the Italian naval base at Taranto. The Italian Navy suffered serious losses from the torpedo-carrying Swordfish aircraft and subsequently relocated its main naval base to Naples. On returning to Alexandria, *Sydney* was dispatched to Piraeus with stores and military personnel, and then rejoined the Seventh Cruiser Squadron on convoy escort duties in the Aegean. After a refit at Malta, *Sydney* made a final sweep along the coast of North Africa and then patrolled the waters off Mogadishu on its return home. *Sydney* arrived in Fremantle on 5 February 1941 and then returned to Garden Island where the ship's company was feted by the press and people. The ship dubbed the 'Stormy Petrel' had been replaced in the Mediterranean by *Perth*.

As the exchange of cruisers was being effected, Captain H.M.L. Waller RAN was appointed to command the Mediterranean Fleet's Inshore Squadron consisting of the six Australian destroyers and HMS *Terror*, together with a flotilla of minesweepers, anti-submarine trawlers and smaller craft. His task was to support land operations against the Italians, who were attempting to advance from Egypt into Libya. The squadron was subjected to surface attack and shore battery fire. *Stuart*, *Vampire* and *Voyager* were all involved in the assault on Tobruk in January 1941, and the entry into Benghazi the following month. By this time, *Perth* had been damaged by the Germans while in port in Malta. In early March 1941, the ship had been repaired and served with the Australian destroyers in the defence of Greece. Air attacks were becoming more frequent as German forces tried to reverse the Italian losses. On 28 March, an Allied cruiser force that included *Perth* was operating south of Crete to protect Allied troop convoys between Egypt and Greece when it engaged the Italian Fleet off Cape Matapan. The leading Italian ships had been damaged by air attack and *Stuart* was detached with three other destroyers to sink them. By the next morning, the Italians had lost five warships and more than 2400 men.

In contrast to the Allied naval successes against Italy, German military advances in Greece prompted the withdrawal of Allied forces in late April. *Perth* assisted in the evacuation of troops from Porto Rafti on the night of 24–25 April, and at Kalamata on 28–29 April; *Stuart* and *Voyager* were sent to the port of Navplion where they engaged German combat aircraft and protected Allied shipping sent to transport troops; *Waterhen* and *Vendetta* recovered troops from Megara, and later joined *Stuart* and *Vampire* to escort convoy GA 12 from Suda Bay in Crete to Alexandria. German dominance in the air and control of Greece rendered naval operations in the Aegean extremely hazardous. The Germans sought to enhance their already strong position by occupying Crete. As the small Allied garrison on the island resisted a major German airborne landing, Allied control of the waters surrounding Crete was strengthened with the arrival of two new N Class destroyers, *Napier* and *Nizam*. Together with *Perth*, they prevented the landing of any German reinforcements on the island. But as the situation on land gradually deteriorated, the decision was made to withdraw the remaining Allied troops during the last week of May 1941. The Luftwaffe was not far away. An officer from *Nizam* recalled:

> *As dawn broke we were proceeding at 30 knots towards Kasa Straits [off the southern coast of Crete]. We sighted the first enemy reconnaissance aircraft at 0445, and from 0530 until 0800 were bombed by the single aircraft from about 15 000 feet. As we approached the straits about 30 dive bombers took up the battle, and we had a merry hour and a half with them, shooting down two and damaging one. Luckily the only damage to our force was one hit, and two near misses on a British destroyer, reducing her speed to 22 knots. This was somewhat alarming as at 1000 hours we were only 15 miles from Crete. However, we were left alone, apart from two high-level bombing attacks by single aircraft. We entered harbour at 1700, oiled and embarked provisions and ammunition throughout the night.*

When water was discovered in the oil fuel tanks the next day, it became apparent that *Nizam* had sustained minor hull damage after a near miss.

With 1188 troops on board the following night, *Perth* was bound for Alexandria when a bomb exploded in a boiler room and killed four sailors and nine soldiers. The next night, *Napier* and *Nizam* were again off the southern coast of Crete when they were attacked by twelve German dive-bombers. *Napier* was hit and damaged. With only one operational engine, the stricken destroyer managed to make Alexandria. After defeats in Yugoslavia, Greece and Crete, the only Allied successes were the defeat of Italian forces in Abyssinia and Somaliland. This allowed warships, including *Parramatta*, operating south of the Suez Canal to be deployed into the Mediterranean, and secure the rich oilfields adjacent to the Persian Gulf.

The Allies needed the port of Abadan on the Shatt-el-Arab to remain open at all costs. The waters of the Gulf would also attract enemy submarines, hunting tankers proceeding to and from the principal oilfield ports. Although Allied shipping was again being convoyed to and from the Gulf and enjoyed some protection from surface raiders, by early 1940 both the German and Italian navies had submarines beyond the Straits of Hormuz. For its part, the Iraqi

Government had finally acceded to a British request to have troops stationed in the country when the regime was toppled by a *coup d'etat* on 3 April 1941. Britain responded by dispatching troops in anticipation of an opposed landing. *Yarra* escorted the troopships.

Placed under the operational control of the Senior Naval Officer Persian Gulf, Commodore Cosmo Graham RN, *Yarra* spent the first three weeks of May 1941 supporting the land forces occupying Basra at the head of the Shatt-el-Arab and its port of Ashar. On 24 May, *Yarra*'s captain, Commander W. Hastings Harrington RAN, commanded the naval force which would 'attack and disperse all enemy found on the right bank of the Shatt-el-Arab in the vicinity of Habib Shawi (seven miles up river from Ashar) and inflict maximum casualties'. Two companies of Gurkhas would be put ashore, with *Yarra* to bombard other targets. The night before, six sailors from *Yarra* disguised as Arab fishermen had taken soundings of the river to aid the landing. The attack was successful, with Iraqi opposition and several fortifications destroyed. *Yarra* fired 43 4-inch high explosive shells and over 750 smaller rounds. When the armistice with Iraq was signed on 31 May, the Australian sloop was at anchor off Ashar. For their efforts, 25 of the ship's company were rewarded with malaria.

To prevent Germany from attacking the oilfields from the north, the British decided to invade Syria on 8 June 1941 with *Perth*, *Stuart* and *Nizam* supporting the invasion force. But no sooner had the Allies reached an agreement with the Iraqis than the Persians (Iranians) started to augment their defences along the Shatt-el-Arab and the island of Abadan after refusing to expel German and Italian nationals. The British planned a landing of troops supported by a naval force including *Yarra* and the Australian-manned armed merchant cruiser HMS *Kanimbla*, which arrived from the East Indies Station on 7 August. The operation had three aims: to capture the naval base at Khorramshahr; to occupy Abadan without damaging its refinery or oil installations; and capture Axis shipping at the port of Bandar Shapur at the terminus of the Trans-Persian railway from the Caspian Sea. Captain W.L.G. Adams RN in *Kanimbla* was told by Commodore Graham that 'You will be—must be—in charge of the Bandar Shapur party', while *Yarra* would be in the Khorramshahr force. With the operation set to begin on 25 August, *Yarra* remained in Basra with *Kanimbla* lying at anchor south of the Shatt-el-Arab.

Kanimbla arrived at Bandar Shapur as the Germans were beginning to scuttle their ships. Prompt action by Australian boarding parties prevented all but one of the ships from sinking, while the crews of several Persian gunboats surrendered. The captured ships were sailed to India and subsequently made a useful contribution to the Allied war effort. *Yarra* proceeded to Khorramshahr independently. Arriving undetected in the dark, Harrington observed the Persian sloop *Babr*, which *Yarra* attacked to prevent her resisting the landing. After ten salvos the sloop was set on fire and later sank. The Australian ship then proceeded up the Karun River and silenced gunfire from a naval barracks before forcing two Persian gunboats to surrender. By the early evening, Khorramshahr had been occupied and the Allies had achieved their objectives.

Two days later *Yarra* was sent to capture the Italian merchant vessel *Hilda*, which was at anchor off Bandar Abbas, on the northern shore of the Strait of Hormuz. Although the Italian ship was engulfed in flames when *Yarra* arrived, the fire was gradually brought under control. To the amazement of Harrington, *Yarra* was instructed to tow the *Hilda* towards Karachi, which he did at 2.5 knots. After being relieved of the merchantman, *Yarra* proceeded to Kuwait with a kitten and a Sind gazelle rescued from the burning Italian ship. This swift and successful operation resulted in the resignation of the Persian Government, with its successor ordering resistance to cease the following day. The oil supplies, so vital to the Allies, were safe. It also opened a new line of communications with the Soviet Union; something that was vital at this point in the war. By November, and with their work nearly done, *Yarra* was in the Mediterranean while *Kanimbla* was in Singapore. Both Captain Adams and Commander Harrington were awarded the Distinguished Service Order (DSO).

As the action against Iraq came to an end, naval support for the besieged Allied garrison at Tobruk continued. The defence of Tobruk, mainly by the Ninth Division of the Second AIF, was considered crucial to the course of the war in the Western Desert. In the 139 'runs' against fierce enemy opposition completed by RAN ships including *Stuart*, *Vampire*, *Vendetta*, *Parramatta*, *Waterhen*, *Voyager*, *Nizam* and *Napier*, 1532 troops were transported to Tobruk, 2951 men were withdrawn and 616 tons of supplies were delivered. A member of *Stuart*'s ship's company described the routine 'ferry runs' to Tobruk:

> *The following fits any or all of the runs. Morning of the first day, sailed from Alexandria with troops, ammunition and stores. Air attacks at so and so during the day. Arrived Tobruk after dark, unloaded and took on so many wounded, 200 troops and ammunition empties and proceeded to Mersa Matruh. Air raid at Mersa.*

> *Next day embarked ammunition and stores and sailed for Tobruk. Air attacks . . . Arrived Alexandria. And then 36 hours later, the same thing all over again.*

Twenty-six warships and five merchant vessels were lost in the defence of Tobruk including *Waterhen*, sunk off Salum after dive-bomb attacks on her last run from Alexandria, and *Parramatta*, sunk by the German submarine *U 559* with very heavy loss of life. *Vampire* had earlier been sent to Singapore for a refit to be followed by *Voyager* and *Stuart*. *Hobart* replaced *Perth* in July 1941.

The heavy cruiser HMAS Canberra *in Sydney Harbour during the 1930s.*

Back in Australia, German raiders threatened international and local trade. This meant that *Canberra* was never too far from local waters. The first fifteen months of the war until the end of 1940 were frustrating for the heavy cruiser's ship's company. Spending very long periods at sea in convoy and escort work, the task of tracking down German raiders had so far been fruitless. The beginning of 1941 saw *Canberra* back in the Indian Ocean and engaged in convoy duties, when a report was received indicating that the German pocket battleship *Admiral Scheer* had entered the Indian Ocean on 3 February. Just over a week later *Scheer* fuelled from the Norwegian tanker *Ketty Brovig*, captured by the Germans a month earlier, north of Madagascar. With a flotilla of Allied ships including *Canberra* making for her last known position, *Scheer* returned to the Atlantic and *Canberra* was again denied action.

On 4 March, while patrolling to the north of the Saya de Malha Banks near the Seychelles, *Canberra* launched her Walrus reconnaissance aircraft to search for enemy ships. Just before 5.00 p.m. the aircraft reported sighting a tanker with what appeared to be an armed raider in company. The suspected raider, *Coburg*, went to the north, *Ketty Brovig* to the south. The cruiser's aggressive commanding officer, Captain Harold Farncomb RAN, altered course and closed at 25 knots. He ordered both ships to stop but this was ignored even after warning shots were fired. Keeping his ship at a range of about ten miles to avoid becoming an attractive torpedo target, Farncomb unleashed *Canberra*'s 8-inch guns on *Coburg*, which he still thought was a raider. Eliminating a tanker and an armed raider would have been a useful boost to Allied morale and would have dented German confidence. Ten minutes later the suspected raider was identified as an ordinary supply ship. There was considerable disappointment, which was made worse by a later report that *Coburg* had started scuttling action as soon as *Canberra* had fired her warning shots.

The Australian cruiser then set off after the tanker. *Ketty Brovig*'s crew had also attempted to scuttle her. To prevent her loss, *Canberra*'s Walrus aircraft was landed on the sea alongside. Despite the presence of sharks the flight observer, Lieutenant Charles Malleson, jumped into the water and boarded the sinking vessel. While looking for code-books and ciphers, Malleson came to the conclusion that the tanker could be saved and requested a salvage party. Unfortunately, *Coburg* was too severely damaged and quickly sank. Deciding that *Ketty Brovig* was also a lost cause, Farncomb in *Canberra* hastened her end with gunfire. Those in *Canberra*'s engine room were kept informed of the action by the bridge. For a time, the engineer commander later remarked, it 'held the ratings' interest more than [would] a broadcast description of a Test match with Bradman batting against Larwood'.

This was *Canberra*'s first action against the enemy and good practice for the day she would meet a more formidable foe. But some 215 8-inch rounds had been fired, a very large number considering the nature of the opponents and the fact that they had contributed to their own demise. It prompted the Deputy Chief of Naval Staff, Captain Joseph Burnett RAN, to remark: 'Fancy wasting all those bricks on two harmless freighters'. The Second Naval Member, Commodore John Durnford RN, stated that ammunition might have been saved if *Canberra* had closed to a more effective range, while the two valuable ships might not have been lost if *Canberra* had been closer. Despite the hollowness of *Canberra*'s success, it would be over two months before the Germans found out about the sinking of *Ketty Brovig*. With one less tanker and the Allies having some success, German raider operations were curtailed and were not to recover until the end of 1941. After further patrols in the Indian Ocean and convoy duties around New Guinea and the Java Sea, *Canberra* ended 1941 on her way to a long overdue refit. The three German raiders were eventually sunk: *Pinguin* in May 1941, *Atlantis* in November 1941 and *Admiral Scheer* by Allied aircraft at Kiel in April 1945.

As *Canberra* tasted action for the first time, *Sydney* resumed convoy work off the coast of Western Australia. After escorting the giant transport *Queen Mary* to Jervis Bay in early April, *Sydney* proceeded to Port Phillip Bay where the Chief of Naval Staff, Admiral Sir Ragnar Colvin, embarked for a secret passage to Singapore, arriving on 19 April. By the end of the month, *Sydney* was back in Fremantle and Collins relinquished command to Captain Burnett. The new commanding officer was fortunate that the first four weeks were taken up with relatively straightforward convoy escort work in the Indian Ocean. On 24 June, *Sydney* sailed for Port Jackson and escorted a Pacific Ocean convoy, before docking for minor maintenance. On 8 August, *Sydney* resumed her escort duties, on this occasion sailing with *Awatea* to Auckland and Suva. The cruiser was back in her home port by the end of the month before escorting convoy US 12A, consisting of the transports *Queen Mary* and *Queen Elizabeth*, from Jervis Bay to a rendezvous with *Canberra* in the Great Australian Bight. *Sydney* was back in Fremantle at the end of September and proceeded to the Bight for a rendezvous with convoy US 12B, which was to be escorted into the Indian Ocean.

Meanwhile, the 6700-ton troopship *Zealandia* with nearly a thousand men of the Australian Eighth Division reinforcements and an RAAF detachment on board, sailed from Port Jackson in company with the cruiser *Adelaide* bound for Singapore. On her return to Fremantle, *Sydney* received orders to sail into the Bight to escort *Zealandia* into the Sunda Strait, which lies between the Indonesian

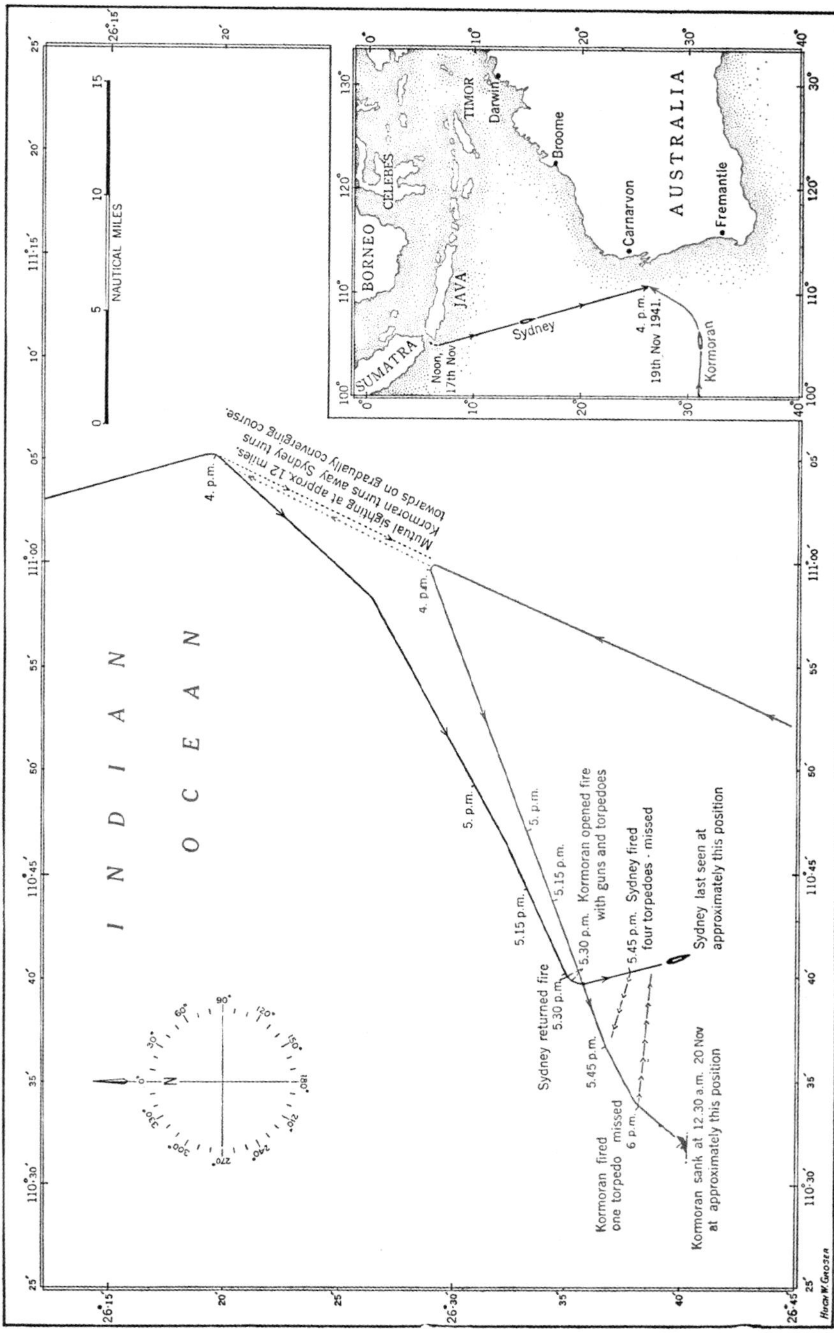

The official naval historian's representation of the Sydney–Kormoran *action on 19 November 1941.*

islands of Java and Sumatra. *Sydney* was to be relieved by the cruisers *Danae* and *Durban*, which would then escort *Zealandia* to her final destination of Singapore. On 8 November, *Canberra* departed Fremantle with *Queen Mary* and *Queen Elizabeth* bound for a rendezvous with the cruiser HMS *Cornwall* near the Cocos Islands. Three days later, *Sydney* departed Fremantle with *Zealandia*. After an incident-free run, *Sydney* detached *Zealandia* on 17 November. By this time *Canberra* had returned to Fremantle and was on her way back to Port Jackson. In the absence of any signal amending her arrival time, *Sydney* was expected back in her home port of Fremantle on the afternoon of Thursday, 20 November.

On the afternoon of 19 November, *Sydney* was in the Indian Ocean south-west of Carnarvon proceeding on a south-easterly course when an unidentified merchant ship was sighted on the horizon. It was the German auxiliary cruiser HSK *Kormoran* preparing to lay a pattern of mines off the coast of Western Australia. When hailed by *Sydney*, *Kormoran* attempted to pass herself off as a Dutch freighter, *Straat Malakka*. The interrogation continued at long range, but when the suspect ship was unable to hoist the Dutch ship's secret code letters, *Sydney* closed to a range of 1500 yards. The reasons for this are the subject of speculation, but perhaps *Sydney* was intending to board *Kormoran*. Whatever the reason, once they had lured *Sydney* into a vulnerable position, the *Kormoran*'s well-trained and disciplined crew dropped the raider's camouflage and fired on the light cruiser with devastating effect. After a short engagement, both *Sydney* and *Kormoran* were badly damaged. *Kormoran* was scuttled six hours later. The German survivors observed that *Sydney* was on fire and making her way slowly over the horizon to the north-east. Most of *Kormoran*'s ship's company were recovered several days later and became prisoners of war. In contrast, *Sydney* was lost with all hands (645 men) and practically without trace. Despite many attempts to find the wreck, *Sydney* has never been found.

The sinking of *Sydney* has proved extremely difficult to explain because the only first-hand evidence of the engagement came from the *Kormoran* survivors. There were many unanswered questions. Mindful of his criticism of Farncomb's sinking of *Ketty Brovig*, why did Captain Burnett in *Sydney* forfeit the huge tactical advantage of his superior firepower by bringing his ship so close to *Kormoran*? Why was *Sydney* lost with all hands and virtually without trace? In the absence of any reliable evidence, the loss of *Sydney* remains one of those mysteries locked forever in the oceans. Theories about what

Survivors from HSK Kormoran *after being recovered from the sea off the Western Australian coast. (RAN official)*

might have happened to her were rife in Navy Office and all around the nation during the war years. Her loss remains the most controversial single event in Australian naval history.

Despite the public criticisms made of Burnett, the first two years of war had demonstrated the ability of Australian officers and sailors in naval combat. Australians were now commanding the RAN's cruisers. Within two years of the outbreak of hostilities, John Collins had been made a Companion of the Order of the Bath (CB) for his skill during the sinking of *Bartolomeo Colleoni*; Captain H.M.L. Waller, described by Admiral Sir Andrew Cunningham as the finest destroyer captain of all time, had received a Distinguished Service Order (DSO) and Bar; Commander A.S. Rosenthal had also received the DSO and Bar for his 'skill and enterprise against enemy submarines'; Captain H.L. Howden, Lieutenant T.K. Morrison and Commissioned Shipwright E.V. Gooch had been honoured for their service with the Somaliland Force; Commanders L.S. Dalton, H.J. Buchanan and J.C. Morrow, among others, were awarded the DSO for operations in numerous theatres; Lieutenant Commander G.G.O. Gatacre and Lieutenant W.G. Wheeler received the Distinguished Service Cross (DSC) for service in British ships in the sinking of the German battleship

Bismarck; Sub-Lieutenant F.M. Osborne, a young Reserve officer, received the DSC for daring while serving in armed trawlers on the Norwegian coast; four chief petty officers and two junior sailors were awarded the Distinguished Service Medal (DSM) for their service in *Sydney* during the sinking of *Bartolomeo Colleoni*; three petty officers and a steward were decorated for their actions during operations in the Persian Gulf; nearly a dozen officers and senior sailors were honoured with the George Medal (GM) for their work with mine clearance and explosives demolition teams; and nearly twenty senior and junior sailors were given the British Empire Medal (BEM) for acts of bravery, courage and devotion to duty. Another 167 personnel were Mentioned in Dispatches and a further ten formally commended. There was ample evidence that RAN personnel were every bit the equal of their British, French and Dutch counterparts. While there was much to rejoice in their successes, the celebrations were muted as the RAN death toll steadily increased and fears of a new foe entering the fray escalated.

As news of *Sydney*'s tragic loss resonated around the nation and the *Kormoran* survivors were being interrogated, a Japanese carrier task force moved secretly towards the main American naval base at Pearl Harbor. Japan needed the vital resources that had been denied to it by an international embargo following its invasion of Indochina. Planning a southwards thrust towards the oil, tin and rubber supplies in the East Indies had commenced, with the objective being to seize and occupy a zone covering the territory and waters enclosed by a perimeter that ran from Burma, south through Malaya, the East Indies, New Guinea, the Bismarck Archipelago, the Gilbert Islands and up to Kamchatka to the north. To secure this zone, the Japanese would occupy Thailand, mount an amphibious invasion on Malaya and capture Singapore before driving towards the Philippine Islands. The United States Asiatic Fleet would be destroyed in the waters around the Philippines and the approaching Pacific Fleet would be attacked by Japanese carrier-borne and shore-based aircraft. Having achieved undisputed command of the seas, Japan would resume the southward advance through the Dutch East Indies to New Guinea and the Bismarck Islands. The enclosed zone would give Japan unfettered access to the resources it needed to guarantee economic independence and fortify the defensive perimeter.

The greatest threat to Japan's achievement of this objective was Allied naval power. The Commander-in-Chief of the Combined Fleet of the Japanese Imperial Navy, Admiral Isoroku Yamamoto, was concerned about the inadequate size of the Japanese merchant fleet and his navy's ability to contain the US Navy until the defensive perimeter had been established. When asked about Japan's chances of winning a war against America and Britain in September 1940, Yamamoto replied: 'If I am told to fight regardless of consequences, I shall run wild for the first six months or a year but I have utterly no confidence for the second or third year'. What was needed was a bold and devastating strike at the heart of American naval power; a blow from which it would take some considerable time to recover.

8

The continent under threat

1942–45

A surprise attack on Pearl Harbor was included in the Japanese war plans finalised in October and endorsed on 1 December 1941. It had been decided in early November that 7 December would be the optimum date to destroy the most American warships. On 22 November, units of the Japanese Carrier Fleet rendezvoused off the Kurile Islands in the North Pacific, setting a course to the east until 3 December when the fleet would turn towards the south and its target of Pearl Harbor. The Japanese hoped to destroy the US Pacific Fleet in one swift blow. With the American carrier capability in tatters, the Japanese believed they could quickly establish and exploit command of the Pacific Ocean. On 6 December, Vice-Admiral Chuichi Nagumo, commander of the Carrier Striking Force, was informed that the carriers *Lexington, Enterprise* and *Saratoga* were at sea. However, since they would probably return to base before the attack, the planned strike was to go ahead.

Over an eight-hour period, the Japanese would simultaneously attack the east coast of Malaya at Kota Bharu, the Philippines, Guam, Hong Kong and Wake Island. The key element was surprise and the attack on Pearl Harbor was planned for early Sunday morning when the ships were alongside and the Americans least ready to defend their assets. When the air-raid alarm was sounded at 7.58 a.m., the first wave of 213 Japanese aircraft armed with torpedoes and bombs attacked the moored American battleships. In just two hours, 1763 men from the fleet were killed and a further 900 killed ashore. Of the battleships that represented the primary target, *Arizona* was sunk at her berth. *Oklahoma*, *California* and *Utah* capsized, but were later salvaged; however, *Oklahoma* was deemed beyond economical repair. Although they inflicted substantial losses on the US Navy, the Japanese failed in their primary objective as most of the battleships survived and the aircraft carriers were untouched.

As the Japanese offensive began, *Vampire* and *Vendetta* were in Singapore with four recently commissioned *Bathurst* Class corvette-minesweepers *Burnie*, *Goulburn*, *Bendigo* and *Maryborough*. The armed merchant cruiser *Manoora* was also alongside, with *Kanimbla* inbound from Penang. At 3.00 p.m., the Japanese attacked Singapore for the first time. The British and American governments immediately suspended trans-Pacific merchant ship sailings. The British battleship *Prince of Wales* and the battle cruiser *Repulse* had arrived in Singapore on 2 December and had sailed on the evening of 8 December, in company with *Vampire* and the British warships *Tenedos*, *Electra* and *Express*. A Japanese naval air strike force based in Vietnam attacked the two British capital ships with high altitude and torpedo bombers. The following morning both *Prince of Wales* and *Repulse* were sunk with the loss of 840 officers and sailors. By 14 December the Allied position in the Pacific was in disarray. Cooperation was poor and communications between the British Eastern Fleet (Vice-Admiral Sir Geoffrey Layton) and the US Asiatic Fleet (Admiral Thomas Hart USN) were inadequate. In any event, they lacked the ships to challenge the Japanese. *Hobart*, *Yarra* and the three corvettes *Wollongong*, *Toowoomba* and *Ballarat* were ordered to Singapore for escort, patrol and minesweeping duties. They were subjected to constant threat of air attack.

As the Japanese asserted their control of the western Pacific, the US Asiatic Fleet could not remain in Manila. The British and Dutch wanted it based in Batavia (now Jakarta) or Surabaya in the Dutch East Indies (now Indonesia). Darwin had also been mentioned. Admiral Hart's instructions from Washington nominated Surabaya, for which he departed in the submarine USS *Shark* on 26 December. Several days later his senior staff officers also sailed from Manila, embarked in the submarine *Swordfish*. The remaining staff officers sailed the following day in the submarine *Seawolf* bound for Darwin. It was to become the operating base for the submarine squadron attached to Hart's fleet. However, when the Americans arrived they found some local resistance to their presence, because some felt it would undoubtedly draw a Japanese attack. By 29 December Darwin was playing host to six American submarines, two submarine tenders, three cruisers and eight destroyers. But this concentration of naval power did not remain in Darwin for very long.

At the close of 1941, Allied naval power had been divided into four widely separated groups and their respective commands: the US Pacific Fleet at Pearl Harbor to the east; the British Eastern Fleet at Trincomalee; the small American–British–Dutch–Australian (ABDA) Force (including three American, three Dutch, one British cruiser and HMAS *Hobart*); and the Anzac Force (three Australian and one British cruiser). At the same time, Admiral Chester Nimitz USN became Commander-in-Chief of the US Pacific Fleet (CINCPACFLT) and sought to prevent a southward Japanese advance on Rabaul by striking at the Marshall Islands on the Japanese flank. Little damage was done in the operation but the US had taken the offensive.

After Australian protests that Australian waters were excluded from the designated American naval zone in the Pacific, Prime Minister Winston Churchill confirmed Britain's view on 3 January 1942: the US Navy area should extend to the Australian coast. As the new Chief of Naval Operations (CNO), Admiral Ernest King USN, had only recently gained full authority over the whole US Navy, Churchill believed he would accede to the British request that American naval authorities should accept responsibility for Australian waters. When King did consider the issue, he established an 'Anzac Area' which contained the north-east portion of the Australia Station. The US Navy commander of the area was to be assisted by a British flag officer whose appointment was approved by Australia and New Zealand.

On 15 January 1942, Admiral Hart arrived in Surabaya and took charge of the naval branch of ABDA with the title 'ABDAFLOAT'. This terminated the responsibility of the CINC Eastern Fleet for naval operations in the ABDA area. In the exercise of ABDA naval command, maritime forces in the area would operate under their own national commanders with operational tasking being coordinated by ABDAFLOAT. But these was no doubt that the allocation of commands and the arrangement of Allied naval forces was in need of a fundamental revision. In early 1942, Australian Prime Minister John Curtin argued strongly for the formation of an Anglo-American fleet in the Pacific. The Advisory War Council also condemned the Allied plan to have 'two inferior fleets, one in the Indian [the British Eastern Fleet] and the other in the Pacific [the American Asiatic and Pacific Fleets]' which 'at the best will impose on us a defensive and not offensive strategy'. The British were negotiating the possibility of basing the Eastern Fleet on the Australian coastline, while the US Pacific Fleet would not extend its area of responsibility to east Australian waters despite Curtin's insistence that it should. For their part, the Americans appreciated their attractive strategic position on Japan's eastern flank. Although the US Navy finally accepted responsibility for east Australian waters, as has been noted, it planned to contribute only one cruiser to its defence. After examining the British appreciation of the situation in the Far East in the period to February 1942, the Australian Chiefs of Staff stated that the prevailing strategic outlook 'was most unsatisfactory . . . In other words, the US Pacific Fleet, on which we had based great hopes is unable and unwilling to assist'.

The defence of Singapore proved to be a challenge for the Allies as Japanese surface units and naval aircraft converged on the strategic base. *Canberra* and *Vampire* had escorted the liner *Aquitania* to Singapore with Australian troop reinforcements. *Napier*, *Nizam* and *Nestor* escorted the aircraft carrier *Indomitable*, with Hurricane fighters and aircrew embarked for service in Malaya where her aircraft were launched. *Yarra*, *Bendigo* and *Wollongong* were involved in the local defence and reinforcement of Singapore and the rescue of ships sunk by the Japanese as they fled to the south. Some key elements from the surviving Allied naval forces in the South-West Pacific were formed into the Anzac Squadron based at Suva in Fiji. Consisting of *Australia*, HMNZS *Achilles*, HMNZS *Leander*, USS *Chicago* and two American destroyers, this was the first time that naval units from the three nations (Australia, New Zealand and the US) had operated together under a unified command, in this case Rear Admiral J.G. Crace, Rear Admiral Commanding the Australian Squadron (RACAS).

Nearly seventy days had elapsed since the attack on Pearl Harbor. The Allied defence based on a British battle fleet, integral to the success of the Singapore strategy, had not materialised. HMS *Prince of Wales* and HMS *Repulse* were at the bottom of the sea. Thailand, Malaya and the Philippines had been invaded. The capture and occupation of Singapore on 15 February 1942 was crucial to Japanese war plans. The fall of Singapore took with it the bulk of the Eighth Division of the Second AIF and the axis of Allied naval operations moved from the 'Malay Barrier' to the waters surrounding and enclosing the Dutch East Indies. The Japanese forces moved relentlessly on and landed in New Guinea and on New Britain. The war came to Australia's shores on 19 February, when Darwin, with 47 naval and merchant vessels in the harbour, was bombed. The American destroyer *Edsall* had earlier sunk the Japanese fleet submarine *I 124* off Darwin. When Japanese Zero fighters and bombers attacked the port and city, *Swan* and *Warrego* were able to raise steam and get underway as USS *Peary* was hit and exploded into flames. Five British merchant ships were lost in the action in addition to HMA Ships *Mavie* and *Kelat*. The hospital ship *Manunda* was also damaged.

When the ABDA command had been dissolved on 2 February 1942, there was a naval force of eight cruisers around Java. These were formed into an Allied striking force for operations in Dutch East Indies waters which comprised American, Dutch, British and Australian units, including *Perth* and *Hobart*. After encountering the Japanese in a number of minor actions, on 25 February Allied aircraft noted two convoys approaching Java: one making for the east of the island and the other for the west. The Dutch naval commander, Vice-Admiral Conrad Helfrich, divided this force into an Eastern and Western Force. Commodore John Collins RAN, the commander of British naval forces in Java, deployed the Western Force against the Japanese western group. While on passage through the Sunda Strait between Sumatra and Java islands on the night of 28 February–1 March 1942, *Perth* and USS *Houston* encountered the Japanese Western Invasion Convoy consisting of six cruisers, twelve destroyers, two aircraft carriers and one minelayer. After a desperate gun and torpedo battle between the two Allied ships and the much larger Japanese force, both *Perth* and *Houston* were sunk with heavy loss of life. Tragically, 353 Australian officers and sailors were lost in the action and a further four later died ashore. Also, 324 men became Japanese prisoners of war. Ten days later, *Yarra* was escorting a small convoy south of Java when she was engaged by three Japanese heavy cruisers. After ordering the ships to scatter, Lieutenant Commander Robert Rankin RAN turned towards the enemy group and engaged the Japanese in an attempt to give the convoy a chance to flee. *Yarra* was severely damaged by the vastly superior Japanese forces and sunk. A total of 138 officers and sailors were lost; only thirteen were rescued by a Dutch submarine five days later.

While the Allies were seeking to restrict their losses, the Japanese were considering their next conquest. Japan held vast areas of land but, more importantly, had begun to exert control over the Pacific and Indian Ocean basins. It seemed that nothing could stand in the way of the victorious Japanese. Recognising that the Japanese Navy had to bring the US Navy to a decisive engagement, the Commander-in-Chief of the Japanese Combined Fleet, Admiral Yamamoto, planned an attack on the American naval base at Midway Island. He believed that this would draw the Americans into the decisive battle he sought. The victory he envisaged at Midway would secure command of the seas for Japan and allow it to consolidate its recent gains. But before this plan, codenamed 'MI', could be executed, New Guinea needed to be completely cleared of Allied forces and Port Moresby captured. This latter plan, codenamed 'MO', would be executed simultaneously with an attack on the Solomon Islands. Although the Japanese carrier strength available for MO was limited to *Shokaku* and *Zuikaku*, and the light carrier *Shoho*, Yamamoto was confident that the element of surprise he had enjoyed at Pearl Harbor would be sufficient to ensure that MO would be likewise successful. This strategy was also preferred over a cross-country march from the northern coast of New Guinea, which the Japanese already held.

The Japanese expected to succeed and to isolate Australia. They had already decided against invading or occupying Australia for the following reasons, outlined in a report prepared by the Japanese Imperial General Staff in 1942:

> *If the invasion is attempted, the Australians, in view of their national character, would resist to the end. Also because the geographic conditions of Australia present numerous difficulties in a military sense, it is apparent that a military venture in that country would be a difficult one. To alter the plan already in force, and to employ a force larger than the one employed in the southern area since the outbreak of the war, to suddenly invade Australia which lies 4000 nautical miles away would be a reckless adventure, and is beyond Japan's ability.*

This is why Japan sought to capture New Caledonia, Fiji and Samoa, and to establish a seaplane base in the Louisiade Archipelago—150 miles south-east of the 'tail' of New Guinea. The fact that the Japanese did not intend to invade Australia is immaterial to any overall assessment of the plan's strategic significance. Australia was a focus for shipping across the two ocean basins, the Indian and Pacific, either side of the continent. Japan could achieve its ends, severing sea communications to the north-east and north-west of Australia, without conquering continental territory.

On 3 April, a Japanese invasion fleet entered the Indian Ocean via the Sunda Strait bound for Ceylon, while a second passed through the

Malacca Strait heading for the Bay of Bengal. As part of its campaign to invade and hold Burma, the Japanese Navy was tasked with destroying Allied forces in and around Ceylon and southern India, and disrupting the sea lines of communications in the Bay of Bengal. On 9 April near Trincomalee, Japanese aircraft sank the British aircraft carrier *Hermes* before engaging her consort, HMAS *Vampire*. An overwhelming force converged on *Vampire*, which eventually suffered a direct hit in the boiler room. After the order was given to abandon ship, another bomb broke the ship's back. The commanding officer, Commander W.T.A. Moran RAN, and seven sailors were killed. It seemed that the Japanese were incapable of error as Australia lost yet another ship. But soon, for the first time in the war, good fortune would be with the Allies as they prepared for a major Japanese offensive.

Having broken the Japanese naval communications codes and anticipating a possible thrust towards Port Moresby and Australia, two Allied carrier task forces and a cruiser striking force were concentrated in the Coral Sea–New Hebrides area. It was now the Allies who enjoyed the element of surprise. Moreover, the Japanese were relying on intelligence to the effect that only the carrier *Saratoga* was able to mount a counter-attack. In fact, *Saratoga* was completing a refit at Puget Sound, 7800 miles from Noumea. Although by mid-March the islands adjacent to the sea lanes had been garrisoned by the Allies, the Japanese realised the key to their success was destroying the American carriers. By the end of April, the Allied position had further deteriorated and Australia was directly threatened for the first time. After the loss of the cruisers *Dorsetshire* and *Cornwall* in the Indian Ocean, the British naval shield had dissolved completely.

On 3 May 1942, further intelligence was received that the Japanese were landing at Tulagi Harbour in the Solomon Islands. Meanwhile, a Covering Group, under Rear Admiral Goto, and a Support Force, commanded by Rear Admiral Marushige, sailed for the Jomard Passage and entry into the Coral Sea off the north-east coast of Australia. In company with the Port Moresby Invasion Group, commanded by Rear Admiral Kajioke, the whole group would subsequently alter course to the west and start the offensive against Port Moresby. If *Saratoga* did appear and attempt to offer resistance, the two carriers of Vice-Admiral Takagi's Carrier Striking Force would converge on the American carrier and launch an attack with dive-bombers and torpedo bombers.

The Japanese commander, Vice-Admiral Shigeyoshi Inouye, was embarked in his flagship, the cruiser *Kashima*, alongside in Rabaul. At the time of what became known as the Battle of the Coral Sea he was simultaneously in command of the Japanese Fourth Fleet and the South Seas Force. Opposing Inouye in the Coral Sea was Rear Admiral Frank Fletcher USN, the commander of Allied Task Force 17. On the morning of 4 May, Task Force 17, consisting of the American carrier *Yorktown*, the heavy cruisers *Astoria, Chester* and *Portland*, and six destroyers, was within 100 miles of the Japanese invasion force and planes from *Yorktown* attacked Tulagi and Gavutu Harbour. One Japanese destroyer was sunk and another badly damaged. Five enemy landing craft were sent to the bottom, a minelayer was damaged and several aircraft shot down. During 5–6 May, Allied ships commenced refuelling from the fleet tanker USS *Neosho* in preparation for another engagement. This was discontinued on 6 May when news of an advancing Japanese naval force was received. The Allied ships were then reorganised into three groups: the Attack Group; the Air Group based around the carriers *Yorktown* and *Lexington*; and the Support Group, which included *Australia* and *Hobart* commanded by Admiral Crace.

On the morning of 7 May, scout aircraft of the Attack Group located a large Japanese force based on three carriers which appeared bound for Port Moresby. Immediately, 92 planes from the American carriers were launched. They succeeded in destroying the Japanese carrier *Shoho*. However, Japanese aircraft from *Zuikaku* and *Shokaku* attacked and sank the tanker *Neosho* and the destroyer *Sims*, the former being mistaken for an American light carrier which had been detached to the south. A lull in the action followed while each carrier force tried to locate the other. There were several aerial clashes but neither side's carrier aircraft could locate the opposing surface forces. In the early morning of 7 May, Japanese land-based air forces concentrated their efforts on the Allied Support Force, deployed to intercept the Port Moresby Invasion Force in the Jomard Passage. Three Japanese bombing and torpedo attacks were sustained by Crace's force, attacks which would otherwise have been mounted on the more highly valued Allied carrier force. The Japanese operational plan was in disarray by the end of 7 May. Having received reports of Crace's force and the existence of two carrier battle groups in the Coral Sea, Admiral Inouye ordered the Port Moresby Invasion Group to turn back from the Jomard Passage until the American carrier strength had been neutralised. Emphasis was now on finding and destroying the American carriers.

Early the next morning, 8 May, air patrols from both sides simultaneously located the surface forces and the battle reached its crucial stage. Allied planes mounted a fierce attack on the carrier *Shokaku* and inflicted severe damage, while *Lexington* was abandoned after large leakages in aviation fuel put her in immediate danger of explosion. The Japanese had lost considerably more carrier fighter aircraft and Inouye was unwilling to risk his carriers further. He was also unwilling to send the Invasion Force through the Jomard Passage against Crace's force and was concerned about the likelihood of attack from Allied land-based aircraft. As a result of the heavy losses sustained by both sides, the Allies and the Japanese withdrew the major part of their forces. With the Invasion Force returning to Rabaul, *Shoho* sunk, *Shokaku* damaged and *Zuikaku* withdrawn to the south, Yamamoto was left with no choice but to confirm Inouye's effective cancellation of Operation MO. Had Yamamoto ordered the Invasion Force to turn again towards Port Moresby, it stood a very good chance of success. With *Lexington* sunk and *Yorktown* bound for Noumea, the likely Allied air resistance would have been a fraction of that anticipated on 6 May. However, Yamamoto had received orders on 5 May that Operation MI was to proceed as planned and set about preparing for the most decisive engagement of the Pacific War.

The Battle of the Coral Sea was a strategic victory for the Allies. As naval air power and carrier warfare emerged as the key to future Allied success, the absence of two big carriers at Coral Sea weakened Japan's capacity to launch a strike on Midway less than one month later. It was also a tactical success in that Japan was forced to fight a land campaign in New Guinea—an advance that highlighted the poor support it was able to provide for its troops so far from home. Japanese plans for taking Fiji, Samoa and New Caledonia were shelved and the sea route to the north and east of Australia remained open. The naval success at Coral Sea was also an overwhelming psychological victory for the Allies. For the first time in six months, the Japanese had been stopped—and stopped where they least expected—at sea. But the time for celebration had not yet arrived. The Australian Advisory War Council surprisingly described the result of the Coral Sea Battle as 'rather disappointing' when it met to discuss the outcome of the operation in late May 1942. Given that the Allies had advance notice of Japanese intentions, the Council saw the battle as a missed opportunity where the Allies 'should have been able to concentrate the superior strength necessary to have ensured a complete victory'.

The level of fear of the Japanese Navy within Australia was such that Sydney Harbour was the scene of frantic naval activity. While preparations were being made for another major engagement in the

Pacific a mysterious reconnaissance aircraft flew over Sydney in the early morning of 30 May 1942. It circled the cruiser USS *Chicago*, which was then at Number 2 Buoy to the east of Garden Island. Within minutes of the sighting in Sydney, a similar aircraft flew over the battleship HMS *Ramillies*, which was lying at anchor in Diego Suarez Harbour in Madagascar. A torpedo from a midget submarine hit and damaged *Ramillies* on 30 May. The plane seen and heard over Sydney was from the large Japanese fleet submarine *I 21*. It had taken off from a position 35 miles to the north-east of North Head. Enjoying the apparent safety of Sydney Harbour at that time were the American ships *Chicago*, *Perkins* and *Dobbin*, the Australian cruisers *Canberra* and *Adelaide*, the armed merchant cruisers *Kanimbla* and *Westralia*, the corvettes *Whyalla* and *Geelong*, the minelayer *Bungaree* and the Indian corvette *Bombay*. The Dutch submarine *K 9* was adjacent to the depot ship *Kuttabul*, lying alongside at the south-east corner of Garden Island. At sunset, the submarines *I 22*, *I 24*, and *I 27* each released a midget submarine from a position seven miles east of Sydney Heads.

At 8.15 p.m., the midget submarine from *I 27* became entangled in the anti-torpedo net between Georges Head and Green Point. At 9.52 p.m., the channel patrol boat HMAS *Yarroma* reported a 'suspicious object in net' which was confirmed at 10.30 p.m. to be a submarine. At 10.35 p.m., demolition charges were fired in the midget submarine killing the two crew and destroying the submarine. The midget submarine from *I 24* had passed through the harbour entrance at 9.58 p.m. After the general alarm was sounded at 10.27 p.m. and again at 10.36 p.m., the port was closed and ships were instructed to take anti-submarine precautions. At 10.50 p.m., *Chicago* noticed a submarine's periscope 500 yards away. Under heavy pom-pom fire, the Japanese steered a course that took them just 200 yards off Garden Island.

With all this activity going on, the midget submarine from *I 22* entered the harbour. At 10.52 p.m., 'a flurry on the water' was sighted. Two minutes later a submarine was noticed but it appeared to be damaged as it turned slowly to starboard in the harbour entrance adjacent to Hornby Light on the tip of South Head. The anti-submarine vessel *Yandra*, which was fitted with one 4-inch gun and 31 depth charges, attacked the submarine at 11.07 p.m. The Naval Officer Commanding Sydney, Rear Admiral Christopher Muirhead-Gould, ordered the ferries to continue operating to 'keep the submarines down till daylight'. He failed to issue the direction to 'darken ship', however, which meant that vessels on the harbour continued to show their lights while the floodlights illuminating the dockyard construction site gave the Japanese a clear silhouette of their targets. The order to 'darken ship' was finally issued at 11.14 p.m. and the dockyard lights turned off at 11.25 p.m. At 11.30 p.m., an underwater explosion rang out, the shock waves from which wrecked the depot ship *Kuttabul*, then being used to accommodate naval defaulters. Nineteen naval personnel were killed and ten were wounded. Muirhead-Gould had blundered.

At 1.58 a.m. the midget submarine from *I 24*, her torpedoes fired and mission complete, attempted to leave the harbour and return to the fleet submarines. At 3.00 a.m., the midget submarine from *I 22* made a desperate effort to enter the harbour channel for the first time after recovering from the depth charge attack from *Yandra*. After 3.00 a.m., all was quiet until two hours later a suspicious object was investigated in Taylor Bay. For the next three-and-a-half hours there were repeated depth charge attacks. The midget submarine from *I 22* lay on the harbour floor. It had been pounded by depth charges and its torpedoes were jammed in the tubes. Both its crew were dead, although the submarine's engines continued to run throughout the day. They had committed suicide with their service revolvers.

The fleet submarines lying outside the harbour were more successful in their campaign, sinking several merchant ships off the coast between Newcastle and Gabo Island. On 3 June *Iron Chieftan* was sunk; she was joined on the bottom by *Iron Crown* the next day. *Arunta*, *Kalgoorlie*, *Rockhampton*, *Doomba*, *Moresby*, *Bingera*, *Yandra*, *Kybra* and *Whyalla* combined to escort ships proceeding along the New South Wales coast. During the early hours of 8 June, one of the large submarines fired ten shells into the Sydney harbourside suburbs of Rose Bay and Bellevue Hill, while another fired some shells into Newcastle. Neither attack did any serious damage. After sinking the Panamanian ship *Guatemala* off Sydney on 12 June, the submarine flotilla departed.

The two wrecked midget submarines lying in Sydney Harbour were later recovered and a single complete submarine constructed from what remained. The bodies of the four dead submariners were recovered and cremated at Rookwood Cemetery in Sydney. The third wrecked submarine has eluded every attempt to locate it. The shock felt by the people of Sydney following the attack was best summed up by an American naval officer who wrote: 'So, by a combination of good luck and aggressive counter-attack, an extremely well-conceived enemy operation succeeded only in underlining to the embattled

Australians their front row seat in the Pacific War'. The attack brought home to the civilian population the extent to which the war was now on Australia's doorstep; that the conduct of the war was a matter of great urgency; and that the ocean waters held the key to an Allied success or defeat.

Although the southward advance to Port Moresby through the Coral Sea had failed, Admiral Yamamoto held firmly to his contentious plan to attack the American naval base on Midway Island from which he hoped to threaten Pearl Harbor. The island would also serve as a base for the subsequent capture of Fiji, New Caledonia and Samoa, thereby isolating Australia and further threatening the already vulnerable Allied trade routes. Still unaware that the Allies had broken Japanese naval communications codes, Yamamoto believed that the Allied forces would be at their usual base in Pearl Harbor until news was received of the attack on Midway. The approaching Allied fleet would then be attacked and destroyed by the Japanese Navy. With incomplete intelligence covering the disposition of Allied naval forces before the action began, Yamamoto's fleet suffered heavy and debilitating losses. Four carriers were sunk. By mid-1942, the Japanese carrier force and its naval air power had been effectively marginalised. Midway was described as the 'beginning of the end' for Japan, which had lost its chance of gaining supremacy over the US Navy. Major Japanese advances had been halted and Allied counteroffensives could soon be launched.

The character of the war had changed decisively but it was far from over. On 16 June 1942, Prime Minister John Curtin stated:

> *I do not think the enemy can now invade this country, we have proved that, with the resources we have had, together with the command of the sea established by the gallant US Navy, by decisive victories at Midway Island and the Solomon Islands. We are not yet immune from marauding raids which may cause much damage and loss. I believe, however, that we can hold Australia as a base from which to launch both limited and major offensives against Japan.*

With the Japanese naval thrust halted, the Allies attempted to use their superiority at sea to recapture key territories and bases held by Japan in the South-West Pacific. The amphibious assault on Guadalcanal on 7 August 1942 was the first Allied offensive landing of the Pacific War. It was an operation aimed at preventing the Japanese from building and operating an airfield on Lunga Plain; at securing the trans-Pacific supply routes to Australia; and was the first step towards dislodging the Japanese from their stronghold at Rabaul. The naval forces available for the landing, although strong by comparison with earlier Allied naval efforts in the Pacific, were by no means overwhelming.

The task of the Allied naval forces was twofold: to screen and escort forces from the amphibious groups to the landing area; and to defend against a Japanese counteroffensive. The assault and landing of troops was successful. The Japanese were defeated at Tulagi and at Guadalcanal on 7 August but, as expected, they were swift to react. A naval task force had been hastily gathered under Vice-Admiral Mikawa (Commander of the Outer South Sea Fleet) to attack the Allied beachhead and recover Guadalcanal. On the night of 8–9 August, Mikawa's fleet engaged the Allied force consisting of *Australia*, *Canberra* and *Hobart*, and US Ships *Astoria*, *Vincennes*, *Quincy*, *Chicago* and *San Juan*. Mikawa based his attack on surprise and the Japanese Navy's superior night-fighting ability. After successfully passing at 25 knots a mere half mile from the radar pickets—which failed to detect the ships—Mikawa's force passed Savo Island and engaged the southern patrol force led by *Canberra* and *Chicago* off the northern coast of Guadalcanal. *Canberra* drew intense Japanese fire from ranges of between 4500 and 9000 yards and may also have been torpedoed. A controversy later developed around the claim that the Australian ship was fired upon mistakenly by American naval units. The Japanese then proceeded to engage the northern patrol force and pounded the American cruisers *Quincy*, *Vincennes* and *Astoria*. Having seized the important tactical initiative by effectively using the cover of darkness, Mikawa's ships sailed out of Savo Sound.

By 6.45 a.m. the next morning, *Canberra*'s surviving ship's company of 744 men had been transferred to the American destroyers *Patterson* and *Blue*, and then to the transports *Barnett* and *Fuller* anchored off Gaudalcanal. When the order to 'Abandon ship' was given, *Canberra* was listing more than 25 degrees to starboard and on fire amidships. The destroyer USS *Selfridge* was ordered to sink *Canberra*. After taking hits from 263 rounds and four torpedoes, the heavy cruiser remained defiantly on the surface. A further four torpedoes fired at close range from the destroyer *Ellet* were needed to complete the task. At 8.00 a.m. the largest Australian warship lost during the war turned over to starboard and sank by the bow. Eighty-four men were killed, including Captain F.E. Getting RAN, and a further 109 men were wounded. Four hours later *Astoria* joined

Vincennes and *Quincy* on the floor of what became known as 'Ironbottom Sound'. The Battle of Savo Island was described by *Time* magazine as the US Navy's 'worst bluewater defeat'.

Despite the number of warships sunk, Mikawa was criticised for not attacking the transports. He defended himself on the grounds of fearing an unequal encounter with Fletcher's carrier aircraft at dawn and wanting to be well clear of the area. Although the Allies were able to hold Guadalcanal, a costly land battle would be waged over the next six months for possession of the island with the success of the Allies decided largely by their greater ability to supply and reinforce troops on shore.

Between 12 and 15 November 1942, a renewed naval attack was launched to prevent Japan from reinforcing its position. Only 3000 of the 10 000 Japanese troops sent to Guadalcanal in transports were landed, a success which led the American official naval historian Samuel Morison to remark, 'the US Navy felt it could never be defeated'. Roosevelt declared after the second Guadalcanal offensive that 'it would seem that the turning point in the war at last has been achieved'. By the end of 1942, the main strength of the US Navy was in the Pacific, a fact which was welcomed in Australia. The RAN had lost three of its six cruisers, and with them much of its offensive firepower, within ten months. A number of other ships had also been lost. The destroyer *Voyager* ran aground in Betano Bay on the south-west coast of Timor on 23 September while transporting supplies to Australian commandos engaged in guerrilla actions against the Japanese. The ship's company destroyed the ship on 25 September after two concerted efforts to refloat the destroyer failed. The corvette *Armidale* was attacked and sunk by Japanese aircraft on 1 December 1942 while attempting to evacuate the 2/2nd Independent Company from Timor. Although no one from *Voyager* was seriously injured, 100 men were lost when *Armidale* was sunk. To replace the steadily increasing combat losses, a number of new destroyers, corvettes and requisitioned merchant ships had entered naval service, and more were on their way as the Australian dockyards worked to full capacity.

In early 1943 the Allies consolidated their position in preparation for a series of offensive landings in the Solomons, the Trobriands, New Britain and the east coast of New Guinea near Lae. While the operational shortcomings and tactical deficiencies of the joint naval task units in the Pacific had been largely overcome by this time, the Americans undertook some larger scale reorganisations of their forces. On 13 March 1943, Admiral King introduced a new numbering system for the American fleets: the Pacific fleets were odd numbered and those in the Atlantic even numbered. The South Pacific Force under Vice-Admiral William Halsey USN became the Third Fleet; the Central Pacific Force under Vice-Admiral Raymond Spruance USN was redesignated the Fifth Fleet; while Naval Forces South West Pacific under Vice-Admiral Carpender in MacArthur's command were renamed the Seventh Fleet, although it consisted only of the cruisers *Australia*, *Hobart*, USS *Phoenix* and seven American destroyers. It was a fleet in name only. Each American fleet was subsequently divided into task forces of which the first digit represented the parent fleet. Task Force 44 was redesignated Task Force 74 and was strengthened in May 1943 by the arrival of the new Australian Tribal Class destroyers *Warramunga* and *Arunta*.

Following the decisive action at Midway and eventual Allied success at Guadalcanal, there was a lull in the fighting for several months. In the Solomons, the Japanese established bases at Munda on New Georgia Island and Vila on Kolombangara, while concentrating on re-establishing air superiority over the South and South-West Pacific. The Japanese Navy would lead the next campaign, known as Operation I, having been strengthened by the transfer from the carriers of 96 Zeros, 65 dive-bombers and several squadrons of torpedo planes to Rabaul and Bougainville. The first attacks were directed against Tulagi and Guadalcanal, but only succeeded in sinking an American destroyer, a tanker and the New Zealand corvette *Moa*. Attention then turned to targets in New Guinea, including Port Moresby, Buna and Milne Bay. Exaggerated reports by Japanese pilots led Admiral Yamamoto to believe the operation, which he had personally commanded, had been a success. Two days after the offensive was concluded, the Allies received intelligence that Yamamoto would be flying into the Solomons with a number of his staff. The aircraft carrying Yamamoto was intercepted and shot down. The Japanese naval Commander-in-Chief was killed, badly affecting the Imperial Japanese Navy's morale. Japanese naval tactics also became more extreme.

In the pre-dawn darkness of 14 May 1943, the hospital ship HMAS *Centaur* was torpedoed and sunk with the loss of 268 lives. It was the worst maritime disaster to occur off the east coast of Australia during the Second World War. There were only 64 survivors. The Australian people reacted very differently to news of *Centaur*'s loss than they had to the demise of *Waterhen*, *Vampire*, *Parramatta*, *Sydney*, *Yarra*, *Armidale*, *Perth* and *Canberra*. These were warships and it was to be

The hospital ship HMAS Centaur *which was sunk by the Japanese submarine I 177 on 14 May 1943 with heavy loss of life. (RAN official)*

expected that they would engage the enemy and possibly be lost. There was also a likelihood of merchant ships being sunk by submarines, raiders or mines. In the first half of 1943, 21 ships were attacked off the east coast of Australia between Cairns and Gabo Island by Japanese submarines. International law accepted that merchant ships engaged in the war effort were usually legitimate targets for enemy action. However, *Centaur* was different; she was not only a non-combatant vessel, but a *hospital* ship. Her sinking was a breach of international humanitarian law and a *prima facie* war crime of enormous gravity. There was, not surprisingly, outrage at the news.

Prime Minister John Curtin described the sinking as 'deliberate, wanton and barbarous' while the UAP leader, Billy Hughes, stated that 'the callous sinking of *Centaur* will fill every Australian heart with horror'. Perhaps in disbelief that the Japanese could be so cold-hearted, rumours immediately started that *Centaur* had been carrying troops and war materials, and that the Japanese were aware of this breach in protocol. These were probably fuelled by witnesses observing ambulance drivers carrying personal arms. Despite incontrovertible evidence to the contrary, the rumours lingered. Of course, the Imperial Japanese Navy was not prepared to admit that one of its submarines had been responsible for the atrocity, and in December 1943 issued a statement formally denying responsibility. After the war, speculation about the culprit settled on two boats, *I 178* and *I 180*, both of which were in Australian waters at the time. Volume 83 of the official Japanese *War History Series* published in 1979 named the perpetrator: '*I 177* sank the British hospital ship *Centaur*'. The captain of *I 177*, Commander Hajime Nakagawa, would survive the war to face war crimes charges. Although he refused to confirm that his boat sank *Centaur*, he was tried for ordering his men to fire on survivors from torpedoed ships in the Indian Ocean later while in command of *I 63*. Nakagawa was subsequently found guilty of war crimes and sentenced to six years' imprisonment at Sugamo. His defence, that he was only following orders issued by his superior, Vice-Admiral Shiro Takasu, failed at the War Crimes Tribunal.

A number of statements were made in Nakagawa's defence. The first was that he might not have known that *Centaur* was a protected ship. The submarine's weapons officer stated that he 'didn't see any sign to indicate the ship was a hospital ship'. He was in a position to observe *Centaur* because *I 177* was on the surface when she first spotted the hospital ship. The officer who relieved Nakagawa in command said that he heard no rumours about *I 177* sinking a hospital ship. At any rate, he maintained that Japanese naval officers were meticulous in observing international law. David Jenkins argues in *Battle Surface: Japan's Submarine War Against Australia 1942–44*, that only a man who was both culpably incompetent and criminally determined could fail to identify a hospital ship and then send her to the bottom without giving any thought to those sailing in her. Nakagawa's determined silence in the face of these allegations probably speaks loudest of all about his guilt. But such tactics could not reverse Japan's fortunes. It was now losing the war it had started.

Japanese industry could not build warships at the rate they were being sunk by the Allies. In addition to lacking ships of various classes, Japanese tactics were proving to be erratic and inferior. When the Japanese had attempted to resupply their troops in New Guinea in early March 1943, American and RAAF aircraft attacked a convoy of eight transports escorted by eight destroyers sailing from Rabaul to Lae on the north-east coast. All eight transports were sunk together with four of the destroyers. More than 3000 men perished at what became known as the Battle of the Bismarck Sea. Japanese land forces in New Guinea were increasingly isolated and forlorn. Germany and Italy were also facing defeat. Rommel's army had suffered a decisive defeat at the Battle of El Alamein, while the new Q Class destroyers, *Quiberon* and *Quickmatch*, were supporting Allied landings on the North African coast and attacking Italian supply convoys. The German invasion of Russia had been contained and the Allies were achieving notable successes against the submarine threat.

By the middle of 1943, the Allies were prepared for their own series of major offensives in the Pacific. On 30 June, Allied forces were transported in landing craft from Buna on New Guinea's north-eastern coast to Nassau Bay, 30 miles south of Lae at the head of the Huon Gulf, in the first of a number of amphibious advances that exploited American sea superiority. *Australia*, *Hobart* and *Arunta* were engaged in patrols in the Coral Sea to prevent Japanese surface units disrupting Allied lines of communication. While proceeding to Espiritu Santo in Vanuatu on 20 July, *Hobart* was torpedoed by a Japanese submarine and sustained considerable damage. Seven officers and six sailors were killed, and the ship required an extensive refit. With *Hobart* out of action, the RAN was reduced to two cruisers: *Australia* and the aged *Adelaide*. To supplement its firepower, the Naval Board accepted the Admiralty's offer of another County Class heavy cruiser, HMS *Shropshire*, as a replacement for *Canberra*. Despite its lack of larger combat ships, the RAN nonetheless consisted of 83 fighting ships, with its primary capability found in the ten destroyers and 48 corvettes then in service. As in the First World War, Australian warships were now serving across the world, although the majority were deployed in waters nearer to home. With the Italian Fleet's surrender in September 1943, the Allies had gained the upper hand in the Mediterranean, the Atlantic and the Arctic Circle campaigns. This allowed greater Australian emphasis on prosecuting the war against Japan.

Between mid-1943 and mid-1944, the Allies captured the 1500-mile northern coastline of New Guinea and strategically important offshore islands which would be used as a springboard for retaking the Philippines. By securing complete command of air space and adjacent waters, the Allies were able to isolate the Japanese fortress base of Rabaul and defer a costly attack on its garrisons. At the end of October 1943, the Allies exercised command of South and South-West Pacific waters which they used, together with overwhelming superiority in the air, to support the advance of MacArthur's land forces. However, in the Central Pacific, the success at Midway was followed by a stalemate which had existed for more than twelve months. It was only when the Central Pacific Force under Admiral Nimitz had been sufficiently reinforced with new carriers, battleships and cruisers that the impasse in the Central Pacific could be overcome. At the same time it offered an alternative to MacArthur's island-hopping strategy. Whereas the US Navy would play a secondary role in MacArthur's plan by providing protection for convoys and transports, undertaking shore bombardment and guarding MacArthur's seaward flank, the considerable carrier air power available to the Pacific Force would allow it to plan and undertake amphibious missions at a pace exceeding that which could be achieved by MacArthur. Although MacArthur would proceed as previously agreed, the primary line of advance towards the Japanese home islands was adjusted and would run from Pearl Harbor through the Micronesian island groups to Formosa (Taiwan) and Okinawa. The northern Pacific was less of a concern as the Japanese had already been forced from the Aleutian Islands.

In late 1943, Admiral Mineichi Koga, Yamamoto's successor, proposed that the Bismarck Archipelago must be held, in order to buy sufficient time to strengthen the 'inner line' of Japanese defence and fight a decisive fleet action. This 'inner line' ran through the Marianas, Truk, the Solomons, New Guinea, Timor, the Dutch East Indies and Burma, and would allow Japan to prepare for a counteroffensive in April–May 1944. But even as Japanese planning was proceeding, the Allied position was improving daily. On 1 November 1943, US Marines landed on Bougainville in the northern Solomon Islands. Seven weeks later, another large contingent of Marines landed at Cape Gloucester in New Britain, a Japanese stronghold. *Australia, Shropshire, Warramunga* and *Arunta* supported the landings. Over the next few months, Allied naval forces cut the supply lines to many of Japan's island garrisons which were already isolated and vulnerable. On 29 January 1944, the Allies landed on the Admiralty Islands in the Bismarck Sea to the north of New Guinea. Two months later, the Admiralties were finally captured and would play an important role as a Pacific naval base. The Allies were then able to isolate Rabaul completely and avoid the great loss of life that would have occurred in recapturing it. With the retaking of Hollandia in Dutch (West) New Guinea in April 1944, the occupation of the island of Biak to the north-west of New Guinea in May, and a successful naval offensive on the

Mariana Islands, in the Central Pacific during June, the Allies were ready to recapture the Philippines. Earlier, on 27 March 1944, Vice-Admiral Thomas Kinkaid USN, who had succeeded Admiral Fletcher, reorganised his fleet with most of the American units in Task Force 74 forming Task Force 75. The only remaining American units in Task Force 74 were the destroyers *Mullany* and *Ammen*.

The RAN's role in these operations, which began in mid-1943, was twofold. The first was to provide ships for charting and beach survey work prior to the landings. The second was to deploy ships capable of serving with the Allied naval covering and support forces. *Australia*, *Shropshire*, *Arunta* and *Warramunga* were part of Rear Admiral Sir Victor Crutchley's Task Force 74 and were part of all the major actions in this period, while HMAS *Westralia*, recently converted for service as a Landing Ship Infantry (LSI), landed US forces at Arawa in Bougainville on Christmas Day 1943. Japanese resistance was crumbling. At the Allied 'Octagon' Conference in September 1944, the Combined Chiefs of Staff agreed on a timetable for the final defeat of Japan.

> 15 September, *South West Pacific forces occupy Morotai; Central Pacific forces occupy Peleliu in the Palau Islands; on* 5 October, *occupy Yap with Ulithi to follow;* 15 October, *South West Pacific forces occupy Talaud Islands;* 15 November *land at Sarangani Bay, Mindanao;* 20 December *at Leyte. South West Pacific and Central Pacific forces then combine to occupy either (1) Luzon to secure Manila by* 20 February 1945, *or (2) Formosa and Amoy on the China coast by* 1 March 1945.

The major Allied landing in the Philippines was to be staged at Leyte Gulf. The Allies assembled 550 landing and support ships with surface and air protection provided by the US Third Fleet. Ships of the RAN provided the only Australian participation in the operation. *Australia*, *Shropshire*, *Arunta* and *Warramunga* were involved as elements of Task Force 74 with the three Australian LSIs—*Westralia*, *Manoora* and *Kanimbla*—tasked with landing troops from the US 21st Regimental Combat Team. The frigate *Gascoyne* and *HDML* (Harbour Defence Motor Lanch) *1074* were engaged in surveying and mine-sweeping duties; the destroyers *Norman* and *Quiberon* were part of a diversionary operation conducted by the Eastern Fleet; and the Australian auxiliaries *Poyang*, *Yunnan*, *Bishopsdale* and *Merkur* were part of the Seventh Fleet's Service Force. At 9.00 a.m. on 20 October

1944, an armada of boats and destroyers made for the beaches of Leyte Island. *Australia*, *Shropshire*, *Arunta* and *Warramunga* provided naval gunfire support during the landing. In one of the most theatrical moments in military history, General MacArthur waded ashore in the afternoon to fulfil his promise to the Filipino people that he would return. Early the following day, commemorated within the RAN as Trafalgar Day, a Japanese kamikaze aircraft struck *Australia*'s main superstructure. There was an explosion and intense fire which wrecked the bridge and foremast. Thirty men were either killed outright or died later of their wounds; one of these was Captain E.F.V. Dechaineux RAN. Another 64 were injured. Within four days of the first landing 144 800 American troops were ashore on Leyte Island.

Having anticipated an American assault on the Philippines, the Japanese assembled three separate task forces, which converged on Leyte Gulf on 25 October. Poor coordination and faulty intelligence meant that the Japanese failed to press their tactical advantage and suffered heavy losses in aircraft carriers and battleships. A powerful Allied force consisting of six American battleships and including *Shropshire* and *Arunta* engaged and destroyed the Japanese fleet that had been ordered to enter Leyte Gulf through the Surigao Strait. The Allies now exercised almost complete control of the seas: having established a strong position at Leyte, their next objective was Luzon Island in the northern Philippines, which was to be captured after a landing planned for 9 January 1945 at Lingayen Gulf. The seven major RAN units that had been involved in the Leyte Gulf operation, including the hastily repaired *Australia*, were also present for the Lingayen landings.

En route to the landing, *Australia* was located a hundred miles west of Subic Bay on 5 January when she was attacked by yet another kamikaze. Despite concentrated anti-aircraft fire, the Japanese plane plunged into the cruiser's upper deck amidships. *Australia* again suffered a severe loss of life but was able to continue operating. Another kamikaze struck *Arunta*, killing two men. On 6 January, the RAN contingent, strengthened by *Warrego* and *Gascoyne*, entered Lingayen Gulf and engaged in a pre-landing bombardment. The ill-fated *Australia* was hit again by a kamikaze in the late afternoon and twice more on 8 January. *Australia*'s courageous ship's company had managed to make running repairs before the landing. After yet another kamikaze attack on the day of the Lingayen landing, *Australia* was withdrawn and would never again fire her guns in anger. A total of 44 men had died in the kamikaze attacks. As the flagship returned

"Jap carrier be damned! It's the *Australia*."

By "Olly"

A wartime cartoonist managed to find a lighter side to the RAN Flagship HMAS Australia*'s kamikaze attacks.*

home, the hard-working N Class destroyers *Norman*, *Nepal* and *Napier* were taking part in operations to regain control of Burma.

While the Allies were planning the final onslaught against Japan, the British were able to turn more of their attention to the East and the need for a unified campaign in the Central Pacific. The British Pacific Fleet, the largest British naval force ever deployed to the region, was placed under the command of Admiral Sir Bruce Fraser at Trincomalee on 22 November 1944. He assumed the title Commander-in-Chief, Pacific Fleet and flew his flag in the battleship HMS *Howe*. The fleet arrived in Fremantle on 4 February 1945. It was led by the battleship *King George V* and consisted of four fleet aircraft carriers, three cruisers and ten destroyers. The RAN's representation was substantial: the destroyers *Quiberon* and *Quickmatch* comprised part of the Fourth Destroyer Flotilla; there were sixteen RAN ships in the 21st and 22nd Minesweeping Flotillas; and *Napier*, *Norman*, *Nepal* and *Nizam* further enlarged the Australian contingent. The Pacific Fleet saw action for the first time in late March in an operation to prevent Japan from reinforcing the island fortress of Okinawa. As the fleet was engaged in the major actions against the Japanese in waters encircling the home islands, RAN ships including destroyers, frigates, corvettes and the LSIs were involved in a number of mopping up operations around New Guinea, Bougainville and Borneo. By July 1945 Australian ships were operating in Japanese home waters with *Quickmatch*, *Quiberon* and the four N Class destroyers shelling Japanese territory. The end was near.

Closer to home, a sense of calm had been restored. It had been six months since a merchant ship had been attacked off the Australian coast. The German U-boat *U 862* had sunk the American liberty ship *Peter Sylvester* on 6 February 1945, several hundred miles off Fremantle. Although various defensive measures remained in force, coastal shipping was steaming without interference. Australian industry was also in a position to support the final advance on Japan. Work on the dry dock at Garden Island had continued throughout the war, hampered only by the Japanese midget submarine attack. The Captain Cook Graving Dock was ready for initial flooding in September 1944. Three 60-inch centrifugal pumps designed to discharge 70 500 gallons per minute allowed the dock to be emptied of its 50 000 000 gallons of water in about four hours. The construction was sufficiently advanced to allow the emergency docking of the aircraft carrier HMS *Illustrious* on 2 March 1945, three weeks prior to its official opening by the Governor-General, His Royal Highness the Duke of Gloucester. To mark the occasion, the bow of the new River Class frigate, HMAS *Lachlan*, broke a ribbon extended across the entrance to the dock. The Chief of Naval Staff, Admiral Sir Guy Royle, provided a clear statement of the role the graving dock would play in the present war and in Australia's future.

> *The envisaging of a capital ship dock for Australia was a recognition of the extent to which the defence of the Commonwealth depends, and must always depend, upon seapower. The island-continent itself has 12 000 miles of coastline. Its geographical position makes the sea at once its rampart and its weakness. If*

ocean highways linking us with the rest of the world can be policed and protected, then our security from occupational invasion is assured. If those highways come under domination, then we are constantly and directly menaced. It is the function of seapower to preserve the use of the seas for one's own ships, and to deny that use to the enemy. But seapower cannot be exercised to the full if the warships which are its most potent instrument cannot be assured of an adequate haven for docking, repairs and maintenance. A dock which cannot accommodate ships of all sizes is not an effective ancillary to seapower.

The dock indeed performed a vital role until the end of the war. One of the last major wartime repair tasks undertaken by the dockyard was on the British aircraft carrier HMS *Formidable*. A kamikaze had crashed into the carrier's flight deck, opening up the deck and buckling the special 3-inch thick armour plate. It was an enormous repair job, requiring great skill. Two armour plates weighing fourteen tons each were removed and straightened while a third was replaced by a plate of lesser thickness although of similar quality steel. By the end of its first year in operation, the graving dock would have accommodated the biggest warship it has ever docked: the battleship HMS *Anson* displacing 45 360 tons. It also repaired five other British capital ships: *Indomitable*, *Duke of York*, *Implacable*, *Indefatigable* and *King George V*.

As General MacArthur planned for an invasion of the Japanese home islands in 1946, the dropping of atomic bombs on Hiroshima (6 August) and Nagasaki (9 August), and the Soviet Union's belated declaration of war on Japan brought the war in the East to its inevitable conclusion. On 15 August 1945, Japan accepted an unconditional surrender. The war was finally over after 55 million people had died. The Naval Board sent a general signal announcing the end to hostilities:

The Naval Board send to the RAN their warm appreciation of the fighting spirit, devotion to duty and cheerfulness which have been shown by all officers and men during nearly four years of intensive warfare against the Japanese enemy. Sea power assisted by air power stemmed the Japanese advance which in 1942 threatened Australia. The relentlessness of sea power has been largely responsible for destroying the enemy's power of aggression and desire to carry on the war, thus causing him to surrender. In this

> *application of sea power the RAN has played its part with conspicuous efficiency, producing a record of which we can feel justly proud.*

When the Japanese surrender was signed on board USS *Missouri* on 2 September 1945 in Tokyo Bay, nine RAN ships were present. At similar ceremonies throughout South-East Asia and the South-West Pacific—the last on board HMAS *Diamantina* at Ocean Island—Australian warships represented the nation's contribution to the war and the central role that sea power had played in defeating Japan.

When hostilities had commenced in 1939, the RAN had just over 5000 officers and men. This number had peaked at 39 650 on 30 June 1945, including 2617 women serving in the WRANS and 57 in the RAN Nursing Service. With 337 ships in commission, the RAN was the fourth largest navy in the world. During the war, three destroyers, six frigates, 60 corvettes (four for service in India), four boom defence vessels, 35 *Fairmile* motor launches, and nine HDMLs were built in Australia. A total of 1911 naval personnel died as a result of hostilities. Sixteen officers and 111 sailors were killed in action; ten officers and 35 sailors died of wounds inflicted in combat; a further 144 officers and 1407 sailors were missing presumed dead; 4 officers and another 65 sailors were drowned; and six officers and 113 sailors of the 324 men captured by the enemy died as prisoners-of-war. It is noteworthy that, over four years of combat, only one American officer, the liaison officer lost in *Canberra*, had been killed while serving in an Australian warship. Thirteen British officers and 22 sailors were killed in RAN ships during the war.

In contrast to the First World War, Australians had accepted greater responsibility for the conduct of the naval war effort at sea and ashore. RAN officers and sailors had shown themselves to be every bit the equal of their British counterparts, and worthy of the trust placed in them by the parliament and the people. The war left many legacies. The RAN's order of battle was larger and more diverse than ever before; shore infrastructure around the continent and in New Guinea had been expanded to include docking and maintenance facilities, complemented by a string of naval bases and depots to support maritime defence activity.

The RAN would also enjoy the political and public support of the many thousands of men and women who had worn naval uniform during hostilities, and who had developed an abiding affection for the navy that would be crucial to its future wellbeing. The many ex-service associations that were formed after 1945 were testimony to the fellowship of the sea many had unexpectedly embraced when the nation called them to arms in the most cataclysmic struggle the Western world had ever known.

With the fighting over, it was now time to preserve the peace.

9

Wars and rumours of wars 1946–64

When the Japanese surrendered on 15 August 1945, the Emperor also agreed to an Allied occupation of his country and the disarmament of its military forces. Two days later, the Australian War Cabinet agreed to provide the British Commonwealth Occupation Force (BCOF) with two cruisers and two destroyers, to be based at the port of Kure on the Japanese inland sea. From February 1946 until June 1950, fifteen RAN ships were detached to BCOF in addition to those involved in repatriating Australian troops and prisoners of war. Their duties were diverse. *Quiberon* was involved in the sinking of seventeen Japanese submarines off Kyushu as part of Operation Bottom. *Quadrant* assisted in the disposal of Japanese chemical weapons in Operation Lewisite. Most of the RAN ships were part of the 'Kyushu Patrol' aimed at preventing the prohibited movement of Korean nationals into southern Japan. Most of the illegal immigrants had assisted the Japanese during their occupation of the Korean Peninsula (1911–45) and sought refuge beyond Korea. During her BCOF attachment, *Warramunga* was made available for service in China, where Communist forces were gaining ascendancy over the Nationalist forces of Chiang Kai-shek, on the condition that the ship was used 'for mercy purposes only'. *Warramunga* provided a naval presence in Nanking as the Communists advanced, while four HDMLs were dispatched to Hong Kong to strengthen the Local Defence

Flotilla. When the Indian and New Zealand contingents were withdrawn, responsibility for the Kure naval base rested largely with Australia and it became known as HMAS *Commonwealth*.

Corvettes attached to the 21st and 22nd Minesweeping Flotillas based in Hong Kong cleared shipping lanes and engaged in anti-piracy patrols in Chinese waters. The 20th Minesweeping Flotilla, led by *Swan* and consisting mainly of corvettes, HDMLs and General Purpose Vessels (GPVs), commenced its postwar operations in December 1945. It operated along the coast of Australia, particularly the Great Barrier Reef and Bass Strait, and went as far afield as New Guinea and the Solomon Islands. In three years a total of 1816 Allied and enemy mines were detected and destroyed. It was hazardous work. On 13 September 1947, the corvette *Warrnambool* struck one of the 116 mines laid in a defensive field by HMAS *Bungaree* off Cockburn Reef, Cape York in November 1943. The ship was sunk, with the loss of four men and another 25 wounded. Mines washed ashore or sited in inaccessible locations around the Australian coast and in the South-West Pacific were the responsibility of the Rendering Mines Safe Organisation (RMSO) based at naval shore establishments in Townsville, Port Madang, Thursday Island and Port Moresby.

The two main areas of operations overseas were Rabaul–Tarangau immediately after the war and as part of a navy–army unit in the Solomon Islands from 1950 to 1953. The work carried out in the Solomons followed *Warramunga*'s visit to Guadalcanal (the main island in the group) in 1947 to provide a 'steadying influence' during local political unrest and *Shoalhaven*'s goodwill visit to Malaita in 1948. Several Australian ships were deployed to the Dutch East Indies. As Indonesian nationalists had proclaimed their independence after the Japanese surrender, it was vital that no Australian ship should be seen as contributing to the fortunes of either side in the conflict between the Indonesians and the Netherlands. The corvette *Gladstone* transported Dutch troops from Darwin to West Timor while her sister ship *Gawler* anchored off Celebes to prevent open conflict breaking out between Dutch and Indonesian nationalist forces. The River Class frigate *Macquarie* was deployed to the South-East Asian Command (SEAC) in 1946. She was tasked with transporting war crimes investigation units, prisoner-of-war search parties and war graves registration units. (SEAC units were withdrawn on 30 November 1946.) The following year, the frigate *Barcoo* transported an Australian official delegation to East Timor as part of a reciprocal goodwill visit by the Portuguese Governor, and visited the

Dutch administrative centre in West Timor. Fisheries protection in Australia's northern waters also resumed after the war together with patrols aimed at preventing smuggling and gun-running.

The only new area of activity for the RAN was on the continental shelf of Antarctica. *Wyatt Earp*, originally an American-owned research vessel that would later serve as an examination vessel under the name HMAS *Wongala*, was commissioned as HMAS *Wyatt Earp* in November 1947 to support the Australian National Antarctic Research Expeditions (ANARE). Unfortunately, the ship sustained severe damage on transit through the Southern Ocean and was withdrawn from Antarctic work. The Landing Ship Tank (LST) 3501, later renamed HMAS *Labuan*, completed the first of seven voyages for the ANARE in 1947 with the commanding officer, Lieutenant Commander G.M. Dixon RANVR, claiming possession of Heard Island for Australia on 22 December 1947. Scientific stations were established at both Heard and Macquarie Islands. *Labuan*'s final voyage concluded when the ship arrived at Fremantle on 1 March 1951.

By this time, almost all those men and women who had joined the RAN for war service had been demobilised. Although the Australian Army and the RAAF had rapidly shed large numbers of men and women within twelve months of the war ending, only 20 per cent of naval personnel had been discharged. The navy did not reach its lowest postwar strength—10 188 personnel—until June 1949. The size of the fleet had, however, been drastically reduced with more than 200 ships being decommissioned or returned to civilian service. From a wartime peak of 337 ships, by October 1947 the RAN numbered 27 ships in commission with 34 at various levels of availability in reserve.

As the ships which were still in commission attended to a variety of duties, the Naval Board was confronted with the complex question of the shape and structure of the forces Australia should maintain in peacetime for its own defence and in the light of the continuing part it would play in regional and global strategy in which the United States had replaced Britain as the pre-eminent power. This presented a challenge to the traditional relationships shared by Australia and the RAN with Britain and the Admiralty, both of which still played an important role in guiding local naval development after 1945. The imperial connection would preserve a vital element of continuity with prewar policies and ensured that 'Australia remained involved in the security problems of the United Kingdom and the Commonwealth'.

The specific principles underlying the postwar British Commonwealth defence network were determined at the April–May 1946

Prime Ministers' Conference. These principles made mention of the United Nations (UN), but were silent on the form of cooperation Britain or the Commonwealth should seek or expect from the United States. The principles did, however, make clear that each Commonwealth member assumed the primary responsibility for its own strategic environment and for providing the bulk of forces needed to maintain the right of self-defence incorporated within Article 51 of the UN Charter. It was not until after the conference that Australian Prime Minister Ben Chifley told Federal Parliament that 'the approach to a common scheme of defence for this area should be by agreement between the United Kingdom, Australia, New Zealand, and thereafter with the United States of America, and later with other nations with possessions in this area'. The initial problem was determining with some precision the nature and direction of threats to Australia in the foreseeable future.

In the early postwar years Australia, and to varying degrees the Commonwealth as a whole, saw its potential enemies simply as the proponents of international communism. As the threat was perceived to be global, Australia's defence considerations centred on its possible contribution to the global strategies of its major allies and the forces needed to support this larger role, more so than those required for regional or local defence. In its 1946 review of Australia's strategic circumstances, the Defence Committee concluded:

> *. . . the basic ingredient of Australia's defence must be Empire Cooperation since the size of this country demands for its defence, armed forces and an industrial potential quite beyond our present capacity . . . [Australia's military forces] should be so organised and trained that they can fit in as complete units with Empire Forces in any theatre, keeping particularly in mind the Pacific Theatre.*

In response, the Chifley Government stated that Australia would maintain a military capability consisting of

> *the forces to be placed at the disposal of the United Nations for the maintenance of international peace and security, including regional arrangements in the Pacific; the forces to be maintained under arrangements for cooperation in British Commonwealth defence; and, the Forces to be maintained to provide for the inherent right of individual self defence.*

The main message was that Australia would consider its security objectives on two levels, global and regional, as Sir Frederick Shedden, the Permanent Head of the Department of Defence, explained in 1947.

> *The United Kingdom has not the capacity and strength she formerly possessed . . . The British Commonwealth could not fight a major war without United States cooperation. A world system of collective security must be made effective and supplemented by a series of regional arrangements. It is in respect of a regional arrangement in the South-West Pacific that Australia can play a leading part in Empire cooperation and in collaboration with the United States and also other nations with possessions there.*

Yet planning for this scheme of common defence—expressed within the terms of the ANZAM Pact—did not commence until 1948. ANZAM was essentially an informal security arrangement entered into by Britain, Australia and New Zealand for the defence of the Malayan area, which had become the target for Communist-inspired insurgency. Britain's involvement was integral to Malaya's status as a British possession. The Malayan 'Emergency' was declared in June 1948 and would last for twelve years. Among the British proposals for ANZAM was the recommendation that the protection of the sea lines of communication between Commonwealth nations should be a joint responsibility. Therefore, Australian planning for ANZAM was 'at first limited to the defence of sea and air communications in the region, while co-ordination was conducted at service level and did not involve firm commitments by the Governments concerned'. This accorded with the 1947 Strategic Basis paper prepared for the Government. It noted:

> *Australia is situated at the end of a series of islands extending from South East Asia. Except for those islands to the north and the north-west, she is surrounded by oceans. Her geographic position, therefore, is such that no hostile power without possessing command of the sea and local air superiority could successfully invade Australia.*

Having identified Australia's maritime geography as an asset, the Chifley Government concluded:

> *the security of Australia depends ultimately on the command of sea communications . . . The provision of seapower for the defence*

> *of seaborne trade simultaneously furnishes a deterrent against seaborne raids. As adequate naval strength is of fundamental importance to Empire and Australian defence, the RAN should be maintained at a strength which is an effective and fair contribution to Empire defence.*

With this strategic guidance endorsed by the Government, the RAN's specific postwar force structure was set in place by the announcement in 1947 of a five-year plan including provision for two light fleet carriers. Some progress had already been made on the acquisition of an Australia naval aviation capability. In September 1946, the Chief of Naval Staff, Vice-Admiral Sir Louis Hamilton, was authorised to discuss the RAN's requirements with the Admiralty. The Admiralty recommended the acquisition of two light fleet aircraft carriers and three carrier air groups made up of Firefly and Sea Fury aircraft that would move between a naval air station and an operational carrier. In June 1947, the Naval Board received permission to proceed with the first stage of the naval aviation plan and ordered two *Majestic* Class carriers. The first, laid down in April 1943 as HMS *Terrible* and launched in September 1944, was renamed *Sydney*. At almost 700 feet in length and displacing 19 550 tons, *Sydney*'s complement was 1343 officers and sailors. After being modified to meet Australian requirements the carrier was commissioned on 16 December 1948 and accepted for service in the Royal Australian Navy on 3 February 1949, by Captain R.R. Dowling RAN. The 20th Carrier Air Group, formed on 20 August 1948 at the Royal Naval Air Station at Eglinton in Northern Ireland, completed its pre-embarkation work-up in March 1949. *Sydney* sailed from Glasgow on 12 April 1949, arriving in Australia on 25 May. The aircraft were then off-loaded to HMAS *Albatross*, the new RAN Air Station at Nowra on the New South Wales south coast, commissioned on 31 August 1948. The carrier returned to Britain in July 1950 and embarked two more squadrons—808 Squadron (Sea Furies) and 817 Squadron (Fireflies).

The second carrier was laid down in April 1944 as HMS *Majestic* and launched in February 1945. The RAN purchased *Majestic* in 1949 and renamed her HMAS *Melbourne*. In order for the ship to operate the latest jet aircraft, a substantial modification program was initiated: the flight deck lifts were enlarged; an angled flight deck was constructed; a steam catapult was fitted; and a mirror landing system was installed. *Melbourne* was commissioned on 28 October 1955. The carrier air group consisted of Sea Venom fighters, Gannet anti-submarine aircraft and Sycamore helicopters. In 1952 the *Colossus* Class carrier HMS *Vengeance* came to the RAN on loan, while *Melbourne* was being completed. For a brief period in 1955, Australia had three aircraft carriers. This was quite an achievement for a navy which had no naval aviation capability at the end of the Second World War.

The second HMAS Melbourne *at sea with naval aircraft embarked. The two other RAN carriers are in line astern. (RAN official)*

But the acquisition of two aircraft carriers and the general policy on which it was based seemed to reflect operational thinking and tactical concerns rather then strategic priorities. There was a tension between specific force structure acquisitions and the wholly collective outlook of Commonwealth defence. Rather than examining ways of integrating the RAN into larger fleet organisations or agreeing to construct ships in Australia which might have compensated for the operational weaknesses of its allies and major operating partners, Australia tried to establish a capability for independent naval operations while conceding that it could not mount such operations for very long on such a scale. It should be pointed out, in mitigation, that the naval force which America would devote to any Asia-Pacific conflict was undisclosed. Consequently, Australian defence planning had to allow for this uncertainty by maintaining forces capable of undertaking some of the roles that Australia might have expected the United States to fulfil.

The Admiralty was also aware of this uncertainty. When Prime Minister Robert Menzies met with the British Chiefs of Staff in July 1950 to discuss the coordination of strategic planning, the First Sea Lord, Admiral Sir Bruce Fraser, remarked that

> *one of the greatest difficulties presented to Australia in deciding on the deployment of forces outside Australia was the lack of information of US plans for the defence of the Pacific. Before sending troops outside their own country Australia would naturally want to know what reliance could be placed on the Americans for defending their coastline.*

It became apparent that Australian defence planning would proceed on a much firmer basis if some firm undertaking or agreement were given by the United States. This was already proceeding in the naval sphere of operations.

British Commonwealth ANZAM officers had already made good progress in joint planning for the defence of sea communications in the region. Indeed, coordinating naval activity in the ANZAM and Pacific regions had been the subject of discussions between the newly appointed Chief of Naval Staff, Rear Admiral John Collins (the first Australian-trained officer to hold the post), and American naval commanders during the Australian Admiral's visit to Pearl Harbor in 1948. Collins met with the Commander-in-Chief Pacific (CINCPAC), Admiral Dewitt Ramsey USN, and agreed on a plan to regulate naval control of shipping with an accepted boundary for this purpose between the ANZAM region and the CINCPAC area of command. Admiral Collins later told Lord Fraser:

> *I had a very enjoyable and fruitful visit to Pearl Harbor and found that they were thinking on much the same lines as ourselves. For your own information the limits to our proposed area of responsibility on the North and East, were decided in consultation with Commander-in-Chief, Pacific Fleet [Admiral Arthur Radford USN] so as to have some workable arrangement in the event of the only possible trouble.*

While these talks were proceeding, higher level discussions were taking place between representatives of the same three nations with the objective of negotiating a formal defence pact for the Pacific. American concerns about Asia and its desire to have Australia support the terms it was proposing for a peace treaty with Japan led to a more flexible American view on such an arrangement. These talks resulted in the ANZUS (Australia, New Zealand, United States) Treaty, signed in mid-1951 and formally ratified in April 1952. At the same time, since British Commonwealth security arrangements held that Australian and New Zealand maritime forces would be deployed to the ANZAM area, the discussions then in progress between Admiral Arthur Radford USN (as CINCPAC) and Vice-Admiral (later Sir) John Collins continued.

> *A secret conference was held in Hawaii from 26 February to 2 March 1951 for the purpose of coordinating peacetime operational naval responsibilities between the two commands. Since Australia had been delegated leadership in the development of Commonwealth plans for the defence of sea communications in the ANZAM region, Collins represented the British Commander-in-Chief, Far East and the British Chiefs of Staff; Radford represented the US Navy; and, Commodore Frank Ballance, a Royal Navy officer seconded to the RNZN, represented New Zealand as its Chief of Naval Staff. The two admirals continued their discussions until September 1951 when they signed a service level agreement providing for peacetime liaison, naval planning and provisions for the security of sea communications in the Pacific between the two Allied commands. Peacetime liaison was limited to the exchange of naval officers between Honolulu and Melbourne (the location of Navy Office) with provision for further exchanges of naval officers to Wellington and Singapore in wartime. The RNZN had associate status in this agreement until 1978 while the Royal Navy remains a formal party (although of undefined status) as well, despite the withdrawal of its permanent naval presence from the region in September 1975.*

Specific 'areas of maritime responsibility' were established by the Radford–Collins Agreement which were used for naval planning, but which did not constitute regions of national responsibility as delivered by formal international treaty. As a peacetime arrangement, the ANZUS navies directed their efforts to the reconnaissance of their respective areas and surveillance of hostile warships, submarines and merchantmen. For wartime contingency purposes, the three parties developed plans for the control and protection of Allied shipping in the western Pacific and eastern Indian Oceans. At the heart of the agreement was the principle of coordinating national responsibilities to effect a rationalisation of naval resources. In other words, given the fact that the ANZUS Treaty made all three Allied partners equals, in a political sense, each of the three navies assumed an obligation to carry out agreed missions in their own maritime regions. The US Navy was pleased with the outcome of both the ANZUS and the Radford–Collins discussions. Admiral Arthur Radford later commented that he had

> *known of a prospective ANZUS conference for some time and had urged that it be held in Pearl Harbor or nearby. The prime ministers of Australia and New Zealand, and my many military friends in both countries, had all mentioned that they felt rather left out of things. They did not belong to the North Atlantic Treaty Organisation (NATO) and yet had a keen interest in all that went on there. They had been happy to join with CINCPAC in planning for shipping control and other wartime emergencies in the* Radford–Collins Agreement. *But they wanted another connection, and if they could not belong to NATO they wanted to be on their own with the United States, not as partners in a pact including the British.*

The results of the Radford–Collins conferences met with a varied reception in Australia. The Menzies Government was dissatisfied with the outcome because it did not include Australian participation in global war planning, but the participants were able to reach agreement on the need for peacetime naval cooperation in the areas of escort, convoy routing and diversion of traffic, reconnaissance, anti-submarine warfare, local defence and search and rescue. Significantly, even before the ANZUS Treaty was formally ratified, the basis for Allied maritime security and cooperation in the greater South-West Pacific had been established. Both the Radford–Collins Agreement and the ANZUS Treaty also represented American naval and diplomatic dominance in the Pacific region. While planning and some operational aspects had been formalised, it appears that the United States was still a little uncertain as to what relationship it should develop with the Australian and New Zealand forces. In the five years after the Second World War, the American Chiefs of Staff had tended to see Europe as the main area for communist expansion. This created a tension between American objectives in Europe and its responsibilities in the Pacific.

The higher priority accorded to Europe also meant that American naval power experienced waning fortunes in the Pacific. The first major postwar show of American naval power in the East was not until December 1949 when the Chinese Nationalist Government under Chiang Kai-shek withdrew from the mainland to Formosa (later renamed Taiwan) and established the Republic of China. For the next seven months, at least one American carrier would remain on patrol in the Straits of Formosa to defend the Nationalist Government from a possible invasion by the Communist People's Republic led by Chairman Mao Tse-tung. The only occasion on which the US Navy played a direct role in affairs affecting Australia's immediate region was in the negotiations leading to the recognition by the Netherlands of the Indonesian Republic led by President Sukarno. In November 1947, Vice-Admiral Cooke USN, Commander Naval Forces, Western Pacific, was directed to dispatch a ship to receive, accommodate and support a UN Good Offices Committee sent to arrange a peaceful transition from colonial government to independent nationhood. The transport ship USS *Renville* arrived in Batavia on 2 December 1947 and served as a neutral site for the discussions. The truce signed on 17 January 1948 by the Indonesian nationalists and the Dutch on board the transport was known as the 'Renville Agreement'.

In dealing with nations like Australia, the US Navy's greatest problem was having insufficient ships to meet the many competing demands placed upon it. *Basic Naval Establishment Plan No. 1* of 1950 announced that the new super-carrier *United States* was cancelled and that the US Navy's order of battle would be cut from 731 ships to 688 ships, including a reduction in the number of operational carriers from eleven to eight. Two aircraft carriers, six light cruisers, four minesweepers, seventeen amphibious ships and several service force (tenders and auxiliaries) vessels from the Pacific Fleet were all scheduled for reserve. In addition, sixteen destroyers, two attack transports and four major service force ships were selected for redeployment to the Atlantic. Of the eight attack carriers (CVAs) then in the active fleet, only *Boxer* and *Valley Forge* were to remain in the Pacific during 1950, thereby precluding the continuous operation of one carrier in the Western Pacific. The Pacific Fleet would be assigned three of the seven escort carriers (CVEs) but none of the small aircraft carriers (CVLs). The single cruiser assigned to Naval Forces, Far East would be withdrawn in early 1951. The Fleet Marine Force in Naval Forces, Western Pacific—consisting of two landing teams, one fighter squadron and one transport squadron—would also be withdrawn. But the allocation of these assets had to be reconsidered when the North Korean Army unexpectedly invaded South Korea on 25 June 1950.

The existence of two nations on the Korean Peninsula was a direct consequence of the Cairo Declaration signed on 1 December 1943. It provided for the division of the peninsula for the purposes of disarming the occupying Japanese forces at the 38th parallel of north latitude. When the Red Army occupied Manchuria and the northern half of the peninsula in August 1945, it established a communist regime under Kim Il-sung while an ostensibly democratic, capitalist state was created in the south. Tensions between the two fledgling states had not been expected to end in war. Following the communist invasion, the UN Security Council met and, assisted by the Soviet boycott of proceedings, demanded that the Soviet-backed North Korean troops withdraw immediately from South Korea. When there was no reply from Pyongyang, the Security Council adopted a resolution seeking from member states 'such assistance to the Republic of [South] Korea as may be necessary to repel armed attack'. Sixteen nations indicated their preparedness to provide forces for the UN's first major mission in the cause of resisting aggression. The United Nations Command (UNC) was directed by General Douglas MacArthur, still the effective ruler of occupied Japan. Despite the Australian Government's willingness to assist, Australia's armed forces were far from ready for war.

When the fighting began, the frigate HMAS *Shoalhaven*, attached to BCOF, was immediately offered for UN service, along with the destroyer HMAS *Bataan*, which was shortly to relieve *Shoalhaven*. Three weeks later, the Australian Government announced that *Warramunga* would join the UN Force in Korea. In less than a week, the BCOF Commander in Japan, Lieutenant General Sir Horace Robertson, sought guidance as to whether the Commander of the Seventh Fleet, Admiral Arthur Struble USN, could deploy *Shoalhaven* and *Bataan* in the Formosa area. Prime Minister Menzies refused. For the duration of the action, Australian ships were placed within the overall command of General Douglas MacArthur but under the direct operational control of Rear Admiral William Andrewes (and later Rear Admiral Alan Scott-Moncrieff), Flag Officer Second-in-Command of the British Far East Station. Andrewes exercised command off the Korean Peninsula as 'Commander of the West Coast Support Group'

(Task Group 96.8) which consisted of the British Commonwealth ships deployed in the area.

The UN's first objective was to halt the North Korean advance. After UN troops withdrew to the south-eastern corner of the peninsula, American and British carrier strike aircraft, naval gunfire support and maritime patrols halted the advance and prevented the North Korean forces from being reinforced or supplied by sea. Within a week of the invasion, *Shoalhaven* was escorting the American ammunition ship *Sergeant George D. Kearthley* into Pusan Harbour before the arrival of troopships carrying US ground forces from Japan. For the next two months, *Shoalhaven* was engaged in escort and blockade duties until she was relieved by *Warramunga* on 6 September.

Bataan had arrived at Okinawa on 1 July and was ordered to join the US Escort Group at Sasebo. To avoid the peninsula being completely overrun, *Bataan* provided naval gunfire support for an amphibious landing of the First Cavalry Division at Pohang on the south-east coast. After a brief period of anti-submarine patrolling, *Bataan* was the first Australian ship to exchange fire with a shore battery during the war. *Bataan* destroyed four of the seven North Korean guns without sustaining any damage before departing for Kure and a rendezvous with Prime Minister Menzies. When *Bataan* escorted a convoy to Pusan, she met with *Warramunga*, which had also arrived in the theatre of operations. On 15 September, both ships supported the daring UN landings at Inchon leading to the recapture of the South Korean capital of Seoul before the end of the month.

General MacArthur then invaded North Korea and occupied Pyongyang. *Warramunga* was part of a naval gunfire support force assisting the landing of troops at Wonsan. Although hampered by Soviet mines laid in the harbour approaches, the landing was unopposed. *Warramunga* then proceeded with the battleship *Missouri* to Chongjin near the border with China and Russia to conduct a series of bombardments on enemy positions. By this time, the Chinese had entered the war, and had driven MacArthur's forces from North Korea and again occupied Seoul. By the end of the year, *Bataan* and *Warramunga* were blockading the Yalu Gulf to prevent the landing of enemy reinforcements. After the great success of October, the war had turned decisively against the UN. For the next six months, both Australian ships carried out shore bombardments, patrol and escort duties as the UN desperately tried to preserve its hold on the peninsula's south. A stalemate developed with both sides recognising that the line of truce—the 38th parallel of north latitude—was likely to remain the border between the two Koreas.

To bolster the UN's position at the negotiating table, a show of naval strength was ordered in the Han River near Kaesong. HMAS *Murchison* under Lieutenant Commander A.N. Dollard RAN had relieved *Bataan* and was deployed to the Han with HMS *Cardigan Bay* and the Korean frigate *PF62*. After sailing up river, the flotilla shelled a number of communist positions with *Murchison* alone firing 1056 4-inch rounds and 1030 40-millimetre Bofors shells. On several occasions the Australian frigate was engaged at short range by shore batteries, mortars and field guns that attempted to prevent her escape. Despite being hit four times, *Murchison* was not badly damaged. Operations in the Han River were terminated in November 1951. By the end of the year, the aircraft carrier *Sydney* had arrived in Korean waters with the destroyers *Anzac* and *Tobruk*.

The Australian Government agreed to make *Sydney* available as a short-term relief for the British carrier HMS *Glory* whose officers, sailors and air group needed respite after protracted operations. *Sydney*'s Sea Fury and Firefly aircraft launched their initial attacks on 10 October in the Kojo area on the peninsula's south-east coast, inflicting substantial damage on communist supply lines, artillery batteries, troop concentrations and civil infrastructure. The next day, *Sydney*'s air group flew 89 sorties against a range of targets in addition to spotting for a shore bombardment led by the battleship *New Jersey*. Three of *Sydney*'s aircraft were damaged by anti-aircraft fire. After the second day of flying, the British CINC Far East Station (FES) sent a signal to the captain of *Sydney*.

> *Your air effort in the last two days has been unprecedented in quantity and high in quality. It has been a magnificent achievement on which I warmly congratulate you. Though it is invidious to particularise, the [gunnery] spotters did a first class job and USS* New Jersey*—with the Commander of the Seventh Fleet embarked, said that they were the best they had yet seen.*

After enduring the terrors of typhoon Ruth, which damaged aircraft and injured some of the ship's company, *Sydney* flew 474 sorties in the Han River area between 18 and 28 October. Although three aircraft were shot down and 28 damaged by anti-aircraft fire, no aircrew were lost. It was not until 5 November that *Sydney* suffered her first casualty. Lieutenant K.E. Clarkson RAN was killed when his Sea Fury was hit by anti-aircraft fire. A week later, *Sydney* had completed 1000 sorties in just over eighteen days of combat flying. To do this with the loss of just one pilot was a remarkable achievement. In December 1951 and January 1952, a further two pilots were lost as the number of sorties flown from *Sydney* neared 2500. A total of four Firefly and nine Sea Fury aircraft had been lost through enemy action or misadventure by the time the carrier sailed for Sydney with *Tobruk* on 27 January 1952 to be replaced by *Warramunga* and *Bataan*. *Sydney*'s deployment was also noteworthy as the first occasion on which the RAN operated larger American air assets. Two US Navy Sikorsky Dragonfly helicopters and their crews were flown from *Sydney* while on station off Korea. Their purpose was carrier-borne air–sea rescue and communications. Both aircraft were returned to the US Navy before the carrier sailed for Australia.

During the second half of 1952, *Anzac* and *Tobruk* returned to Korea with the frigate *Condamine* arriving for her first Korean deployment in August. The only other vessel to serve in Korean waters, the frigate *Culgoa*, replaced her sister ship *Condamine* in April 1953. By this time the RAN had developed particular expertise in naval gunfire support, joint naval–military operations in confined waters and the enforcement of naval blockades. With the signing of a truce at Panmunjom on 27 July 1953, armed action came to an end. As part of a United Nations force consisting of sixteen nations that had not previously operated together under a unified command, the Australians managed to preserve the Republic of South Korea from one of the most fanatical and ideological regimes of the twentieth century. In three years of fierce fighting, 339 Australians were killed, 29 taken prisoner and a further 1257 wounded. Of that number, three were killed on naval service and another four wounded. Korean losses on both sides were substantial with estimated death tolls of more than 1.5 million men, women and children. As a peace settlement did not follow the truce, a succession of RAN ships including *Shoalhaven*, *Murchison*, *Culgoa*, *Condamine*, *Arunta* and *Tobruk* were all committed to armistice patrols over the next two years. *Sydney* would return to Korea in late 1953 for a six-month deployment.

There were many lessons to be learned by the RAN from the Korean War. Two problems were immediately apparent in deploying with a force that was predominantly American in command and constitution. Both the Royal Navy and the RAN found it difficult to operate under the more rigid US Navy command systems which saw operational orders issued at a higher level and with more detail than either navy had experienced in the past. This was an echo of Admiral Collins' comment on the US Navy during the Second World War.

> *I found the US Navy invariably obeyed orders almost blindly, and the orders were often so detailed as to cramp initiative. For example, some operation orders laid down the actual courses to be steered rather than the position to pass through. There appeared little opportunity left to the subordinate to exercise his discretion.*

The second problem had always been a possibility and it quickly became apparent that British Commonwealth ships could not rely heavily on American logistic support. Their different engineering and ammunition requirements forced them to rely on the British Far East Fleet supply system based in Singapore. In addition to straining the already overworked organisation, the whole system had to be modified to meet the various demands generated by the Korean War. A special ammunition delivery system was also developed using Hong Kong as a base.

While neither problem was insurmountable, the biggest challenge for those serving in the Australian ships was reacquainting themselves with American operating procedures, and tactical signalling and manoeuvring, particularly in the area of screening. There was also the distinct American naval style of operations.

> *[Australian] commanders had to accustom themselves to having much less scope for initiative than they had enjoyed under British command . . . American naval staff officers wrote orders which covered the most minute details and were of self-defeating length. Such large numbers of routine reports were called for by American authorities that the Commonwealth vessels adopted a policy of polite resistance to those demands in order to fulfil their operational tasks.*

It was fortunate that ships from the Commonwealth navies were placed under the command of Rear Admiral Alan Scott-Moncrieff, Admiral Andrewes's replacement. He was a shrewd commander who showed no hesitation in resisting any American methods or practices he considered tactically unsound or wasteful of resources. There is no doubt that the RAN ships operated well under direct British command and control and that both the British and Australian governments preferred it that way. Scott-Moncrieff prevented the RAN ships from being exposed to excessive or unnecessary risk, and was cognisant of the tension that would have been created on a political level between Australia and the United States had an RAN ship been lost in the war. This is reflected in the official historian's conclusions on the Australian naval involvement in the Korean War.

> *The close contact achieved between the British and Australian ships serving in Korea helped to maintain the already strong British traditions in the RAN, although American influence also contributed to the RAN's development. Command relations between the two navies were unmarred by significant problems . . . Out of this experience grew an acceptance by the US and Britain of Australian responsibility for organizing and directing some major naval exercises of the South East Asia Treaty Organisation [SEATO] and other Allied forces. No other ally was given this continuing degree of respect and authority.*

This close relationship was reflected in many of the commendations Australian warship captains received when they commanded small task elements consisting of American ships, which responded readily to Australian tactical control. As the commanding officer of HMAS *Anzac*, Commander G.G.O. Gatacre RAN, remarked: 'I received ready and complete co-operation from the commanding officers of the US Navy ships which served under my operational command. It was indeed a pleasure to have served with them'. The American Commander of the East Coast Blockade and Patrol Group stated in reply that as Commander of the Songjin Element of the UN Force, Gatacre's 'whole-hearted co-operation, marked aggressiveness, and administration of the units under his command contributed materially to the efficiency of the Task Group'.

The Korean War saw the RAN operating almost totally as an adjunct of the Royal Navy under overall American command. The Naval Board in Melbourne determined which ships would serve in Korea and finalised details for their deployment with CINCFES staff. Higher level liaison between Australia and the UN Command for naval operations was conducted through the Royal Navy. The Korean War broadened even further the RAN's exposure to the US Navy, but despite Britain's diminishing profile in Asia it was not a direct stimulus for closer Australian–American naval relations. Of greater significance was the RAN's limited ability for sustained combat operations. The Australian naval involvement in Korea was not extensive, but strained the RAN's ability to maintain a small number of operational units in a remote conflict zone.

After the Korean War and with the growing possibility of communist infiltration in Indochina, Australia saw advantages in a regional defence arrangement to supplement ANZUS. Following the Geneva Conference on Indochina and Korea in 1954, Australia supported American proposals to create a defence organisation in South-East Asia, although not on the scale of NATO. Accordingly Australia, France, New Zealand, Pakistan, the Philippines, Thailand, Britain and the United States all signed the SEATO defence pact just seven weeks after the Geneva Conference. Australia was committing itself to direct involvement in regional military activities. The doctrine of 'forward defence' was now at work. This accorded with Australia's changing view of the world which now focused on South-East Asia. By October 1953, ANZAM council meetings had begun planning for the formation of a Commonwealth Far East Strategic Reserve based in Singapore commencing on 1 April 1955. Australia agreed to contribute two warships, *Warramunga* and *Arunta*. This commitment would be met by rotating two ships through the reserve on six-month deployments with the newly commissioned aircraft carrier and RAN flagship HMAS *Melbourne* making an annual three-month visit. Regular multinational naval exercises were also commenced under the SEATO umbrella. As part of their service with the Strategic Reserve, several RAN ships participated in offensive operations against communist insurgents in Malaya. *Anzac* and *Tobruk* shelled terrorist concentrations south of Jason Bay in Johore during September 1956. The following year *Quickmatch* and *Quiberon* also bombarded terrorist positions at Tanjong Siang in Johore. *Quiberon* later conducted anti-smuggling patrols off North Borneo in 1958. The Malayan Emergency would not end until 1960.

The Strategic Reserve precluded any suggestion that the British Commonwealth did not still play a major role in defining Australia's foreign and security policies. But the significance of former imperial ties was fading fast. When President Gamal Abdel Nasser's Egyptian Government nationalised the Suez Canal in 1956, the British Government (in covert collaboration with both the French and the Israelis) decided to counter Nasser's move by resolving unilaterally to use force. Such an act was in defiance of the United Nations and despite opposition from the United States. The only solid support the

British Government received was from Australia and New Zealand. Although maintaining the old tradition of loyalty among the dominions for Britain, Australia would play no direct naval or military part in resolving the crisis. (Several Australian officers and sailors were on exchange service in Royal Navy ships operating in the area. They were subsequently awarded the Naval General Service Medal with Suez clasp.) The Americans remained opposed to the Anglo-French policy and were unhappy that Australia had become diplomatically involved. This was, however, the last time Australia would involve itself in a conflict in which its own interests were marginal for the sake of showing political or military solidarity with Britain.

From the mid-1950s the concept of a foreign policy equilibrium developed whereby Australia would attempt to lean on both Britain and the United States according to need and circumstance. Australia was increasingly finding common causes with the United States, while Britain's power and ability to pursue any shared concerns began to wane. But the equilibrium, set sliding towards the United States, would travel only so far. The United States could and would never be a substitute for what Britain had been. For Australia, America was a friendly but foreign sovereign nation. It would never be a 'mother country' or a benign imperial master. After the Second World War Australia had become a fellow traveller with Britain and shared an enormous amount of history, heritage, culture and aspiration, but these fellow travellers departed from each other in the mid-1950s as they pursued different paths to different destinations. The particular relationship that now needed to be furthered and protected was that with the US Navy, given that America's physical involvement in South-West Pacific affairs was still minor.

The American naval presence in the western Pacific during the Eisenhower years (1952–60) was achieved at a substantial price to the United States. Serving as the spearhead of American policy for containing communism in the Far East and the Mediterranean, naval ships and their complements (including marine amphibious units) were deployed to foreign stations for considerable periods. Inevitably, operational readiness and morale declined. The average naval task force cruise to the Western Pacific lasted eight or nine months but, more frequently than not, the period was extended because of minor aggressions and other emergencies. These problems partly accounted for the Australian continent not seeing that much of the US Navy. The US Navy usually operated to the north and the east of the Indonesian archipelagoes. At this time the United States was most concerned with continuing Chinese aggression against Taiwan and the deteriorating situation in Indochina. In early 1954, the carriers *Wasp* and *Essex* entered the Gulf of Tonkin to support French forces against the communist Viet Minh. When the French were defeated at Dien Bien Phu in May 1954, the US naval task force withdrew until July 1954 when it returned to assist in the relocation of 310 000 people from North Vietnam to South Vietnam after the country was divided by international agreement. Operation Passage to Freedom involved 109 American ships and aircraft. Also in July 1954, aircraft from the carriers *Philippine Sea* and *Hornet* provided air cover while survivors from a Cathay Pacific airliner, shot down by Chinese communist fighters, were recovered from the sea.

Early in 1955, the US Navy was back off the coast of Taiwan, assisting in the evacuation of some of the Nationalist-held Tachen Islands bombarded by Chinese communist forces. An American carrier was retained permanently in the Straits of Formosa over the following few years to counter a build-up of Chinese communist forces near the adjacent mainland coastline. This was increased to three carriers in September 1957. When the Communists shelled the Quemoy Islands in August 1958 and the prospect emerged of the islands being cut off from Taiwan, six carriers were deployed to the area with Marine forces drawn from Japan. The emergency passed when a cease-fire was accepted on 6 October 1958. This was the largest, but also the last for some time, American show of naval force in the waters separating Taiwan and China. Although carrier groups were occasionally deployed to the Straits of Formosa, the necessity of having a substantial naval force permanently stationed in or around Taiwan had ended. These deployments had been a drain on the US Navy in the decade following the communist victory on the Chinese mainland in 1949 but the respite was short-lived. As soon as the troubles between China and Taiwan ended, conflict broke out between North and South Vietnam, and within Laos where Pathet Lao forces supported by the North Vietnamese had captured several strategically important positions. Both situations attracted the presence of American naval forces in the Gulf of Tonkin, including imposing carrier groups led by *Lexington, Coral Sea* and *Bennington*.

As the US Pacific Fleet was continually under pressure from budget cuts and the great uncertainty of politics and diplomacy in East Asia to fulfil its commitments, there were few occasions when there were sufficient ships available for a small task group to be deployed as far south as Australia. The United States was never overly concerned by events in either Indonesia or Malaya, which were handled predominantly by the British. The land 'Down Under' was simply too far 'down under'. It would not play any substantial role in American naval policy or activity. This presented a series of problems for Australia and its navy. By the end of 1956, the RAN had reached a strategic and technological turning point. From a wartime peak of 337 ships and 39 650 serving personnel, the RAN now consisted of 41 ships and just over 10 000 personnel. The two carriers *Sydney* and *Melbourne*, together with the Fleet Air Arm, were an enormous drain on the Navy's budget and left few resources for other operational requirements. Although a reduction in the size of the fleet had been expected after 1945, the navy had not envisaged the decline continuing for so long.

Of the three ships ordered in the 1930s, the sole surviving Modified *Leander* Class light cruiser, *Hobart*, had been paid off in 1947. The wartime replacement for the heavy cruiser *Canberra*—HMS *Shropshire*—served in the postwar RAN until she was decommissioned in 1949. The flagship *Australia* became the longest serving RAN warship to that time when she was paid off in August 1954 after 26 years. The three Tribal Class destroyers *Arunta*, *Warramunga* and *Bataan* were obsolete and needed replacing. The two Battle Class destroyers *Anzac* and *Tobruk* were due for modernisation or replacement. Four of the Q Class destroyers *Quadrant*, *Queenborough*, *Quiberon* and *Quickmatch* had been converted to fast anti-submarine frigates, but their best days were behind them. The same could be said for the remaining River Class frigates. *Barcoo* had become a survey ship. *Diamantina* and *Gascoyne* were being converted for scientific work. The two *Grimsby* Class sloops were old and tired. *Swan* became the training ship and *Warrego* a survey vessel. The four Bay Class frigates *Condamine*, *Culgoa*, *Murchison* and *Shoalhaven* had all been paid off by 1956. The six LSTs had either been sold or placed in reserve, unlikely ever to return to operational service. The four *Kookaburra* Class boom defence vessels *Kookaburra*, *Kangaroo*, *Karangi* and *Koala* had been laid down before or in the early stages of the Second World War. Their days were numbered. Their cousin, *Kimbla*, was completed in 1956 but would be converted for service as a trials ship for the Naval Research Laboratory in 1958–59. The only substantial naval construction program (other than the two *Battle* Class destroyers) during the postwar period was three 3000-ton *Daring* Class destroyers. They were ordered in 1947 and built largely to serve as escorts for the navy's carriers. The first to be laid down, *Voyager*, would enter service in 1957. *Vendetta* and *Vampire* would be completed in 1958 and 1959.

The principal problem faced by the Naval Board was that too many ships needed replacing at the same time. Not for the first time was the RAN facing the problem of 'block obsolescence'. To make matters worse, a planned upgrade to allow the carrier *Sydney* to operate new classes of jet aircraft was cancelled. After a brief period operating as a flying training ship, *Sydney* was to be paid off in May 1958. At the same time there was a proposal to disband the Fleet Air Arm and decommission the recently arrived *Melbourne*. Things were not looking too hopeful for the navy. By 1959 the RAN was on the verge of being reduced virtually to a coastguard. Much had changed since 1939 when the navy was the premier Australian service. The RAN was now considered of inferior status to the army and air force and was portrayed, predominantly by senior RAAF officers, as inappropriate to Australia's strategic circumstances and irrelevant to modern war fighting tactics and operations. Although the Naval Board believed it had marshalled some very cogent arguments to support the retention of *Sydney* and *Melbourne*, Cabinet remained unconvinced of the need for fixed-wing naval aircraft. In any event, the navy needed new ships to replace those at the end of their operational service. A decision was made to build four new anti-submarine frigates similar in design to the British Type 12 Class. Two would be built at Cockatoo Island and two at Williamstown. The first two, *Yarra* and *Parramatta*, were laid down in early 1957; construction of the second two ships, *Stuart* and *Derwent*, commenced in 1958 and 1959. These ships were, however, at the lower end of the capability spectrum other than in anti-submarine warfare. The RAN still needed a front-line surface combatant class.

With Britain unable to supply Australia with the newest and best weapons and platforms, and in the absence of a sufficiently developed local industrial and technology base, there was no alternative to approaching the Americans. This had first been mooted in 1951 when the First Sea Lord, Admiral Fraser, informed Vice-Admiral Collins that he was unable to meet the RAN's request for the loan of several *Daring* Class destroyers and advised against purchasing small American destroyers in making good any deficiencies in the RAN's escort strength.

> *You will understand, I am sure, when I say that we would much prefer that the RAN stuck to British built or British type ships. The reasons are many—standardisation of equipment and subsequent logistic problems, training problems, and last but not least, tradition and sentiment. What is more important is that the US ships*

> *are a great deal more expensive than ours. Once a move towards the US had been started I feel it might be difficult to resist further diversions.*

The emotional dimensions of the bond between the RAN and the Royal Navy were never more publicly stated or acutely felt. There was great reluctance in turning to the Americans as Collins' successor, Vice-Admiral Sir Roy Dowling, told the British Chief of Naval Staff, Lord Louis Mountbatten:

> *In the past we have depended entirely on the United Kingdom as you know, and . . . would prefer to keep it that way. We are fully conscious of the help always afforded by the Admiralty, of the fact that we have benefitted from Admiralty research, design, production, know-how and even detailed blue prints for every ship built or weapon manufactured in Australia. We have also deliberately and consistently worked on the principles of complete interchangeability with the Royal Navy in all respects, including officers, men, ships, equipment and logistics generally. We now find ourselves at the crossroads solely because we very much doubt whether the United Kingdom can provide us with what we want in the future.*
>
> *We have no wish to become Americans but there is a strong belief in this country that the sensible course of action for Australians is to acquire war equipment from the United States now. Our very telling reason is of course that, certainly in a global war, our salvation in the Pacific will depend chiefly on the aid of that country. For that we are not less loyal members of the Empire.*

A grasp of the hard political and economic realities in 1957–58 dictated an Australian approach to the US Navy.

The real cost to Australia would not be the initial purchase price of the ships but maintenance and technical support. Australian logistic arrangements and dockyards were designed and equipped to conform to British standards. This had been set out clearly in a memorandum of 1950: 'Royal Navy policy . . . has a bearing on any consideration of the immediate future Naval shipbuilding program in Australia, as Australian naval policy is to conform to Royal Navy types of ships and equipment'. Acquiring American ships would entail an enormous expense in terms of shore infrastructure and logistics management. But if it needed to happen, the Americans were more than happy to assist. As the Australian Naval Attaché to Washington in 1955 remarked, the US Navy was prepared to make a great deal of information available to the RAN.

> *The only restriction on my access to US Navy affairs would be the 'need to know'. Thus, I would not be given access to information on nuclear weaponry, for example, because the RAN had no nuclear capability and therefore no 'need to know'. The arrangement worked very well; I cannot recall a single request being denied me; I do recall being given unstinted help, and guidance. I started sending monthly reports to the Naval Board, as well as separate reports on special subjects.*

The basis of a strong bilateral naval relationship had begun to emerge. But it *could* have been emphasised and furthered both during and after the Korean War. Weaning the RAN off the Royal Navy *could* have begun immediately on cessation of hostilities in Korea, as it was obvious that the demise of British naval power in the East was only a matter of time. The Naval Board *could* have examined the prospects and possibilities of standardisation with the US Navy in 1953–54 and considered buying or building American-designed ships which would be more readily integrated into a joint naval task group. The absence of long-term vision among some Australian naval officers tied the RAN to a declining Royal Navy that was always prepared to exploit the continuing emotional ties between the two navies for its own self-interested ends. The Americans were of course no less self-interested. Nonetheless, the political and diplomatic framework necessary for a bilateral naval partnership between Australia and America to flourish had already been established.

The first fruit of the new relationship was the Naval Board's recommendation that Australia purchase two (later three) *Charles F. Adams* Class guided missile destroyers (DDG-2s) then being built at Defoe's shipbuilding yard in Michigan. The first two ships were ordered on 6 January 1962 and the third just over a year later. They would be named *Perth*, *Hobart* and *Brisbane*. By 1963 it appeared as though the worst of the navy's troubles were over. The three *Daring* Class destroyers had entered service and were proving to be reliable ships. Two new Australian-built frigates, *Yarra* and *Parramatta*, had been commissioned and trials on new weapons systems were under way. The three DDGs were under construction and expected to enter service after 1965. *Sydney* had been converted for operations as a fast troop transport and, much to the relief of the Naval Board, recommissioned in March 1962. Six Ton Class minesweepers—*Curlew*, *Gull*, *Hawk*, *Ibis*, *Snipe* and *Teal*—were also acquired from the Royal Navy in 1961. They were suited for Australian conditions and performed a number of General Duties functions in addition to minesweeping and later minehunting. The Fleet Air Arm was also given a reprieve. The RAN did not have a great deal of depth in its order of battle but the Naval Board had averted its reduction to a mere coastguard.

By 1964, however, the Board was facing another serious systemic problem. This had little to do with hardware or equipment and would potentially take longer to address. After 1957, there was an appreciable erosion of public confidence in the navy's professional standards, caused by a series of mishaps and accidents beginning with an explosion on board the LST *Tarakan* alongside at Garden Island in 1950. Nine sailors were killed and the ship was subsequently found to be beyond economical repair. In 1956, the frigate *Queenborough* collided with the submerged submarine HMS *Tabard*, damaging the submarine's conning tower. In 1958, the newly completed destroyer *Vendetta* crashed into the dock caisson at Williamstown Naval Dockyard in Melbourne. Two years later during a gunnery exercise off Jervis Bay, a shell fired from *Anzac* unintentionally struck her sister ship *Tobruk*. The veteran of combat in Korea was later declared beyond economical repair. A month later the ammunition carrier HMAS *Woomera* blew up off Sydney and sank, with the loss of two sailors. In October 1963, five junior officers under training from *Sydney* were drowned in the Whitsunday Islands during a boating exercise. In January 1964, the engine room of the fleet tanker HMAS *Supply* was flooded and the ship settled to the bottom alongside Garden Island. But all these incidents were overshadowed by the events of 10 February 1964.

In preparation for service in the Strategic Reserve, *Melbourne* and *Voyager* were engaged in a night flying exercise twenty miles off Jervis Bay, prior to the re-embarkation of the air group following the carrier's refit. After experiencing some difficulty in 'finding the wind', *Melbourne* ordered *Voyager* to a new flying course and to assume plane-guard station. *Voyager*'s subsequent movements were inexplicable. At 8.56 p.m., *Melbourne* collided with *Voyager* at high speed. *Voyager* was cut in two; the bow section sank quickly with the stern section remaining afloat for three hours. Tragically, 82 men serving in the destroyer lost their lives in what became the greatest peacetime naval disaster in Australian history. Prime Minister

The damaged bow of HMAS Melbourne *after her collision with the destroyer HMAS* Voyager *on 10 February 1964. (RAN official)*

Menzies established a Royal Commission to inquire into the circumstances of *Voyager*'s loss. After 50 days of public hearings, the Royal Commissioner, the Honourable Sir John Spicer (Chief Justice of the Industrial Court), found that *Voyager* was to blame for the collision. But he also criticised the actions of three officers who were on the carrier's bridge at the time of the collision: Captain R.J. Robertson (the commanding officer), Acting Commander J.M. Kelly (*Melbourne*'s navigator) and Sub-Lieutenant J.A. Bate (a young officer-of-the-watch). These criticisms were unexpected, unjustified and unreasonable.

When the Spicer Report was tabled and debated in Federal Parliament in September 1964, Prime Minister Menzies outlined a number of reforms in naval operations and administration that were already being implemented, while many others were planned. There was to be no repeat of this terrible tragedy. In a motion moved by Opposition leader Arthur Calwell censuring the Government for the succession of naval accidents that had culminated in the loss of *Voyager*, Victorian Liberal backbencher John Jess was critical of the Government's handling of the tragedy. He was disappointed with the conduct of the

Royal Commission, the quality of its report and the treatment of Captain Robertson, who was appointed to the command of the Sydney shore training establishment HMAS *Watson*. Considering his posting to be a demotion and effectively an expression of a lack of confidence in his ability, Robertson sought permission to resign from the navy on 28 September 1964. The circumstances of his departure from the navy meant that he was ineligible for a pension. With Robertson gone and believing the collision to be an isolated incident of poor judgement, the Naval Board members hoped that *Voyager* would be soon forgotten by the Parliament and the people. They were wrong.

As the navy was preoccupied with handling the fall-out from the parliamentary debate of the Spicer Royal Commission and the many reforms the Parliament and media were pressing upon the Naval Board, the strategic situation in South-East Asia continued to deteriorate. After 1963, when the new nation of Malaysia arose out of a federation of the former colonial states of Malaya, Sabah (North Borneo), Sarawak and Singapore (which later withdrew), Indonesian President Sukarno embarked on a policy of 'Confrontation'. He considered the new nation to be part of a 'neo-colonialist plot' and later threatened to crush Malaysia, whose navy was initially commanded by RAN officers on secondment. Australian ships deployed to the Strategic Reserve were immediately made available for Malaysia's defence against Indonesian insurgents. *Yarra* and *Parramatta* were deployed in patrols off Malaysia in April 1964 to intercept any unauthorised craft. They were joined later in the year by all six Ton Class minesweepers and *Sydney*, which transported troops, ammunition, anti-aircraft guns and stores to Malaysia. By the end of 1964, Indonesia had dispatched paratroopers to Malaysia and was attempting to land armed infiltrators by sea in a number of locations. In the Singapore Straits, a vessel that made for Indonesian waters fired on *Teal*. The minesweeper returned fire and arrested the vessel, subsequently handing over the crew to the Singapore police. The security situation showed no signs of improving. The Coalition Government's long respite from adequate defence spending was over.

On 10 November 1964, Prime Minister Menzies announced that there had been 'a deterioration in Australia's strategic situation'. He explained that substantially increased spending on national defence was required. Although public attention was drawn to the most controversial element in the new defence program—the reintroduction of National Service (conscription) for the army—the RAN was to be enlarged by more than 3000 officers and sailors by 1967 and made the principal beneficiary of the funds provided for the acquisition of new and expanded capabilities. Despite the *Voyager* disaster and the public disquiet it had caused, the Government had expressed a powerful vote of confidence in the Naval Board and in the RAN's officers and sailors.

In the first year, there was an increase of 40 per cent in the navy's capital equipment budget. *Melbourne* was to be upgraded, while the Fleet Air Arm would take delivery of its third generation of new aircraft: Grumman S2 Tracker anti-submarine aircraft and McDonnell Douglas A4 Skyhawk fighter-bombers. The possibility of *Melbourne*'s replacement was raised, but no firm plans were made. The navy was awaiting the imminent arrival of *Perth* and *Hobart* from the United States. The DDGs possessed a formidable anti-air and surface warfare capability. After more than three decades without a submarine capability, the RAN's offensive capability would be strengthened by four new *Oberon* Class submarines, *Oxley*, *Otway*, *Ovens* and *Onslow*, to be built in Scotland. As there was also an emphasis on effective escort

An A4 Skyhawk about to be launched off the flightdeck of HMAS Melbourne. *(RAN official)*

vessels, the RAN was pleased to accept delivery of HMS *Duchess* from the Royal Navy as a short-term replacement for the *Daring* Class destroyer it had lost. (The US Navy had offered the Second World War destroyer USS *Twining* as a possible replacement.) Two new *River* Class frigates, *Swan* and *Torrens*, were ordered as permanent replacements for *Voyager*. This would give the navy ten escort vessels of which seven could be expected to be operational at any one time. The new fleet would be supported by the maintenance ship *Stalwart* being built at Cockatoo Island; the Tide Class replenishment ship *Supply*, which had recently entered service after several years as a Royal Fleet Auxiliary; and twenty new *Attack* Class patrol boats to replace gradually a number of old vessels including the wartime HDMLs. In overcoming 'block-obsolescence', a new fleet was being built. Many of the ships being paid off were also kept in 'strategic reserve' or 'mothballs' with the expectation that they could be returned to service within months in the event of an emergency.

Twenty years after the end of the Second World War, the RAN was a very different kind of navy preparing to fight a very different kind of war.

10

'Up top'

1965–72

Twelve months into its biggest peacetime expansion, the RAN was under pressure to meet increasing operational demands. Would the new navy be sufficiently large and capable when all of the new ships, submarines and aircraft entered service? Writing in the *Bulletin* during November 1965, Professor Tom Millar outlined a compelling case for a stronger navy with more diverse capabilities and the need for the Government to continue with its injection of additional funds into the RAN.

> *Perhaps the key question is the extent to which we can or should rely upon our allies to fill the gaps in our naval defence and strike capacity. This is not an easy strategic problem, but political factors compound the difficulty. There are important political reasons why we should have a more independent and more comprehensive capability than we have at present. In South-East Asia at any one time there are between 700 and 2700 Australian naval personnel, and between six and ten of Her Majesty's warships. They receive little of the publicity attracted by the Army's combat units but they make a steady contribution to the security of the area and to the Army's ability to stay there. They have helped deter or prevent Indonesian assaults on Malaya and Singapore. They are a reminder of our permanent presence and interest in the region.*

The scope of Australian naval activity was about to become even broader.

On 29 April 1965, Prime Minister Menzies announced in Federal Parliament that the Australian Government had received a request for military assistance from the Government of South Vietnam. In indicating the Government's intention to respond favourably with the offer of an infantry battalion for combat operations, the Prime Minister stated that 'the takeover of South Vietnam would be a direct military threat to Australia and all countries of South and South-East Asia. It must be seen as part of a thrust by Communist China between the Indian and Pacific Oceans'. The United States had already committed itself to offensive combat operations. President Lyndon Johnson had earlier suggested that Australia might provide minesweepers and landing ships for service in Vietnamese waters. The minesweepers were fully committed to the defence of Malaysia after May 1964, while the RAN did not have an amphibious warfare vessel. The naval contribution would initially be limited to the troopship HMAS *Sydney*. The converted aircraft carrier would transport the officers and soldiers of the First Battalion, Royal Australian Regiment (1RAR) together with equipment and stores to Vung Tau on the coast of Phuoc Tuy province in South Vietnam. The dockyard refit then in progress was curtailed and preparations were hastily made for the 27 May 1965 departure date. The newly commissioned HMAS *Duchess* would escort *Sydney* to her destination. This was not the first time Australian ships had entered a Vietnamese port. *Vampire* and *Quickmatch* had visited Saigon in 1962 to demonstrate Australian support for the imperilled South Vietnamese Government. The US Navy had already been involved in Vietnam for more than a decade.

The first formal detachment from the US Navy, eight officers and men, arrived in Saigon in 1950 as part of the navy section of the Military Advisory Aid Group (MAAG). Their task was to assist the Vietnamese and the French Navy in Vietnam. This pattern continued until 1963, by which time there were still only 742 American naval officers and men in South Vietnam. Units of the US Navy had been continuously deployed to waters off Vietnam since the early 1960s while the political situation in South Vietnam deteriorated and the US assigned its military personnel to South Vietnamese units in the field. The American naval presence was significantly strengthened after the destroyer USS *Maddox* was attacked on 2 August 1964 by North Vietnamese torpedo boats in the Gulf of Tonkin, 28 miles off the coast. The following day, another attack was staged on American warships although on this occasion they were 60 miles from the North Vietnamese coast. The two attacks, which became known as the Gulf of

HMAS Sydney, *en route to South Vietnam in June 1965, refuels from the fleet tanker HMAS* Supply. *Her escort, the destroyer HMAS* Duchess, *is also taking on fuel. (RAN official)*

Tonkin Incident, prompted retaliatory strikes from aircraft launched from the carriers USS *Constellation* and USS *Ticonderoga*. This retaliatory action lasted until February 1965 when a combined naval and air force started a campaign, Operation Rolling Thunder, of high-intensity bombing over North Vietnam. By September 1968 naval operations were under way off the demilitarised zone between North and South Vietnam, in the Gulf of Tonkin aircraft carriers were deployed for air strike and interdiction missions, and in the Mekong Delta anti-riverine infiltration operations were also in progress. By that time the US Navy had 38 386 personnel serving in or around Vietnam.

Sydney arrived in Vung Tau for the first time on 8 June 1965. After unloading 1RAR's personnel and equipment, *Sydney* sailed for the Singapore naval base. One of *Sydney*'s junior sailors, Able Seaman Neil McInnes, described the passage to Vung Tau:

> *As we got progressively closer to Vietnam, in the mornings we would go to action stations, called 'class three', in preparation for*

> *any defensive movements that would have to be made by the ship. As we got closer the intensity of the action stations would start to step up. Action station red was the imminent one in preparation for an enemy attack. The guns were 40/60mm anti-aircraft Bofors. These guns were on the sponsons on the side of the ship. The ship was so old that if they fired one all the decking around it fell into the sea because it was so rusty. We had a lot of small weapons on board; plus we had choppers armed with depth charges. When we got closer we would usually pick up an escort of American fighters, which would escort us right into Vung Tau.*

In her first two voyages to South Vietnam, *Sydney* transported 827 Australian troops, 1935 tonnes of cargo and 400 vehicles. For the next eighteen months, *Sydney* sailed to and from Vietnam in support of Australian land operations and became known affectionately as the 'Vung Tau Ferry' despite the hot and overcrowded conditions on board. Over the next seven years, *Sydney* would sail to Vietnam on 23 occasions accompanied by twelve RAN ships including *Quiberon*, *Queenborough*, *Anzac*, *Vendetta*, *Vampire*, *Duchess*, *Yarra*, *Parramatta*, *Stuart*, *Derwent*, *Swan* and *Torrens*. The Australian National Line (ANL) ships MV *Jeparit* and MV *Boonaroo* provided logistic support. *Jeparit* was commissioned into the RAN in December 1969 and made 42 voyages to South Vietnam between June 1966 and March 1972. *Boonaroo* sailed twice to South Vietnam in 1967.

Indonesia's 'Confrontation' with Malaysia continued as the war in South Vietnam steadily escalated. In early February 1965, the Australian Government decided to send an infantry battalion and a squadron from the Special Air Services Regiment (SASR) to Borneo where there had been a substantial build-up of Indonesian land forces. In March 1965 the destroyer escorts *Parramatta* and *Derwent* combined with *Melbourne* and other Commonwealth forces in a deliberate demonstration of sea and air power off Malaysia. The minesweepers maintained vigilant patrols in the Johore, Malacca and Singapore Straits, and in waters off North Borneo. In June 1965, *Yarra* bombarded eastern Sebatik Island off Sabah to harass and deter Indonesian infiltrators who had crossed the border. In three operations, *Yarra* fired 70 rounds at the retreating Indonesian forces in the border area of Sebatik. An attempted coup by Indonesian communists on the night of 30 September 1965 proved to be the turning point. In the wake of the failed uprising, there was considerable violence and devastating reprisals against the communists and their sympathisers. Although a number of RAN ships engaged Indonesian forces throughout 1966, the 'Confrontation' ended in August 1966 when Indonesia and Malaysia signed a peace agreement. There were now twelve RAN ships in the South-East Asian area with 3584 officers and sailors embarked. The overall strength of the navy had increased to 14 714, a rise of 1211 over the previous year.

With a steady increase in personnel and the delivery of new ships, the RAN's essentially minor role in South Vietnam was expanded when the Australian Government sent the first of a series of six-member clearance diving teams. Clearance Diving Team (CDT) 3 was sent to South Vietnam in February 1967 under the command of Lieutenant M.T.E. Shotter to serve with the US Navy as an explosive ordnance disposal (EOD) team. Initially based at Vung Tau but later relocated to Da Nang in Quang Nam province, CDT 3 was tasked with the various aspects of harbour defence. However, the divers also destroyed a number of Viet Cong bunker complexes and recovered sunken aircraft. In the four years that the eight contingents were in South Vietnam, 7441 ships were searched and made safe from mines and underwater sabotage by the 49 RAN clearance divers. There were several minor casualties but only one death by misadventure.

Several weeks after CDT 3's initial deployment commenced, the Minister for the Navy, Don Chipp, announced that HMAS *Hobart* would be the first RAN ship to serve as an operational unit with the US Seventh Fleet off Vietnam. The navy would now be involved in combat operations rather than support duties. Minister Chipp further stated that this would be a regular deployment with a destroyer to be rotated through the operational area every six months. *Hobart* arrived off South Vietnam in late March 1967 and was immediately sent into action against a Viet Cong stronghold in Quang Ngai province. The following day *Hobart* assisted a US Marine patrol pinned down by the Viet Cong and a week later offered similar support to the South Vietnamese Second Infantry Division north of Cap Mia. *Hobart* fired 27 rounds in the second operation and killed fifteen Viet Cong. Within a fortnight, the Australians had shown their efficiency and their ability to handle the new American ships.

The *Charles F. Adams* Class destroyers were ideally suited for operations off Vietnam. In addition to being new ships employing the latest technology, many of the officers and sailors who manned the ships in Vietnam had been part of the ships' companies which had taken delivery of the vessels from the builders in Michigan and participated in rigorous post-delivery trials with the US Navy. By the time *Hobart*

The destroyer HMAS Hobart *on the gunline off South Vietnam. (RAN official)*

arrived off Vietnam in 1967, a pattern of deployments had begun which would continue for over four years and bind the RAN and the US Navy together as never before. There were four main types of operations involving the Australian ships: the first two involved participating in longer term US Navy operations: Market Time (as an unattached participant) and Sea Dragon; the third and fourth, which occupied most of the operational service of the ships deployed after 1968, involved screening American aircraft carriers operating in the Gulf of Tonkin and providing naval gunfire support (NGS), as part of

Task Unit 70.8.9, on the 'gunline' off the Vietnamese coastline in support of land offensives and against enemy shore targets.

Operation Sea Dragon commenced in October 1966. The objective was to prevent the North Vietnamese from using the waters of the Gulf of Tonkin north of the Demilitarised Zone (DMZ) to ferry supplies, ammunition and personnel to South Vietnam. This had become a more important supply route for the North Vietnamese as the Allies had subjected the land routes to heavy bombing and deforestation campaigns. At first, Sea Dragon units were only permitted to fire on coastal batteries in North Vietnam in self-defence, while North Vietnamese fishing boats were exempt from attack. By the time *Hobart* arrived, the Sea Dragon force, enlarged to a cruiser and four destroyers, was authorised to fire on shore targets which were supporting coastal supply movements as far north as Thanh Hoa, a provincial centre less than 100 miles from the major North Vietnamese port of Haiphong. Until 1 November 1968 when President Lyndon Johnson suspended direct attacks on targets in North Vietnam, Sea Dragon units were kept extremely busy patrolling coastal waters off central Vietnam and interdicting waterborne logistic craft. The Australian ships were integrated fully into this operation, with the Australian destroyer captains frequently acting as tactical commander for the Sea Dragon forces.

While the RAN destroyers were not formally deployed to Operation Market Time, they gave assistance when their primary mission allowed them to do so. This was often the case when the Australian ships were deployed to the gunline. Market Time was an operation aimed at preventing the resupply of North Vietnamese or Viet Cong units from the sea. Although there were regional surveillance centres to which US Navy, Coast Guard and South Vietnamese Navy units were attached, the operation covered the entire length of the South Vietnamese coastline. The main focus of surveillance was in the Gulf of Tonkin and in the Gulf of Thailand. The Australian ships frequently tracked suspicious vessels and supported Market Time forces on an opportunity basis.

The third mission undertaken by some of the RAN ships—*Hobart* in her first deployment; *Perth* in her second deployment; and *Brisbane* in both her deployments—was screening the American carriers which were operating between Hainan Island and North Vietnam, designated 'Yankee Station'. There was nothing new in this duty for the RAN ships and their personnel who were experienced in escorting HMAS *Melbourne*. In addition to providing an anti-submarine and anti-aircraft screen, both threats being considered low, the destroyers were able to render assistance to the American carriers when required or recover the aircrew from any aircraft which ditched into the sea during launch or recovery from the carrier.

The main task of the RAN ships during the four-and-a-half years of operations was providing naval gunfire support. This applied to every destroyer sent to Vietnam. With detachments from the US Marine Corps First Air and Naval Gunfire Liaison Company posted to all military regions in South Vietnam, gunfire from the ships deployed on the gunline would be requested and then corrected by teams of shore spotters. The almost entirely computerised gunnery and fire control system in the Australian DDGs presented no special problems for gunline operations. The Australian ships rapidly distinguished themselves in this mode of operation, especially for their surface gunnery as *Perth*'s commanding officer during her second deployment, Captain (later Vice-Admiral) D.W. Leach, recalled.

> *The US Marines and Army forward spotters were always very complimentary about the RAN's bombardment accuracy and I'm sure that this was not just because we were valued allies, as some of the opening salvoes from US Navy ships needed rather dramatic corrections. It was the RAN's reputation for 'Firing for Effect' after an average of two ranging salvoes which led to a big US Navy drive for accuracy in concentrating more on ballistics, wind and battery alignment.*

Throughout their deployment to Vietnam, the RAN ships were fully supported with ammunition, fuel, food and other stores by the Seventh Fleet Mobile Logistic Support Force. This allowed the destroyers to remain at sea for extended periods. There were, however, some minor difficulties as *Perth*'s commanding officer during her third deployment, Captain (later Commodore) I.M Burnside, commented.

> *With regard to items not on the US Navy inventory, or which were outside normal US Navy coverage, we had to rely on Australian supplies. Here we did have problems, particularly when they had to come through Manila or Saigon. In the case of Manila we did not always have good support from the Embassy staff and, with Saigon, the marathon of their customs procedures was often impossible to master.*

While the Australian DDGs could be easily integrated into US Seventh Fleet operations off Vietnam, a greater challenge was the deployment of a British-designed ship to an American fleet. This would give a good indication of how important it was for the RAN to consider greater standardisation of its ships with those of its major operating partner. In August 1968, the Director of Plans at Navy Office in Canberra advised the Naval Board that, owing to maintenance cycles and other operational commitments, it would be extremely difficult to have another DDG replace *Brisbane* when that ship was due to be relieved off Vietnam in the second half of 1969. The prospect of sending a non-American-designed ship to the Seventh Fleet so concerned the Board that it dispatched a team of officers to Subic Bay to investigate the problems and difficulties associated with the deployment of a *Daring* Class destroyer. During an earlier visit to South-East Asia, the new Minister for the Navy, Bert Kelly, had spoken with a number of US Navy authorities who advised him that they 'regarded logistic support for the *Darings* as merely a problem to overcome'. With the expectation that any obstacles could be overcome, the necessary modification work began on *Vendetta* in late 1968.

At its second meeting in 1969, the Board decided *Vendetta* would indeed be deployed to Vietnam and that such a deployment would serve three purposes:

> *a) It would improve morale by allowing the crews of ships, other than DDGs, to participate in 'front-line' operations; b) It would be a test of the capacity to provide logistic support for a ship not built in the United States; and, c) It would give operational experience of the attachment of a* Daring *to a US task force.*

One could also have added that it would help the RAN to overcome its fleet planning problems. The cost of modifying *Vendetta* was justified by the board's earlier intention to effect such modifications during the ship's approaching half-life refit. The principal problem was the supply of 4.5-inch ammunition with the appropriate fuses fitted. Careful planning by the Fleet Staff in Sydney ensured an adequate supply of ammunition was provided to *Vendetta* with minimum modification to US resupply procedures. Despite her older and more cumbersome gunnery and fire control system, *Vendetta* nonetheless made an impressive contribution to the Allied effort, participating in a range of operations as wide as that of the DDGs, while firing some

13 709 rounds from her main armament. The *Daring* trial had been an unqualified success. After a series of rotations, the last RAN destroyer to serve in Vietnamese waters was *Brisbane*. Her deployment lasted from April to September 1971 and involved carrier escort duties and NGS. *Brisbane*'s return to Sydney on 15 October brought to an end four-and-a-half years of sustained destroyer operations.

After announcing the destroyer deployments in 1967, Navy Minister Don Chipp intimated that the RAN commitment to Vietnam would be further increased with the dispatch of a specially formed aviation unit, to be known as the RAN Helicopter Flight Vietnam (HFV). The RAN HFV arrived in South Vietnam in October 1967 under the command of Lieutenant Commander N. Ralph RAN and was fully integrated into the US Army 135th Assault Helicopter Company. The Australians flew troop-carrying helicopters and gunships. A detachment of RAN pilots also served with the RAAF's No. 9 Squadron based at Vung Tau between May 1968 and April 1969. The RAN unit to suffer the largest number of casualties in the Vietnam War was the RAN HFV.

Lieutenant Commander P.J. Vickers RAN was killed on 22 February 1968 when his Iroquois was hit by ground fire during an extraction of South Vietnamese troops at Xuan Loc. Lieutenant A.A. Casadio RAN and Petty Officer O'Brien Phillips and two American aircrew were killed on 21 August 1968 when their low-flying Iroquois crashed and burned. It was later discovered that a rocket-propelled grenade had hit the helicopter's engine. A fourth member of the RAN HFV, Sub-Lieutenant A.J.H. Huelin RAN, was killed on 4 January 1969 when his helicopter hit power lines near Saigon in bad weather. The last member of the flight to be killed was Leading Aircrewman N.E. Shipp. The gunship in which he was embarked crashed while engaging enemy troops south-west of Long Dinh. Another seven personnel were wounded in action and three injured in accidents. Given the highly dangerous and consistently hazardous missions allocated to the RAN HFV, the number of fatalities could easily have been much larger by the time the unit returned to Australia in June 1971.

While service with the US Army was in some senses an unconventional role for naval aviators, this did not deter the Naval Board from seeking a wider role for Australian aircrew. Having recently acquired the Skyhawks and the Trackers, both American built and configured, the RAN sought an opportunity for the aircraft and aircrew to be experienced and tested in battle conditions. Accordingly, in mid-1968, the Naval Board planned to offer six of its Skyhawk pilots and maintenance personnel for six aircraft to the US Navy. The plan, however, did not receive the Government's endorsement, and there were no further offers of naval aviators. *Melbourne* was, however, usefully deployed elsewhere providing a substantial Australian presence in the region. With so much operational activity keeping the navy fully occupied, there had not been much time to dwell on the loss of *Voyager* as the third anniversary of the collision came around. But *Melbourne*'s former captain, John Robertson, was still pursuing justice.

As part of his campaign to challenge Sir John Spicer's Royal Commission findings, in 1965 Robertson had interviewed Peter Cabban, *Voyager*'s executive officer throughout 1963, about the health and general wellbeing of the destroyer's commanding officer, Captain Duncan Stevens. After a tumultuous year serving alongside the volatile Stevens, Cabban retired from the RAN as a lieutenant commander and became a management consultant. After the loss of his old ship, Cabban had spoken with several of the survivors and had been told that Stevens had consumed a triple brandy shortly before the collision. He was stunned, as it was RAN policy for watchkeepers not to drink at sea. Cabban was just as surprised when he was not called to give evidence at the Royal Commission. In a dictated background statement, Cabban reported a number of incidents during the year before the collision when Stevens had consumed excessive amounts of alcohol ashore and had become unwell as a result. This information found its way into the hands of several Liberal backbenchers in Canberra, who pressed the Government for a fresh inquiry into the collision. After a dramatic parliamentary debate in which Prime Minister Harold Holt interrupted one of his own backbenchers, Ted St John QC, who delivered his maiden speech on the need for a new inquiry, the Cabinet agreed to a second Royal Commission to be conducted by three judges. Over 85 days, almost every aspect of the navy's corporate culture was analysed and assessed. The royal commissioners found that the sole cause of the collision lay with *Voyager*; no blame could be attached to any person serving in *Melbourne*; alcohol had not been one of the causes of the collision; but that Stevens had been unfit to command *Voyager* owing to ill-health. The Naval Board established a 'Committee on Public Relations' to develop a media strategy for handling the fall-out from the second inquiry. Following its first meeting, the committee told the Board that there was not much goodwill toward the navy within the media, that the commission's findings would be reported by journalists so as to emphasise its criticisms and that the navy's public image could only be restored gradually. Cabinet decided to offer Robertson an ex gratia payment of $60 000 as compensation for not being granted a pension. The Royal Commission report was debated in Federal Parliament in early April 1968. When it ended, an editorial in *The Australian* was headed '*Voyager*—Still Too Many Doubts'.

One week after the lively parliamentary debate was adjourned, HMAS *Hobart*, under the command of Captain K.W. Shands, arrived off the Vietnamese coast. On 13 April 1968 the Australian destroyer relieved USS *Henry B. Wilson* in the NGS task unit off the DMZ. Five days later *Hobart* participated in Sea Dragon operations off Cap Lay, coming under enemy shore battery fire on two occasions. After firing 3000 rounds in seventeen days of operations, *Hobart* sailed on 1 May for maintenance periods in Taiwan and Hong Kong before returning to the gunline on 20 May in support of land operations around Da Nang. *Hobart* deployed north to waters adjacent to the DMZ on 26 May for operations around the old Vietnamese capital city of Hue, and Cap Lay. On 2 June, the ship departed for Subic Bay and the replacement of her main armament gun barrels; six days later she was back off Vietnam for gunfire support operations with South Vietnamese and US Army units.

On 11 June, the Australian destroyer returned to Sea Dragon operations with Captain Shands acting as task unit commander. After coming under enemy shore fire during an attack on targets northwest of Cap Lay on 14 June, *Hobart* and two American destroyers, *Theodore Chandler* and *Edson*, were deployed the following day for surveillance of Tiger Island, a small rocky island thirteen miles off the coast from Cap Lay and five miles north of the DMZ. The island was suspected of being used by the North Vietnamese as a site for radar-monitoring of the Allied ships involved in Sea Dragon and NGS missions. As the ships were stretched to the limit in operational tasking, intelligence suggested that the North Vietnamese were supplying the surveillance unit stationed on Tiger Island under the cover of darkness. *Hobart* and the two American destroyers deployed with her were to prevent this resupply from occurring in addition to normal Sea Dragon operations.

While in waters between Tiger Island and Cap Lay in the early hours of 17 June, *Hobart* detected by radar an aircraft approaching from the west over Cap Lay. While over the Vietnamese mainland, the aircraft's 'Identification Friend or Foe' (IFF) transponder, which transmitted its identity, was turned off. When the aircraft reached the Gulf of Tonkin, the IFF transponder was turned on. While *Hobart* was attempting to confirm its initial assessment that the fighter was American, the aircraft fired a missile. It struck the Australian destroyer amidships on the starboard side. The warhead passed through a lower deck and penetrated the pantry of the chief petty officers' mess, a radar room and the missile director control room. It also seriously damaged the secondary conning position. The body of the missile then passed through the outer skin of the after funnel, damaging its uptakes, and ended up in the forward funnel.

With *Hobart*'s ship's company rushing to action stations, the still unidentified aircraft made another pass over *Hobart* and fired a further two missiles at short range. The second missile, striking *Hobart* three minutes after the first, penetrated the transom but resulted in little comparable damage as the missile warhead failed to explode. The third missile entered the destroyer very near to where the first had caused so much damage. It passed through the fan space, missile director equipment room and Number 2 director. The Ikara missile magazine was also damaged. In all, there were over two hundred holes in the destroyer's superstructure. Chief Electrician R. Hunt and Ordinary Seaman R. Butterworth were killed. A number of other sailors were injured, including Petty Officer D.J.T. Raymond, Leading Seaman W. Mieszkuc, Engineering Mechanic G.H. Sculley, Able Seaman K.R. Laity, Engineering Mechanic E.J. Holmes, Able Seaman J.R. Parker and Ordinary Seaman R.F. Davidson. They were not the first Australian sailors injured in ships deployed off Vietnam. Four members of *Perth*'s ship's company were injured during the ship's first Vietnam deployment when an enemy 3-inch shell sliced through the corner of the after 5-inch gun turret and exploded in an empty compartment.

When the attacking aircraft turned towards *Hobart* and appeared set for another attack, the destroyer's main armament engaged with five rounds. The aircraft fled when fired upon by *Hobart*. Although badly damaged, *Hobart* steamed towards the cruiser USS *Boston* and, in company with the destroyer USS *Blandy*, formed an anti-aircraft screen in the event of further air attack. A helicopter from USS *Enterprise* was then sent to convey Able Seaman Parker, Mechanic Holmes and Able Seaman Laity to a hospital in Da Nang. News of the incident and the ship's condition was then relayed to Australia.

> *Material damage put weapon and direction radars out of action; missile system and one mounting out of control, whilst one mounting was able to fire in local control. Main machinery was not*

> *damaged.* Hobart *has made repairs to 5-inch gun system, SPS 40 radar and missile system.* Hobart *has examined rocket fragments and at present assesses weapons as being of United States origin.*

Three watertight bulkheads, two watertight hatches and a number of non-watertight bulkheads had been holed. The ship's company collected rocket fragments after *Hobart* was relieved of her task unit command by *Edson* and proceeded to Subic Bay for repairs. It later emerged that *Hobart* had not been as unlucky as it first appeared. During the previous night, an American patrol boat participating in Market Time operations, *PCF 19*, was sunk near the DMZ with the death of five personnel. Shortly after *Hobart* had been attacked on 17 June, friendly aircraft also engaged *Boston* and *Edson* with *Boston* sustaining a missile hit but no serious casualties. Later in the same night the US Coast Guard Cutter *Point Dume* and another patrol boat, *PCF 12*, were also attacked.

The US Navy held an inquiry that was immediately broadened to include events on the two nights prior to the attack on *Hobart* when ground observers on the Vietnamese coast had reported sighting a number of enemy helicopters. These reports were apparently confirmed by surface radar in the vicinity. The suspect enemy 'helicopters' were fired upon by US Air Force fighters, which later reported possible destruction of the targets. During the inquiry it emerged that the aircraft which engaged *Hobart* was an F-4 Phantom fighter from the US Seventh Tactical Air Force based in Thailand. It had fired three of its four Sparrow semi-active homing, air-to-air missiles at *Hobart* from short range. The inquiry into the incident concluded that:

> *Positive reaction to a reported enemy air threat, difficulty in discriminating between air and surface targets on fighter aircraft radar in the low altitude attack environment, and inadequate coordination between friendly forces involved in the action contributed to the inadvertent attacks on friendly forces. No physical evidence of helicopters destroyed has been discovered in the area of activity nor has extensive reconnaissance produced any evidence of enemy helicopter operations in or near the DMZ.*

In the wake of the attack on *Hobart*, the RAN announced that:

> *Actions have been taken to provide improved coordination and control to minimise the possibility of such an occurrence. These*

> *include more effective methods for assuring that control centres ashore have full and timely knowledge of the location of all friendly naval vessels in the area. In addition, improved measures have been instituted for determining the precise location of all friendly aircraft, vessels and ground forces prior to issuing clearance to engage.*

The Naval Board accepted the inquiry's report and agreed with the steps taken by the US Navy to minimise the possibility of any repeat of the incident. The repairs to *Hobart* in Subic Bay took four weeks. This was followed by three days of sea trials where the gunnery system was tested and found to be working effectively. On 25 July 1968, *Hobart* was back on the southern gunline engaging shore targets near Da Nang where she remained until 10 August when transferred to Sea Dragon exercises.

While *Hobart* was being repaired in Subic Bay, *Melbourne* was undergoing an extensive refit and modernisation at Garden Island Dockyard to operate the new generation of aircraft. On 14 February 1969, the flagship was recommissioned and began a work-up off Jervis Bay before departing for South-East Asia on 5 May 1969 for multinational naval exercises. The legacy of *Voyager* was in the mind of every Australian ship's captain engaged in fleet operations with the carrier. There could be no repeat of the 1964 collision or anything like it.

On the night of 2–3 June 1969, *Melbourne* was exercising in the South China Sea with a combined naval force. The SEATO exercise, called Sea Spirit, consisted of *Melbourne* operating her aircraft with five escorts: three American ships, *Keys*, *Larson* and *Frank E. Evans*; the New Zealand cruiser *Blackpool*; and the Royal Navy destroyer *Cleopatra*. Shortly after 3.00 a.m., *Melbourne*'s commanding officer, Captain J.P. Stevenson, ordered *Evans*, which was ahead of the carrier, to take up plane-guard station astern. Stevenson and the Fleet Commander (FOCAF), Rear Admiral G.J.B. Crabb, had given strong warnings to all of *Melbourne*'s consorts prior to the exercise not to turn towards the carrier when taking station. Using voice radio, *Evans* was informed that *Melbourne*'s course was 260 degrees. The carrier's navigation lights were then turned to full brilliance. Unlike the hapless *Voyager*, *Evans* was not working up and had performed the manoeuvre four times already that night.

For 30 seconds after receiving the signal, *Evans* neither altered course nor speed. She was some 3600 yards ahead of *Melbourne* on her port bow. The destroyer's first alteration of course was to

HMAS Melbourne *in company with HMA Ships* Voyager *and* Vendetta. *(RAN official)*

starboard—towards the carrier. When she continued in this direction, Stevenson took immediate action to warn the destroyer over voice radio that she was standing into danger: 'Watch it, you are on a collision course.' At the same time, he directed *Melbourne*'s operations room to 'watch *Evans*. She appears to be on a steady bearing'. Stevenson had done everything that Captain Robertson, *Melbourne*'s commanding officer when she collided with *Voyager*, was criticised for not doing in 1964 when a collision with *Voyager* appeared imminent. In *Evans*, her captain, Commander Albert McLemore USN, was asleep in his bunk with two very inexperienced watchkeeping officers, Lieutenants Ronald Ramsey and James Hopson, on the bridge. Ramsey, aged 24, was not a qualified officer of the watch (OOW). Hopson, aged 28, was at sea for the first time as an officer. With *Evans* now on a steady course towards the carrier producing a relative closing speed of over 40 knots, *Melbourne* expected the American destroyer to take action on the warning signal acknowledged by *Evans*'s bridge staff.

As the destroyer maintained her course, a collision seemed inevitable and Stevenson took action to best protect his ship. Realising that putting *Melbourne*'s engines astern was pointless, Stevenson altered the carrier's course to port signalling with two blasts on *Melbourne*'s siren that her rudder was hard to port. It appeared as though the carrier's turn would allow *Evans* to pass narrowly ahead of her. But maintaining her stationing speed of 22 knots, the destroyer then reversed her wheel to starboard and under the carrier's bows. For the second time in five years, the luckless *Melbourne* cut another plane-guard destroyer in half. *Evans'* bow section sank very quickly, while her stern, which was tethered to the carrier after the collision, remained afloat for several days. She was then stripped of parts and sunk for target practice. Of the 273 members of the ship's company, 74 sailors were lost. Nearly all were located in the forward section. The Wessex helicopter squadron embarked in *Melbourne*, HS 817, received the US Navy Meritorious Unit Citation for its role in the rescue of 38 American survivors.

The Australian press, recalling the highly controversial *Voyager* disaster, featured headlines with the 'Here we go again' theme. *Melbourne* was tagged the 'jinx' ship while reporters alleged a strange hoodoo surrounded her every move. A USN–RAN Joint Board of Inquiry was established, presided over by Rear Admiral Jerome King USN. The five other members were Rear Admiral H.D. Stevenson RAN, Captain K.W. Shands RAN, Captain J. Davidson RAN and two USN captains. Unfortunately, the inquiry would prove to be one of the most disappointing incidents in the naval and national relations between Australia and the United States. The Americans appeared determined to reduce the culpability of the destroyer's captain, Commander McLemore. Lieutenant A.R. Vincent RANVR, sent to the inquiry to assist the RAN's legal adviser, Commander H.H. Glass QC RANVR, would say later of Admiral King's performance: 'I hope that if any Australian officer conducted a Board of Inquiry in this fashion his conduct would be described as disgraceful'.

There was little doubt that privately the Americans accepted full responsibility. Publicly, their attitude was very different. Having provided Stevenson with a copy of the Joint Board's report, excluding its opinion as to responsibility for the collision, Admiral Crabb informed Stevenson that charges would be framed with a view to his court martial. The Naval Board believed that a court martial

> *was the only really satisfactory method of providing Stevenson with the opportunity of having the imputations against him judged*

> *professionally. He had already stated that he intended to rebut any criticism of his conduct if such were made in the report.*

There was some political opposition to the decision among those who did not understand the traditional purpose of the court martial for clearing an officer's name. At his court martial, *Melbourne*'s captain pleaded not guilty with his counsel, Gordon Samuels QC, submitting that Stevenson had 'no case to answer'. This was accepted. Stevenson gained no pleasure from his acquittal, however, and continued to believe he had been made a scapegoat for American incompetence. He later resigned, protesting that his posting to a shore job in Sydney after relinquishing command of *Melbourne* was professionally demeaning. The similarities to the John Robertson saga were all too obvious.

Three officers from *Evans*, Commander McLemore and Lieutenants Hopson and Ramsey, faced trial by court martial after a pre-trial investigation had found that each had a case to answer. Hopson pleaded guilty to the charges brought against him and was reprimanded for dereliction of duty and negligence. One week later, Ramsey entered the same plea and was found guilty of negligence. Both officers were relegated to lower positions on the promotion list. McLemore pleaded not guilty, but was subsequently found guilty of dereliction of duty and negligently hazarding his ship. He was formally reprimanded and his naval career was effectively over. The loss of *Frank E. Evans* and its appallingly managed aftermath soured Australian–American naval relations. It was all the more regrettable because the controversy could have been avoided easily. However, the continuing war in and around Vietnam provided both navies with ample opportunity to heal the wounds that each had suffered from the collision. That the RAN–US Navy relationship could sustain the attack on *Hobart* and the loss of *Frank E. Evans* was a testimony to its strength, durability and continuing importance to both nations.

The RAN's involvement in the Vietnam War was also important because, for the first time, Australians were not fighting alongside the Royal Navy. A sound working arrangement was established between the Australian CNS and the Commander-in-Chief Pacific Fleet (CINCPACFLT) for the deployment of the RAN destroyers within the US Seventh Fleet organisation. The Australian ships came under the operational command of the Commander, Seventh Fleet except when released for visits elsewhere in South-East Asia when they reverted to routine Australian Naval Board control. However, administrative control continued to be exercised through the Australian Fleet Commander, who also retained control over HMAS *Sydney*. CDT 3 came under the operational control of the Commander, Naval Forces in Vietnam (COMNAVFORV)—a US Navy officer. The only restriction placed on the deployment of RAN units in Vietnam by American commanders was that they were not to be deployed in Cambodia or near that country's border. This applied to units of all three Australian services in Vietnam.

The close association between the RAN and the US Navy had a definite influence on the Australian Naval Board and the navy's culture. For example, on 10 May 1968, the Board decided that it would alter the RAN's squadron titles to a system more closely resembling that of the US Navy. The RAN would in future abandon the use of Royal Navy squadron numbers. Thus, the Tenth Destroyer Squadron, consisting of the three *Daring* Class destroyers, would become the Second Australian Destroyer Squadron. The senior ship of the squadron would be its commander and would bear the American style short title, COMAUSDESRONTWO. The DDGs would make up the First Australian Destroyer Squadron. The American system of hull numbering—large white block numbers on the ship's bow and also on the transom (later shifted to the after section of the ship's side)—would be introduced together with the US Navy practice of referring to ships' names by type designator and number. In the case of the three *Charles F. Adams* Class ships, they would be known as DDG-2s after the lead ship of the American class. The only essentially British practice retained was the use of black bands and squadron numbers on the funnel of the lead ship of each squadron.

In general terms the Vietnam War allowed the RAN and the US Navy to observe each other at close quarters for an extended period. The relationship was also helped by the exchange of personnel for short periods during operations off the Vietnamese coast. Australian naval personnel serving in or off South Vietnam learned how the US Navy functioned. It also expanded the experience of Australian officers and sailors.

> *By 1970, the RAN had developed a small pool of officers and sailors who were not only experienced in DDGs but also in Vietnam operations. The posting policy had been developed where personnel served as much as possible in the same class of ship and/or type of equipment. The training advantages of this policy are obvious . . . The Fleet Staff had also acquired a degree of*

> *'Vietnam expertise' by this time and knew how to push a DDG to extremes to ensure that our work-up brought every problem possible before us.*

The RAN had made a notable and highly credible contribution. During the conflict, 2858 members of the RAN served in and around South Vietnam. The destroyers fired 102 132 rounds and received enemy fire on seventeen occasions. There were 26 battle casualties: eight killed and eighteen wounded. Another seven men were injured in battle and another 23 sustained non-combat injuries. There is no doubt that the performance of all the Australian naval units created a most favourable impression with the US Navy, which awarded six commendations to the RAN: two to HMAS *Perth*, one to HMAS *Hobart*, one to HS 817 Squadron, and two to CDT 3.

While the Vietnam War was approaching a stalemate, Australian perceptions of defence and security were changing dramatically. Some of the changes had been prompted by the war in Vietnam and what it meant to broader Australian–American relations. Others were wholly separate from Vietnam and reflected political and economic development in the former European colonies that were now independent South-East Asian nations. The 1968 assessment of the strategic climate marked the start of a new era. The end of forward defence was foreshadowed. The British had indicated their intention to withdraw from east of Suez. Meanwhile, Indonesia, Malaysia, Singapore and Thailand had emerged as securely established states with independent foreign and security policies. Half of the British forces deployed in Malaysia would be withdrawn by 1971, and the remainder by 1976.

President Richard Nixon's 'Guam Doctrine' was also anticipated in Australia for about a year before it was formally announced on 3 November 1969. Australians believed that once the United States had concluded its involvement in Vietnam, it was likely to bring about 'important modifications in its attitudes and policies—particularly the need for the countries of South East Asia to do more to contribute to their own and regional security'. While Nixon stated that the United States would provide a nuclear shield for its friends and allies, in the event of lower level aggression against one of its friends or allies the United States would 'look to the nation directly threatened to assume the primary responsibility of providing the manpower for its defence'. The Guam Doctrine amounted to a limiting of the role the United States would play in international affairs rather than a withdrawal from that role. Nixon also explained the relationship between American interests and commitments, and their effect on US foreign policy. However, the United States would honour its treaty commitments, such as that to Australia and New Zealand under ANZUS.

> *[It] is misleading . . . to pose the fundamental question so largely in terms of commitments. Our objective, in the first instance is to support our* interests *over the long run with a sound foreign policy. The more that policy is based on a realistic assessment or ours and others' interests, the more effective our role in the world can be. We are not involved in the world because we have commitments; we have* commitments *because we are involved. Our interests must shape our commitments, rather than the other way around.*

By 1971 the predicted changes in the level and nature of American and British involvement in South-East Asia had come to pass a little earlier than expected. In particular, the declaration of limited commitment announced by Nixon in 1969 required Australia to focus more on the dynamic forces operating within the region rather than on the influences and roles played by major external powers. With 1970 heralding the start of a more stable decade in the region, Australia offered continuing support to Singaporean and Malaysian security after the withdrawal of British forces, and was a signatory to the Five Power Defence Agreement (FPDA) which included Malaysia, Singapore, Australia, New Zealand and Britain. The FPDA superseded ANZAM, with the military force provided by Australia, New Zealand and Britain. The initial naval commitment consisted of two Royal Navy frigates, one New Zealand anti-submarine frigate and an Australian destroyer. Additionally, Australia would provide one of its new *Oberon* Class submarines to the Malaysia–Singapore region every six months for training purposes. The British contribution ended in late 1975 and SEATO was virtually voted out of existence in 1977, although it had been winding down since 1970. Britain had become a very marginal player.

As the withdrawal of British naval forces was under way, the Australian continent gradually saw more of the US Navy with the frequency of ship visits increasing steadily throughout the 1960s. The types of units entering Australian ports widened as well. On 1 May 1960, USS *Halibut* was the first American nuclear submarine to visit Sydney. She was followed the following year by one of her sisters, *Sargo*. The nuclear carrier battle group of USS *Enterprise* and her consorts, the nuclear-powered cruisers *Long Beach* and *Bainbridge*, visited Sydney in September 1964 with *Long Beach* returning in 1967. The anti-submarine warfare carrier USS *Intrepid* arrived in Sydney on 8 January 1969 with *Bainbridge* returning, with the conventional cruiser *Belknap*, for the Captain Cook Bicentenary Celebrations in April 1970. Shortly afterwards, the carrier *Coral Sea* returned for her third visit to Sydney in less than ten years with the carrier *America*, which arrived on 21 November 1970, ending a major year for interservice liaison. American warships were now frequent visitors to Australian waters, and joint exercise planning had benefited from the many experiences the two navies had shared working with each other in Vietnam. It was a useful foundation on which to base the post-Vietnam phase of Australian–American naval relations, which saw attention diverted from South-East Asia.

By this time the Indian Ocean was becoming the new focus for naval attention. There was press criticism of both the Australian Government and the Naval Board for their long-term neglect of this region. A particularly strident editorial in the *Sydney Morning Herald* on this subject was prompted by reports in late 1969 that the Soviet Union was negotiating to establish naval support facilities in Mauritius and the Seychelles.

> *It is difficult to understand the Government's reluctance to pay more than lip-service to the need to bestir itself to meet the new strategic situation which is developing as Britain moves out of the Indian Ocean and Russia moves in. We have always thought of ourselves as a Pacific Ocean Power; we have now got to remember that we are an Indian Ocean Power too.*
>
> *Our election did extract from [Prime Minister] Gorton the promise to build a naval base in the West, but the hope that this meant that some constructive thought was being given to the Indian Ocean has diminished as subsequent Government 'explanations' have progressively watered down the role and importance of Cockburn Sound [naval base].*
>
> *The defence answers of the sixties have little relevance to the seventies, when the whole structure of power in our region will change. There is no evidence that our naval planners are sufficiently aware of this, any more than our political masters are. There seems to be a nervous reluctance in Australian naval circles to press for recognition of the fact that the RAN will be a more*

> *important service in the seventies than it has been for the past 20 years. The 1960s was the decade of the Army; the 1970s ought to see the Navy come into its own.*

If the RAN was to regain its place as the pre-eminent Australian service, elevate maritime defence concerns to the forefront of public and political thinking and be prepared for operations in the Indian Ocean, it would need to give the Government a broad range of new options for dealing with an ever-increasingly complex set of defence and diplomatic concerns in the region and beyond.

11
Finding a niche
1973–89

Australian military involvement in Vietnam began to wind down several years before *Sydney*'s last trip to Vung Tau in March 1972. In November 1970, 8RAR returned to Australia without replacement. Four months later, the army's tank squadron was withdrawn together with the RAAF Canberra and Caribou squadrons. Then followed the navy's guided missile destroyers, the HFV, and further battalions until all that remained were two army units: the 150-member Australian Assistance Group and the long-serving Australian Army Training Team—Vietnam (AATTV). Towards the end of 1972 the controversial National Service scheme was terminated and the remaining Australian military personnel were withdrawn. In early 1973, President Richard Nixon announced that 'peace with honour' had been achieved in South Vietnam. A cease-fire was announced and Australia established diplomatic relations with the North Vietnamese leadership in Hanoi. The last American troops left Vietnam on 29 March 1973. Just over two years later, the Australian embassy would be closed as communist forces captured Saigon. On 30 April 1975, the nation of South Vietnam was no more. Many would wonder what the Australian participation had all been for.

With the end of 'Confrontation' in 1966 and the conclusion of Australian involvement in the Vietnam conflict in 1972, questions were being asked about the navy's relevance. Other than the very general threat of Soviet naval expansion, there were no obvious maritime threats to Australia's own waters or its unfettered use of the seas. But the answers were soon apparent. During the 1970s and 1980s, the RAN would demonstrate that warships were very effective ambassadors in peacetime and could promote Australia's national interests in an endless number of ways. Diplomacy more than combat, restraint rather than force, would remain the orders of the day for two decades.

There were three separate strands of 'naval diplomacy'. The first was 'flying the flag' through ship visits and joint exercises at sea and ashore with friends and allies. The second was the assertion of Australia's territorial sovereignty and national interest regardless of whether they were being directly challenged. The third was displaying humanitarian concern through a range of relief and assistance operations. Each was significant in demonstrating the capabilities of warships and the nuances that could be reflected in their presence.

There was nothing new about naval diplomacy for the RAN, which already possessed long experience in assisting diplomatic initiatives and missions. Even before the end of hostilities in Vietnam, the RAN's contribution to the security of South-East Asia had begun to change. In 1971, the frigate *Swan* arrived for service with the Australia–New Zealand–United Kingdom (ANZUK) Force which succeeded the long-running Commonwealth Far East Strategic Reserve. The ANZUK Force was based at Singapore until 1974. There were concurrent ship deployments to Malaysia and Singapore until 1977 in support of the Five Power Defence Agreement. A submarine was also deployed to Singapore for part of each year.

In 1973, HMAS *Supply* sailed in company with the RNZN frigate *Otago* (later replaced by *Canterbury*) to Mururoa Atoll as a protest against French atmospheric atomic testing in the Pacific. *Supply* spent 180 days at sea and brought worldwide attention to trans-Tasman opposition to the French Government's indifference to the concerns of South Pacific nations directly affected by fall-out from the test site. Atmospheric testing at Mururoa would be discontinued in 1974. Following the transfer of the first RAN *Attack* Class patrol boat to Indonesia in 1973, the first combined naval exercise in Australian waters involving ships of neighbouring navies, including Indonesia, was held in 1974. Several of the RAN's landing craft later assisted Indonesia with survey operations. As a virtual continuation of Second World War mine clearance operations, Australian minesweepers and clearance divers were made available for clearing minefields and destroying other explosive ordnance throughout the 1970s in New Guinea and the Solomon Islands. During the late 1970s, deployments 'up top' were less frequent although the Soviet Navy occupied Cam Ranh Bay and the Vietnamese invaded Cambodia. At the same time, there were growing concerns about the security of Australia's northern waters and offshore resources. From 1973, *Attack* Class patrol boats, RAN Tracker aircraft and RAAF maritime patrol aircraft were deployed in waters between Broome and Cape York for fisheries protection duties. In the years that followed, fishing vessels from a number of countries including Indonesia, Taiwan and Japan were arrested and impounded for illegal fishing activity.

In what were often described as the most enjoyable deployments for the participants, HMA Ships *Stalwart* and *Supply* were present for the proclamation of Papua New Guinea's independence from Australia in 1975. Soon after, *Supply*, *Hobart*, *Vampire* and *Stuart* sailed to the United States for the bicentenary celebrations of the American declaration of independence from Britain. In 1976, the survey ship *Moresby* represented Australia at the Seychelles' independence celebrations. The next year, *Melbourne* and *Brisbane* took part in the Spithead Review to mark Queen Elizabeth's silver jubilee. In 1978, *Derwent* visited Darwin to coincide with the granting of self-government to the Northern Territory. *Yarra* sailed to Vanuatu for that country's independence celebrations two years later. The following year *Swan* became the first RAN ship to visit the People's Republic of China and *Vampire* and *Jervis Bay* were deployed to South Pacific waters to act as 'splashdown observers' during China's test of an intercontinental ballistic missile (ICBM).

The navy was equally adept at assisting a number of civilian authorities. Navy divers were dispatched by HS748 aircraft to Hobart in January 1975 after the freighter *Lake Illawarra* struck a bridge pylon over the Derwent River and sank. A number of cars plummeted into the river after a section of the bridge collapsed. The navy launched its biggest peacetime relief operation on Christmas Day 1974 in the wake of Cyclone Tracy's devastation of Darwin. Operation Navy Help Darwin involved *Melbourne*, *Supply*, *Hobart*, *Brisbane*, *Vendetta*, *Stuart*, helicopters and HS748 aircraft, the hydrographic ship *Flinders*, which checked and surveyed the harbour approaches; and six heavy landing craft (LCH), which transported stores and equipment. HMAS *Arrow* was anchored in Darwin harbour as the cyclone struck. She was driven under a wharf and destroyed. Two sailors were killed. Late the following year, *Supply*, *Vendetta* and *Vampire* were deployed to Darwin in case they were needed to evacuate refugees after Indonesia's invasion of East Timor. *Parramatta*

The patrol boat HMAS Arrow *was deemed to be beyond repair after suffering severe damage in Cyclone Tracy. Two sailors were killed. (RAN official)*

provided relief to earthquake victims at Bali in July 1976. Nearer to home, Bass Strait oil rig surveillance (BSORS) operations by patrol boats and Tracker aircraft commenced in 1980 and *Flinders* surveyed a new 80-mile passage through the Great Barrier Reef adjacent to Mackay in 1981–82. The ‘Hydrographer’s Passage’ saved 220 miles on a return trip to Japan, which represented a substantial savings to ship operators. While all of this non-warlike activity was underway, a long-running and expensive war continued. After 120 years, the Russians were again the source of Australian anxiety as the RAN fought the ‘Cold War’.

The Soviet Navy had expanded at an unprecedented rate after the Second World War and was increasingly perceived by Western nations as a growing threat to global sea lines of communication and world peace. As the Soviet Navy’s attempts to spread its influence focused on the Indian Ocean and the western Pacific, Australia was an important Cold War ally for the United States as it developed a similar fear of encroaching Soviet sea power. Traditionally subordinated to the needs of the Red Army, by the mid-1950s the Soviet Navy was the fourth largest in the world following those maintained by the US, Britain and France. When Admiral Sergei Gorshkov became Commander-in-Chief of the Soviet Navy in 1955, he initiated an enormous transformation of the seagoing fleets, presiding over the construction of offensive fleet assets, nuclear-powered submarines, and cruisers and destroyers armed with advanced surface-to-surface missiles (SSMs). Gorshkov also formulated a sweeping vision of the Soviet Union's imperial future resting on the state's naval power—not unlike what Admiral Mahan did for the Americans 60 years before. Drawing on Mahan's dictum that 'a Navy is well suited for an active and useful role as an instrument of state policy in peacetime as well as wartime', Gorshkov stated:

> *Navies . . . are constantly being utilised as an instrument of state policy in peacetime. In this regard, navies have assumed particular significance under today's conditions. The mobility of the fleet and its flexibility in the event limited military conflicts are brewing, permit it to have an influence on coastal countries, to employ and extend a military threat to any level, beginning with a show of military strength and ending with the landing of forces ashore.*

But the Soviet Navy was not a balanced fleet like the US Navy. It was, in fact, distinctly unbalanced. It boasted a massive nuclear and conventional submarine capability. Between 1949 and 1972, the Soviet Navy developed 24 new classes of submarine. Once under way, the production rate for nuclear submarines was fifteen or sixteen boats each year. By 1980 the Soviet Union deployed 280 nuclear and nuclear ballistic missile carrying submarines. Three-quarters of the Soviet submarine fleet was nuclear powered. But the Soviet fleet lacked aircraft carriers, while the surface fleet suffered from vastly deficient air protection. The size and potency of the submarine fleet was, however, sufficient to cause a reorientation of force structures in most Western navies.

Having developed and enhanced its capabilities, the deployment of the Soviet Navy was steadily extended beyond local waters. In 1965, Soviet warships began calling at a number of Indian Ocean ports. After the 1967 Arab–Israeli war, the pro-Soviet Government of South Yemen instructed Britain to withdraw its forces from Aden. Seven days later a small detachment of ships from the Soviet Pacific Fleet began a deployment to the Indian Ocean calling at ports in India, Pakistan, Iran, Iraq, Ceylon, Somalia and South Yemen, the latter then serving as a Soviet staging base in the Indian Ocean basin. Of the 32 Indian Ocean littoral states, many were underdeveloped and considered susceptible to Soviet 'assistance'. To demonstrate national resolve and partly to reveal its intentions, the Soviet Navy launched Operation Okean in 1970. This was the first worldwide Soviet naval exercise. A total of 150 surface ships, 50 submarines and a large number of maritime aircraft were deployed at the one time to test the capabilities of the Soviet Navy, and to gauge the American response. The exercise demonstrated that the Soviet Navy was now a global force with five specific roles: nuclear strike deterrent; sea denial; control of Soviet sea frontiers; presence; and seaborne power projection. As the world's seas were one and control of them deemed indivisible, the Cold War had been enlarged to wherever control of the seas could be contested.

With the British withdrawal from east of Suez to be completed before 1971, the vast Indian Ocean basin held great potential for further warship 'goodwill' visits and the spread of Soviet political and economic influence. Through an adventurous application of naval diplomacy, by 1975 the Soviet Union had gained an important tactical presence in the basin without having to encounter any Western navy operating in strength. The opposing American naval force in the immediate region was small and limited in range. The Middle East Force, based at Bahrain, consisted of two elderly destroyers and a seaplane tender. Its role to that time had been making goodwill visits to the Gulf states. It was ill equipped for a more substantial role and was certainly not in a position to oppose encroaching Soviet hegemony. In fact, while the US Navy that faced the burgeoning Soviet Fleet in the early 1970s was a shadow of what it had been a decade earlier, the 'Carter Doctrine' of the late 1970s defined the Persian Gulf and the northern Indian Ocean as an area vital to American interests. But the Pacific Command, from which most of the forces required for operations in the Persian Gulf were drawn, actually shrank during the Carter years. Additionally, as the departure of the British had left the US Navy in the position of sole Western guardian of the Indian Ocean, the 'one-and-a-half ocean' navy was forced to face a three-ocean contingency. This caused not a little concern in Canberra.

Successive Australian governments had shown little interest in the Indian Ocean or the territorial defence of Western Australia. When Paul Hasluck, a Western Australian journalist and former diplomat, entered Federal Parliament in the 1950s and argued that the Indian Ocean rather than the South Pacific was likely to be the decisive ocean in Australian defence 'during the next half century', there was little public or parliamentary reaction. By 1967, however, the Australian Government was seeking American involvement in Indian Ocean affairs. This was materially assisted in 1967 when the Johnson Administration and US Navy finalised an agreement with the British Government and the Royal Navy for the development of naval base facilities on the island of Diego Garcia in the Indian Ocean. It was not until 1970 that construction of a communications facility began. While Australia offered the US Navy use of Cockburn Sound, south of Fremantle, for development as a naval base in the wake of the 1971 India–Pakistan war, the Americans preferred to negotiate directly with the Soviet Union to limit naval activity in the Indian Ocean. But there was an unmistakeable message in this for Australia. The United States was clearly reluctant to commit itself to costly infrastructure in the Indian Ocean at a time when Soviet designs and activities in the region were still uncertain. It was nonetheless apparent that the Soviet naval presence would be concentrated in the north-western parts of the Indian Ocean and would rely either on the port facilities of its client states, particularly around the Horn of Africa, or on deep ocean mooring buoys.

By this time the presence of 'stray' Soviet ships in or near Australian waters had become an almost annual occurrence. In 1968, the patrol boats *Attack* and *Advance* shadowed a Russian trawling vessel for two months in the Gulf of Carpentaria. The following year, the submarine *Ovens* shadowed a Soviet oceanographic submarine off Tasmania and *Hobart* followed three Soviet ships off the Queensland coast. Conscious of widening Soviet interest in the Indian Ocean, Exercise Swan Lake was conducted in 1970 to test the Australian Fleet's ability to deploy west and operate in the Indian Ocean. There were significant logistic support difficulties to overcome. Three years later, *Perth*, *Derwent* and *Supply* completed a goodwill cruise of the Indian Ocean littoral. While these deployments were useful, the general proliferation of Soviet submarine activity in the Indian and Pacific Oceans produced a requirement among the ANZUS navies for an improved surveillance reporting system able to track more accurately the movements of the Soviet surface and sub-surface fleets. The RAN had been receiving environmental data on ocean conditions from the US Navy's Anti-submarine Warfare Environmental Prediction Centre in Guam since 1964. The 1977 ANZUS Maritime Surveillance and Reconnaissance Agreement was a product of a shared concern over Soviet submarine activity and became the leading edge of Australian–American Cold War collaboration. While most of these efforts were centred on the Pacific, there remained the problem of what to do about the Indian Ocean. Australia did not need to work hard in persuading the Americans to show a greater interest in the Indian Ocean.

Spreading Soviet influence in the mid-1970s could not be ignored when there was a distinct shift in relative capabilities from the Black Sea and Baltic Fleets to the Pacific Fleet, which also operated in the Indian Ocean. The acquisition of the abandoned American naval facilities at Cam Ranh Bay on the southern coast of Vietnam in 1977 was crucial to this process. Development of the site gave the Soviets an ice-free Pacific port with facilities to host the largest concentration of communist naval power outside the USSR. In 1985, HMAS *Canberra* shadowed the passage of the giant Soviet battle cruiser *Frunze* through the South China Sea en route to Vietnam. In less than ten years of Soviet tenancy, approximately 25 to 30 naval units—including surface combatants, conventional and nuclear-powered submarines and naval auxiliaries—were based at Cam Ranh Bay. The adjacent air base supported long-range naval reconnaissance, strike and tactical fighter aircraft. The base also provided the Soviets with a strategic geographic position from which to follow US and Allied operations in the South China Sea, and the Indian and Pacific Oceans. The Soviet Pacific Fleet increased in size and importance, and its deployments to the South-West Pacific became more regular.

The Soviet invasion of Afghanistan in late 1979 added impetus to American efforts in the Indian Ocean, while greatly contributing to the growing momentum for Australia to play a larger role in monitoring and containing Soviet maritime power. Prior to the Afghan invasion, Prime Minister Malcolm Fraser had announced during a visit to Washington that he had offered US naval forces the use of Cockburn Sound. By this time, the navy had developed Garden Island (not to be confused with the Garden Island in Sydney Harbour) as a naval base. Located five miles off the coast and adjacent to Cockburn Sound, the 'other' Garden Island was connected to the shore by a long causeway. The guided missile cruiser USS *Oklahoma City* became the first foreign warship to visit the West Australian Naval Support Facility on 19 April 1976. In 1978, the facility was commissioned as the shore establishment HMAS *Stirling*. In April 1980, the US Defense Department dispatched an evaluation team for a cost-effectiveness study of HMAS *Stirling* as an alternative site to other proposed bases for American naval units patrolling the Indian Ocean. The following year saw twelve American attack submarines visit *Stirling*. Following the Soviet invasion of Afghanistan, an Australian task group based on *Melbourne* sailed for the north-west littoral of the Indian Ocean on an extended 'flag flying' deployment. A major surface unit remained in the region to demonstrate Australia's concern. But the increasing Western naval presence in the Indian Ocean was not without some reverberations elsewhere.

In October 1980, Australia withdrew from the Beacon Compass naval exercises scheduled to be conducted with American and British naval units in the Persian Gulf, opting instead to conduct 'national exercises' further south in the Indian Ocean. The reason given was that Australia was unwilling to disrupt its growing commercial relationships with certain Middle Eastern states. The involvement of RAN ships in patrols around the Gulf of Oman in conjunction with American carrier patrol groups had also strained Australian relations with India. For their part, the Indians were unwilling to host or supply Australian ships that had been operating with the US Navy. Had the RAN become too close strategically or too tied logistically to the US Navy? Although Australia tried hard to prevent itself from being seen as a stalking horse for the British or an American proxy, India made a defence and diplomatic issue of the Australian–American alliance. As a retired Indian naval officer and strategist, Vice-Admiral M.P. Awati, told a seminar at Canberra in 1984, the RAN 'would be most welcome to Indian Ocean littoral states provided it is operating as a totally self-contained independent group . . . not in any way dependent on [the USN] for supply and support'. But India's emerging naval power was itself becoming a source of concern.

From the mid-1980s, the Indian Navy embarked on an ambitious naval construction program at a time when the United States was pondering a retreat from the Indian Ocean. The program included aircraft carriers, submarines, destroyers, frigates, amphibious vessels, corvettes and attack craft. Minesweepers and maritime patrol aircraft were also being acquired from the Soviet Union. In 1988, India acquired a Soviet-built nuclear-powered submarine that it renamed *Chakra*. (The submarine was returned to the Soviet Union after a twelve-month trial period when India decided against operating a nuclear-powered navy.) India was poised to become the world's third-ranking naval power after the United States and the Soviet Union. It was widely feared that India would soon possess the capability to conduct sustained operations throughout the region, eventually dominating the ocean basin. This did not eventuate but the fear would remain for some time.

Naval officers attempted to place India's actions within a broader context. Vice-Admiral M.W. Hudson, the long-serving Australian

Chief of Naval Staff, remarked during a visit to India: 'To a large extent the Indian Navy is replacing obsolete ships and going through a similar program of re-equipment that we are going through in Australia. They do, of course, have a very large maritime commitment, their coastline is long, they rely heavily on their sea lines of communication and it is certainly no surprise to me that they would wish to be able to protect that maritime area'. In an interview with Indian defence correspondent Dr Manoj Joshi, published in the *Hindu*, Admiral Hudson stated further that India's naval force structure was 'appropriate to India's strategic circumstances' and denied that a 'power vacuum' would develop following the further decline of superpower presence in the region. Although India had hinted that it was willing to play the part of regional policeman, littoral or island states did not give India any encouragement to fulfil such a role. Similarly, the possibility of the Indian Navy being used to aid an Indian ethnic population beyond its immediate region, such as in Fiji, was rejected forcefully by those nations with a sizeable Indian ethnic population.

In any event, the Indian Navy ranked third in spending priority behind the army and air force. Within its allocation, ship construction accounted for around 20 per cent of the navy's spending. In relative terms, this was lower than Australia where construction hovered around 28 or 29 per cent in the same period. However, India had a navy three times as large, including a capable Fleet Air Arm. But its ability to project power and influence was constrained by its small operating budget and infrequent ship visits. Nevertheless, Australia had officially embraced a 'two-ocean navy' policy in an effort to increase its profile in the Indian Ocean. This meant the fleet needed to be more capable of self-reliant operations. The navy of the 1980s needed newer and different kinds of ships.

The first task was to replace the ships acquired during the early to mid-1960s. The *Daring* Class destroyers were nearing the end of their operational service. After conversion to a training role in 1974, *Duchess* was paid off in 1977 and replaced as a training ship by the ANL vehicle ferry *Australian Trader*, which was renamed HMAS *Jervis Bay*. *Vendetta* was paid off in 1979 and *Vampire*, which had assumed a training role in 1980, left service in 1986 to become a museum ship at the Australian National Maritime Museum at Darling Harbour in Sydney. The *Oliver Hazard Perry* Class guided missile frigates (FFG-7) replaced the *Darings*. The first four ships—*Adelaide*, *Canberra*, *Sydney* and *Darwin*—were built in Seattle. These ships were designed to serve mainly as anti-air and anti-submarine ships, capable of

The Guided Missile Frigate (FFG) HMAS Adelaide *in Sydney Harbour. (RAN official)*

defending a replenishment ship or carrier battle group. *Adelaide* was launched in 1977 and commissioned in 1980. The next three ships arrived in Australia over successive years and were later modified to operate larger helicopters on their flight decks. Another two sister ships—*Newcastle* and *Melbourne*—were later built in Australia.

The carrier-cum-troopship *Sydney* had been paid off in 1973 without any alternative capability being made available. It was not until 1981 that the RAN acquired a dedicated troop transport vessel with the commissioning of HMAS *Tobruk*. Based on the British *Sir Bedevere* design, the Australian-built *Tobruk* offered a heavy lift capability and the facilities for supporting an amphibious landing. Eight Landing Craft Heavy (LCH) had earlier entered service. Although originally intended for army operations, *Balikpapan* (the only ship to actually serve with the Army Water Transport Squadron), *Brunei*, *Labuan*, *Tarakan*, *Buna*, *Salamaua*, *Wewak* and *Betano* were capable of lifting three battle tanks, 23 quarter-tonne trucks or thirteen armoured personnel carriers. Commissioned in 1973–74, these versatile ships were also ideal for transporting cargo and supplies from ships lying offshore to water terminals or across beaches. *Buna* and *Salamaua* were transferred to the newly independent Papua New Guinea in 1975.

The hard-working *Attack* Class patrol boats proved to be inadequate for more demanding tasks and were eventually replaced by the larger *Fremantle* Class. The first of this class, HMAS *Fremantle*, was built in Britain and commissioned in 1980, while the other fourteen were constructed in Cairns. The last ship of the class, *Bunbury*, was commissioned in December 1984. A number of the *Attack* Class boats were earlier offered to Australia's neighbours as part of the Defence Cooperation Program. *Aitape*, *Ladava*, *Lae*, *Madang* and *Samarai* were given to Papua New Guinea in 1975; *Acute*, *Archer*, *Attack*, *Bandolier*, *Barbette*, *Barricade* and *Bombard* were transferred to Indonesia between 1974 and 1985. It was decided that HMAS *Cook* would replace the Second World War veteran *Diamantina* as the oceanographic research ship and that the trials ship HMAS *Kimbla* would be scheduled for decommissioning in 1985. Meanwhile, a replacement was planned for the replenishment vessel *Supply* and thought turned to a new class of minehunting vessel to replace the ageing Ton Class. The three DDGs and the six destroyer escorts together with the four FFGs were the mainstay of the RAN's offensive capabilities. But most controversial was the decision to replace the flagship HMAS *Melbourne*.

By 1980 the carrier had been in service for 25 years. As the ship was originally laid down in 1943, the hull was more than 35 years old. *Melbourne* was one of the smallest aircraft carriers operating fixed-wing aircraft anywhere in the world. But as a capital ship, she allowed the RAN to claim membership of an elite group. It was a costly privilege. *Melbourne* not only needed extensive maintenance, she was expensive to operate and her aircraft would need upgrading within a decade. A project team was working on replacement options. At the same time, the Royal Navy was asking similar questions about naval aviation. It operated three carriers, the aged *Hermes* and the newly commissioned *Invincible* and *Illustrious*. Another new carrier, *Ark Royal*, was under construction and would replace *Hermes* on completion. In 1981, the British Government offered to sell *Invincible* to the Commonwealth Government as a replacement for *Melbourne*. It would be renamed HMAS *Australia* and was due to arrive at Sydney in late 1983. As plans were initiated to decommission *Melbourne*, Argentina invaded and occupied the Falkland Islands in the South Atlantic on 2 April 1982. Although it was a remote and little-known British possession, Prime Minister Margaret Thatcher announced that Britain would reclaim the Falklands by force. A substantial naval task group led by HMS *Invincible* sailed from Portsmouth on 5 April. After a short, sharp campaign, the Argentine occupation force was defeated and Britain regained possession of the islands in June. The victory was not without a considerable cost to Britain. Two Royal Navy destroyers (*Coventry* and *Sheffield*) and two frigates (*Antelope* and *Ardent*) were sunk; six Sea Harriers and four RAF Harriers, 21 naval helicopters and three RAF helicopters were lost; 84 British naval personnel had been killed. The Royal Fleet Auxiliary *Sir Galahad* was also sunk with the loss of 50 lives. In contrast to the 1956 Suez Crisis, all RAN personnel on exchange duty with the Royal Navy were replaced before the ships in which they were serving reached the operational zone. During the war, HMAS *Jervis Bay* was made available for the seagoing training of Royal Navy midshipmen.

In the wake of the Falklands War, Prime Minister Fraser indicated he would accept London's decision to retain *Invincible* should the British Government deem the ship necessary to the United Kingdom's continuing security interests. Prime Minister Thatcher decided to keep *Invincible* and her air group to ensure that Britain had two operational carriers available at all times. By now a major refit for *Melbourne* had been cancelled. The carrier's squadrons had been transferred to the Naval Air Station at Nowra and the flagship was prepared for decommissioning prior to being scrapped. In 1983, the newly elected Hawke Labor Government announced that *Melbourne* would not be replaced. In a further blow, the RAN would cease operating fixed-wing aircraft from 30 June 1983 (with the exception of two HS 748 electronic warfare aircraft) although four Skyhawks were to be retained for target-towing duties with some of the Trackers deployed on Bass Strait oil platform patrols. On 30 June 1984, the remaining Skyhawks and Trackers ceased flying permanently. The Trackers then rotted on a tarmac at the Naval Air Station in Nowra while awaiting disposal; the Skyhawks were sold to the Royal New Zealand Air Force (and came back to Nowra with the RNZAF for fleet support duties) and later decommissioned and listed for private sale (2002). The only bright news for Australian naval aviators was the Government's decision to acquire eight S-70B Sikorsky Seahawk helicopters for anti-submarine warfare service. A contingent of Aerospatiale AS 350B Squirrel helicopters was also to enter immediate service for training and light utility work on board the FFGs. Four Iroquois UH-1B helicopters would remain in service for training and utility tasks. While these decisions were being made, the once proud *Melbourne* was stripped of useful fittings and towed from Sydney Harbour by the tug *De Ping* in 1985. Many grieved her undignified departure for scrapping in China; just as many were glad the ill-fated ship had finally gone. But the loss of an important war-fighting capability was significant.

The navy had developed and refined considerable expertise in carrier operations over more than 30 years. Other than rotary aircraft operating from the FFGs, *Stalwart* and *Tobruk*, the RAN was no longer a major player in naval aviation. A symbol of naval potency—the aircraft carrier—would no longer head the navy's order of battle. There was widespread disappointment and despondency and no hesitation in accusing both political parties and the other two services, especially the air force, of bad faith and moral duplicity. Could the Government be persuaded to change its mind? Perhaps another type of ship could be acquired to perform carrier-like operations. The finality of the decision took some years to sink in. But the alleviation of the considerable financial burden that *Melbourne* had become gave the RAN an opportunity to broaden its capabilities. If the loss of the carrier achieved anything, it allowed the navy to tackle its foremost problem: mobility.

While developing the 'two-ocean Navy' policy, Australia continued to rely on American naval power, particularly in the Indian Ocean. Such reliance did not conflict with American policies. In the early 1980s, the Reagan Administration was seeking to strengthen US long-range surveillance capabilities, with a specific interest in guaranteeing continued American access to petroleum production centres in the Middle East while safeguarding Western commercial and naval shipping against Soviet submarine warfare capabilities and other forms of interdiction. HMAS *Stirling* was ideally placed to support such an effort. No sooner had the Soviet presence been checked in the Indian Ocean than a new direction in Soviet foreign policy demanded a return of emphasis on what had previously been regarded as an American 'lake'—the Pacific Ocean.

Soviet interest in the Pacific had historically been confined to the North Pacific and restricted to whaling and fishing but, from the mid-1980s, there was an appreciable interest in the South-West Pacific where the Soviet Union sought to increase its profile with fishing agreements negotiated with Kiribati and Vanuatu. Maintaining its traditional high profile in the North and Central Pacific, the United States pursued low-key policies in the South Pacific abbreviated by stronger stances over tuna fishing disputes. Although America was a major supplier of regional aid and had an interest in the preservation of secure sea lines of communication throughout the western Pacific basin, the US Navy was nonetheless content to have Australia play the major public role, while emphasising the threat posed by Soviet interference in regional affairs. This was the main message conveyed by Admiral David Jeremiah USN (CINCPACFLT), who visited Australia in 1988.

> *The Pacific is the only theatre in which the USSR has direct access to a major ocean and the only one in which the US and the Soviet Union face one another across a common border—the 2000-mile maritime frontier that extends from the Bering Strait to the north coast of Japan. These key characteristics require US forces to be forward deployed throughout the region to succeed with our national strategy to deter aggression by demonstrating our resolve through presence and to respond promptly and forcibly if aggression occurs, in order to keep open the sea lanes.*

By this stage, however, the US Pacific Fleet was in a better position to oppose the Soviet Navy, with a national strategy that sought to deny its superpower rival command of the seas. In June 1985 Defense Secretary Caspar Weinberger declared that 'the US has made a fundamental decision that we are a Pacific nation, that we will remain a Pacific power and a force for peace and stability in the region. Our nation's future does indeed lie in the Pacific . . . let no one misread the past or misjudge our resolve'. The strengthening of the Pacific Fleet and the creation of a '600-ship Navy' was an integral component of the United States 'Maritime Strategy' outlined publicly in the early 1980s by the Secretary of the Navy, John Lehman.

The 'Maritime Strategy' stressed that the United States would achieve deterrence if it had the ability to take any fight to the Soviet homeland. This required a naval emphasis in the northern Pacific and the northern Atlantic, and the creation of a 600-ship navy built around fifteen large-deck carrier battle groups. The US Navy was riding the crest of a wave. New classes of ships were being built with the encouragement of forceful political support from a United States government determined to pursue a more assertive foreign policy. The only concern for the US Navy was the attitudes of a number of foreign governments which were either reconsidering their involvement in Western nuclear defence or reassessing their alliances and agreements with the United States. For the greatest part, Australia had been a willing participant. But there were some occasional misgivings. The Holt Coalition Government had declined approval for the nuclear-powered cruiser *Truxton* to visit Australia in 1967 after the US Navy refused to disclose details of either its power plant or weapons fit. In 1973 the Whitlam Labor Government criticised the American nuclear missile test program in the Pacific and prohibited the docking of American warships in Australian ports after the US Navy insisted on maintaining its policy of neither confirming nor denying the presence of nuclear weapons in its vessels. In 1976, the incoming Wran Labor Government in New South Wales banned American nuclear-powered ships from entering Sydney Harbour. Although unable to change the policy in New South Wales where the Labor Party remained in power, the newly elected Fraser Coalition Government reinstated American docking permissions suspended by Whitlam. But the growing electoral appeal of anti-nuclear policies and the emergence of strident anti–American sentiment in Australia during the late 1970s and early 1980s raised the profile of the Australian–American alliance and intense public debate followed. It appeared that most Australians were very comfortable with the alliance and believed it was crucial for national security. However, they wanted some official assurance that their safety was not adversely affected by the presence of American military facilities on Australian soil at North West Cape, Nurrungar and Pine Gap.

In 1983, the incoming Hawke Labor Government initiated a review of Australia's relationship with the United States and the effect of the ANZUS alliance on the nation's contribution to the global strategic balance and regional stability in the Pacific. The review's findings were endorsed by the Minister for Foreign Affairs, Bill Hayden, who told Parliament that: 'The Review has led to a firm and unequivocal reaffirmation of the Alliance as fundamental to Australia's national security and foreign defence policies'. Soon after he became Minister for Defence in 1985, Kim Beazley outlined the Government's view of ANZUS and the tangible benefits a close defence relationship with the United States brought to Australia, particularly in the maritime area.

> *The ANZUS Treaty provides a background for a wide range of mutually beneficial defence co-operative activities that significantly improve our practical defence competence and operational capability. In addition, it assures our access to a level of technology needed for the development and acquisition of weapons systems which provide an opportunity for our small population to be able to defend a large continent.*

The following year, Beazley commissioned defence and security analyst Dr Paul Dibb to produce a comprehensive review of Australia's defence capabilities, including an assessment of the Government's existing strategic guidance to the Defence Department. The Dibb Review expressed the realities of the ANZUS alliance in frank terms.

> *Our close relationship with the United States is significant for our security and the development of our defence capability, but for over a decade we have recognised that the United States is a global power with a variety of interests, none of them centred on Australia. There are potential situations where we would not expect the United States to commit combat forces on our behalf and where we need a demonstrably independent combat capability.*

However, the review played down the significance of seaborne trade and the security of the sea lines of communication at the heart of the 1951 Radford–Collins Agreement. The navy regarded this agreement as fundamental to the management of Australia's vast maritime area. Dibb remarked:

> *Radford–Collins is possibly a useful peacetime planning measure to exercise procedural doctrine and command and control, but it has particular limitations in time of threat. Its convoying and escort connotations . . . suggest a disproportionate commitment of scarce resources which may be only marginally related to our national interest and capabilities. Under Australian treaty*

practice, the Agreement would not be categorised as a treaty. Therefore, it does not create binding rights and obligations.

American concerns about the Dibb Review seem to have been prompted as much by what the review was seen to represent as by what it actually said. Admiral James Lyons USN (CINCPACFLT) and other American officers criticised the review for confining force capability to operational requirements within Australia's neighbourhood. As well, there was concern about Dibb's treatment of the Radford–Collins Agreement. What seems to have aroused more anxiety than the review's recommendations was the widely held impression that it represented a unilateral attempt to redefine Australia's security interests in ways that were indifferent to, or that might even damage, American interests. The regional reaction to the Dibb Review reflected a similar concern about Australia becoming 'isolationist'. But this was simply a review not government policy.

Having consulted widely, the Government issued a Defence White Paper in 1987, which would serve as the blueprint for Australian defence and security planning for the following decade. It stated that Australia's defence strategy was one of self-reliance within the framework of Australia's alliances and regional associations. It also reaffirmed Australia's alliance with the United States and the importance of a close naval relationship between the two nations.

Australia is part of the Western community of nations. Australia therefore supports the ability of the United States to retain an effective strategic balance with the Soviet Union . . . Defence co-operation will continue to be sustained with the United States in peacetime . . . The practical benefits Australia and the United States gain from our alliance during peacetime need to be clearly understood . . . For example, port visits by US warships provide opportunities for combined exercises with advanced technology vessels while at the same time providing rest and recreation facilities for US Naval deployments in our region . . . The United States gains information important to its global maritime intelligence system from Australian surveillance and intelligence gathering activities in an area extending from the eastern Indian Ocean to the South West Pacific.

The White Paper also affirmed the continuing importance of the Radford–Collins Agreement for the protection of trade in the designated

Australian area of responsibility. Whereas Dibb suggested that joint exercises were no longer needed, the White Paper stated that Australian forces 'will continue to develop their interoperability with those of the US'. Higher level cooperation would continue as well.

> *The Joint Facility at North West Cape permits reliable transfer of messages to both US ships and submarines operating in the Indian Ocean and Western Pacific as part of a complex system of communications supporting the global balance. This Government believes that Australia makes a most effective contribution to Western security as a whole by its particular and immediate contribution to regional stability. An effective capacity for Australian self-defence frees our ally of concern for our immediate security and in turn develops capabilities relevant to our wider regional security.*

All of this pleased the navy and delineated a very clear set of responsibilities. But there were problems across the Tasman Sea.

Despite the long and close relationship that had existed between New Zealand and the United States, New Zealand Prime Minister David Lange said during a speech at Yale University during April 1989 that his nation's involvement in ANZUS was 'dead'. The alliance had gone into its terminal decline when Lange's Labour Government refused the destroyer USS *Buchanan* entry into New Zealand ports until the US Navy had confirmed or denied whether the ship carried nuclear weapons. In line with their stated policy, the Americans refused to make any such statement. *Buchanan* subsequently berthed in Sydney on 4 March 1985. The American ship, a *Charles F. Adams* Class DDG almost identical to those serving in the RAN, was not carrying nuclear weapons (I spent some time on board the ship while alongside) and the New Zealand Government privately knew as much. During the 1970s and 1980s, the US Navy frequently removed the nuclear weapons from their smaller ships bound for Australia or New Zealand at Subic Bay in the Philippines.

The New Zealand Government's actions had created an unnecessary security crisis. Lange had engaged in a deliberate political stunt to score domestic electoral advantage. This was despite conceding that the Soviet Union had a long-term subversion plan in the South Pacific using fishing agreements with small island states as a tool for gaining influence. The Australian Government was unimpressed. Kim Beazley stated: 'The Australian Government has stated clearly its complete disagreement with New Zealand's policy on port access for Allied nuclear powered or armed vessels. The Australian Government looks forward to a full resumption of a tri-lateral ANZUS relationship as soon as this is feasible'. For its part, the RAN exploited every opportunity for bilateral training with the US Navy and the chance to play an even greater role in regional naval affairs. In addition to the ANZUS joint naval exercises which were held annually in February, there was the Kangaroo Exercise series conducted every three to four years around northern Australia and the biennial RIMPAC naval exercises off Hawaii. Other intermittent contact consisted of rest and recreation visits by American carrier battle groups and single ships on passage through Australian waters. This contact with the US Navy ensured the RAN remained proficient in its war-fighting skills and able to participate in multinational naval taskforces.

But closer to home, there were growing concerns about the internal stability of several small Pacific island nations. The military coup in Fiji in May 1987, led by Lieutenant Colonel Sitiveni Rabuka, led to Operation Morris Dance. Five RAN ships already in the vicinity of the Fijian islands were instructed to remain near the capital city of Suva as part of a contingency plan for the possible evacuation of Australian nationals. A company of soldiers from the Operational Deployment Force in Townsville was embarked in *Tobruk* and detached to the other RAN ships on arrival in Fiji. As it turned out, the security situation did not necessitate the evacuation of Australian nationals and political calm returned, although a second coup was staged in 1989. Operation Sailcloth followed the deterioration of political stability in Vanuatu in 1988. *Jervis Bay* and *Stalwart* were diverted to waters off Port Vila in the event that Australian nationals needed to be evacuated. Although the two ships were able to remain offshore for 25 days, the crisis itself was brief and the vessels were allowed to resume their training program after two days. In 1990, *Jervis Bay* was prepared for the possible evacuation of Australians during the early stages of the violent uprising in Bougainville that would eventually erupt into a civil war. While these operations were largely reactive, the RAN wanted to play a more proactive and productive role. Vice-Admiral Hudson claimed that 'Australia is uniquely placed to provide a steadying influence in the South Pacific region assisting in the development of a community spirit. It is here that we see a host of newly emergent nations keen to express their newly acquired statehood and subject to the tensions that may follow'.

It was clear that the navy was capable of exerting a positive influence. The 1987 Defence White Paper had foreshadowed the need for a naval presence in the region and presumed the RAN would be sufficiently mobile to provide it. In the late 1980s, warships were used extensively to reinforce Australia's diplomatic and economic policies, to prevent unwanted interference in regional affairs by a non-resident power and to provide an appropriate level of force in the right place at the right time. In 1987, there were 67 ship visits to South Pacific ports. That number increased to 92 in 1988. South-East Asian ports received 35 ship visits in 1987 and 42 in 1988. From early 1989, one and sometimes two RAN ships were deployed to Singapore in support of the Five Power Defence Agreement. Ship maintenance facilities at the Lumut naval dockyard in Malaysia were made available to the RAN. The navy's influence was further consolidated by the Pacific Patrol Boat project which provided for the construction of vessels for Papua New Guinea, Vanuatu, Tonga, Fiji, Tuvalu, Palau, Kiribati, the Solomon Islands, the Marshall Islands, the Cook Islands and the Federated States of Micronesia. Twenty patrol boats were delivered between May 1987 and May 1997. In addition to the construction and periodic maintenance of the small patrol boats, the navy agreed to provide specialist hydrographic surveying services and general advice on maritime surveillance.

Despite fears about the resurgence of 'gunboat diplomacy' and the alleged initiation of a regional naval arms race, the Australian people were quick to express their pride in, and satisfaction with, the navy during a year-long celebration of the RAN's seventy-fifth anniversary in 1986. The principal event was an international naval review held on Sydney Harbour. Twenty-seven ships from seven nations including the United States, Britain, France, Canada, New Zealand and Papua New Guinea, and led by the 16-inch gun *Iowa* Class battleship USS *Missouri* and the British aircraft carrier HMS *Illustrious*, participated in what was a rehearsal for the Bicentennial Naval Salute, a much bigger and more ambitious naval review planned to coincide with the Australian Bicentenary.

Twelve nations accepted invitations to send their ships to Sydney in October 1988. The US Navy sent the battleship USS *New Jersey*. The Royal Navy was represented by the aircraft carrier HMS *Ark Royal*, while the smaller Pacific island navies were also represented.

An armada of 50 ships converged on Sydney Harbour. It was a magnificent spectacle that showcased Australia's hospitality, Sydney's picturesque harbour, and the high regard in which the RAN was held around the world. It also allowed the RAN to parade its newest acquisition. Earlier in the year Prime Minister Hawke had accepted the

The sail training ship Young Endeavour *in Sydney Harbour with trainees embarked. (RAN official)*

44-tonne two-masted brigantine *Young Endeavour* as Britain's bicentennial gift to Australia. The RAN would operate the sail training ship on behalf of the *Young Endeavour* Youth Scheme. Designated an RAN tender and flying the Australian naval white ensign, the ship's captain, navigator, doctor, engineer, cook and watch leaders were members of the RAN. The crew would consist of 24 trainees aged between 16 and 23 years. In 1992, *Young Endeavour* began a voyage to mark the 500th anniversary of Christopher Columbus' discovery of the New World. *Young Endeavour* called at ports in the Indian Ocean, Africa and the Mediterranean before arriving in Greece in March 1992. The ship then proceeded to Genoa in Italy to join an international fleet of sailing ships for a short passage to Cadiz in Spain. From Cadiz, *Young Endeavour* participated in the 'Grand Regatta Columbus', sailing to Puerto Rico via the Canary Islands. She then made for the east coast of America, culminating in the largest gathering of such vessels ever seen on 4 July 1992 in a 'Parade of Sail' on New York Harbour. The ship returned to Australia in December 1992 after transitting the Panama Canal and crossing the Pacific Ocean. She had visited 30 ports in 20 countries.

The Bicentennial Naval Salute was a public relations success. On the eve of the naval review, Professor Geoffrey Blainey remarked in the *Weekend Australian*:

> *We live in a phase of world history when naval power seems temporarily silent. Furthermore, we live in a nation where yacht, kayak, speedboat and water-ski capture the imagination more than big ships . . . Even the battle of the Coral Sea has faded from the public imagination. More than half of the present population of Australia probably has not heard of it. If the Australian navy had been the main opponent of the Japanese fleet in the Coral Sea, the victory might have lived in folklore . . . So here we are, a nation of islanders who de-value seapower. We should take more interest in it. The sea still counts.*

And the RAN allowed the Australian Government to make the most of the opportunities presented by the nation's maritime geography.

12

Across the seas

1990-2003

With the astonishing collapse of the Soviet Union after 1989 and a sudden end to four decades of Cold War, the new Russian Government decided against renewing the Soviet lease on the Cam Ranh Bay naval base in Vietnam after its expiration in 2004. Accordingly, Australian security policy concentrated on credible lower-level contingencies and acknowledged that the nation would need to plan for a range of operations without direct support from its superpower ally. This meant that the force structure of the RAN in particular would reflect regional needs with less emphasis on previously maintained war-fighting capabilities. The initial outcomes of this policy shift were the abandonment of any interest in the acquisition of an aircraft carrier and the replacement of larger specific-purpose ships in favour of smaller multifunction units. Having accepted a measure of responsibility for preserving stability within and among the small South Pacific island states, Australia found itself engaged in a series of operations that sought, among other things, to avoid the conflicts that might attract third-party involvement. But threats associated with challenges to the right of free passage through the northern archipelagic waters served as a reminder that sound relations with Australia's most important neighbour, Indonesia, could never be taken for granted.

With these more immediate local concerns drawing closest attention and prompting concerted action, the thought of RAN involvement in a major Middle Eastern conflict would not have been in a single

Australian mind as a new decade dawned. The brutal and unprovoked Iraqi invasion of Kuwait on 2 August 1990 on the pretext of assisting a 'free provisional government' produced an immediate international reaction of disbelief and determination. Four days after the UN Security Council passed Resolution 661 on 6 August which imposed trade sanctions on Iraq, the Australian Government announced that two RAN frigates and a replenishment ship would deploy to the Middle East to assist in enforcing these measures against Iraq. The frigates *Darwin* and *Adelaide* sailed from Sydney on 13 August, with the tanker *Success* to follow the next day. While the two Australian ships were proceeding to the Gulf, the UN Security Council passed Resolution 665 authorising member states to deploy maritime forces to enforce the trade blockade by whatever measures were necessary to halt and inspect all inbound and outbound shipping. When they arrived in the operational zone on 3 September, the Australian ships were to 'identify, contact, interrogate and warn' vessels which might have been carrying prohibited cargo to Iraq or Kuwait in breach of the UN resolution. Command and control of ships and their individual responsibilities were now considered in detail. There was no clear multinational organisation or concept of operations in force at that stage. The first meeting of the Multinational Naval Force was held on 5–6 September and resulted in an agreement on the designation and allocation of a number of patrol areas.

The RAN Task Group was allocated an area in the Gulf of Oman, astride the major shipping routes leading to Khawr Fakkan in the United Arab Emirates and to the Straits of Hormuz. Although the Royal Navy had deployed its ships, there appears to have been no specific consideration given to deploying British and Australian units to the same or adjacent areas. The ties that had bound the two navies together for so long had unravelled. As *Darwin*'s commanding officer, Captain (later Vice-Admiral) R.E. Shalders, wryly noted: 'The Royal Navy tended to try to locate themselves wherever the action was likely to be most interesting'. The Multinational Naval Force (MNF) agreed to work under an arrangement, or 'loose association', which was created to reflect that a large group of ships had been deployed with varying political commitments by their governments and with different rules of engagement. Ships remained under national control while tactical and operational control was exercised by on-scene Task Group commanders.

An RAN liaison officer, Commander A.E. Flint, was also appointed to the staff of Vice-Admiral Henry Mauz USN, Commander US Naval

Forces Central Command (COMUSNAVCENT), who was embarked in his flagship, the specially fitted-out command and control ship USS *Blue Ridge*. Admiral Mauz's appointment was in addition to his command of the US Third Fleet. Commander Flint's role was to participate in the COMUSNAVCENT battle watch organisation as a surface warfare officer in addition to serving as a liaison officer to other Coalition naval commanders in the Gulf. During sanction enforcement operations, Admiral Mauz coordinated operations from *Blue Ridge*, which remained alongside at Bahrain. While the interrogation of merchant ships was their primary task, the RAN units also exploited opportunities to work with a number of the navies participating in the MNF.

On 6 September, *Darwin* and *Adelaide* entered the Gulf of Oman. Just over one week later, *Darwin* conducted the first RAN interception of a prohibited vessel, the Iraqi merchant ship *Al Fao*. On 18 September, an Australian medical team made up predominantly of RAN personnel embarked in the US Navy's giant hospital ship USS *Comfort*. During October, shipping interception missions increased as the Iraqi merchant fleet started returning to the Persian Gulf in large numbers. On 8 October, *Darwin* and Royal Navy forces intercepted and boarded the Iraqi tanker *Tadmur*. On the same day, *Adelaide* fired a number of warning shots during the interception and boarding of another Iraqi merchantman, *Al Wasitti*. Boardings of the tankers *Al Mutanabbi*, *Al Bahar*, *Al Arabi* and *Amuriyah* followed. After 28 October, almost all Iraqi merchant traffic was laid up in numerous ports with only two ships attempting to reach Iraq. During these long periods of patrol the RAN was second only to the US Navy in the tempo of operations. Captain Shalders later stated: 'The Australian Task Group achieved a ratio approaching 90 per cent of time at sea. Other Multi-National Naval Force navies aimed for a much reduced tempo of around 50 per cent'.

As the prospect of hostilities increased, *Brisbane* and *Sydney* left for the Gulf to relieve *Darwin* and *Adelaide*. While they were en route, the UN Security Council passed Resolution 678 authorising the use of force to remove the Iraqi army from Kuwait. Australia's response was immediate. The Leader of the Government in the Senate, Senator John Button, informed its members that

> *Australia is prepared to make our naval task force available to serve with Allied forces in operations authorised by Resolution 678, should that become necessary. Accordingly . . . our ships*

> *would be available to participate in action with the Allied fleet in the Gulf, where they would be in a position to make an important contribution to its air-defence capabilities . . . These steps need to be taken now because they are essential to ensuring that our ships are fully prepared to operate as safely and effectively as possible should conflict erupt. They do not formally commit Australian forces to any action; [the RAN] units will remain at all times under Australian national command. Our ships will operate principally with ships of the US, Britain and Canada, under US operational control. This is normal under such circumstances, and will contribute both to the effectiveness and to the safety of our ships and men.*

As the deadline for the withdrawal of Iraqi forces drew near, *Darwin* and *Adelaide* were relieved and *Brisbane*, *Sydney* and *Success* sailed towards the Persian Gulf on 16 December to begin familiarisation with anti-air warfare (AAW) operations. The Australian ships were readily integrated into the air surveillance program being conducted by the MNF. With the expectation of action with Iraqi fighter aircraft, further command briefs for *Brisbane* and *Sydney* were conducted on board USS *Bunker Hill*, an AEGIS cruiser, which was the anti-air warfare commander. She was stationed closest to the threat as a picket. A quickly established rapport with *Bunker Hill* and other US Navy ships greatly assisted the smooth and rapid integration of the Australian units into a very active and complicated AAW picture.

On 26 December, *Sydney*, in company with US Ships *Oldendorf*, *Fife*, *Curts*, *Trenton* and *Shreveport* and the Royal Navy frigate HMS *Brazen*, intercepted the *Ibn Khaldoon*, the Libyan-sponsored 'peace ship'. It was carrying prohibited cargo in addition to over 240 civilian men, women and children, accompanied by an international media contingent. Four days later, as Iraqi combat aircraft began sorties over the northern Persian Gulf, *Sydney* acted as the primary intercept ship for the boarding of the Iraqi merchant ship *Ain Zalah* and, with the Australian Task Force Commander, Commodore (later Rear Admiral) C.J. Oxenbould embarked as 'On Scene Commander', exercised tactical control over US Ships *Guam*, *Trenton* and *Fife*. Hostilities seemed imminent and a meeting of the commanders of the various national task forces was held in HMAS *Success* alongside at Dubai.

> *This important meeting took place on 9 January and was also attended by Rear Admiral March USN, who had been designated*

as the US Navy Battle Force Commander. The continuation of Multi-National Force operations was a key issue . . . The Multi-National Force task group commanders were asked to indicate their ability to assign units to the battle force and those who were requested to have their ships take up stations by 12 January in the lead up to the impending deadline.

With a deadline for the withdrawal of Iraqi forces set for 15 January, *Sydney* joined *Brisbane* in escorting the American carrier USS *Midway*. The only other nation to have its ships making up *Midway*'s protective screen was the Netherlands. By this time COMUSNAVCENT, Vice-Admiral Stanley Arthur USN, who had relieved Admiral Mauz, had completed his operational planning and had organised and deployed an amphibious task force, six carrier battle groups and several flotillas of surface ships which were also stationed in the Red Sea and the Gulf of Oman. Tactical control of all Australian units deployed to the Gulf had earlier, on 13 January, been formally passed to Rear Admiral Daniel March USN, who was embarked in *Midway*.

The issue of command and control in the event of hostilities was settled without fuss.

Ability to operate within the operational control of the Commander of the Multi-National Force will be exercised and the operating procedures refined. The previously successful arrangements under which national command is retained by Australia will also continue.

The following day, all three Australian ships joined Battle Force Zulu as part of the MNF. The operational plan devised by COMUSNAVCENT was immediately implemented with three carrier battle groups conducting simultaneous flying operations within the Persian Gulf. The MNF was an imposing armada. With six aircraft carriers, two battleships, fifteen cruisers, 67 destroyers and frigates, and over 100 amphibious, auxiliary and support vessels, it was the most awesome display of naval power since the end of the Second World War.

The naval forces opposing the MNF were not large. At the time it invaded Kuwait, Iraq was known to have a small frigate, six *Osa* fast attack craft armed with Styx surface-to-surface missiles, and several very old torpedo boats and patrol boats acquired from the Soviet Union in the 1950s and early 1960s. It was also likely that the Iraqis had captured remnants of the Kuwaiti Navy, consisting of six fast attack craft armed with Exocet missiles and five large patrol craft, which might have been fitted with surface-to-surface missiles. This small force would not have posed any serious threat to the MNF, although the power of the missiles deployed in the fast attack craft could not be discounted.

When hostilities commenced, Prime Minister Hawke stated at a press conference:

> *Fellow Australians, you will recall that on the 4th of December last, I told Parliament that Australia was prepared to make our naval task force available to serve with Allied forces in operations authorised by Resolution 678 of the United Nations Security Council should that become necessary . . . With profound regret I must now inform you that the necessity which I foreshadowed in the Parliament five weeks ago has come about. As a consequence, therefore, the Australian naval task force in the Gulf is now, with other members of the United Nations, co-operating in armed action to fulfil the United Nation's resolution to enforce the withdrawal of Iraq from Kuwait.*

From the commencement of Operation Desert Storm on 17 January until early February, *Brisbane* and *Sydney* continued as consorts to *Midway* under the tactical control of Admiral March. The only departure from this routine was when *Sydney* was released from the carrier screen to escort USS *Niagara Falls* to the northern part of the Persian Gulf. By the end of January, the threat to naval forces from Iraqi air attack had subsided. Over a hundred Iraqi fighter aircraft were reported to be in Iran while most of the Iraqi Navy's ships had been sunk or severely damaged. This allowed the American carriers to operate some sixty miles closer to Kuwait.

> *As the carriers moved north,* Brisbane *and* Sydney *restationed into the northerly sectors of the screen immediately south of the Zagros Mountains gap and within sight of the Iranian coast. The Australian units thus became the first line of defence for both air and surface threats coming from Iran, all combat air patrol aircraft being concentrated on the main threat axis in the direction of Iraq. This tasking demonstrated considerable trust by the US Navy in RAN capabilities as the threat of short or no warning attack from aircraft in or over Iran, was at the time considered very real.*

On 14 February both Australian ships proceeded to new stations close to the Kuwaiti coastline. This led to *Sydney* being one of the northernmost ships in the Persian Gulf. In effect, the deployment of the Australian frigate was no different from its US Navy equivalent. *Sydney*'s commanding officer, Commander (later Commodore) L.G. Cordner, remarked during the war that: 'We should be playing our part fully which is what our Government intends us to do. So we should be prepared to carry out any role that an American frigate could undertake and that is what we have done'.

A staff officer serving with the RAN Task Force commander commented: 'RAN ships escorted high-value units and patrolled the Battle Force screen. The confidence placed in the two RAN combatants was demonstrated by the fact that they were generally stationed "up threat". This employment included, when the actions of Iraqi aircraft in Iran were still unclear, being stationed only some fifteen miles off and within sight of the Iranian coast'. It was while patrolling in the northern Gulf area that *Sydney* was able to render assistance to two American warships, the cruiser *Ticonderoga* and the landing ship *Tripoli*, both of which struck mines in mid-February. On 24 February, the ground war was launched. Saddam Hussein's 'mother of all battles' lasted for a hundred hours. The Iraqi Army was disorganised, badly led, poorly equipped and dispirited. It proved no match for the Coalition, which exerted its superiority in the air and from the sea. A cease-fire was called, by which time the RAN's Clearance Diving Team (CDT) 3 had arrived in the area of operations. On 3 March, CDT 3 commenced port-clearing operations. At the conclusion of its deployment CDT 3 had dived for 231 hours, cleared 2 157 200 square metres of seabed and rendered safe 60 sea miles. The RAN divers had worked closely with their Royal Navy and US Navy counterparts to clear mines from around a number of ports. The four main areas were the ports of Mina'ash Shu'Aybah and Ras al Shuwaik, the Kuwaiti naval base at Ras Al Qualai'ah and the boat harbour of South al Ahmadi. Over the next three months, *Brisbane*, *Sydney*, *Success* and her replacement *Westralia*, the medical teams serving in USS *Comfort* and CDT 3 gradually returned to Australia. On 9 March 1991, Rear Admiral March relinquished tactical control of the ships making up the MNF.

The RAN contribution continued after the hostilities of the Gulf War were formally over. As part of Australia's contribution to the MNF remaining in the Gulf to enforce trade sanctions against Iraq, *Darwin* served throughout most of mid-1991 as a fully interoperable unit of the MNF and during June as part of the USS *Nimitz* carrier battle group in the central Gulf area. When opportunity allowed, Australian personnel were exchanged with their American counterparts from the carrier *Nimitz* and the cruiser *Ticonderoga*. In late June, *Darwin* proceeded to the northern Persian Gulf to commence escorting merchant ships through the still active minefields around Kuwait to the port of Mina'ash Shu'Aybah. The *Knox* Class frigate USS *Whipple* led *Darwin* through a short familiarisation period.

Admiral Charles Larson USN, Commander-in-Chief Pacific, told the US Senate Armed Services Committee shortly after hostilities ended that 'Australia quickly and easily integrated its naval and medical units with US units in the Gulf, proving the value of our relationship and interoperability'. The Commander of the Australian Task Force, Commodore Oxenbould, echoed this sentiment: 'The integration of allied forces was impressive. The control of such a massive force with very few real problems reflected the considerable benefit of large multi-national exercises such as RIMPAC'. The Gulf War was testimony to the wisdom and foresight which had insisted that the RAN operate closely with the USN throughout the 1980s. It was a triumph for interoperability and a means whereby the RAN could consolidate its already considerable familiarity with US Navy tactics and operating procedures.

Australia's active participation in the Gulf War was relatively inexpensive. Four combatant ships were rotated through the conflict zone with support from two replenishment units. Of the latter, HMAS *Success* was the longest serving ship in the Allied taskforce. Australian naval ships found no difficulty in operating with the vast international force under complex rules of engagement and detailed command and control arrangements. There were no accidents and none of the ships suffered major mechanical or technical problems. Every operational responsibility was met and, most importantly, not a single Australian life was lost or seriously threatened. Given the military cost of the Gulf War to other nations, particularly those with ground forces, Australia was numbered among the Coalition partners but at a very small price.

The Gulf War was an opportunity for the navy to prove itself in a demanding and diverse operational setting. If it was in any sense a test, the RAN passed with flying colours. At the same time, the Australian people observed the considerable diplomatic and political benefits of having a navy able to participate in multinational operations while demonstrating a very high level of operational professionalism. Prime

Minister Hawke spoke of the warships' performance as a 'job gloriously well done' which had added 'another glorious chapter in the history of the Royal Australian Navy'. But it was a chapter still being written. For the next decade, RAN ships would be rotated through a multinational Maritime Interception Force (MIF) to enforce UN trade sanctions against Iraq. This was another kind of challenge for the navy. As history had shown, blockading operations are usually long, largely repetitive and frequently unexciting.

After 1991, all merchant ships inbound or outbound from the Gulf of Aqaba in the northern Red Sea were liable for boarding and inspection. After an initial interrogation conducted by maritime VHF radio to determine the ship's last port of call, present destination, cargo carried and nationality, a decision would be made by the MIF coordinator on whether to inspect the ship. Ships nominated for inspection were ordered to heave to and to have the crew muster in a clearly visible location on the upper deck. When the crew was accounted for, a boarding party would be dispatched by either a rigid inflatable boat or by Seahawk or Squirrel helicopter. The boarding party either scaled the ship's side by ladder or descended to the upper deck by rope before splitting into three teams. The Bridge Team, led by a boarding officer, would obtain details of both the ship and her cargo. The Sweep Team would ensure the ship's superstructure was clear of any hazards or threats to the boarding party. The Security Team would proceed to the crew muster position and verify the crew count. Once the ship and crew were properly secured, the Sweep Team would conduct the physical inspection of the vessel. Searching a large ship with a varied or containerised cargo could take up to eight hours and require a boarding party with 30 members. On completion, the vessel would be either allowed to proceed to her destination or diverted to another port if found to be carrying prohibited cargo. Australian boarding parties boarded and searched thousands of ships in all weather conditions.

As the RAN would be contributing to the enforcement of trade sanctions against Iraq for the next decade, the 1990s saw a shift in focus from war-fighting to a range of 'peace operations'. Although these were something new for most naval personnel, the RAN had contributed to a number of peace missions over the previous four decades.

The first RAN peacekeeper was Commander H.W. Chesterman, who was sent to the Dutch East Indies in September 1947 as part of a UN mission during the conflict between Indonesian nationalists and the Dutch colonial authorities. Chesterman returned to Australia in

January 1948. The RAN contributed personnel for service with the United Nations Emergency Force (UNEF) II in the Sinai from 1976 to 1979. From 1982 to 1986, Australia and New Zealand provided eight Iroquois helicopters for the Multinational Force and Observers (MFO) in the same area. *Tobruk* transported the contingent's helicopters and essential stores to the Sinai. RAN specialist personnel also participated in the UN's weapons inspection teams in Iraq (UNSCOM) in the immediate aftermath of the Gulf War. Over the next few years, small contingents of specialist RAN personnel were involved in a series of peace missions. Operation Gemini was the Australian contribution to the UN mission in Cambodia (UNTAC) in 1992. RAN personnel were attached to the Force Communications Unit and the Movement Control Unit based at Cambodia's major port of Sihanoukville and at the headquarters in Phnom Penh. Operation Solace was Australian support for two UN missions, UNITAF and UNOSOM I, in Somalia during 1993. *Tobruk* and *Jervis Bay* were tasked with transporting troops, armoured personnel carriers, heavy equipment and vehicles from Townsville to Mogadishu and to provide continuing logistic support. Operation Lagoon saw *Tobruk* and *Success* provide command and control afloat and logistic support for peacekeeping talks in Bougainville during 1994. *Ipswich*, Sea King helicopters and CDT 1 were also involved. In 1997–98, *Tobruk* returned to Bougainville and was the venue for the signing of a peace accord. In the years that followed RAN ships and personnel were deployed to the island to assist with implementing the agreement. In 1994, six RAN medical personnel were posted to UNAMIR—the UN's mission to Rwanda after the genocide of 780 000 mainly Tutsi men, women and children. These were all in addition to Operation Damask, the RAN's contribution to the enforcement of UN sanctions against Iraq, which was the largest Australian peacekeeping operation in terms of the number of participating personnel.

By this time, the navy needed to replace the remainder of the ships acquired during the major fleet build-up of the 1960s, while paying off manpower-intensive ships it could no longer afford to operate. The 1991 Force Structure Review concluded that only three-quarters of the forces envisaged in the 1987 Defence White Paper could be funded within the existing budget. As the Government was unwilling to increase the defence budget to cover the new acquisitions, the 1996 Defence Efficiency Review and the 1997 Defence Reform Program were initiated to find more money within the existing financial allocation to pay for the new ships and equipment. It was hoped that savings of $1 billion per annum could be achieved through a range of measures, including reducing the navy's personnel strength. None of these measures were popular: shore bases were either closed or their functions amalgamated; some uniformed functions were civilianised as the naval workforce was reduced; command and control arrangements were streamlined; and higher defence management was reorganised, with a number of senior officers offered early retirement. Economy drives and cost cutting became a preoccupation as money had to found. But how much was too much? A fire in HMAS *Westralia* on 5 May 1998 which killed four crew members was partly attributed to inadequate expenditure in routine maintenance, and to defective liaison between naval staff and commercial contractors.

However, the fifth and sixth FFGs, *Melbourne* and *Newcastle*, were shortly to enter service. Their efficient and economical completion was an important achievement for Australian naval defence and local industry. From the 1960s until the mid-1980s, Garden Island, Williamstown and Cockatoo Island dockyards were notorious for poor performance and debilitating industrial relations anarchy. In Sydney, 'Fleet Base East' was separated from Garden Island with the dockyard staff becoming employees of a new Government-owned company known as Australian Defence Industries. The Cockatoo Island Dockyard was closed in 1991 after 80 years of shipbuilding that began with the River Class destroyer *Huon* and ended with the replenishment ship *Success*. The Williamstown Naval Dockyard was sold to AMECON—a merger of three Australian public companies: Eglo Engineering, ICAL and Australian Shipbuilding Industries. After a three-month closure, the dockyard reopened with a new outlook and the number of unions represented on the site reduced from 23 to three. Work on *Melbourne*, halted when the dockyard changed hands, was resumed and the ship delivered ahead of the contract date. Similar success with *Newcastle* demonstrated that AMECON was a successful shipbuilder and Williamstown a preferred site for warship construction. In the space of a few years, a near revolution had been completed in the Australian shipbuilding industry. The company was in a good position to tender as prime contractor for the new class of frigate that was to replace the River Class destroyer escorts. *Yarra*, the last furnace fuel oil (FFO) burning ship to serve in the RAN, was listed for scrapping in late 1985. *Stuart* was paid off in 1991 after firing the last Seacat missile and hitting the designated target. The last destroyer escort to go was *Torrens*. The hull was stripped and sunk by a Mark 48 torpedo fired from the submarine HMAS *Farncomb* on 14 June 1999.

AMECON was the winning tenderer for the *Anzac* ship project in November 1989. The *Anzac* Class was a variant of the German Meko 200 Class. Turkey, Greece and Portugal had also placed orders for ships of this innovative design. Eight of the 3600-tonne ships were to be built for the RAN—*Anzac*, *Arunta*, *Warramunga*, *Stuart*, *Parramatta*, *Ballarat*, *Toowoomba* and *Perth*—and two for the RNZN. Their main armament was a single 5-inch gun mount, ship-launched torpedoes and the Sea Sparrow point defence missile. They would also be able to embark the Seahawk helicopter and be fitted with the Rapid Assist and Traverse (RAST) recovery system to allow helicopter operations to take place even in rough seas. The first frigate, appropriately named HMAS *Anzac*, entered service in 1996. As the *Anzac* Class frigates were completed, the high fuel-consuming and manpower-intensive DDGs were retired. *Perth*, *Hobart* and *Brisbane* were among the longest serving ships in the RAN's history. Many believed they were the best. They were also the last ships to fire the Australian-designed Ikara anti-submarine missile which had been phased out several years before. All three had rendered outstanding service during the Vietnam War, and *Brisbane* was deployed to the 1991 Gulf War with great distinction. *Brisbane*'s decommissioning in October 2001 brought a golden era to an end. The nation had reason to be grateful for the ingenuity and forethought of the Navy Minister, Senator John Gorton, and the Chief of Naval Staff, Vice-Admiral Sir Henry Burrell, who had ordered the ships nearly four decades earlier.

The six *Oberon* Class submarines were also to be replaced. The first to be completed, *Oxley*, was more than eleven years older than the last, *Otama*. The new *Collins* Class were named to commemorate gallant Australian naval personnel: *Collins* (Vice-Admiral Sir John Collins), *Farncomb* (Rear Admiral Harold Farncomb), *Waller* (Captain 'Hec' Waller—killed in HMAS *Perth* during 1942), *Dechaineux* (Captain Emile Dechaineux—killed in HMAS *Australia* in 1944), *Rankin* (Lieutenant Commander Robert Rankin—killed in HMAS *Yarra* in 1942) and *Sheean* (Ordinary Seaman 'Teddy' Sheean—killed in HMAS *Armidale* in 1942). The construction of a complete class of submarines in Australia was a complex and challenging undertaking. Although submarines had been refitted and modernised in Australia, none had been built from plans. Shortly after *Collins* entered service, a number of serious shortcomings were reported in the submarine's

HMA Submarine Collins *heads to sea for trials. (RAN official)*

operational capabilities, especially excessive hull noise and shortcomings in the combat system. These became the subjects of public controversy and disquiet; the *Collins* Class were the most expensive vessels Australia had ever built. Rear Admiral P.D. Briggs was appointed to head a 'Submarine Capability Team' whose challenge was to fix the problems. Now that the design and technical problems have been progressively remedied, the *Collins* Class provides the RAN with the most advanced conventional-powered submarine capabilities in the world.

Having recognised the indispensable service provided by *Tobruk* over the previous fifteen years, the RAN acquired two *Newport* Class amphibious transport ships from the US Navy in 1994. USS *Saginaw* and USS *Fairfax County*, launched in 1970, were substantially rebuilt, converted to an amphibious transport and training role, and renamed *Kanimbla* and *Manoora*. A midships helicopter hangar was fitted to accommodate four Black Hawk helicopters or three Sea King helicopters. The 34-metre bow ramps and horns, intended for 'over the beach' amphibious operations, were removed and a 70-tonne crane installed forward of the bridge to handle two LCM8 landing craft. The tank deck provided 810 square metres of storage through a stern door. The modernisation and conversion of these two major ships took much longer than planned and placed a considerably greater demand on already strained resources than had been expected. After a varied career with many unexpected deployments in company with *Tobruk* or as a stand-in for her, the training ship *Jervis Bay* was paid off in 1994 and sold. The engines were worn out and the ship contained a great deal of asbestos fibre.

The last three Ton Class ships in service—*Snipe*, *Ibis* and *Curlew*—were belatedly replaced by two Australian-designed Bay Class inshore minehunters (MHI). *Snipe* left service in 1983 and *Ibis* the following year. *Curlew* was the last to be paid off in 1990. *Rushcutter* and *Shoalwater* were built at the Carrington Slipways in Newcastle and entered service in 1986–87. They provided some of the capabilities provided by the Ton Class although displacing only 170 tonnes and having a ship's company of just thirteen. Built as catamarans and intended for inshore waters, they proved to be too unstable for effective minehunting in other than calm seas. A plan to build another four vessels was cancelled. Six coastal minehunters based on the *Gaeta* Class built for the Italian Navy were ordered for delivery after 1998. They would be commissioned as *Huon*, *Hawkesbury*, *Norman*, *Gascoyne*, *Diamantina* and *Yarra*. Much larger ships than the MHIs, their principal task was to keep the nation's focal points for trade—harbours and ports—free from the threat of mines. They would be supported in this work by a number of commercial vessels refitted for service as auxiliary minesweepers. The navy's long-serving hydrographic ships, *Flinders* and *Moresby*, were also to be replaced by two new vessels, *Leeuwin* and *Melville*, and complemented by the four survey motor launches that entered service between 1989 and 1990: *Paluma*, *Mermaid*, *Shepparton* and *Benalla*. *Moresby* was decommissioned in October 1997 after 34 years' service and *Flinders* in October 1998.

The fleet tanker *Supply* had been paid off in 1985 and was replaced by *Success*, the largest ship built for the RAN in Australia. To make the 'two-ocean navy' policy a reality, a second replenishment vessel was acquired. *Appleleaf* served in the Royal Fleet Auxiliary from 1979, including a deployment to the South Atlantic for the Falklands War in 1982, until being transferred to the RAN as HMAS *Westralia* in 1989. The ship was leased for five years before being purchased outright in 1994. After the 1998 engine room fire, the ship was repaired and modified before returning to operational service in early 2000. The fleet tender *Stalwart* and the perennially unreliable oceanographic ship *Cook* were paid off without immediate replacements in 1990 and 1991. The former National Safety Council of Australia (Victorian Division) vessel *Blue Nabilla* was acquired by the navy and converted for service as a safety and trials ship with the new name *Protector* in March 1991. She would assist the work of the Defence Science and Technology Organisation (DSTO) and with trials of the new *Collins* Class submarines. She was decommissioned in 1998 and reappeared as a civilian-manned training ship at the RAN College, HMAS *Creswell*.

The 380-tonne fast catamaran *Jervis Bay* was acquired by the navy and commissioned in June 1999. This aluminium ship was built in Tasmania for civilian use as a fast car ferry. *Jervis Bay* was capable of 43 knots and was leased for two years as a short-term supplement for the RAN's sea-lift capability while the conversion of *Manoora* and *Kanimbla* continued. (*Manoora* began a series of trials in early 2000.) The acquisition of *Jervis Bay* was well timed. Her short period of naval service almost completely coincided with a security and humanitarian crisis previously unseen in the region.

After years of violence and unrest, the Indonesian Government agreed to a ballot being held on 30 August 1999 to determine whether the East Timorese people wanted to remain within Indonesia or seek independence. When it became clear the East Timorese

The fast catamaran HMAS Jervis Bay *became known as the 'Dili Express' after her service in East Timor. (RAN official)*

had voted overwhelmingly for independence, pro-Indonesian militia members, encouraged and supported by the Indonesian Army (TNI), went on a rampage across the country. Hundreds of people with pro-independence sympathies were killed and public and private property wantonly destroyed. Pictures of the death and destruction being inflicted upon the East Timorese were relayed across the world. The international community was appalled by the brutality of the militias and the indifference of the Indonesian authorities to the devastation. On 15 September 1999, the UN Security Council resolved unanimously to create a multinational force to restore peace and security in East Timor while providing humanitarian assistance. The multinational force was to be 'replaced as soon as possible by a UN peacekeeping operation'. Following some heated diplomatic exchanges, an Australian-led multinational force known as INTERFET (International Force East Timor) arrived in Dili to restore order on 20 September. Australia contributed over 5500 personnel and displayed its ability to command and to coordinate a joint military force. This would be the first occasion in which an Australian government was accountable to the UN for the outcome of a peacekeeping mission.

Operation Stabilise involved elements of all three Australian services. Fifteen RAN personnel were deployed to Dili to form the Naval Component Command (NCC) under Commodore J.R. Stapleton. (Commodore B.D. Robertson succeeded him on 21 November 1999.) The NCC controlled a force of 35 ships, coordinated the activity of eight ships operating purely in support of INTERFET, assisted in the management of more than 30 merchant ships, and acted as the harbour authority for all East Timorese ports from 20 September. *Success* sailed from Darwin on 19 September bound for Dili. The tanker was deployed to refuel ships on station and to provide fuel for use ashore. Also embarked in *Success* was the three-member Hydrographic Office Detached Survey Unit, which advised that Dili harbour was safe for navigation. The unit remained in East Timor for ten weeks and provided much useful data for landing sites along the East Timorese coast. Six members of an eight-member detachment from CDT 4 were also landed on the first day to check the wharfage and harbour bottom at Dili and to identify other landing sites. The other two members of the detachment were deployed to Dili in an RAAF C-130 Hercules and were the first Australians to reach the port area. The detachment officer-in-charge, Lieutenant Commander Peter Tedman, described the scene:

The landing craft HMAS Labuan *unloads a Second Cavalry Regiment ASLAV in Dili Harbour. (RAN official)*

> *The conditions on the wharf and in the wharfside buildings were something that had to be seen to be believed. Some 5000 refugees had been herded onto the wharf to await forced relocation. They were living in absolutely appalling conditions under the guns of a company of Indonesian marines and the militia. In the first few hours the team cleared the wharf and surveyed and marked a beach landing site adjacent to the wharf.*

Anzac, *Adelaide* and *Darwin* led the Australian naval contribution with warships also provided by the United States, Britain, New Zealand, France, Portugal, Singapore, Italy and Thailand. *Newcastle* and *Melbourne* were both to serve as guardships at the East Timorese enclave of Oecussi in West Timor. In addition to providing a strong naval presence and demonstrating the resolve of the INTERFET Commander, Major General Peter Cosgrove, the warships provided maritime surveillance and secured the sea lines of communication. The navy was also involved in the initial insertion of INTERFET troops at Dili and later at Suai, on the southern coast, and at Oecussi. This involved *Tobruk*, *Balikpapan*, *Brunei* and *Jervis Bay*. Three other LCHs—*Betano*, *Wewak* and *Labuan*—later served in East Timor together with the survey motor launches *Mermaid* and *Paluma*. *Jervis Bay*, known affectionately as the 'Dili Express', initially carried only personnel and light cargo and was manned by rotating crews. With the setting of mooring buoys in Dili harbour, the ship was able to discharge cargo through the stern door onto the wharf. Personnel were followed by equipment. Significantly, 97 per cent by weight and 93.2 per cent by volume of all equipment used in East Timor was transported by sea.

On completion of the INTERFET mission and the commencement of a new mandate—UNTAET (United Nation's Transitional Administration East Timor)—General Cosgrove and Commodore Robertson sailed from Dili on board *Jervis Bay* on 23 February 2000 in company with the frigate *Melbourne*. *Jervis Bay* continued to assist the UN mission until August 2000, and carried over 6600 passengers and 3200 pallets of supplies between Darwin and Dili. The catamaran sailed for Hobart where she was paid off on 11 May 2001. *Brunei* supported operations in East Timor for a total of fifteen months and was awarded the Meritorious Unit Citation. Writing towards the end of his NCC service, Commodore Robertson remarked:

> *East Timor was certainly a challenging episode in the ADF's history, including that of the Navy. Much of great value was learnt (and inevitably some lessons were re-learnt). The need for modern amphibious forces has been demonstrated. Operation Stabilise was not, however, a valid test of the RAN's war-fighting capability or proficiency and one must be cautious not to draw the wrong conclusions from this experience.*

But the operation clearly demonstrated the ADF's competence in command of a highly visible international joint operation, and the extent of the Australian public's support for humanitarian interventions. As the RAN commitment to East Timor was reduced, the navy continued to support Operation Bel Isi II in Bougainville, with the periodic deployment of an LCH and the auxiliary minesweepers.

While these operations were publicly popular, the RAN's public profile would be affected by two related events in September and October 2001. They had to do with the Government's use of the navy to enforce the nation's immigration laws. For naval officers and sailors, there was nothing new in this kind of work. From 1977, the RAN had assisted a number of civil agencies in dealing with the arrival of refugees from Indochina, especially after the Vietnamese invasion of Laos and Cambodia. In that year, *Moresby* intercepted a vessel carrying

47 Vietnamese refugees. Navy Tracker aircraft were then deployed to Darwin for aerial surveillance operations. In 1988, *Swan* rescued 72 Vietnamese refugees in the South China Sea. The following year, *Melbourne* rescued another 99 in the same waters. In 1990, *Bunbury* rescued 118 Indochinese refugees off the Kimberley coast. During the 1990s, increasing numbers of people were arriving on Australia's shores seeking asylum. In the period 1999–2000, RAN patrol boats and Australian Customs vessels apprehended 51 'suspected illegal entry vessels' (SIEVs) carrying 2663 passengers from fourteen nations, at Ashmore Reef, 360 miles north of Broome. Most of the SIEVs were Indonesian fishing vessels owned or chartered by criminal organisations seeking to defy Australian immigration laws to make large sums of money from 'people smuggling'. The work of apprehending SIEVs was described by one commanding officer as being among the 'hardest tasks undertaken by patrol boat ship's companies'. While in command of *Geelong*, Lieutenant Commander J.J. Williams remarked:

> *To the uninitiated, nothing can prepare for the shock of that first boarding of a suspected illegal vessel. The money is made from the number of people delivered, so as many people as possible are crammed into the vessel for the often long, and always dangerous voyage, through an unforgiving Timor Sea. The bilges quickly fill with human waste and the effects of seasickness. Vermin and parasites thrive in the filth, adding to already unhealthy conditions. By the time they arrive at Ashmore Reef and are apprehended, the passengers are generally in a very poor state both physically and emotionally. The presence of mothers with children often adds to an already sad situation.*

As the 'suspected unlawful non-citizens' (SUNCs) had broken Australian law by arriving at Australia in this manner, the SIEV was treated as a crime scene and evidence collected for subsequent legal proceedings. The patrol boat captain then determined whether the SIEV was capable of being steamed or towed to a destination where the SUNCs were received, charged formally with illegally entering Australia and any claims for asylum evaluated. The crew, usually Indonesian, were also charged with violations of Australia's immigration laws.

As the number of illegal arrivals increased during 2000–01, the Howard Coalition Government decided to send a clear message, particularly to Indonesian people smugglers, that Australia would refuse them entry. On 26 August 2001, the Norwegian merchant ship MV *Tampa* recovered a group of SUNCs from the stricken Indonesian vessel KM *Palapa I* in the Timor Sea south of Java. The *Tampa*'s master, Captain Arne Rinnan, wanted to land the SUNCs at the nearest Indonesian port but was pressured by the *Palapa* survivors to sail for Christmas Island to enable them to seek residence in Australia. The Commonwealth Government advised Captain Rinnan that he was not to approach Christmas Island or to enter Australian waters. *Arunta* was deployed to Christmas Island in the event she was needed to prevent *Tampa* from entering Flying Fish Cove. On 28 August, the National Security Committee of Cabinet directed the Commander of the Australian Theatre, Rear Admiral C.A. Ritchie, to prepare 'a maritime control and response plan to detect and intercept and warn vessels carrying unauthorized arrivals for the purpose of deterring SIEVs from entering Australian territorial waters'. Plans for Operation Trump, later renamed Operation Relex, were hastily devised. To avoid the need for *Tampa* to enter Australian waters, the *Palapa* survivors were transferred to *Manoora* and conveyed to the Pacific island of Nauru where their claims for asylum in Australia would be assessed. The '*Tampa* crisis' rapidly became an international controversy. Opposition politicians and sections of the Australian media accused the Government of manipulating the incident for electoral advantage prior to the 10 November 2001 Federal poll.

On 11 September, terrorists linked to the radical Islamic al-Qa'ida movement hijacked four domestic airliners in the north-eastern United States. One crashed into a Pennsylvania forest. One was flown into the Pentagon in Washington. Two were flown into the twin towers of the World Trade Center in New York. More than 3000 people were killed. The world had never before seen terrorism on this scale. Western security had been breached and ordinary people were frightened by what was depicted as religious extremism of the most brutal and callous kind. In Australia there was a massive outpouring of sympathy for the American people. The Australian Government declared its solidarity with the American people and its willingness to assist with a 'War on Terrorism'. The immediate aim of the campaign was the capture of those who had assisted the '9/11' perpetrators. When suspicion fell on Osama bin Laden and the al-Qa'ida terrorist network based in Afghanistan, the US Government demanded that the Taliban regime surrender bin Laden for prosecution. When the defiant Taliban refused, the United States issued an ultimatum that continued unwillingness to cooperate would lead to military action. While Prime Minister Howard pledged Australian support for US-led offensive operations in Afghanistan, he insisted that Operation Relex remained the Government's foremost security priority. Attention then returned to the Indian Ocean.

With the SUNCs from *Palapa* in custody, the navy was asked to establish a virtual naval blockade of the waters between Australia and Indonesia by providing surveillance, interception and transport of illegal immigrants taken into custody off the north-west coast of the continent. Operation Relex involved over a dozen RAN ships. During September, three SIEVs carrying a total of 489 potential illegal immigrants (PIIs) were intercepted. In October, a further six SIEVs with another 959 PIIs on board were intercepted. In November and December, only three SIEVs were intercepted, with 340 PIIs taken into custody. These operations were difficult and distressing for all concerned. Those seeking to enter Australia by these means, whatever the merits of their claims for asylum, were desperate to succeed. It was apparent to their supporters and opponents that they were prepared to go to extreme lengths, even risking death, to achieve their goal.

Political passions were inflamed on 7 October 2001 when *Adelaide* attempted to turn back the Indonesian fishing boat *Olong* (designated 'SIEV 4') then bound for Christmas Island. The vessel was taken in tow as the Immigration Minister, Philip Ruddock, and Prime Minister Howard told journalists that those on board *Olong* had thrown children overboard in an attempt to frustrate the navy's efforts to return the boat to Indonesia. This revelation was met with outrage, although no evidence of the claim was made public. The Prime Minister was adamant: people who imperilled the lives of their children in this way would never be welcome in Australia. *Olong* began to sink on 8 October. With human lives at risk, there was no alternative but to transfer the 223 men, women and children on board the stricken vessel to *Adelaide*. Shortly afterwards, pictures were released claiming to substantiate the claim that children were thrown overboard. In fact, they depicted the rescue of children from *Olong* as the boat was sinking. As the 'children overboard' claims gained currency, Commander Norm Banks in *Adelaide* tried to correct the record. He claimed to have seen children being held over the side of the sinking *Olong* rather than being thrown into the water. By the time of the 10 November election, serious doubt had been cast over the sensational claim. On 8 November, Rear Admiral G.F. Smith, the Maritime Commander, advised Vice-Admiral D.J. Shackleton, the

Chief of Navy, that 'there was no evidence to support the allegation that a child had been thrown overboard, and that the photographs that had been used were a misrepresentation of that alleged incident'. Shackleton had not realised that night film footage of the incident did not confirm claims that children were thrown overboard until he actually saw the video earlier that day.

While the 'children overboard' saga was fast becoming a national political issue, the navy's attention was not unreasonably directed elsewhere. After 11 September, the ADF's focus had shifted to the 'War on Terrorism' and Australia's likely contribution. The navy was tasked with the deployment of three major fleet units and devising plans for a subsequent rotation. HMAS *Anzac*'s extant deployment had to be extended. The ship's tasking and rules of engagement also had to be modified. Security arrangements were reassessed and new measures were being proposed to ensure ships and shore establishments were not easy targets for terrorists. The Federation Naval Review was cancelled. In the context of these very pressing operational demands, the political controversy brewing over the 'children overboard' incident did not receive priority attention.

In any event, the Coalition parties achieved a comfortable victory at the polls. Debate continued for weeks about the extent to which the '*Tampa* crisis' and the 'children overboard' affair had influenced the election result. Some commentators asserted that it had worked significantly in the Coalition's favour by appealing to historic Australian paranoia about the threat posed by foreigners arriving in boats. And some were asking if Operation Relex was really the kind of work the navy ought to be doing and whether the operation had effectively politicised the service. These were very serious concerns that deserve an extended reply.

In answer to the first question: responding to any perceived threat or actual violation of Australia's national sovereignty is a matter for the navy in the absence of a coastguard service. (The navy believed that Opposition Leader Kim Beazley's proposal for an Australian coastguard would result in duplication of effort and draw funds away from the RAN.) And in answer to the second: if the use of force is the continuation of politics by another means, and given the navy operates under political control within the law, most of its activities have a political dimension. But these questions obscured two principles of much greater import.

The first was the requirement that the navy accept any and every task allotted to it by government without question or qualification.

Other than to ensure the task does not violate Australian and international law or unduly expose servicemen and women to danger or harm, those commanding the armed forces must remain completely subservient to the will of the people as expressed by Cabinet or Parliament. This is because there are very grave dangers associated with allowing any officer, sailor, soldier or airman to express any view of any task allotted by government. The service might reasonably advise government that any direction in fulfilling an allotted task might be inefficient or ineffective, that it might cost human lives or be done a better way. But ultimately, commanders must not be given discretion to determine those tasks they will accept from government and those they will reject. If the people decide that the Government has not used the armed services appropriately or adequately, they can make that judgement at the ballot box. Operation Relex is distressing for everyone concerned, including the officers and sailors of the RAN who are tasked with its conduct. It is unpleasant work that no one likes doing, involving long periods at sea with little respite. But most significantly, the navy carried out the Government's directions without commenting on, or criticising, the policies upon which they were based. That the RAN's performance at sea did not draw any political comment was much to the navy's credit.

The second principle flows from the first. There is no doubt that some naval officers and sailors believed that Operation Relex was morally wrong, practically inefficient and politically opportunist. Others were convinced that Australia needed to stem the apparently endless flow of SIEVs from Indonesia in particular and that, quite apart from whether those illegally entering Australia ought to have their claims for asylum granted in Australia or offshore, people smugglers were endangering the lives of hundreds if not thousands of desperate people by taking them offshore in unseaworthy vessels. Quite apart from their personal views, there is no evidence that naval officers or sailors performed their duties in a manner that reflected either support for, or opposition to, the Government's policies. The navy was given a job to do and every man and woman involved in its execution upheld the navy's high standards of personal and professional conduct. At the senior levels of command and notwithstanding the 'children overboard' affair of which more will be said in a moment, there was never any suggestion that Admiral C.A. Barrie (the Chief of Defence Force), or Admirals Shackleton, Ritchie or Smith, were ever motivated by a concern to help the political fortunes of one party or to hinder those of another. While there may have been some shortcomings in the management of their interactions with politicians and public servants, they remained above party considerations and allegations of partisanship.

In these two critical respects, the navy handled Operation Relex very well. Whether the navy should have been put in such a complicated position is another matter. It would appear that events conspired to make this operation more controversial than it needed to be. The confluence of the '*Tampa* crisis', the 'children overboard' affair and a federal election that the Labor Party desperately hoped to win, created a volatile environment in which everything that naval ships did and everything that naval officers and sailors said would be given a political connotation and be exploited for some partisan advantage. This is inherent in the conduct of Australian politics and particularly prevalent in electioneering. For the most part, the Australian people recognised that the navy was simply carrying out the will of the elected government. It was clearly a difficult task which many people believed the navy executed with competence and compassion. The navy retained the nation's respect and even won its sympathy until the Senate held an inquiry into a 'Certain Maritime Incident'—as the 'children overboard' affair was also known—in early 2002. This long and acrimonious inquiry led to eroded esteem and diminished trust in the navy.

It now appears that many within the navy were aware that claims of children being thrown overboard from *Olong* were false within 48 hours of them first being publicly uttered. Either to avoid political controversy or to save face, inadequate action was taken to advise Prime Minister Howard and Immigration Minister Ruddock that their public statements were without foundation. In the weeks that followed, the 'children overboard' affair was exploited politically even as some senior officers attempted to correct the public record. Immediately before the federal election, Vice-Admiral Shackleton cast doubt on the truthfulness of the 'children overboard' story. This created a political storm only made more turbulent when he issued a clarification. It appeared to the media that the Chief of Navy had contradicted the Government and was then directed to retract what he knew to be the truth. Internal inquiries were conducted by the public service and the ADF into the handling of information conveyed ashore by those in *Adelaide* relating to the actions of those on board *Olong*. Both concluded that children were not thrown overboard from *Olong*, but that this information had not reached Defence Minister Peter Reith. This finding was met with thinly veiled disbelief.

There have been ministers who have come to the Navy or Defence portfolios without a personal interest in security questions, and those with a specific brief to achieve certain policy changes or administrative reforms. There have been some very poor ministers whose short-term political objectives have wreaked long-term operational harm. Few ministers have, in any event, made much of a contribution to the shape and direction of the navy. Since the Second World War, John Gorton and Kim Beazley are probably the only two. They remained in the portfolio for sufficient time to initiate and execute changes in policy and to ensure the acquisition of the most suitable equipment for the navy's present and future needs. They also developed a personal affection for the navy and genuine sympathy for its people. This was reflected in the political support they offered in parliament and the extent to which they defended the service against unjustified or unreasonable public criticism. Gorton and Beazley stood with the navy in good times and difficult times. This made them different.

The majority, however, did not stay long enough to make a difference or they were overwhelmed by the size and complexity of the task before them or they were unable to manage the complicated interface between politicians and service officers. But a small minority of ministers did not just perform poorly, they left a legacy of ill-will and distrust. The relationship between the RAN and the Government had certainly been strained during John Moore's time as Defence Minister. The Chief of Navy, Vice-Admiral D.B. Chalmers, had not had his two-year appointment extended for the customary third year while Rear Admiral D.J. Shackleton had been a surprise choice as his successor on 3 July 1999. The subsequent sacking of Dr Paul Barrett as Secretary of the Department of Defence made many fear that loyalty was a conditional commodity that could not be presumed.

The Senate inquiry beginning in February 2002 was more wide-ranging and far-reaching than the two previous assessments of the 'children overboard' affair. Although largely established for political purposes, the inquiry revealed much to be lamented. It became increasingly clear that a number of senior ADF officers had been prevented or persuaded not to correct the false claims made about children being thrown overboard by senior government leaders. This did not reflect well on the ADF or its most public face, Admiral Chris Barrie, who told the Senate in late February that he still believed that children had been thrown overboard when all the available evidence suggested otherwise. He stated that the initial report was very believable and there was no reason to doubt its accuracy. Furthermore, he commented that his subordinate commanders had ample opportunity to advise him formally that the report was either inaccurate or untrue but had not done so. At a press conference on 27 February, held after he conceded that children were not thrown overboard from *Olong*, veteran political commentator Laurie Oakes asked Admiral Barrie whether he 'felt like a dill'. This was an ignominious conclusion to a long and distinguished naval career. In a series of polls and surveys, there was clear evidence that the public standing of the ADF as a whole and the navy in particular had fallen as a consequence of a 'certain maritime incident'. It was, in fact, a low point in the navy's relationship with the Australian people. Blame can be properly laid at the feet of both the Coalition parties and the ADF's senior leadership. This damage to the navy's professional reputation could and should have been avoided as RAN ships continued to enforce sanctions in the Persian Gulf, while a multinational Coalition, including Australian ground forces, launched a military strike against the Taliban regime in Afghanistan.

After a short sharp campaign with a lengthy aftermath, remnants of the now defeated Taliban were driven from the principal cities of Kabul and Kandahar, and forced to seek refuge in mountains near the Pakistan border. Osama bin Laden had not been captured but the ability of al-Qa'ida to conduct terrorist campaigns had been substantially reduced. The War on Terrorism continued as attention returned to Iraq and its continuing frustration of UN efforts to verify its non-possession of weapons of mass destruction (WMDs). President George W. Bush urged the UN in September 2002 to insist that Iraq comply with sixteen specific Security Council resolutions demanding its disarmament or 'action would be unavoidable'. In November 2002, the UN Security Council passed resolution 1441 giving Iraq 30 days to provide the UN with a full and accurate declaration of all aspects of its weapons programs and to give UN arms inspectors complete and unhindered access to any site suspected of being part of a WMD program. Iraq agreed and the inspectors returned on 26 November with Saddam Hussein's regime warned of the serious consequences that would follow any hindrance of the arms inspectors led by Dr Hans Blix. The frigates *Darwin* and *Anzac*, already deployed to the northern Persian Gulf as part of the Maritime Interception Force (MIF), were joined in late 2002 by the amphibious transport ship *Kanimbla* as the Australian Government lent its weight to international resolve. By this time Captain P.D. Jones had assumed command of Maritime Interception Operations in the northern

Arabian Gulf. He was initially embarked in the American destroyer USS *Paul Hamilton*. (He subsequently transferred to *Kanimbla* on her arrival in Bahrain.) Although international attention had shifted to possible war, the Australian ships and personnel remained committed to preventing smuggling and the passage of prohibited trade. By the end of January 2003, command and control arrangements together with specific taskings were being devised in the event of war, while operational liaison was well under way with a number of Gulf states. The foremost threat seemed to be Iraqi mines. These concerns were heightened by the movement of Iraqi naval and government ships as war became imminent.

On 17 March 2003, President Bush gave Saddam Hussein and his sons 48 hours to leave Iraq or face military attack. The following day, Prime Minister Howard announced that as part of Operation Falconer, the Government had committed ADF elements in the Middle East to the coalition of military forces preparing to enforce Iraq's compliance with its international obligations to disarm. As expected, there was intense political debate on whether a war against Iraq was justified. The Government argued that Iraq possessed WMDs and was likely to use them if not disarmed immediately. As Australia shared in the benefits of Western security, the Government argued, it was obliged to contribute to its maintenance. The Opposition claimed that UN weapons inspectors should have been given more time to ensure Iraq did not possess WMDs, but would support Australian involvement in a strike against Iraq if supported by a UN resolution. Other political groups alleged that the war was actually about control of oil supplies and America's desire to reconfigure the political map of the Middle East. Most significantly, all parties were adamant that opposition to the war should not be translated into ill-will against service personnel. At least one lesson had been learnt from the bitter experience of Vietnam three decades earlier. However, some protest groups nevertheless engaged in irresponsible behaviour as ships departed Sydney Harbour, while others showed scant regard for the feelings of families and friends as they prepared to farewell deployed loved ones.

After a succession of ignored ultimatums, a 'Coalition of the Willing' led by the United States and consisting of British and Australian naval, ground and air forces, launched an offensive operation against Iraq on Thursday, 20 March 2003. At midnight, US Special Forces seized Iraq's two major offshore oil terminals, Kaaot and Mabot, off the coast of the Al Faw Peninsula. A mass breakout of Iraqi steel-hulled ships and mostly wooden dhows had occurred before hostilities began. Rather than being turned around, the vessels were inspected and the Khawr Abd Allah (KAA) waterway was cleared for combat operations. During the night of 20–21 March, *Anzac* in company with the British frigates *Marlborough*, *Chatham* and *Richmond* proceeded sixteen miles up the KAA waterway conscious of the threat posed by mines. As 40 Commando of the Royal Marine Battalion was landed on the peninsula to begin the ground assault on southern Iraq, *Anzac* was ordered to provide naval gunfire support (NGS) at 6.04 a.m. For the first time in 31 years, an RAN ship had engaged in NGS as shells from the 5-inch mounting were directed at Iraqi bunkers, artillery positions and key military installations ashore. Over the next three days, *Anzac* conducted seven fire support missions against Iraqi military installations and artillery positions. The Australian frigate's highly accurate NGS assisted in the seizure of the township of Al Faw and Iraq's southernmost deep water port of Umm Qasr. Moreover, small craft from *Kanimbla* patrolled the coastal waters and encountered a tug carrying 86 different types of mines, AK-47 assault rifles and boxes of ammunition. The tug's crew of 50 men was held in *Kanimbla* until transferred ashore. Had the mines been released in the harbour approaches, the initial landing and subsequent safe passage of Coalition ships would have been severely hampered.

With Iraqi opposition reduced to sporadic sniper fire, 32 members of CDT 3 were deployed to Umm Qasr, with the US Navy's Special Clearance Team 1 and the RN's Fleet Diving Team 2. In completely blacked-out underwater conditions, the divers conducted a tactile search for an Iraqi minelayer sunk with her mines on board. After several dives, the mines were located, recovered and destroyed at a remote site. The Australians then assisted with explosive ordnance disposal in the nearby town. The port of Umm Qasr was declared open on 9 April with the divers moving north to the port of Khawr Az Zubayr two days later. The team was withdrawn in mid-May after clearing 135 square kilometres of Iraqi territory of mines and unexploded ordnance. In May *Darwin* and *Anzac* returned to Australia to tumultuous welcomes and were replaced by *Sydney*. *Kanimbla* returned in June. At the time of writing, the long-term future RAN presence in the Persian Gulf had not been determined. In 2000, there were, once again, immediate security concerns demanding a response nearer to home. And again, it was the strife-torn Solomon Islands.

In June 2000, *Manoora* and *Tobruk* had been deployed to the Solomon Islands for Operation Plumbob following a coup on 5 June that led to the resignation of Prime Minister Bart Ulufa'alu and a deterioration of civil law and order in the small Pacific nation. *Tobruk* evacuated 480 Australian civilians and 'Approved Foreign Nationals' from Honiara, the Solomons' capital, and conveyed them to Australia. The ship was severely overcrowded and conditions were difficult for all on board. The hard-working *Tobruk* returned to Honiara a week later to support the Australian High Commissioner's efforts to secure a cease-fire between the leading dissident factions in the Solomons: the Malaita Eagle Force and the Isatabu Freedom Movement. An agreement was signed on 2 August 2000 and *Tobruk* was permitted to sail after 41 consecutive days at anchor off the main island of Guadalcanal. But the Solomons remained in the grip of domestic conflict, corruption and disorder which appeared to reach another crisis in 2001. As part of Operation Trek, *Sydney*, *Newcastle*, *Tobruk*, *Darwin*, *Kanimbla*, *Manoora* and *Melbourne* were all deployed for brief periods to the Solomon Islands in support of the Peace Monitoring Council and the International Peace Monitoring Team (IMPT) to prevent the further escalation of violence and to provide a neutral safe haven for the warring parties to negotiate a peace agreement. The IMPT was tasked with disarming the militants and ex-militants in accordance with the Townsville and Marau peace agreements.

Throughout 2002, civil disorder and internal chaos continued. It appeared as though the Solomon Islands was headed for social disintegration and political anarchy after Australian peacekeeping personnel were withdrawn in March 2002. The Government's authority was defied routinely, the treasury was virtually bankrupt, criminal gangs operated with impunity and ethnic violence was unrestrained. There was an emerging fear in Australia that the Solomons might have become a haven for terrorists and drug-runners. In June 2003 at the request of the Solomon Islands Government, plans were developed for an Australian-led military and police peacekeeping force to restore law and order in the troubled nation. New Zealand, Papua New Guinea, Tonga and Fiji offered to provide personnel for what was designated a 'Regional Assistance Mission'. All sixteen members of the Pacific Island Forum endorsed Australia's plan at a meeting held in Sydney on 21 July 2003. Prime Minister Howard indicated that the mission could be a precedent for further military–police security force deployments in the region: 'it will send a signal to other countries that help is available if it is sought, that we do have a desire to help all the peoples of the Pacific to have conditions of law and order and hope and peace and stability for their future generations'. The following day, HMAS *Manoora* sailed from Townsville bound for the Solomon Islands. Embarked were 300 troops from 2RAR. The physical presence of *Manoora* in Iron Bottom Sound symbolised Australia's firm commitment, while giving personnel ashore reassurance as they moved around the capital. A week later, the patrol boat *Whyalla* arrived off Guadalcanal as the mission established its base to the east of Honiara. The coastal minehunter, *Hawkesbury*, and the LCHs *Wewak* and *Labuan* were subsequently sent to the Solomons to assist with two Navy Sea King helicopters also provided by the RAN's HS 817 Squadron at HMAS *Albatross*. The LCHs, once considered for disposal, demonstrated the importance of the navy retaining a flexible transport and logistic support capacity for deployments around the Pacific. During a three-month deployment, *Hawkesbury* was involved in the collection of 333 weapons and over 1800 rounds of ammunition during the gun amnesty period. The ship also provided humanitarian aid support, maritime surveillance and boarding operations, maritime transport, search and rescues, medical evacuations, disposal of dangerous ordnance, beach landings, airfield surveys and other support tasks.

At the time of writing, the mission was continuing with considerable success. It was apparent that the navy was again giving the Australian Government an ability to influence events and people far beyond the nation's shores. A century after he outlined the potential of a navy to further Australia's interests, the words of William Creswell still resounded with wisdom: 'For a maritime state furnished without a navy, the sea, so far from being a safe frontier is rather a highway for her enemies; but with a navy, it surpasses all other frontiers in strength'. Australia remains a maritime nation and its navy is at the forefront of implementing national policy.

13

The new millennium

As the centenary of Federation approached, the Commonwealth Government released the first Defence White Paper since 1987. It identified a number of priority tasks. The *first* was the defence of the continent, offshore islands and contiguous waters with a self-reliant defence force able to assert sovereignty over the air and sea approaches. The *second* priority was contributing to the security of the immediate neighbourhood, including maritime surveillance, evacuations and disaster relief. The *third* priority for Australia's forces was supporting the nation's wider interests and objectives by being able to contribute effectively to international coalitions of forces to meet crises beyond the immediate neighbourhood. The *fourth* was the provision of humanitarian aid and assistance to Australia's nearest neighbours in time of natural disaster or internal crisis. In an introductory letter, dated 6 December 2000, Prime Minister Howard said the Government's policy

> *recognises that Australia's most basic strategic premise and a fundamental responsibility of government is the defence of Australia by Australians. It also recognises that the ADF has in recent years faced new and increasing demands for operations such as humanitarian relief, evacuations, peacekeeping and peace-enforcement and that this trend is likely to continue . . . Working together with our foreign, trade, economic and social policies, our defence policy will help Australia continue to develop as a country which is confident and self-reliant and engaged within the region as a cooperative, respected and influential partner.*

The key element in the paper was an increase in defence spending of an average of 3 per cent per annum in real terms throughout the ensuing decade with an immediate increase of $500 million in 2001–02 and $1000 million in the following year. The paper provided for a capability upgrade for the *Collins* Class submarines and a new class of at least three air-warfare destroyers to replace the FFGs when they begin to leave service in 2013. (In a subsequent statement, the Government announced that the two oldest FFGs, *Adelaide* and *Canberra*, would leave service much earlier, possibly in 2006.) A replacement for the *Fremantle* Class would enter service in 2004–05 with plans announced to replace *Westralia* in 2009, *Tobruk* in 2010, *Manoora* and *Kanimbla* by 2015 and *Success* in 2015. History provides ample evidence that such replacements are rarely delivered on time or at the estimated cost. But the existence of detailed force structure plans represents a departure from past practice and reason to believe that the navy will be given the ships it requires to fulfil the public's expectations of the roles it needs to discharge.

In line with the Government's broad policy intentions, *RAN Doctrine 1—Australian Maritime Doctrine* was released just prior to the Defence White Paper. This was the first time the navy had sought to produce such a comprehensive statement of its charter and key responsibilities. The document explained:

> *Distance is the most striking single fact about Australia's* strategic geography *[original emphasis retained]. Australia is very big and very difficult to defend. It is also very difficult to attack. Nevertheless, Australia's interests involve even greater issues of distance than do our imperatives of territorial defence alone.*

In contrast to the vagaries of a century before about what an Australian navy was meant to achieve, the RAN's mission beyond 2000 was stated succinctly: 'to fight and win in the maritime environment as an element of a joint or combined force, to assist in maintaining Australia's sovereignty and to contribute to the security of our region'. This demanded the possession of 'a worldwide reputation for excellence as a sea power; a well-equipped, professional team of highly motivated people, serving Australia with honour, supported by a nation proud of its Navy'.

Within the next decade, the navy will begin to absorb another new generation of ships and people. Very soon, the RAN will be completely without the first-hand expertise of those who served during

'Confrontation' or off South Vietnam. Officers and senior sailors whose operational experience was gained entirely in peacetime will make up the bulk of the navy's senior leadership. In a decade, only those who saw active service in the two Gulf wars will have participated in combat operations. Those who fought off Kuwait in 1991 and Iraq in 2003 were not placed in obvious or imminent danger. And yet, the level of training and degree of professionalism was such that each and every task was fulfilled without fuss or failure. While war is the best training for war, successive generations of Australian officers and sailors have shown the capability of the nation to produce men and women with both the aptitude and ability to operate a navy able to achieve and maintain world's-best practice in naval operations. For a nation of 20 million people, this is a singularly spectacular but rarely celebrated achievement. RAN officers have served in exchange postings with every major Western navy and, more recently, most regional navies. They have commanded British squadrons and in the case of Malaya, entire navies. Australian sailors have never shown any difficulty in being able to operate technologically advanced equipment or technically complicated machinery. They have become adept at maintaining aircraft and manning submarines, and have displayed a genuine willingness to get the job done. Without such individuals, and the ability of the Australian mindset to adapt to the rigours of naval life, the RAN would be more of an idea than a reality a century after the *Defence Act* was first passed by the Federal Parliament.

The navy can be trusted with the implementation of national policy because it is capable, self-reliant and experienced in working with Australia's friends and allies. There are few countries able to maintain the security of their sovereign waters or to control the passage of people and goods across their borders. Because of the Royal Australian Navy, Australians can still say with a sense of reassurance and perhaps even a measure of relief: 'our home is girt by sea' *and* guarded by Australian warships for whom life at sea remains 'no pleasure cruise'.

FURTHER READING

Official histories

Arthur Jose, *Official History of Australia in the War of 1914–18*, vol. IX, *The Royal Australian Navy*, Angus & Robertson, Sydney, 1928; George Hermon Gill, *Official History of Australia in the War of 1939–45, The Royal Australian Navy, 1939–42*, Australian War Memorial, Canberra, 1957; George Hermon Gill, *Official History of Australia in the War of 1939–45, The Royal Australian Navy, 1942–45*, Australian War Memorial, Canberra, 1968; Robert O'Neill, *Australia in the Korean War 1950–53*, vol. II, *Combat Operations*, AGPS, Canberra, 1985; Denis Fairfax, *Navy in Vietnam*, AGPS, Canberra, 1980; Jeffrey Grey, *Up Top: the Royal Australian Navy and the South-East Asian conflicts, 1955–1972*, Allen & Unwin, Sydney, 1998; David Stevens (ed.), *Australian Centenary of Defence*, vol. III, *The Royal Australian Navy*, Oxford University Press, Melbourne, 2001.

General works

Frank Broeze, *Island Nation*, Allen & Unwin, Sydney, 1998; Alun Evans, *A Navy for Australia*, ABC Enterprises, Sydney, 1986; Alun Evans, *The Royal Australian Navy*, Australians at War Series, Time Life Australia, Sydney, 1988; Henry Feakes, *White Ensign, Southern Cross*, Ure Smith, Sydney, 1951; Peter Firkins, *Of Nautilus and Eagles: A History of the Royal Australian Navy*, Hutchinson, Melbourne, 1983; Tom Frame, *Pacific Partners: A History of Australian–American Naval Relations*, Hodder, Sydney, 1992; Tom Frame, James Goldrick and Peter Jones (eds), *Reflections on the RAN*, Kangaroo Press, Kenthurst, 1991; Tom Frame and Kevin Baker, *Mutiny: Naval Insurrections in Australia and New Zealand*, Allen & Unwin, Sydney, 2000; Ross Gillett (ed.), *Australia's Navy: Past, Present and Future*, Child & Henry, Sydney, 1986; R. Jones, *Seagulls, Cruisers and Catapults*, Pelorus, Hobart, 1989; Lew Lind, *Historic Naval Events of Australia Day-by-Day*, Reed, Sydney, 1982; George Lionel Macandie, *The Genesis of the Royal Australian Navy*, Government Printer, Sydney, 1949; Frances McGuire, *The Royal Australian Navy: Its*

Origins, Development and Organisation, Melbourne, 1948; George Odgers, *The Royal Australian Navy: An Illustrated History*, Child & Henry, Sydney, 1982; Peter Plowman, *Across the Sea to War: Australian and New Zealand Troop Convoys from 1865 through two World Wars to Korea and Vietnam*, Rosenberg, Sydney, 2003; J. Ross, *The White Ensign in New Zealand*, Reed, Wellington, 1967; David Stevens (ed.), *Maritime Power in the Twentieth Century: The Australian Experience*, Allen & Unwin, Sydney, 1998; David Stevens and John Reeve (eds), *Southern Trident: Strategy, History and the Rise of Australian Naval Power*, Allen & Unwin, Sydney, 2001; David Stevens and John Reeve (eds), *The Face of Naval Battle*, Allen & Unwin, Sydney, 2003; Bruce Swain, *A Chronology of Australian Armed Forces at War, 1939–45*, Allen & Unwin, Sydney, 2001.

Colonial

John Bach, *The Australia Station: A History of the Royal Navy in the South West Pacific, 1821–1913,* University of New South Wales Press, Kensington, 1986; Charles Bean, *Flagships Three*, Alston Rivers, London, 1913; P.M. Cowburn, 'The British Naval Officer in the Australian Colonies', *Journal of the Royal Australian Historical Society*, March 1968; K.M. Dallas, 'The first settlements in Australia: considered in relation to sea power in world politics', *Tasmanian Historical Research Association Monograph*, no. 3, 1952; Wilson Evans, *Deeds not Words*, Hawthorn, Melbourne, 1971; V. Fitzhardinge, 'Russian naval visitors to Australia, 1862–1888', *Journal of the Royal Australian Historical Society*, June 1966; Alan Frost, *Convicts and Empire: A Naval Question, 1776–1811,* Oxford University Press, Melbourne, 1980; Ross Gillett, *Australia's Colonial Navies*, Naval Historical Society of Australia, Sydney, 1982; Meredith Hooper, 'The Naval Defence Agreement 1887', *Australian Journal of Politics and History*, vol. 14, no. 1, April 1968; Robert Hughes, *The Fatal Shore*, Harvill Collins, London, 1987; Robert Hyslop, 'War Scares in Australia in the 19th Century', *Victorian Historical Journal*, vol. 47, no. 1, February 1976; B.A. Knox, 'Colonial Influence on Imperial Policy, 1858–1866, Victoria and the *Colonial Naval Defence Act*, 1865', *Historical Studies*, vol. 11, no. 41, November 1963; Colin Jones, *Australia's Colonial Navies*, Australian War Memorial, Canberra, 1986; Bob Nicholls, *Boxers and Bluejackets: Australia's Naval Expedition to the Boxer Uprising*, Allen & Unwin, Sydney, 1986; Norman Pixley, 'The Queensland Maritime Defence Force', *Journal of the Royal Historical Society of Queensland*, 1960–61.

World wars

Chris Coulthard-Clark, *Action Stations, Coral Sea*, Allen & Unwin, Sydney, 1991; Eric Feldt, *The Coast Watchers*, Oxford University Press, Melbourne, 1946; Tom Frame and Greg Swinden, *First In, Last Out! The Navy at Gallipoli*, Kangaroo Press, Kenthurst, 1986; David Jenkins, *Battle Surface! Japan's Submarine War Against Australia 1942–44*, Random Century, Sydney, 1992; T.M. Jones and I.L. Idriess, *The Silent Service*, Angus & Robertson, Sydney, 1944; David Hamer, *Bombers and Battleships*, Allen & Unwin, Sydney, 1998; Bruce Loxton and Chris Coulthard-Clark, *The Shame of Savo: the Sinking of HMAS* Canberra, Allen & Unwin, Sydney, 1994; F.M. and D.P. McGuire, *The Price of Admiralty*, Oxford University Press, Melbourne, 1962; W.D. McIntyre, *The Rise and Fall of the Singapore Naval Base, 1919–42*, Macmillan, London, 1979; S.W.C. Pack, *The Battle of Matapan*, Batsford, London, 1961; Ray Parkin, *Out of the Smoke*, Hogarth, London, 1960; David Stevens (ed.), *The Royal Australian Navy in World War II*, Allen & Unwin, Sydney, 1996; Dan van der Vat, *The Last Corsair: The Story of the* Emden, Hodder & Stoughton, London, 1983; Denis and Peggy Warner, *Kamikaze: the Sacred Warriors 1944–45*, Oxford University Press, Melbourne, 1983; Denis Warner and Sadao Seno, *Disaster in the Pacific; New Light on the Battle of Savo Island*, Naval Institute Press, Annapolis, 1992; Ray Worledge (ed.), *Contact! HMAS* Rushcutter *and Australia's Submarine Hunters, 1939-46*, Anti-submarine Warfare Officers' Association, Sydney, 1994. See also the wartime series produced by the Australian War Memorial *HMAS*, *HMAS Mk II–IV*.

Ship histories

John Bastock, *Australia's Ships of War*, Angus & Robertson, Sydney, 1975; L.E. Clifford, *Leader of the Crocks*, Cheshire, Melbourne, 1945; Ralph Diamond, *The History of HMAS* Voyager *I*, Southern Holdings, Huonville, 1992; Ross Gillett, *Australian and New Zealand Warships 1914–1945*, Doubleday, Sydney, 1983; Ross Gillett and Colin Graham, *Warships of Australia*, Rigby, Adelaide, 1977; A.W. Greig, 'The First Australian Warship', *Victorian Historical Magazine*, vol. 9, September 1923; T. Hall, *HMAS* Melbourne, Allen & Unwin, Sydney, 1982; Geoffrey Ingleton, *Watchdogs Infernal and Imperial*, Golden Lantern, Sydney, 1934; Ronald McKie, *Proud Echo*, Angus & Robertson, Sydney, 1953; Brian Ogle, *The History of HMAS* Maryborough, privately published, Sydney, 1992; Arthur Parry, *HMAS* Yarra*: the Story of a Gallant Ship*, Angus & Robertson,

Sydney, 1944; W.S. Robinson, *Tamworth's Times: A Chronology*, privately published, Sydney, 1991; Frank Walker, *HMAS* Armidale*: The Ship that Had to Die*, Kingfisher, Budgewoi, 1990; Michael White, *Australian Submarines: A History*, AGPS, Canberra, 1992; M. Wilson, *Royal Australian Navy: Major Warships*, Topmill, Sydney, 1994. See also the many monographs published by the Naval Historical Society of Australia.

HMAS *Sydney*

In order of publication: G.H. Johnston, *Grey Gladiator: HMAS* Sydney *with the Mediterranean Fleet*, Angus & Robertson, Sydney, 1941; John Ross, *Stormy Petrel*, Patterson, Perth, 1946; G. Scott, *HMAS* Sydney, Horwitz, Sydney, 1962; Michael Montgomery, *Who Sank the* Sydney*?*, Cassell, Melbourne, 1981; Barbara Winter (Poniewierski), *HMAS* Sydney*: Fact, Fantasy and Fraud*, Boolarong, Brisbane, 1984; Tom Frame, *HMAS* Sydney*: Loss and Controversy*, Hodder, Sydney, 1993; Joint Standing Committee on Foreign Affairs and Trade, *Report on the Loss of HMAS* Sydney, the Parliament of the Commonwealth, March 1999; Richard Summerrell, *The Sinking of HMAS* Sydney*: A Guide to Commonwealth Government Records*, NAA, Canberra, 1999; Wesley Olsen, *Bitter Victory: the Death of HMAS* Sydney, University of Western Australia Press, Perth, 2000; Peter Hore (ed.), *HMAS* Sydney *II: The Cruiser and the Controversy in the Archives of the United Kingdom*, Papers in Australian Maritime Affairs No. 9, RAN Sea Power Centre, Canberra, 2001.

Post 1945 operations

G.M. Dixon, 'Voyage to Heard and Kerguelen' and 'Heard Island Relief', *The Navy: Australia's Maritime Journal*, Melbourne, vol. 11, no. 4, April 1948, pp. 20–2, 52, and vol. 12, no. 4, April 1949, pp. 12–15; Tom Frame, *Where Fate Calls: The HMAS* Voyager *Tragedy*, Hodder & Stoughton, Sydney, 1992; John Foster, *Hands to Boarding Stations: The Story of Minesweeper HMAS* Hawk*, Confrontation with Indonesia 1965–66*, Australian Military History Publications, Sydney, 2003; Harold Hickling, *One Minute of Time*, Reed, Auckland, 1965 and *Postscript to* Voyager, Reed, Auckland, 1969; Colin Jones, *Wings and the Navy*, Kangaroo Press, Kenthurst, 1997; David Marr and Marian Wilkinson, *Dark Victory*, Allen & Unwin, Sydney, 2003; Jo Stevenson, *No Case to Answer*, Alpha, Sydney, 1970. The *Navy Annual* produced since 1991 is a valuable source of information and insight.

Biographies

Henry Burrell, *Mermaids Do Exist*, Macmillan, Melbourne, 1986; John Collins, *As Luck Would Have It*, Angus & Robertson, Sydney, 1965; William Creswell (edited by Paul Thompson), *Close to the Wind*, Heinemann, London, 1964; Galfrey Gatacre, *Reports of Proceedings*, Nautical Press, Manly, 1982; Robert Hyslop, *A Very Civil Servant*, Clarion, Binalong, 1998; Barbara Poniewierski, *Commander Long*; John Ross, *Lucky Ross*, Hesperian, Perth, 1994; Sir Victor Smith, *A Few Memories of Sir Victor Smith*, ANI Press, Canberra, 1992; Stephen Webster, 'Creswell, the Australian navalist: a career biography of Vice Admiral Sir William Rooke Creswell, KCMG, KBE (1852–1933)', Unpublished doctoral thesis, 1975. Awards for bravery and gallantry to RAN personnel during wartime are contained in J.J. Atkinson, *By Skill and Valour*, Spink, Sydney, 1986.

Policy and administration

Brian Beddie, 'The Australian Navy and Imperial Legislation', *War and Society*, vol. 8, no. 2, September 1987; Ian Cunningham, *Work Hard, Play Hard*, AGPS, Canberra, 1988; John J. Dedman, 'Encounter over Manus', *Australian Outlook*, vol. 20, August 1966, pp. 135–53; Tyler Dennett, 'Australia's Defence Problem', *Foreign Affairs*, New York, vol. 18, no. 1, October 1939, pp. 116–26; F.B. Eldridge, *History of the Royal Australian Naval College*, Georgian House, Melbourne, 1949; Alfred Festburg, *Heraldry in the Royal Australian Navy*, Silverleaf, Melbourne, 1981; Tom Frame, *The Garden Island*, Kangaroo, Kenthurst, 1990; Tom Holden, *The Administration of Discipline in the RAN*, RAN, Canberra, 1992; Robert Hyslop, *Australian Naval Administration, 1900–1939*, Hawthorn, Melbourne, 1973 and *Aye, Aye, Minister: Australian Naval Administration 1939–59*, AGPS, Canberra, 1990; John Jeremy, *Cockatoo Island: Sydney's Historic Dockyard*, UNSW Press, Sydney, 1998; David Stevens (ed.), *In Search of a Maritime Strategy*, SDSC, Canberra, 1997; Josef Straczek, *The RAN: Ships, Aircraft and Shore Establishments*, Navy Public Affairs, Sydney, 1996.

INDEX

Index

Index

Index